The China Information Technology Handbook

Patricia Ordóñez de Pablos · Miltiadis D. Lytras
Editors

The China Information Technology Handbook

 Springer

Editors
Patricia Ordóñez de Pablos
Departamento de Administración de
Empresas y Contabilidad
Facultad de Ciencias Económicas
Universidad de Oviedo
Avd del Cristo, s/n
33.071 Oviedo-Asturias
Spain
patriop@uniovi.es

Miltiadis D. Lytras
University of Patras
Research Academic Computer Tech. Inst.
Computer Engineering & Informatics
Dept.
Patras
Greece
lytras@ceid.upatras.gr

ISBN: 978-0-387-77742-9   e-ISBN: 978-0-387-77743-6
DOI: 10.1007/978-0-387-77743-6

Library of Congress Control Number: 2008929612

Printed on acid-free paper

springer.com

To Haido and Dimitris Miltos
To Elvira and Joaquín Patricia

Foreword

Miltiadis D. Lytras and Patricia Ordóñez de Pablos

Department of Computer Engineering and Informatics, University of Patras, Greece
Dept. of Business Administration and Accountability, University of Oviedo, Spain

China is a fast-growing emerging economy and current impressive economic growth rate of almost 9 percent annually. Its contribution to global GDP growth since 2000 has been almost twice as large as that of the next three biggest emerging economies (India, Brazil and Russia) combined. Some even refer to China as the mother of emerging markets and transition economies.

Directly or indirectly the Chinese economy has influenced interest rates, prices for raw materials and wages in the western established economies. Currently China is the most R&D intense of emerging market countries and is seventh of all countries in the world. Its economic power is exemplified by the fact that it is expected to be the fifth largest source of outward foreign direct investment during 2004- 2007.

Working with Chinese firms has become a reality for the vast majority of managers in Western countries. With its high growth rate, the presence and impact of the Chinese economy will only become larger.

With China's importance on the global scale set to grow faster than ever – shows a unique window to observe the changes that will chart the course of the future in this region of the world. One of the keys to dealing with China is understanding the complex dynamic between rapid change and tradition.

In a world were traditional business practices are reconsidered; economic activity is performed in a global context; new areas of economic development are recognized as the key enablers of wealth and income production; the quest for collaboration and exploitation of synergies is recognized as an Information Technologies Primer; this book brings together academics, researchers, entrepreneurs, policy makers and government officers aiming to contribute to the debate on Sustainable Development and Strategic Management through Information Technology in China.

Over recent years, China's IT economy has poised for a new round of development, which in some respects characterizes a large number of offshore software outsourcing for scale and low cost. The phenomenon of global software development has intensified more than ever before, turning into an increasing dispersion of software development activities across geographies. To be more competitive or simply survive in such a rapidly evolving environment, IT companies have been looking to innovate and differentiate themselves by resorting to new development methodologies.

The strategic management of IT in China needs in our days to be justified and promoted through a multi-focus approach. The scholar value of this proposed book in anchored in the following key pillars: 1) The focus of the analysis is performed by exploiting state of the art and emerging trends in Theory and Technology; 2) It provides to IT students and academics as well to other target market an excellent match of theory and practice. The publication strategy of this book as explained in a later stage in tentative tables of contents promote this vision: and 3) It gives an excellent opportunity for discussing some of the top/hot topics in IT and providing fresh ideas on how real world business challenges set new frontiers for IT and management

So the development of this reference book is targeting to huge audiences aiming to communicate knowledge on a timely topic. The contribution to the literature of IT will be significant: Current publications do not focus jointly in the two areas and also they don't apply a combined IT and China Perspective.

THE CHINA INFORMATION TECHNOLOGY HANDBOOK aims to timely respond to the high demand of our society to adopt Emerging Technologies in all the aspects of Business and Economic activity towards innovative solutions to research problems and high performance systems. The key characteristic of the book is that brings together the experts of the IT industry, IT practitioners and researchers in High Tech Research centres and Academia promoting a sound contribution to the IT literacy as demanded by real users.

The book is formed by 22 chapters that address key topics from social networks and IT companies, mobile telecommunication services and innovation networks, logistics and IT services in China to electronic goverment and e-commerce. The chapters of the book are: Chapter 1: "Guanxi And Information Technologies Companies In China: Understanding Social Connections Structures" (Miltiadis D. Lytras and Patricia Ordóñez de Pablos); Chapter 2: "Enterprise Risk Management: Information Technology Outsourcing Risk with the Trend in China" (Desheng Wu, David L. Olson and Dexiang Wu); Chapter 3: "Chinese Consumers' Attitudes and Adoption of Online and Mobile Banking" (Sylvie Laforet); Chapter 4: "International Patterns in Manufacturing Strategies" (Ruth Alas, Tomas Eklund, Mikael Collan and Ants Kraus); Chapter 5: "The Term Innovation and its Front End – Is There a Specific Asian View?" (Alexander Brem); Chapter 6: "Research on Establishing Beijing International IT R&D Hub" (Zhao Jing-Yuan); Chapter 7: "Absorptive Capability, Local Innovation Networks and International R&D Spillovers: An Empirical Study on the Chinese ICT Industry" (Shouhua Wei, Xianjun Li, Guisheng Wu); Chapter 8: "Analyzing Growth of Mobile Telecommunication Services in China" (V. Sridhar); Chapter 9: "3D Virtual World Success in Mainland China. Second Life vs. HiPiHi"(Xi Zhang, Doug Vogel, Zhenjiao Chen, Zhongyun Zhou); Chapter 10: "The Role of China in Requirements Research" (Alan M. Davis and Ann Hickey); Chapter 11: "Chinese Cultural Characteristics And Effective Business In China". Maria Fernanda Pargana Ilhéu; Chapter 12: "The Impact of Information Technology on Organizational Forms" (Liang-Hung Lin); Chapter 13: "Intellectual Capital and Competitive Advantage in the Globalization Context. An Empirical Analysis of creative industries in China" (Ru-Yan

Hong and Xiao-Bo Wu); Chapter 14: "The Innovest Ratings of Chinese Organizations: A Benchmarked Analysis" (Edward J. Lusk); Chapter 15: "Language-divides and Global Inequalities: Problems and a Solution" (Pak Hung Mo); Chapter 16: "Agricultural Informationization in China" (Wensheng Wang, Guangqian Peng and Guangmin Lu); Chapter 17: "Market Characteristics of Mobile Communications Market in China" (Sunanda Sangwan, Guan Chong and Louis-Francois Pau); Chapter 18: "Logistics and IT Services in China: Outsourcing in the Manufacturing Industry" (Yen Chun); Chapter 19: "China's Perspectives on the Development of Information Technology" (Hou Ying and Hao Yufan); Chapter 20: "Electronic Government in China: History, Current Status, and Challenges" (Yue "Jeff" Zhang, Li Richard Ye and Zhiyang Lin); Chapter 21: "Software Evolution for Evolving China" (Hongji Yang, Feng Chen, He Guo, Yong Zhou and Mingyan Zhao); and Chapter 22: "E-Commerce In China: Culture And Challenges" (Jeffrey Hsu).

We wish readers to enjoy this variety of topics on IT in China. We are looking forward to have your attention in our next book concerning Business in China and in Arab World which will be published in 2009.

Don't miss the special edition of China Insights Today for the Beijing Olympics, which you can download from http://www.chinainsightstoday.com. Additionally if you are interested in 1st International Conference for the Web Science, please have a look at http://icws2009.org

We would be happy to receive your comments and suggestions. Feel free to drop us a mail at miltiadis.lytras@gmail.com and patriop@uniovi.es.

Contents

Chapter 1
Guanxi and Information Technology Companies in China: Understanding Social Connections Structures

Miltiadis D. Lytras[1] and Patricia Ordóñez de Pablos[2]

[1] Department of Computer Engineering and Informatics, University of Patras, Greece
[2] Dept. of Business Administration and Accountability, University of Oviedo, Spain

Abstract Companies must understand how social connections or "guanxi" are created and deployed in China. The goal of this chapter is to analyze the literature addressing the dynamics of social networks in China, as well as the positive and negative aspects associated with them. The chapter concludes with a discussion of why managers should make an effort to understand social connections and their dynamics when doing business in Confucian societies, like China.

1 Introduction - China and Information Technology Companies

China's IT economy has been poised for the last few years for a new round of development; as evidence of this pending "new launch", one observes a large number of offshore software firms created and sustained by the IT outsourcing elections made by many multinational corporations. The phenomenon of global software development has significantly intensified largely due to the low salary/high skill outsourcing possibilities in many countries such as India and China.

To be more competitive or simply just to survive in the rapidly evolving and dynamic IT environment, IT companies have found it necessary to innovate and so differentiate themselves. Despite the unprecedented market and profit potential of the software sector, IT companies are experiencing major deployment difficulties in China. As Haoyang Che (The Institute of Software at the Chinese Academy of Sciences) states, 'among the most important obstacles, we can highlight that many Chinese IT-related companies are still governed by an ingrained officialism that disallows just enough methods'. Also contributing to deployment impediments is the fact that China is not an English-speaking country and so most of its software [SW] developers are non-native speakers of English. Thus, many SW firms must wait for the Chinese IT versions to be published to obtain the needed information; in addition considerable time is needed to do the translations and to test their efficacy. This translation and testing process can take upwards of six months.

P.O. de Pablos, M.D. Lytras (eds.), *The China Information Technology Handbook*,
DOI: 10.1007/978-0-387-77743-6_1, © Springer Science+Business Media, LLC 2009

Needless to say such a SW development lag in the dynamic and rapidly developing SW markets contributes significantly to deployment difficulties. Also, there is a "trust" issue. Local and overseas SW developers come from different institutional frameworks and so have different cultural orientations. This fact often makes mutual trust very hard to achieve. Finally, language differences act to deepen the existing communication chasms between the two. The sum total of these communication and deployment issues add an extra level of complexity to doing business in China for IT companies.

This chapter will bring together research which contributes to the debate over what *guanxi*, or social connections, means in the Chinese society, discuss its implications and analyze its major benefits, risks, ethics dimensions regarding Information Technology [IT] companies.

2 Definitions of Guanxi

Let us examine the basic lexicon of *guanxi* and then, review the relevant literature that has been put forward on this topic.It is possible to trace some of the fundamental meanings of guanxi to ancient Chinese philosophies, especially to the writings of Confucianism (Confucius, 1915). An important term that we need to explain in order to enrich our understanding of guanxi is "lun" which captures the essential aspects of the ancient Chinese social system and its political and moral philosophy.

The root meaning of "lun" derives from the paramount importance accorded to human relationships in Confucianism. Countries like China, Taiwan as well as overseas Chinese communities, share a heritage of Confucianism which states that the following five major relations or *wu-lun* govern all human relationships: emperor-subject, father-son, husband-wife, elder-younger brothers and friend-friend. To ensure social harmony, order and stability, appropriate behaviors are needed. The practice of *guanxi* or social connections is pervasive; one finds it not only in China but also in other Asian cultures like Korea and Japan.

The second meaning of "lun" is social order or what Fei (1992) calls differentiated order. In a similar way to natural order, social order or stability lies in differentiation, which can be interpreted hierarchically and horizontally. In hierarchical differentiation, members of each relationship enjoy differential or "unequal" rights and obligations. For instance, a sovereign, father, husband, elder brother, or senior friend has more prerogatives and authority than the subject, son, wife, younger brother, and the junior friend. This is the same idea as we find in western cultures as the "pecking-order". Horizontally, the self is "at the center of a series of concentric circles" (Redding and Wong, 1986), where socially-related-others are differentiated in terms of their "closeness to the self". In the traditional Chinese family context, closeness is based on blood ties such as family membership, clan membership, close relatives, or distant relatives.

Finally, "lun" also refers to moral principles regarding interactive behaviors of related parties. Just as these relationships are highly differentiated, so are the corresponding moral principles. There are no universal moral standards applied consistently to all human relationships and therefore each relationship operates under its own moral principles.

At this point, it is necessary to introduce a clear definition of the term *guanxi*. The word *guanxi* is formed by two Chinese characters: Guan and Xi. "Guan" means door or gate. "Xi" means to tie up. Generally guanxi refers to relationships or social connections based on mutual interests and benefits (Bian, 1994; Gold et al., 2002; Yang, 1994). The term "guanxi" carries several different important connotations.

In the most general sense, *guanxi* simply means relationships. The second usage refers to subsets of relationships that work according to norms of reciprocity. A third usage expresses a pejorative connotation. It refers to "the usage of someone's authority to obtain political or economic benefits by unethical person(s)" (Xinci Xinyu Cidan, 1989). *Guanxi* or *guanxixue* represents a way to bypass regulations, laws ("fa"), or norms through personal connections with people who control limited resources (Gold, 1985).

In this paper, we will focus primarily on the second usage of the term *guanxi*. Thus, here the term refers to a special relationship one that bonds partners through reciprocal exchange of favors as well as mutual obligations (Alston, 1989; Luo, 1997; Ordóñez de Pablos, 2005; Ordóñez de Pablos and Lytras, 2007).

2.1 Dimensions of guanxi construct

Hwang (1987) suggests that *guanxi* is a multidimensional concept formed by three analytical dimensions or ties: affective, normative and instrumental.

The affective dimension of *guanxi* refers to the development of close relationships with another person solely due to the existence of affective ties/bonds between them. Usually, these affective ties are gender specific. The normative dimension indicates that *guanxi* often develops because two particular individuals are tied to each other through some kind of prescriptive relationship categorized as being friends or relatives. Finally, the instrumental dimension stands in opposition to the affective tie. When a person tries to develop an affective tie with another person, then such a tie is the goal itself. However, when the person attempts to establish an instrumental tie, then the relationship serves only as a means or an instrument to attain other goals. Therefore, this relationship is usually unstable and temporary. (Hwang, 1987: 950).

This three-dimensional view of *guanxi* is only useful for analytical distinctions. In fact, when we analyze a particular *guanxi*, we usually uncover a mix of the three dimensions. It is this combination of dimensions that determines the nature, strength and stability of a particular guanxi. The instrumental, affective and normative dimensions are not necessarily aligned or run in the same direction. Nevertheless, as Chung and Hamilton state "inconsistency among the three dimensions does not prevent the development of a guanxi relationship". It is the case, however, that a guanxi with dimensions going in different directions will be weaker than if they were to be aligned. On the other hand, as noted above, a relationship that is purely instrumental is generally short-term but can be modified. Therefore, if the firm desires to transform an instrumental relationship into guanxi, then it needs to strengthen either the affective or normative dimension or both.

2.2 Categories of guanxi

A set of specialized terms has arisen in China related to *guanxi*. Some examples are: "la guanxi", "gua guanxi", "meiyou guanxi", "guanxi gao jiang", "lisun guanxi", "you guanxi", "youde shi guanxi", "guanxi wang", and "guanxi hu". Table 1 shows the translation of these terms and their meanings (McInnes, 1992).

Table 1 Different types of guanxi

TERM	TRANSLATION	MEANING
"La guanxi"	"To pull" guanxi	It means to get on the good side of someone, to store political capital with them, and carries no negative overtones
"Gua guanxi"	"Work on" guanxi	It means roughly the same but with a more general, less intensive feeling and usually carries negative overtones.
"Meiyou guanxi"	"Without" guanxi	It has become an idiom meaning "it does not matter".
"Guanxi gao jiang"	Guanxi "made ruined"	It means the relationship has done badly, usually because of a lack of flexibility of those involved.
"Lisun guanxi"	"Straighten out" guanxi	It means to put a guanxi back into proper and normal order, often after a period of difficulty or awkwardness.
"You guanxi"	"To have" guanxi	It means to have access to needed influence.
"Youde shi guanxi"	"What one does have" or "the one thing one does have"	It is sometimes negative, meaning that one has all the guanxi one needs, but something else special is lacking.
"Guanxi wang"	Guanxi "net"	It means the whole network of guanxi through which influence is brokered
"Guanxi hu"	Guanxi "family"	It means a person, organization, and even government department, occupying a focal point in one's guanxi network.

Source: Adapted from McInnes (1992)

There is one typology of *guanxi* based on the closeness of the parties involved in the relation. Thus, the term *jiaren* represents the extended family, *shuren (non-family members)* and implies connections with people from the same town, former classmates and the like. Finally, the term *shengren* refers to strangers. Other scholars propose the following categories of *guanxi*: urban/rural *guanxi*, husband/wife *guanxi*, mother-in-law/daughter-in-law *guanxi*, all-female *guanxi*, classmate *guanxi* and owner/tenant *guanxi*. Each relation carries its own nuanced connotations.

2.2.1 Renqing or favor

To fully understand *guanxi* and its managerial implications at the firm level, it is also necessary to analyze the concept of *renqing* or favor. *Renqing* is a set of social norms "by which one has to abide in order to get along well with other people in Chinese society" (Hwang, 1987:954). This term emphasizes the value of maintaining personal harmony and social order among those situated in hierarchically structured relationships. Another way of understanding this principle is that *renqing* implies not only a normative standard for regulating social exchange but also a social mechanism that an individual can use to strive or compete for resources within a stable and structured social fabric. The basic logic of *guanxi* is reciprocity. However, the logic of reciprocity is not proximal and so is to be worked out over time.

2.2.2 Xinyong and business

The Chinese word *xinyong* literally means the use or usefulness of trust. At a general level, *xinyong* "refers to integrity, credibility, trustworthiness, or the reputation and character of a person. In business circles, *xinyong* refers to a person's credit rating" (Yang, 1994:84). There is an obvious and important link between *guanxi* and *xinyong*. Simple put: Good *Guanxi* fosters the development of Reliable *Xinyong*. Why? In China the actions of government are more unpredictable and the outcomes of any legal action uncertain. The arbitrary nature of formal law and government leads to the development of informal rules. Thus, the importance of personal trust emerges as a result of the lack of confidence in the legal system.It is important to understand that trust or *xinyong* is not a static concept. After the establishing trust, its development and maintenance is dependent on the performance of the parties involved in these relationships; here the key word is *perseverance*. The time taken to build trust depends on the quality of the *guanxi* already developed.

2.2.3 Guanxi base

Guanxi begins with a *guanxi base* defined as: "a base which two or more persons have a commonality of shared identification" (Jacobs, 1979: 243). Three elements are key for building these bases: kinship, friendship and other personal relations. Additionally, there are two basic ways to build this base: group identification and altercasting. First, the creation of a *guanxi* base generally demands the existence of some common identity, entailing either a blood relationship or the same social interconnection. The first type of connections represents "ascribed" or inherited *guanxi*. Kinship as well as locality are the two most common forms of ascribed *guanxi* bases. The second type of connections refers to "achieved" or "cultivated" *guanxi* (Tsang, 1998).Another way to develop *guanxi* is through altercasting. This term refers to "the building of *guanxi* between individuals who have no ascribed commonalty" (Yeung and Tung, 1996:61-62). Thus, to attain this goal, individuals must rely on an intermediary. Often, this person is a mutual friend of both individuals who vouches for the behavior and sincerity of these individuals.

Research suggests that there are six major *guanxi* bases: locality/dialects, fictive kinship, kinship, work place, trade associations/social clubs, and friendship. These bases have varying significances over time. Alternatively, Wong and Leung, 1992 identify eight stages to transform a relationship from an outsider to an insider: availability, association, acceptance, affective, affordable, affirmation, assurance and actualization.As implied above, the maintenance of *guanxi* requires continual social interaction. One way to ensure these continual social interactions is to add more bases to the *guanxi*. Thus multiple *guanxi* relations increase not only the opportunity for interaction but also the feelings of commonality between parties and so make it easier for *ganqing* (and *xinyong*) to develop. Bringing multilateral interactions into the picture of dyadic exchange is a major step to understanding the implications of how these ties and reciprocal relationships act to define the social fabric and the organizational culture in the Chinese institutional framework. And so it is necessary to address *"third-party effects"*, which often come from those who are not commonly connected to the two sides of a social exchange (Lin, 2002). Specifically, Gold et al. 2002, conclude that there are four basic strategies for maintaining *guanxi*: tendering favors, nurturing long-term mutual benefits, cultivating personal connections and cultivating trust. Their study reports that 85% of the 19 firms studied indicated that trust was a basic condition for building and sustaining *guanxi*. These strategies are not mutually exclusive but complementary. Thus six of the 19 firms stated they adopted an integrated approach to *guanxi*, using the four strategies.Additionally, firms need to remember that it is more effective to develop multiple connections rather than single-linkages. Such "multiplexing" cultivate more commonalties—more *guanxi* bases—between two parties, so that the ties become stronger, more permanent, and more irreplaceable (Wong and Leung, 1992:65).

In the art of *guanxi*, usually three things are exchanged: gift, banquets or favors. In the art of *guanxi-giving* three elements need to be taken into account: kinds of gifts given, occasion and form of gift-giving, and discreetness in the occasion and the means of presenting the gift. Thus, elements like the following are important: timeliness of the gift, rarity of the gift, the status of the giver, the intensity of the relationship between giver and recipient, and the extent of the recipient indebtedness to the donor (Yang, 1994:126).Finally, the value of *ganqing* and *guanxi* is not static but changes over time. Both are conditioned upon the continued social interaction and mutual help.

2.3 Advantages and risks of guanxi

Several empirical studies have examined the outcomes of *guanxi*. Most studies focus **only on the positive outcomes** from developing *guanxi*. For example, Xin and Pearce, 1996 suggest three major benefits that arise from the establishment of *guanxi*: key sources of information, sources of resources and other areas, such as: smoothing transport arrangements, smoothing collection of payments and building up the firm's reputation and image. Other studies analyze both positive and negative aspects of *guanxi*. For example, recently, Pae, Wong and Lee (2001) developed and tested a model to analyze factors that positively affect *guanxi* as well as the impact of *guanxi* on organizational performance. They state that once *guanxi* is established, it has positive effects on organizational performance. In particular, it offers good means of facilitating transaction by allowing access to limited resource/information, preferential treatment in business dealings, and protection from external threats [...] they also report on the negative aspects of *guanxi* including: corrupt behaviors, favoritism, and nepotism) (Pae, Wong and Lee, 2001:52).

What factors influence *guanxi*? According to the findings of a study, *guanxi* is positively affected by a firm's decision-making uncertainty and perceived similarity, such as: mutual understanding, common interests and shared values and experiences, while negatively affected by: opportunism, job mobility and monitoring industrial companies.There is a dark-side to guanxi. There is a close association between certain types of guanxi and bribery. In this sense, some researchers and managers state that guanxi is synonymous with corruption. It may benefit a few at the expense of the many and so reduce societal well-being. Others suggest that guanxi may or may not be ethically problematic depending on the intentions of its use.

2.4 Guanxi Today

Finally, it is important to highlight two quite lively and unresolved debates over *guanxi*. On the one hand, there is disgreement over the extent to which *guanxi* is something unique to China or if it is a response to specific and historical condictions that happen to develop in China. However, it is unlikely that a protracted theoretical debate of the "Chineseness" of *guanxi* will serve to advance research on the social structure of Chinese society. Currently, there is considerable disagreement over the "fate" of *guanxi* given the economic reforms in the People's Republic of China. As Gold et al., (2002) point out "as the state has loosen its grip on the economy, the role of *guanxi* has expanded in Chinese society. They argue that its role will continue to expand, leading to an economic system that is substantially different from the rational-legal system that defines Western market economies. Others believe that the role of *guanxi* is declining in the era of economic reforms, and that eventually formal rational law will supplant the norms of the personal economy" (pp. 3-4).

3 Conclusions and implications for management in the IT sector

With the growing importance of the Chinese domestic markets to the world economy, and its attraction as a low-cost high-quality production base, a large number of international companies have established operations in China. Many of these companies are in the IT sector.ver the last few years, a number of articles have been published about the Chinese concept of guanxi, sometimes translated as "social connections" and sometimes as "backdoor connections" (DeFrancis, 1997: 211). The word "guanxi" refers to the concept of drawing on connections in order to secure favors in personal relationships. It is richer and certainly more nuanced than a pure interpersonal relationship or friendship; it is a reciprocal obligation to respond to requests for assistance. As a strong tie in social networks, guanxi has played a critical factor in firm's performance in China, affecting the flow of information and a firm's interaction in the partnered and venture driven global context the nexus of which seems to be China. Therefore, a guanxi-based network constitutes part of an organization's core competency and competitive advantages which can increase its overall performance (Luo, 1997).

The principal reason for interest in guanxi is undoubtedly the growing importance of China to the Western business community. How does guanxi works? What does it imply? Answers can be found in the following two Chinese sayings:

"One person honors some other person a linear foot, the other person should, in return, honor him ten feet" (ren jing ni yi chi, ni jing ren yi zhang).

"Receive a droplet of generosity; repay like a gushing spring" (di shui zhi en dang yi yong quan xiang bao). On the other side of this issue consider the words of one of the great Chinese philosophers Sun Tzu: "Know your enemy, know yourself, and you can fight an honored battle with no danger of defeat".

Therefore, a Western firm looking for opportunities in China needs to understand the logic of guanxi or social connections and its associated elements, like renqing or favor, ganqing or emotional feeling, xinyong or trust and gao or reciprocity. Foreigners are, by definition, outsiders and do not belong to the Chinese institutional framework or network. However, once individuals are accepted within this network, then they enjoy its benefits. Therefore, the challenge is to get inside the network. In this sense, guanxi teaches a person to identify an outsider from an insider ("zi ji ren") or collaborator, and prescribes rules for dealing with each kind of person. Finally, one must not forget negative elements associated with guanxi practices in China as discussed above. Zhu (1999) states, that the dominant guanxi culture and mechanisms in China's business practices have resulted in mass managerial misbehavior. With the aim of developing or manteining a good guanxi, reward a favor or beg for a favor, many Chinese managers dine at the expense and to the detriment of enterprise, charge personal expenses to the firm, invest carelessly in expanding projects to curry personal or family favor, risk company funds in the stock markets, and divert state assets to build personal xiaojinku or personal wealth (literally "little gold storage").

References

Alston, J.P. 1989. Wa, guanxi, and inwha: managerial principles in Japan, China, and Korea, Business Horizon, Vol. 32, March-April, pp. 26-31.

Bian, Y. J. 1994. Work and inequality in urban China. Albany: SUNY.

Confucius (1915), The Ethics of Confucius. New York: Putnam.

Che, H. (2006): Software development in China, Online, Last access day: 1/4/2008, http://www.bcs.org/server.php?show=ConWebDoc.3757

Fei, X. (1992). From the Soil. The Foundations of Chinese Society. Translated by Gary G. Hamilton and Wang Zheng. Berkeley, University of California Press.

Gold, T., Doug, G., and Wank, D. 2002. Social Connections in China. Institutions, Culture and the Changing Nature of Guanxi. Cambridge University Press.

Hwang, K. K. 1987. Face and favor: the Chinese power game, American Journal of Sociology, Vol. 92, No. 4,945-974.

Lin, Y-M. .2002. Beyond the dyadic social exchange: guanxi and third-party effect. in Gold, T., Doug, G., and Wank, David. Social connections in china. institutions, culture and the changing nature of guanxi. Cambridge University Press.

Luo, Y. 1997. Guanxi and performance of foreign-invested enterprises in China: An empirical inquiry, Management International Review, 37(1), 51-70.

McInnes, P. 1992. Guanxi or contract: A way to understand and predict conflict between Chinese and Western senior managers in China-based ventures, Paper given at the Symposium on Multinational Business Management, sponsored by Nanjing University and Florida Atlantic University, Nanjing, December 10-12, 1992.

Ordóñez de Pablos, P. (2005): "Western and eastern views on social networks", The Learning Organization- An International Journal, Vol. 12, No. 5 pp. 436-456. Ordóñez de Pablos, P. and Lytras, M.D. (2008), "What managers need to know about social connections and business in China", China Insights Today, Issue 1, January-March 2008. http://www.chinainsightstoday.com/Issue1.pdf

Pae, J. H., Wong, Y.H. and Lee, D-J. 2001. A model of close business relationships in China (guanxi), European Journal of Marketing, Vol. 35, No. 1 (2), pp.51-69.

Tsang, E. W. K. 1998. Can guanxi be a source of sustained competitive advantage for doing business in China?, Academy of Management Executive, 12(2): 64-72.

Yang, M.M. 1994. Gifts, favors and banquets: the art of social relationship in China. Cornell University Press, Ithaca, NY.

Yeung, I.Y. and Tung, R. L. 1996. Achieving business success in Confucian societies: the importance of guanxi (Connections), Organizational Dynamics, 25(2), 54-65.

Redding, G. and Wong, G.Y.Y. (1986), "The psychology of Chinese organizational behavior," in M.H. Bond (eds.), The Psychology of the Chinese People. New York: Oxford University Press, pp. 213–266, 1986.

Zhu, Tian (1999), China's Corporatization Drive: An Evaluation and Policy Implications, Contemporary Economic Policy, 17(4): p530.

Chapter 2
Information Technology Outsourcing Risk Trends in China

Desheng Wu[1], David L. Olson[2] and Dexiang Wu[3]

[1] RiskLab, University of Toronto, CANADA
[2] University of Nebraska, USA
[3] University of Science and Technology of China, CHINA

Abstract The information technology (IT) industry has seen massive changes in the past decade. A great deal of outsourcing of IT has been outsourced, much to India, but also a great deal to China and Russia. The Chinese government has adopted a five-year plan for economic development emphasizing service outsourcing. This paper reviews IT outsourcing risk, considers methods to identify and assess risk, and points to tools for the evaluation of risk, both quantitative and qualitative. Factors specific to China are reviewed.

1 Introduction

Every year we see at least one significant advance in computer speed and computer system storage capacity. Every year we purchase a new cell phone, expecting it to be outdated in a year. Every year we expect that Intel will build a faster chip, leading to a new generation of personal computers. These factors make long term information technology (IT) investment challenging. It is hard to have a rational long-term business plan if the conditions concerning product availability are going to be completely revised. We need to learn to keep up with new developments, which lead to new opportunities. It has always been the case that we need to adapt – but now we need to adapt much faster.

Outsourcing has evolved into a way for IT to gain cost savings to organizations (Gonzalez, et al. 2006). Outsourcing is attractive to many types of organizations. Outsourced IT work from corporate America over the past 5 years has grown from $5.5 billion to over $17.6 billion. Currently India has 80% of this lucrative market (Levensohn 2004). However, according to the 2005 CIO Insight Outsourcing Survey, China is beginning to offer compelling advantages over India since India's original cost benefits are reaching wage and capacity limits (Asia Times Online, 2007). Risk factors specific to IT implementation (specifically of ERP systems) in China were addressed by Yusuf et al. (2006), who suggested solutions to include outsourcing. This paper reviews information systems risk, and presents methods that can be used to evaluate this risk, especially as relating to IT outsourcing to China.

2 Information Systems Risk

Risks in information systems can be viewed from two perspectives. There is a need for information technology security, in the sense that the system function properly when faced by threats from physical (flood, fire, etc.), intrusion (hackers and other malicious invasions), or function (inaccurate data, reporting systems not providing required information to management and/or operations). Physical security is usually dealt with by one group of people, while IT personnel are usually responsible for risks involving intrusion or function. Anderson (2007) called for converging IT and physical security under the direction of a single strategic leader, allowing focus on organizational business objectives. He suggested focus on each organization's unique characteristics considering company size, industry regulations, liability, technical complexity, culture, and risk tolerance. Convergence of physical and IT security are expected to align security efforts with business objectives and allow better risk focus. It also can lead to reduced overhead and administrative duplication. Interaction of system components can lead to better detection of threats, and control of corporate assets. Risk acceptance decisions can be transferred to business units that are most affected.

2.1 IT Risk Identification and Analysis

Information systems involve high levels of risk, in that it is very difficult to predict what problems are going to occur in system development All risks in information system project management cannot be avoided, but early identification of risk can reduce the damage considerably. Kliem and Ludin (1998) gave a risk management cycle consisting of activities managers can undertake to understand what is happening and where:

- Risk Identification
- Risk Analysis
- Risk Control
- Risk Reporting

Risk identification focuses on identifying and ranking project elements, project goals, and risks. Risk identification requires a great deal of pre-project planning and research. Risk analysis is the activity of converting data gathered in the risk identification step into understanding of project risks. Analysis can be supported by quantitative techniques, such as simulation, or qualitative approaches based on judgment. Risk control is the activity of measuring and implementing controls to lessen or avoid the impact of risk elements. This can be reactive, after problems arise, or proactive, expending resources to deal with problems before they occur. Risk reporting communicates identified risks to others for discussion and evaluation.

Risk management in information technology is not a step-by-step procedure, done once and then forgotten. The risk management cycle is a continuous process throughout a project. As the project proceeds, risks are more accurately understood. The primary means of identifying risk amounts to discussing potential problems with those who are most likely to be involved. Successful risk analysis depends on the personal experience of the analyst, as well as access to the project plan and historical data. Interviews with members of the project team can provide the analyst with the official view of the project, but risks are not always readily apparent from this source. More detailed discussion with those familiar with the overall environment within which the project is implemented is more likely to uncover risks. Three commonly used methods to tap human perceptions of risk are brainstorming, the nominal group technique, and the Delphi method.

2.2 Brainstorming

Brainstorming involves redefining the problem, generating ideas, and seeking new solutions. The general idea is to create a climate of free association through trading ideas and perceptions of the problem at hand. Better ideas are expected from brainstorming than from individual thought because the minds of more people are tapped. The productive thought process works best in an environment where criticism is avoided, or at least dampened.

Group support systems are especially good at supporting the brainstorming process. The feature of anonymity encourages more reticent members of the group to contribute. Most GSSs allow all participants to enter comments during brainstorming sessions. As other participants read these comments, free association leads to new ideas, built upon the comments from the entire group. Group support systems also provide a valuable feature in their ability to record these comments in a file, which can be edited with conventional word-processing software.

2.3 Nominal Group Technique

The Nominal Group Technique (Moore 1994) supports groups of people (ideally seven to ten) who initially write their ideas about the issue in question on a pad of paper. Each individual then presents their ideas, which are recorded on a flip-chart (or comparable computer screen technology). The group can generate new ideas during this phase, which continues until no new ideas are forthcoming. When all ideas are recorded, discussion opens. Each idea is discussed. At the end of discussion, each individual records their evaluation of the most serious risks associated with the project by either rank-ordering or rating.

The silent generation of ideas, and structured discussion are contended to overcome many of the limitations of brainstorming. Nominal groups have been found to yield more unique ideas, more total ideas, and better quality ideas than brainstorming groups.

2.4 Delphi Method

The Delphi method was developed at the RAND Corporation for technological forecasting, but has been applied to many other problem environments. The first phase of the Delphi method is anonymous generation of opinions and ideas related to the issue at hand by participants. These anonymous papers are then circulated to all participants, who revise their thoughts in light of these other ideas. Anonymous ideas are exchanged for either a given number of rounds, or until convergence of ideas.The Delphi method can be used with any number of participants. Anonymity and isolation allow maximum freedom from any negative aspects of social interaction. On the negative side, the Delphi method is much more time consuming than brainstorming or the nominal group technique. There also is limited opportunity for clarification of ideas. Conflict is usually handled by voting, which may not completely resolve disagreements.

3 Risk Analysis and Mitigation

Once risk is identified, it then needs to be analyzed and controlled. There are many models that have been proposed for risk analysis, to include multiple criteria analysis such as analytic hierarchy process or outranking methods (Wang and Yang 2007), as well as fuzzy group models (Cong et al. 2008). Olson (2004) includes multiple criteria selection model examples.

3.1 Outsourcing Risks

Viewing enterprise software as a system leads to consideration of the risks involved, and the impact on not only IT costs, but also on hidden costs such as organizational disruption, future upgrades, etc. Further, there are non-cost factors of importance, such as quality, security, and provider proximity (Gonzalez et al. 2006) . Managerial decision makers can then consider mitigation strategies, important in initial system selection, as well as in developing plans for dealing with contingencies (what to do if the system fails; what to do if the vendor raises the price of software support; what to do if the vendor discontinues support for this version of software). An alternative approach is to avoid all of this hassle, and rent an enterprise system from an application service provider (ASP). That involves a whole new set of systemic risks. The overall ERP selection decision involves the seven broad categories of alternatives shown in Table 1 (derived from Olson 2004). Each specific organization might generate variants of selected alternatives that suit their particular needs.

Table 1 Alternative ERP Options

Form	Advantages	Disadvantages
In-house	Fit organization	Most difficult, expensive, slowest
In-House + vendor supp.	Blend proven features with organizational fit	Difficult to develop Expensive & slow
Best-of-breed	Theoretically ideal	Hard to link, slow, potentially inefficient
Customize vendor system	Proven features modified to fit organization	Slower, usually more expensive than pure vendor
Select vendor modules	Less risk, fast, inexpensive	If expand, inefficient and higher total cost
Full vendor system	Fast, inexpensive, efficient	Inflexible
ASP	Least risk & cost, fastest	At mercy of ASP

Outsourcing has evolved into a way for IT to gain cost savings to organizations. This is true for ERP just as it is for other IT implementations. Competitive pressures as motivation for many organizations to outsource major IT functions Bryson and Sullivan 2003). Eliminated jobs make businesses more productive. Often those jobs eliminated are from IT. Outsourcing is attractive to many types of organizations, but especially to those that have small IT staffs, without expertise in enterprise systems. Some organizations, such as General Motors, outsource entire IT operations. There also are on-demand application providers willing to provide particular services covering the gamut of IT applications. Reasons for use of an ASP included the need to quickly get a system on-line (even to bridge the period when an internal system is installed), or to cope with IT downsizing. ASPs can help both small carriers develop new capabilities quickly, as well as providing faster implementations at multiple locations for large companies, and provide access to automatic updates and new applications. They also provide a more flexible way to deal with the changing ERP vendor market. ERP can be outsourced overseas. Overseas outsourcing takes advantage of tremendous cost saving opportunities. As of publication date, India has significant cost advantages over the U.S. and Europe in average programmer salary, while capable of providing equivalent or superior capabilities in many areas. However, relative pay schedules are subject to inflation, and Indian pay rates were expected to increase by double-digit rates over the next few years. ERP skills are one of the areas where higher inflation is expected. However, the expertise available in India still makes them a highly attractive source of IT. Over a period of years, those in other countries such as China are expected to overcome current language barriers and develop sufficiently mature IT skills to draw work from India. As the manufacturing center of the world, China is becoming the winner of most IT outsourcing contracts from developed Asian countries such as Japan and South Korea. It is now poised to compete head-to-head with the traditional outsourcing destination countries, such as India, Ireland and Israel, for the much bigger and more profitable North American and European market.

There is a tradeoff in outsourcing ERP systems, in that costs and some form of risks are reduced by outsourcing, but other companies view ERP as too mission-critical to yield control. The biggest risks of outsourcing are downtime and loss of operational data. Organizations whose systems expand rapidly due to acquisition may find outsourcing attractive for technical aspects of ERP. The tradeoff is between savings in capital investment and technical expertise through ASP, versus control and customization abilities better served through in-house IT. Government use of ERP has its own set of characteristics. The value of outsourcing financial systems in government can be very beneficial in terms of reduced cost (Joplin and Terry 2000). Benefits of application hosting were stated as lower opportunity costs of software ownership, and avoiding problems of developing and retaining IT staff. Additional difficulties faced by governmental IT directors in the governmental sector include the need to be able to defend proposals in public hearings. Such applications also involved the use of ERP to reduce State jobs, which can lead to difficulties with the state information worker union.

3.2 Tradeoffs in ERP Outsourcing

Bryson and Sullivan (2003) cited specific reasons that a particular ASP might be attractive as a source for ERP. These included the opportunity to use a well-known company as a reference, opening new lines of business, and opportunities to gain market-share in particular industries. Some organizations may also view ASPs as a way to aid cash flow in periods when they are financially weak and desperate for business. In many cases, cost rise precipitously after the outsourcing firm has become committed to the relationship. One explanation given was the lack of analytical models and tools to evaluate alternatives. These tradeoffs are recapitulated in Table 2 (derived from Olson 2004):

Table 2 Factors For and Against Outsourcing ERP

Reasons to Outsource	Reasons Against Outsourcing
Reduced capital expenditure for ERP software and updates	Security and privacy concerns
Lower costs gained through ASP economies of scale (efficiency)	Concern about vendor dependency and lock-in
More flexible and agile IT capability	Availability, performance and reliability concerns
Increased service levels at reasonable cost	High migration costs
Expertise availability unaffordable in-house (eliminate the need to recruit IT personnel)	ERP expertise is a competency critical to organizational success
Allowing the organization to focus on their core business.	ERP systems are inextricably tied to IT infrastructure
Continuous access to the latest technology	Some key applications may be in-house and critical
Reduced risk of infrastructure failure	Operations are currently as efficient as the ASPs
Manage IT workload variability	Corporate culture doesn't deal well with working with partners.
Replace obsolete systems	

3.3 Qualitative Factors

While cost is clearly an important matter, there are other factors important in selection of ERP that are difficult to fit into a total cost framework. Van Everdingen et al. conducted a survey of European firms in mid-1998 with the intent of measuring ERP penetration by market (Van Everdingen et al. 2000). The survey included questions about the criteria considered criteria for supplier selection. The criteria reportedly used are given in the first column of Table 3, in order of ranking. Product functionality and quality were the criteria most often reported to be important. Column 2 gives related factors reported by Ekanayaka et al. (2003) in their framework for evaluating ASPs, while column 3 gives more specifics in that framework.

While these two frameworks don't match entirely, there is a lot of overlap. ASPs would not be expected to have specific impact on the three least important criteria given by Van Everdingen et al. The Ekanayaka et al. framework added two factors important in ASP evaluation: security and service level issues.

Table 3 Selection Evaluation Factors

ERP Supplier Selection (Van Everdingen et al.)	ASP Evaluation (Ekanayaka et al.)	Ekanayaka et al. subelements
1. Product functionality	Customer service	1. Help desk & training
		2. Support for account administration
2. Product quality	Reliability, scalability	
3. Implementation speed	Availability	
4. Interface with other systems	Integration	1. Ability to share data between applications
5. Price	Pricing	1. Effect on total cost structure
		2. Hidden costs & charges
		3. ROI
6. Market leadership		
7. Corporate image		
8. International orientation		
	Security	Physical security of facilities
		Security of data and applications
		Back-up and restore procedures
		Disaster recovery plan
	Service level monitoring & management	1. Clearly defined performance metrics and measurement
		2. Defined procedures for opening and closing accounts
		3. Flexibility in service offerings, pricing, contract length

4 Outsourcing Risks in China

China is India's only neighbor in the Far East with a comparable population but far better infrastructure boosted by its fastest expanding economy in the world. China is already the manufacturing center of the world, and the winner of most IT outsourcing contracts from developed Asian countries such as Japan and South Korea. It is now poised to compete head-to-head with the traditional outsourcing destination countries, such as India, Ireland and Israel, for the much bigger and more profitable North American and European market.

According to Gartner Group, the global IT services market is worth $580 billion, of which only 6% is outsourced. India currently has 80% of this market, but other contenders are rising with China now enjoying the biggest cost advantage. On average, an engineer with two to three years post-graduate experience is paid a monthly salary of less than $500, compared with more than $700 in India and upwards of $5,000 in the United States. India also led other countries in the region with the highest turnover rate at 15.4%, a reflection of the rampant job-hopping in the Indian corporate world, especially the IT sector. Other markets with high attrition rates include Australia (15.1%) and Hong Kong (12.1%). Almost all Indian IT firms projected greater salary increases for 2005, according to a recent survey. Table 4 summarizes the labor cost factors, based on Meta Group Consultancy (2001).

Table 4 Relative Labor Costs

	India	China	Other (Ireland, etc.)
Monthly Salary	$700 or more	$500 or less	$600-5,000
Salary Increase	10-15% annually	6-8% annually	7-10% annually
Personnel Turnover	30%	12.6%	10-15%
IT Graduates	150,000 annually	250,000 annually	30,000-50,000 annually
IT Worker Shortage	250,000 by 2010	None reported	20,000-200,000 by 2010

In light of the increasing labor costs, India's response is also moving to China. In fact, most Indian IT firms that operate globally have begun implementing back-door linkages to cheaper locations. IT giants such as Wipro, Infosys, Satyam and Tata Consulting Services (TCS) have all set up operations in China, given the lower wage cost of software engineers due to the excess supply of trained man-power. TCS set up its shop in China in 2002 that employs more than 180 people; a year after making a foray into the country, Infosys (Shanghai) has a staff strength of 200 to cater to clients in Europe, the US and Japan; Wipro set up its Chinese unit in August 2004.

4.1 Business Risks

Two types of risks are perceived in international business operations in China that apply to an ERP IT software company. First, because China is not a full market economy based on a democratic political system, there is some political risk in the government's interfering with free enterprises. Such risks are deemed negligible based on the open and reform policies of the central government in the past two decade, and the economic boom derived from such a more transparent political environment. Second, whereas China's lack of protection of intellectual properties is widely reported, there have been very few cases where business software was pirated. This is due to the requirement of domain knowledge to profit from selling business software.A crucial factor for China's emergence into the global outsourcing industry is government support. The most important central government policy for the software industry is the June 2000 announcement of State Council Document 18, formally known as the "Policies to Promote the Software and Integrated Circuit Industry Development." The document created preferential policies to promote the development of these two sectors. The documented policies for software companies include:

1. Value-added Tax (VAT) refund for R&D and expanded production
2. Tax preferences for newly established companies
3. Fast-track approval for software companies seeking to raise capital on overseas stock markets
4. Exemption from tariffs and VAT for software companies' imports of technology and equipment
5. Direct export rights for all software firms with over USD $1 million in revenues

China has recently adopted the "Thousand-Hundred-Ten Project" of service outsourcing with the aim of promoting their service outsourcing industry (Fa 2006). They intend to develop ten base cities of service outsourcing that are to be internationally competitive. They also want to promote one hundred transnational corporations to transfer their service businesses to China, and to cultivate one thousand large and medium-sized service outsourcing enterprises with international qualification.

5 Conclusions

Information systems are crucial to the success of just about every 21st Century organization. The IS/IT industry has moved toward enterprise systems as a means to obtain efficiencies in delivering needed computing support. This approach gains through integration of databases, thus eliminating needless duplication and subsequent confusion from conflicting records. It also involves consideration of better business processes, providing substitution of computer technology for more expensive human labor.But there are many risks associated with enterprise systems (just as there are with implementing any information technology). Whenever major changes in organizational operation are made, this inherently incurs high levels of risk. COSO frameworks apply to information systems just as they do to any aspect of risk assessment. But specific tools for risk assessment have been developed for information systems. This paper has sought to consider risks of evaluating IT proposals (focusing on ERP), as well as consideration of IS/IT project risk in general. Methods for identifying risks in IS/IT projects were reviewed. We also presented the status and trends of outsourcing risks in China.

References

Anderson K (2007). Convergence: A holistic approach to risk management. Network Security May, 4-7

Asia Times Online: http://www.atimes.com/atimes/South_Asia/FK16Df06.html. Accessed July 2007

Bryson KM and Sullivan WE (2003) Designing effective incentive-oriented contracts for application service provider hosting of ERP systems, Business Process Management Journal, 9:705-721

Cong G., Zhang J., Chen T. and Lai K-K (2008) A variable precision fuzzy rough group decision-making model for IT offshore outsourcing risk evaluation. Journal of Global Information Management 16: 18-34

Ekanayaka Y Currie WL and Seltsikas P (2003) Evaluating application service providers. Benchmarking: An International Journal 10:343-354

Fa SZ (2006) Circular of Ministry of Commerce on Implementing the "thousand-hundred-ten project" of service outsourcing. http://big5.mofcom.gov.cn/gate/big5/tradeinservices.mofcom.gov.cn/en/b/2007-11-20/11152.shtml

Gonzalez R, Gasco J, Llopis J (2006) Information systems offshore outsourcing. Industrial Management & Data Systems 106: 1233-1248

Joplin B and Terry C (2000) Financial system outsourcing: The ERP application hosting option. Government Finance Review 16:31-33

Kliem RL, Ludin IS (1998) Reducing project risk. Gower, Aldershot England

Levensohn A (2004) How to manage risk – Enterprise-wide. Strategic Finance 86: 55-56

Meta Group Consultancy (2001) ComputerWorld, March 19: http://insight.zdnet.co.uk/specials/utsourcing/0,39026381,39150917,00.htm

Moore CM (1994) Group techniques for idea building, 2nd ed. Sage Publications, Thousand Oaks CA

Olson DL (2004) Managerial issues of enterprise resource planning systems. McGraw-Hill/Irwin, Boston

Van Everdingen Y, van Hellegersberg J and Waarts E (2000) ERP adoption by European mid-size companies. Communications of the ACM 43:27-31

Wang J-J and De-Li Y (2007) Using a hybrid multi-criteria decision aid method for information systems outsourcing. Computers & Operations Research 34: 3691-3700

Yusuf Y, Gunasekaran A, Wu C (2006) Implementation of enterprise resource planning in China. Technovation 26:1324-1336

Chapter 3
Chinese Consumers' Attitudes and Adoption of Online and Mobile Banking

Sylvie Laforet

University of Sheffield, UNITED KINGDOM

Abstract This chapter examines the market demand for online and mobile banking in China. The results are presented and discussed, based on a consumer survey conducted in six major Chinese cities. Consumer behaviour, attitude, motivation and cultural influences are studied in relation to Chinese adoption of these services. The chapter is organised as follows: it starts with an overview of new distribution channels in the retail banking industry and their effects on consumer behaviour as well as, the development of online and mobile banking in China. Then, a review of the literature on consumer attitude and adoption of electronic banking with a discussion of the factors predetermining attitudes to online and mobile banking; Followed by an examination of the drivers of online and mobile banking in China as well as, Chinese culture influence on Chinese perception of technology-based financial services. Finally, the survey findings are presented, with a discussion of managerial implications incorporated.

1 New distribution channels and effects on consumer behaviour in the retail banking industry

Traditional retail banking is typically characterised by brick and mortar branches. Competitive advantages came from careful planning of the branch network in the banking industry in early days. Beckett et al. (2000) argued that within the traditional structure and operation of banking services industry, consumers had little choice in selecting delivery channels. The rigid structure of the industry and simple delivery channels meant, consumers were locked into buying patterns and had little incentive to change. However, with the increasing turbulence in the environment, co-operation, changes, globalisation and convergence, as well as changing consumer preferences, many new distribution channels have recently flourished in the banking industry.One of the most significant changes in the banking industry has been the consumer movement from traditional branch banking to electronic delivery channels such as Internet, telephone, and mobile phones in private banking. Although the term electronic banking often refers to online banking,

P.O. de Pablos, M.D. Lytras (eds.), *The China Information Technology Handbook*,
DOI: 10.1007/978-0-387-77743-6_3, © Springer Science+Business Media, LLC 2009

it is an upper construct, including also telephone banking, WAP-banking, as well as iNet-television banking (Karjaluoto et al. 2002). With the help of new technology and the emergence of Internet, which is widely seen as the most important delivery channel in the era, banking is no longer bound to time or geography. Consumers all over the world have relatively easy access to their accounts 24 hours a day, seven days a week. The new types of distribution channels, online and mobile banking provide many benefits to both banks and their customers.

The emergence of new forms of technology have a great impact on consumer behaviour, not only consumers' attitudes and motivations are influenced and affected by several factors such as, their previous experience, IT skills, technology acceptance, etc. but also, consumers' behaviour are more disposed to change and unpredictable with regard to choosing banking services. As a result, how to attract and retain customers are becoming of key importance. Therefore, a better understanding of consumers' attitudes becomes a must for bank providers who want not only anticipate, but also influence and determine consumer buying behaviour.

According to the ORB Special Reports, by most measures, electronic banking is a runaway success. Not only is the penetration growing, but the level of usage is also increasing. It is believed that if done correctly, electronic banking can increase customer satisfaction, boost retention and improve profits. Under these circumstances, online and mobile banking are not only there to change people's financial management habits, but they also use today's computer technology to make available to customers the option of bypassing time-consuming, paper-based aspects of traditional banking in order to manage their finances more rapidly and efficiently.

2 Online and mobile banking in China

In 1997, China Merchants Bank was first to launch the Internet Payment System in China and thereafter, the Internet banking system and telephone banking system spread rapidly within China mainland. Although Chinese proficiency of using the Internet system is relatively low and it is believed that electronic banking is still in the initial stage in this country, with the advantages of being convenient, safe, efficient and economical, Chinese domestic banks have confidence that electronic banking is the perfect extension of traditional banking business. Consequently, they are eager to implement this new technology and services in order to grasp and, penetrate the market and gain competitive advantage. Most Chinese retail banks provide online banking and mobile banking as an add-on service to the existing branch activities.

Electronic banking is a major strategic response from Chinese domestic banks to the increasing competitive environment after the People's Republic of China accession into the WTO. With the opening of retail banking and RMB business to all players by 2007, Chinese domestic banks face powerful competition from foreign banks. Online banking has been seen as a powerful IT tool for Chinese domestic banks to provide better customer services and to enter new markets and expand thus, enabling them to compete better with multinational banks.. Companies' perceived benefits of electronic banking are found to be highly correlated with the increase in Internet banking investment. Banks have viewed electronic banking as an enabler to improve customer services to enhance their ability to compete, to facilitate their new product offering and services as well as, to reduce transaction costs (Lu et al. 2005).

Despite these optimistic views concerning the application and benefits of online and mobile banking in China, there are still many crucial problems which are very difficult to conquer, such as Chinese consumers' attitudes towards technology-based banking services, their attitude towards using credit cards, Chinese traditional belief and habit with regard to personal financial management reflecting in their Confucian-based culture – which will be discussed in the section on 'National culture of China' below and, the low prevalence of Internet in some areas. As far as the Internet penetration among households is concerned, China lags far behind developed countries because the access price is out of reach for many. The cost of access is much higher than in the US partly, as a result of Chinese government policies (Yu 2006 quoting Samisee 1998). A report by China Internet Information Centre (CNNIC) shows that the Internet reached only about 7 percent of the population in mid-2004 (CNNIC 2004).

As far as mobile banking in China is concerned, it is in the initial stage of implementation. The largest mobile network operator in China, collaborated with three leading banks, Bank of China, Industrial and Commercial Bank of China and China Merchants Bank, started to implement this new banking service. The concept of mobile banking is new to most customers, the prevalence, is also relatively low.

3 Consumer attitude and adoption of electronic banking

Consumer adoption of electronic banking has been researched from several perspectives - from the consumer perceptions and expectations of service quality to measuring consumer satisfaction/dissatisfaction using SERVQUAL (Lewis 1991; Holmond and Kock 1996; Aladwani 2001; Jun and Cai 2001) - consumer motives and acceptance of techno-based banking services (Barzack et al. 1997) – consumers' usage, attitudes and behaviours towards online and mobile banking focusing on the socio-economic/demographic factors (Beckett et al. 2002; Howcroft et al. 2002), benefits sought and consumers' attitudes towards online banking (Machauer and Morgner 2001).

Academics also take a different stance in the theories they adopt when exploring consumer adoption of electronic banking. Consumer behaviour, innovation and acceptance of new innovations (for example, Suganthi et al. 2001; Gerrard and Cunningham 2003) as well as relationship marketing (Kapoulas et al. 2002; Mukherjee and Nath 2003) were used. Researchers also focused upon the adopters versus non-adopters and systematically categorised adopters/non-adopters into active users, light and non-users (Sarel and Marmorstein 2003), or into two groups of 'will never adopt' to 'already have' (Kolodinsky et al. 2004).

Consumers' attitudes and motives have by far been more widely studied as Akinci et al. (2004) suggest, "among the fundamental factors influencing consumer buying behaviour and have attracted considerable attention from researchers probing the behaviour of bank customers and their relationship with these institutions". The consumer research also lacks empirical evidence about how consumer behaviour, attitude, motivation affect consumer acceptance of online and mobile banking (Karjaluoto et al. 2002). Given these predispositions, in the following consumer behaviour, attitude and motivation are examined in relation to online and mobile banking adoption. In addition, the author was interested in finding out whether Chinese culture affects adoption of online and mobile banking in China.

3.1 Factors predetermining consumer attitude and adoption of mbanking

Research on consumer attitude and adoption of electronic banking showed, there are several factors predetermining a consumer's attitude towards online and mobile banking such as a person's demographic, motivation and behaviour towards different banking technologies and an individual's acceptance of new technology. Similarly, it has been found that attitudes towards online banking and actual behaviours were both influenced by prior experience of computers and new technology and, other possible factors discussed below.

With regard to demographics factor, Howcroft et al. (2002) revealed that younger consumers value the convenience or time saving potential of online and mobile banking more than older consumers. Younger consumers also regarded the lack of face-to-face contact as less important than older consumers. These authors further found, the educational levels of respondents did not affect the use of telephone or online banking.

However, Karjaluoto et al. (2002) showed a typical user of online banking in Finnish market highly educated, relatively young and wealthy person with good knowledge of computers and especially, the Internet. The results of their study proposed that, demographic factors have an impact on online banking behaviour. Consistently with past studies (Daniel 1999; Sathye 1999) and the Electronic Banking Market Assessment Report showing a clear-cut division between the rich, who would use online banking and the poor, who would possibly prefer televised-banking.

Though, the wide use of geographic, demographic, socio-economic and psychographic variables have not always been accepted as good predictors in predicting buying behaviour in financial services by past and recent studies, which claimed that, the benefits customers seek for in banking services and/or the product attributes should be identified instead (Minhas and Jacobs 1996; Lockett and Littler 1997; Machauer and Morgner 2001). For instance, Machauer and Morgner' study focused on segmenting the consumer in bank marketing by expected benefits and attitudes. Using cluster analysis, these authors separated customers into four groups the 'transaction oriented' group, who have a strong technology but weak information attitude; the 'generally interested', who have a positive technology and online and strong information attitude; 'service oriented' who have both, weak information and technology attitudes; and the 'technology opposed' group, have strong information but weak technology attitudes. But this argument contradicts again with a recent study by Suoranta et al. (2004), showing that household income and education had a significant effect on the adoption of electronic banking among mature Finnish consumers.

Consumers' motives also predetermine consumers' attitudes and behaviours towards different banking technologies. Barczak et al. (1997) studied consumers' motives in the use of technological-based banking services found, four motivational clusters for people's money management philosophies 'security conscious', 'maximizers', 'instant gratification' and 'hassle avoiders'. These four motivational segments had different attitudes and behaviours towards different banking technologies.

With regard to new technology acceptance, the literature points out that unless, the specific need of a consumer is fulfilled, consumers may not be prepared to change from the present setting and familiar ways of operating (Sathye 1999). In the context of online, mobile banking and traditional retail branches, whether consumers would adopt new technology-based delivery channels depends on their attitudes towards each of these channels. Research showed that consumers are not generally predisposed to change their behaviour radically and adopt widespread usage of telephone and online banking. Thornton and White (2001) also, noted that changes in the use of delivery channels would occur as the population matures as knowledge, confidence and computer usage increases.

Karjaluoto et al. (2002) showed that prior experience with computers and technologies and attitudes towards computers influence both attitudes towards online banking and actual behaviours. Their study revealed among these factors, prior computer experience had a significant impact on online banking usage while, positive personal banking experience seemed to have had an effect on both attitudes and usage and, satisfied customers tent to keep up with their current delivery channel.

Research showed attitudes towards electronic banking and actual behaviours were also influenced by factors such as satisfaction/dissatisfaction with current banking services, reference groups (i.e. influence from families and others) and computer attitudes. Thus, it can be argued that these would strongly affect attitudes and behaviours towards online banking.

In the past, Lewis (1991) pointed out that the reasons consumers switched delivery channel from traditional to electronic self-service was the dissatisfaction with their present services. These might include the slow speed of service in branches, inconvenient branch opening hours or places and the small number of branch staff available to serve customers, etc. While a number of recent studies focusing on customer satisfaction with bank services, indicate that early adopters and heavy users of Internet banking were more satisfied with this service compared to other customers (Polatoglu and Ekin 2001).

Others also argued that the delivery of technology services appears to be correlated with high satisfaction where these services were most important to customers (Joseph and Stone 2003). Similarly, the literature suggests that consumers prefer a mix of rather than any one single delivery channel (Howcroft et al. 2002) and that it would be highly important for service providers to understand and improve each channel within the overall service offering rather than concentrating efforts on improving one delivery channel in isolation (Patricio et al. 2003).

Karjaluoto (2002) showed that reference groups have equally affected attitudes and behaviours towards online banking. Measuring attitudes with the Fishbein model, they also suggested that the overall strongly positive attitudes towards online banking are faster, cheaper, easier and more service-oriented.

Finally, a number of studies also found trust and perceived risks have a significant positive influence on commitment (Bhattacherjee 2002; Mukherjee and Nath 2003). Bhattacherjee theoretically conceptualised and empirically validated a scale to measure individual trust in online firms. The author found that one's willingness to transact with an online firm may be predicted by additional variables above, and beyond trust, such as perceived usefulness and perceived ease of use of such transactions. Likewise, one's trust in an online firm may not be derived only from prior familiarity with the firm, but also from calculative, institutional and identification and beliefs about the firm. This is consistent with Howcroft et al. study (2002), claiming that the most important factor in encouraging the use of online banking, is lower fees and improved levels of service, i.e. an error-free service. They also found among the reasons for consumers to be reluctant to use online banking services were concerns over security, lack of awareness of online services offered by banks and complex bank sites. While, Mukherjee and Nath tested a model of trust in India in which 'shared value', 'communication' and 'opportunistic behaviour' were antecedents of trust. They concluded that both shared value and communication played a significant positive role on trust and that trust had a significant positive influence on commitment.

In so far, we have looked at how attitudes, motivations and behaviours influenced electronic banking adoption mainly in a Western and non-Chinese context. Next, we look at the drivers of online and mobile banking in China and the influence of Chinese culture on consumer behaviour.

3.2 Drivers of online and mobile banking in China

The drivers of online and mobile banking in China were underlined in part, by Chinese information technology development, Internet access, computers ownership and especially, the emergent of Internet bankers. Although the number of actual Chinese using Internet banking is expected to remain low by international standards, due to the low Internet penetration above mentioned. This situation would be improved as Chinese bank customers' increase in sophistication, gain greater access to the Internet and adopt new technologies such as, WAP. ACNielsen Consult China Online Banking online survey of 2001, found that the population of emergent Internet bankers has grown 50 percent to 2.5 million, up 900,000 from the second half of 2000. Twenty three percent of regular users are now performing basic Internet banking activities online (including visiting bank websites on the Internet), compared to 17 percent in 2000 and, just over 10 percent in 1999.

Furthermore, a number of authors noted attitudes to online banking in China were changing dramatically (Sandland 2000). Li (2002) also claimed that Chinese were undergoing tremendous changes in their attitudes towards the service. Among the most frequent net surfers, the proportion of those against the online banking system had dropped from 14 percent in 2000 to 6 percent in 2001. The AC Nielsen Online China Report found that the drivers of growth in online banking were a combination of convenience provided to those with easy Internet access, the availability of secure, high standard online banking functionality, cost savings and the necessity of banking services.

Similarly, mobile banking has many advantages such as convenience and low cost savings. Mobile banking service takes place 24 hours a day 365 day a year. Customers only need to pay about 0.1 Yuan for every successful transaction and it only takes a few seconds for the whole process to complete, after the user sends his message.

National culture of China

It is clear that culture makes a difference to the consumer's behaviour and therefore, has an impact on bank marketing; While, Internet banking is compatible with consumers' lifestyles and values. Hofstede's (1991) 'value system' of national cultures represented by four dimensions, have some relevance in the context of China and can help in understanding the consumer's behaviour of new technology-based financial services channels, such as online and mobile banking. Based on the culture analysis from various studies (Chimezie et al. 1993; Muhlbracher et al. 1999), Chinese consumers tend to have strong uncertainty avoidances, which mean there is a great need for strict regulation and legislation to ensure limited uncertainties. However, according to Duff (2002), one barrier that is preventing active online trading participation in China mainland is the lack of regulation. Therefore, Chinese consumers might be more concerned about the risks of new and unfamiliar technology-based financial services, such as online and mobile banking. In addition, Chinese tend to have relatively weak time perspective. Referring to the literature's time and location value of online banking or known as, temporal and spatial flexibility of this service (Heinoken 2007). Since Chinese consumers tend to be more resistant to change, they might prefer and keep on using familiar methods of banking and cash carrying. As China has been known as a cash-centric society, people tend to pay in full in cash for some large items such as cars and even, houses.

Furthermore, personal interaction in purchasing behaviour in China is prevalent. In Confucian-based cultures such as the Chinese, people prefer to deal with someone who either possess the knowledge about the product or who is a member of their social network. The Chinese also have long favoured face-to-face transactions, because they help build trust. This strong preference might have a negative impact on electronic banking, because the latter is impersonal in nature.

Losing face is also an issue in China. It is almost the worst thing imaginable for a Chinese person to lose face in front of others particularly, those whom they know. This has an impact on their attitudes towards using credit cards which, in turn has an effect on electronic banking. Similarly, group influence is very important, as Chinese people are highly collectivists. Despite the national culture and subculture, there are always some individuals who are more inclined to adopt new ways of thinking and behaving than others. Rogers (1995) classified potential customers into five categories: innovators, early adopters, early majority, late majority and laggards. In this context, Chinese consumers can be viewed similarly as any consumers in the world since they can be categorised according to the five groups of potential customers, mentioned above.

4 The survey

Three hundred respondents from six major cities of China, including China's Capital city Beijing were prompted randomly in the streets and interviewed by a small team of interviewers. Respondents verbally replied to a structured questionnaire their answers were recorded accordingly by the interviewers. The technique used was similar to that of high street consumer market research poll. In total, 128 respondents participated in this survey, giving a response rate of 43%. There were two advantages for prompting respondents: the first, questionnaires were fully completed thus reducing non-response items. Second, collection of questionnaires was on the spot as a result no reminders were needed hence, time was considerably saved.

The sample size decisions were primarily based on cost considerations and in line with studies on consumer attitude and adoption of electronic banking, where sample sizes used were between 114 to 1167 respondents. The sample was not necessarily representative of the Chinese population as a whole as it ignored the large rural population. However, the target market for online/mobile banking is likely to be urban and relatively wealthy so, we have a sample which is potentially representative of the target population. Respondents were randomly selected from six major cities was necessary, as less developed regions are difficult to reach and lack Internet infrastructure. It would have not therefore, been realistic to ask for any views on the topic concerned.

The relatively high response rate for this type of consumer study was thought to be attributed mainly, to three factors: a clear and simple design questionnaire translated into ordinary Chinese, respondents were briefed about the content and purpose of the survey and were guaranteed that their replies would be treated in strictest confidence. Lastly, the high response rate was also attributed to the respondents' enthusiasm or willingness to participate obviously, to what they considered as an interesting subject to put their views across.

The survey was concerned with users and non-users of Internet/mobile banking. The items in the questionnaire were constructed based on the consumer attitude and adoption of electronic banking literature, mentioned above. The questionnaire focused on the following main issues: consumers' attitudes and reactions to new technology, consumers' attitudes to the traditional retail banking distribution channel, consumers' perceptions of online and mobile bank product attributes, consumers' expectations and major concerns of online and mobile banking, psychological factors and demographic factors.

4.1 Issues investigated in the study

- Consumers' attitudes to Online and Mobile Banking in China
- Consumers' motivation to use Online and Mobile Banking and their needs and drives
- Whether the customer behaviour and attitude influence the popularisation of a new catalogue of services/products
- To what extent the Internet and mobile industry influence the prevalence of Online and Mobile Banking
- Whether psychosocial factors and cultural context influence consumers' attitudes and behaviours

4.2 Study objectives

- To investigate the market status of online and mobile banking in China
- To identify the target customers for online and mobile banking

- To understand the demographic characteristics of users and non-users of electronic banking
- To compare attitudes of users and non-users towards electronic banking with respect to a number of factors such as technology, security, convenience, prior computer/new technology experience, prior personal banking experience and possession of a credit/debit card and a WAP/CDMA as well as users and non-users' attitudes towards the product attributes and reference groups' influence

4.3 Users/non-users' demographics

The proportion of male and female respondents was almost equally split in this survey, with 53 per cent male and 47 per cent female, aged between 25 to 34 years old (57 per cent) and 35 to 44 years old (20 per cent) and salaried employees (66.5 per cent) with a university education (50 per cent). The high response rate coming from younger consumers indicated that they were more interested in online and mobile banking topics than older consumers and were willing to participate in the survey (Table 1).

Over one-third of the respondents indicated that they were online bank users (33 per cent), among which the majority were males (71 per cent), with an age group between 25-34 years old (71 per cent), were also salaried employees and senior managers (87 per cent), and possessed an annual income of 120K to 128K Yuan (42.5 per cent). In contrast, a high percentage of non-users were females, in the category of 45-54 years old, were small business owners, the retired and other

Table 1 Scores of online bank users/non-users on following statements

			User		Non-user
	N	Mean	Sig. (2-tailed)	N	Mean
Convenience		1.98	0.33		2.15
Ease of use	41	2.37	0.18	86	2.15
Access to a wide range of services free from time/place	42	2.19	0.07	84	2.52
Confidential and secure	42	1.90	0.03*	84	2.79
Hackers or fraud	42	2.79	0.03*	86	3.37
Owning credit/debit card	42	1.05	0.00*	86	1.29
Awareness	42	1.00	0.00*	86	1.26
Computer experience	42	1.29	0.000*	85	2.04
Technical experience	40	1.55	0.000*	85	2.32
Personal banking experience	40	2.23	0.31	85	2.36
Reference group influence	39	2.64	0.09	85	2.96

Note: *Significant beyond 0.05

Table 2 Scores of mobile bank users/non-users on the following statements

		User			Non-user	
	N	Mean	Sig. (2-tailed)	N	Mean
Novelty and usefulness		2.00	0.68	122	2.29
Owning WAP/CDMA	5	1.20	0.05	123	1.63
Awareness	5	1.90	0.02*	122	1.99
Prior computer experience	5	1.20	0.15	120	1.81
Prior technology experience	5	1.40	0.09	120	2.10
Personal banking experience	5	2.00	0.31	120	2.33
Reference group influence	5	2.60	0.54	119	2.87

Note: *Significant beyond 0.05

(Table 2). Although the results revealed that 14 per cent of the respondents were mobile bank users, this makes up nearly half of the online bank users' population, suggesting that mobile banking has almost caught up with the online banking services in China. The mobile bank users were spread among the salaried employees, senior managers and a smaller proportion of small business owners, with an age group between 25-34 and 35-44 (half of the proportion of the 25-34 age groups) and possess an annual income of 60K to 120K Yuan and 120-128K Yuan (Table 3). Another point to note, compared with the online services, is that the 35-44 years old group seems to be using mobile banking services more. Similarly, small business owners also seem to use mobile banking instead of online banking.

4.4 Factors affecting consumer attitude and adoption of m-banking

Education - The results showed no significant difference between the online and mobile bank users and non-users in terms of their level of education (Tables 2 & 3). Hence, respondents' level of education was not found to influence online and mobile banking adoption in China.

Awareness - The results indicated a significant difference between users and non-users of online and mobile banking in terms of their level of awareness of these services (Table 4). The results showed non-users of online banking were not at all aware of this service (two-thirds of the sample surveyed), while about one-third of online bank users adopted mobile banking, two-thirds heard about it but did not use it because they were not clear about its benefits (Table 5). This seems to suggest that online and mobile banking share the same level of awareness, which is generally low.

Possession of a credit/debit card and a WAP/CDMA - The results also, showed a significant difference between online and mobile bank users in terms of their possession of a credit/debit card for online banking and a WAP/CDMA for mobile banking. Online bank users were associated with those who owned a credit/debit card (Table 4) and non-mobile bank users were associated with those who did not own a WAP/CDMA (Table 5).

Table 3 Mobile bank users/non-users demographics

	User		Non-user	
	(%)	N	(%)	N
Gender				
Male	2.5	3	51	65
Female	1.6	2	45.5	58
($p = 0.753$)				
Age				
18–24	0		6.3	8
25–34	8.6	11	48.4	62
35–44	4.7	6	14.9	19
45–54	0.8	1	5.5	7
55+	0		11	14
($- = 0.000$)				
Education				
No qualification	0		1.6	2
College	3.2	4	23.6	30
Undergraduate	8	10	42.5	54
Graduate	2.5	3	29	20
Doctor	0.8	1	1.6	2
Other	0		1	1
($p = 0.225$)				
Income				
>20K	0.8	1	23	28
20–60K	1.6	2	32.8	40
60–120K	5.7	7	22.2	27
120–128K	4.9	6	5.7	5
180K+	0.8	1	2.5	3
($p = 0.000$)				
Occupation				
Student	0		1.6	2
Salaried employee	6.4	8	61.6	77
Senior manager	5.6	9	7.2	7
Small business owner	2.4	3	3.2	4
Retired	0		10.4	13
Other	0		1.6	2
($p = 0.000$)				

Table 4 Scores of online bank users/non-users on following statements

		User			Non-user
	N	Mean	Sig. (2-tailed)	N	Mean
Convenience		1.98	0.33		2.15
Ease of use	41	2.37	0.18	86	2.15
Access to a wide range of services free from time/place	42	2.19	0.07	84	2.52
Confidential and secure	42	1.90	0.03*	84	2.79
Hackers or fraud	42	2.79	0.03*	86	3.37
Owning credit/debit card	42	1.05	0.00*	86	1.29
Awareness	42	1.00	0.00*	86	1.26
Computer experience	42	1.29	0.000*	85	2.04
Technical experience	40	1.55	0.000*	85	2.32
Personal banking experience	40	2.23	0.31	85	2.36
Reference group influence	39	2.64	0.09	85	2.96

Note: *Significant beyond 0.05.

Table 5 Scores of mobile bank users/non-users on the following statements

		User			Non-user
	N	Mean	Sig. (2-tailed)	N	Mean
Novelty and usefulness		2.00	0.68	122	2.29
Owning WAP/CDMA	5	1.20	0.05	123	1.63
Awareness	5	1.90	0.02*	122	1.99
Prior computer experience	5	1.20	0.15	120	1.81
Prior technology experience	5	1.40	0.09	120	2.10
Personal banking experience	5	2.00	0.31	120	2.33
Reference group influence	5	2.60	0.54	119	2.87

Note: *Significant beyond 0.05.

4.5 Chinese consumers' attitudes to online and mobile banking

Attitudes of users and non-users of online and mobile banking were compared with respect to five most common attributes identified in the literature for these services such as convenience, ease of use, access to a wide range of services free from time and place, confidential and security, hackers or fraud. The t-tests conducted on the responses from the users and non-users, no significant attitudinal differences were detected for the above factors, except for confidential and security. This factor was found to significantly differ between the online bank users and non-users. It was also associated with the non-users' population. Among the security concerns, hackers and fraud were identified as the main concerns for not using online banking services.

Past experience with computer/new technology and personal banking - The literature suggested, that previous experience with computer and new technology as well as, previous positive banking experience had an effect on online banking adoption. The results confirmed for two factors past experience with computer and new technology but, did not confirm with previous banking experience factor. The results showed previous positive banking experience had no effects on online and mobile banking adoption in China. The *t*-test showed a significant difference between online bank users and non-users, in terms of their scores for variables prior experience with computers and new technology (Table 4). Non-users tent to rate that they had no prior computer experience while the opposite was true with users. In contrast, with mobile banking the results showed no significant difference between users and non-users for none of the above factors except, for prior technology experience (Table 5).

Reference group influence - Respondents were asked to rate the degree of importance on a five-point-scale, whether families and others would influence their decisions on using online banking. The results showed reference group's influence did not have an impact on online and mobile banking adoption in China (Tables 4 & 5).

5 Managerial implications

The current target market for online and mobile banking in China was found to be relatively small. At least, among Chinese urban population surveyed, 33 per cent used online banking and 14 per cent used mobile banking. Thus, the level of awareness of such services was low in China. This suggests, in line with Trappey and Trappey's (2001) findings on Chinese e-commerce, that there was lack of influence from the marketplace. Nevertheless, the findings indicate a penetration in the target market, i.e. urban, middle class and above therefore, the potential of this market should not be underestimated. Equally, there is some good potential for developing Chinese mobile banking, since the results also indicate the proportion of mobile bank users was nearly half of the proportion of online bank users.The findings showed large discrepancies between China and Western countries in terms of users' demographic characteristics and attitudes towards online and mobile banking which, seems to reflect in the cultural differences between the two blocks of countries. In terms of demographic characteristics, Karjaluoto et al. (2002) found a typical user of online banking in Finnish market highly educated, relatively young and wealthy person with good knowledge of computers. While other studies suggest younger, higher earning and unmarried potential customers are most likely to be early adopters of new mobile services.

Our study found the level of education did not influence online and mobile banking adoption. Especially, with regard to mobile banking, the typical user of such service was aged up to 44-years old. The users were predominantly male, consistent with Singh (2004)'s study conducted in South Africa, which found that more males used internet banking than females. Online bank users were also found among the salaried employees, senior managers and in the case of mobile banking, small business owners. They were also in a high-income earners' group. This information should be used for targeting and positioning these services.With regard to consumers' attitudes to online and mobile banking, perceived risks were found most important factor that encouraged or discouraged Chinese adoption of online banking. The survey results also showed that Chinese consumers did not attach much importance to convenience, ease of use and access to a wide range of services free from time and place than security factor, unlike respondents in other countries to whom these attributes were rated as highly important. Hackers and fraud were further found one of the main barriers of online banking adoption in China. Consistent with Trappey and Trappey's (2001) findings, Chinese consumers tend to have low confidence towards e-commerce and the Internet especially, in the area of personal finance. As well as Yu (2006)'s assertion that Chinese main concerns in Internet transaction, is product quality and online security. Although, the data cannot give an insight into why Chinese consumers' perceived risks of online banking was high, Chinese culture influence and their old beliefs to personal finance, their tradition of cash-carrying reflects in their low possession of a credit/debit card and their lack of regulation in online trading, might have been the main causes. Therefore, in order to improve the rate of online banking adoption in China, security issue must first be addressed.

Two other factors were also found to affect Chinese consumer adoption of online and mobile banking. These were: previous experience with computers and new technology. The findings showed non-users of online banking tend to have no prior experience with computers and no experience with new technology, in the case of mobile banking. This was consistent with the literature suggesting, computer attitudes had an effect on attitudes and behaviours towards online banking. Perhaps as Thornton and White (2001) also suggested, as consumers gain knowledge, confidence and with a gradual increase in computer usage, changes in the use of delivery channels would take place.Clear contrast was also found with China's Asian counterparts. Compared with Singaporeans and Malaysians, for instance, Chinese consumers seem more traditional and less affected by technology advancement. Singaporean consumers have negative perceptions about accessibility and confidentiality but, they have positive attitudes towards and experience of new technology compared to Chinese consumers (Gerrard and Cunningham 2003). Similarly to the latter, more awareness and attitude to change were found to affect Internet banking adoption in Malaysia (Suganthi et al. 2001). In contrast, it has been shown that Taiwanese customers with more positive levels of attitude toward technology, ability to use technology and willingness to adopt technology are more likely to appreciate self-service technology (Lin and Hsieh 2006).

As far as mobile banking is concerned, lack of understanding of its benefits was found significant. Consistent with the literature, perceived usefulness is a factor of electronic banking. Despite this, it was perceived as a novelty. Therefore, perhaps while Chinese bankers should focus on security issue for online banking, their advertising should focus on the novel aspect for mobile banking. Bankers should also consider raising consumer awareness and acceptance of new technology-based banking services more, through advertising and promotion rather than word-of-mouth communication. Although, conventional belief suggests that the more satisfaction customers experience, the more likely they are to use a product again and recommend it to others, this might prove not to be effective in the Chinese context. Since we found reference group influence had little impact on online and mobile banking in China.

Finally, although the outbreak of SARS in 2003 has not been an issue raised in our study, it could provide an unforeseen impetus for consumer technology-based services, as Chinese people tried avoid leaving their domicile. The general benefits of these benefits might have become more apparent to Chinese consumers as a result of this outbreak.

6 Conclusion

As the brand new banking distribution channels to Chinese consumers, online and mobile banking are still at an early stage in China. The current target market for online and mobile banking is relatively small due to its low level of awareness. Nevertheless, this should not be underestimated. There is good potential for introducing dual online and mobile banking services since, mobile banking adoption is not far behind the former. There were many critical issues, which stood out as being obstacles to Chinese consumer adoption of online and mobile banking, among these were: consumers' attitudes. Security factor was found the most important attribute that could motivate consumers' attitudes towards online banking in China. Other barriers to Chinese adoption of online banking were perceived risks, computer and technological skills and Chinese habit of cash-carry banking. As for mobile banking, lack of understanding of the concept and its benefits were the main barriers to its adoption. In contrast to Western countries, Chinese online and mobile bank users tend to be predominantly male, not typically young neither highly educated. Users were also widely spread among the salaried employees, senior managers and small business owners. This chapter gives an insight into online and mobile banking in China, which had not previously been investigated. In particular, the survey findings highlighted issues to assist Chinese bankers and the like, in implementing these services more effectively. As such, more women or a particular customer profile may be targeted. Advertising messages could emphasise security for online banking and novelty for mobile banking. Further research may be carried out to acquire insights into the phenomena, based on a larger sample size and a better distribution of respondents' demographics.

Acknowledgments The author would like to thank Xiaoyan Li for her contribution in the main study on 'Consumers' attitudes to online and mobile banking in China'.

References

Akinci, S., Aksoy, S., Atilgan, E. (2004), "Adoption of internet banking among sophisticated consumer segments in an advanced developing country", International Journal of Bank Marketing, Vol. 22 No.3, pp.212-32.

Barczak, G., Ellen, P.S., Pilling, B.K. (1997), "Developing typologies of consumer motives for use of technologically based banking services", Journal of Business Research, Vol. 38 No.2, pp.131-9.

Beckett, A., Hewer, P., Howcroft, B. (2002), "An exposition of consumer behaviour in the financial services industry", International Journal of Bank Marketing, Vol. 18 No.1, pp.15-26.

Bhattacherjee, A. (2002), "Individual trust in online firms: scale development and initial test", Journal of Management and Information Systems, Vol. 19 No.1, pp.211-41.

Chimezie, A., Osigweh, Y., Huo, Y. (1993), "Conceptions of employee responsibility and rights in the US and People's Republic of China", The International Journal of Human Resource Management, Vol. 4 No.1, pp.14-28.

Daniel, E. (1999), "Provision of electronic banking in the UK and the Republic of Ireland", International Journal of Bank Marketing, Vol. 17 No.2, pp.72-82.

Gerrard, P., Cunningham, J.B. (2003), "The diffusion of internet banking among Singapore consumers", International Journal of Bank Marketing, Vol. 21 No.1, pp.16-28.

Heinoken, K. (2007), "Conceptualising online banking services value", Journal of Financial Services Marketing, Vol. 12, pp.39-52.

Hofstede, G. (1991), Cultures and Organisation: Software of the Mind, McGraw-Hill, London.

Holmund, M., Kock, S. (1996), "Relationship marketing: the importance of customer-perceived service quality in retail banking", The Service Industry Journal, Vol. 16 No.3, pp.287-304.

Howcroft, B., Hamilton, R., Hewer, P. (2002), "Consumer attitude and the usage and adoption of home-based banking in the United Kingdom", International Journal of Bank Marketing, Vol. 20 No.3, pp.111-21.

Joseph, M., Stone, G. (2003), "An empirical evaluation of US bank customer perceptions of the impact of technology on service delivery in the banking sector", International Journal of Retail & Distribution Management, Vol. 31 No.4, pp.190-202.

Jun, M., Cai, S. (2001), "The key determinants of internet banking service quality: a content analysis", The International Journal of Bank Marketing, Vol. 19 No.7, pp.276-91.

Karjaluoto, H., Mattila, M., Pento, T. (2002), "Factors underlying attitude formation towards online banking in Finland", International Journal of Banking Marketing, Vol. 20 No.6, pp.261-72.

Kapoulas, A., Murphy, W., Ellis, N. (2002), "Say hello, wave goodbye: missed opportunities for electronic relationship marketing within the financial services sector?", International Journal of Bank Marketing, Vol. 20 No.7, pp.302-10.

Kolodinsky, J.M., Hogarth, J.M., Hilgert, M.A. (2004), "The adoption of electronic banking technologies by US consumers", International Journal of Bank Marketing, Vol. 22 No.4, pp.238-59.

Lewis, B.R. (1991), "Service quality: an international comparison of bank customers' expectations and perceptions", Journal of Marketing Management, Vol. 7 pp.47-62.

Li (2002), People Daily, available at: www.english.peopledaily.com.cn/business. Lin, J-C, C., Hsieh, P. (2006), "The role of technology readiness in customers' perceptions and adoption of self-service technology", International Journal of Service Industry Management, Vol. 17 Iss. 5, pp. 497-517.

Lockett, A., Littler, D. (1997), "The adoption of direct banking services", Journal of Marketing Management, Vol. 13 No.8, pp.791-811.

Lu, M. T., Liu, C. H., Jing, J., Huang, L. (2005), "Internet banking: strategic responses to the accession of WTO by Chinese banks" , Industrial Management & Data Systems, Vol. 105 Iss. 4, pp. 429-42.

Machauer, A., Morgner, S. (2001), "Segmentation of bank customers by expected benefits and attitudes", International Journal of Bank Marketing, Vol. 19 No.1, pp.6-17.

Minhas, R., Jacobs, E. (1996), "Benefit segmentation by factor analysis: an improved method of targeting customers for financial services", International Journal of Bank Marketing, Vol. 14 No.3, pp.3-13.

Mühlbracher, H., Dahringer, L., Leihs, H. (1999), International Marketing: A Global Perspective, International Thomson Business Press, London.

Mukherjee, A., Nath, P. (2003), "A model of trust in online relationship banking", International Journal of Bank Marketing, Vol. 21 No.1, pp.5-15.

Patricio, L., Fisk, R.P., Cunha, J.F. (2003), "Improving satisfaction with bank service offerings: measuring the contribution of each delivery channel", Managing Service Quality, Vol. 13 No.6, pp.471-82.

Polatoglu, V.N., Ekin, S. (2001), "An empirical investigation of the Turkish consumers' acceptance of internet banking services", International Journal of Bank Marketing, Vol. 19 No.4, pp.156-65.

Rogers, E.M. (1995), Diffusion of Innovation, 4th ed., Free Press, New York, NY.

Sarel, D., Marmorstein, H. (2003), "Marketing online banking services: the voice of the customer", Journal of Financial Services Marketing, Vol. 8 No.2, pp.106-18.

Sandland, S. (2000), "China to be top online banking market by 2004", Computer world, available at: www.idg.com.hk/cw/readstory.

Sathye, M. (1999), "Adoption of internet banking by Australian consumers: an empirical investigation", International Journal of Bank Marketing, Vol. 17 No.7, pp.324-34.

Singh, A.M. (2004), "Trends in South African internet banking", Aslib Proceedings: New Information Perspectives, Vol. 56 No.3, pp.187-96.

Suganthi, Balachandher, Balachandran (2001), "Internet banking patronage: an empirical investigation of Malaysia", available at: www.arraydev.com/commerce/JIBC/0103_01.html.

Suoranta, M., Mattila, M. (2004), "Mobile banking and consumer behaviour: new insights into the diffusion pattern", Journal of Financial Services Marketing, Vol. 8 No.4, pp.354-66.

Chapter 4
International Patterns in Manufacturing Strategies

Ruth Alas[1], Tomas Eklund[2], Mikael Collan[2] and Ants Kraus[3]

[1] Estonian Business School, Estonia
[2] Institute for Advanced Management Systems Research, Åbo Akademi University, Finland
[3] Estonian Business School, Estonia

Abstract This chapter explores and analyses patterns in international manufacturing strategies, based on data from the Fourth International Manufacturing Strategy Survey (IMSS), conducted in 2005. Based on a principal components analysis a selection of the thirty-one most important contributing variables from the IMSS dataset is made, and a self-organizing map (SOM) is used to cluster manufacturing companies according to their strategy, performance, manufacturing and supply-chain practices, and improvement programs. The clusters of companies and patterns of strategies are analyzed and discussed. Special attention is attached to differences between countries. The results reveal four groups (types) of companies: low supply-chain integration companies; integrated supply-chain companies; mass production, high tech companies; and production-oriented low tech companies.

1 Introduction

Manufacturing strategy is a well-established research issue, and according to a comprehensive assessment of 285 survey research articles in operations management since the second half of the 1990'ies two topics have stood out as showing the fastest ascendancy to prominence — operations strategy and supply chain management (Rungtusanatham et al. 2003). Despite the significant body of operations management research (Frolich 2002; Rungtusanatham et al. 2003), how to make use of different types of manufacturing strategies to stimulate the continuous growth of manufacturing competitiveness remains an important topic for all manufacturing firms.

Previous research has also indicated that although companies worldwide have made substantial investments in installing enterprise resource planning (ERP) systems, implementing ERP systems has proven unexpectedly difficult (Yen and Sheu 2004).

P.O. de Pablos, M.D. Lytras (eds.), *The China Information Technology Handbook*,   41
DOI: 10.1007/978-0-387-77743-6_4, © Springer Science+Business Media, LLC 2009

The use of field-based empirical methodologies in the area of production and operations management (POM) has been steadily increasing over the past decade. One of the most prominent among these is the survey research methodology, which has often been used to capture data from business organizations (Malhotra and Grover 1998). One significant survey for studying manufacturing strategies on a global scale and at the national level is the International Manufacturing Strategy Survey (IMSS) (Moattar-Husseini and Brien 2004); the first round of this survey was in 1993 (Lindberg et al. 1998). In this paper we have set out to investigate what kind of manufacturing strategies are used in companies, and how companies can be differentiated by looking at their manufacturing strategies, based upon data from the fourth IMSS survey. The survey data also includes information about how intensively and universally ERP systems are used within manufacturing companies. This research takes this information (differences between companies in ERP usage) into consideration and combines it with differences in manufacturing strategies.

However, as with most surveys, the IMSS survey includes a great number of questions. In addition, the number of questions is likely to increase with each iteration of the survey. Therefore, researchers intending to analyze the results face a considerable challenge in identifying the important parts of the resulting data. Therefore, suitable data reduction methods are required in order to be able to analyze the results. In this paper, we apply a two-stage approach. Firstly, factor analysis is used to reduce the number of variables into a more manageable number. After this, the self-organizing map (SOM) is used to visually cluster and analyze the resulting data.

The SOM is a two-layer unsupervised artificial neural network (ANN) that maps multidimensional data onto a two dimensional topological grid, or map (Kohonen 2001). The data, used to generate the map, are grouped according to similarities and patterns found in the dataset, using some form of distance measure, usually the Euclidean distance. The result is displayed as a series of nodes, or points on the map, which can be divided into a number of clusters based upon the distances between the nodes. As the SOM is unsupervised, no target outcomes are provided, and the SOM is allowed to freely organize itself, based on the patterns identified, making the SOM an ideal tool for exploratory data analysis.

"Exploratory data analysis methods, like SOM, are like general-purpose instruments that illustrate the essential features of a data set, like its clustering structure and the relations between its data items" (Kaski and Kohonen 1996). In other words, the SOM can be said to perform visual clustering of data. The SOM differs from statistical clustering methods in a number of ways although it is similar to k-means clustering. Firstly, when using the SOM the targeted number of clusters does not have to be defined. Secondly, the SOM is more tolerant towards data that do not follow a normal distribution. Thirdly, the SOM is quite efficient, and is faster than most top-down hierarchical clustering methods (Vesanto and Alhoniemi 2000). And perhaps most importantly, the SOM is a very visual method of clustering and hence especially suitable for exploratory clustering analyses.

So far the SOM has primarily been applied in engineering (Oja et al. 2003), but the method has been also applied in various other fields, e.g., in medicine (e.g., in breast cancer diagnosis, Chen et al. 2000), text retrieval (Kohonen et al. 2000; Visa et al. 2000) and a variety of tasks relating to financial analysis. SOM has been applied, e.g., in credit analysis (Martin-del-Brio and Serrano-Cinca 1993; Back et al. 1995; Kiviluoto 1998), in financial benchmarking (Back et al. 1998; Eklund et al. 2003), and in macroeconomic and macro environment analysis (Kasabov et al. 2000; Costea et al. 2004; Länsiluoto et al. 2004). The self-organizing map has also been applied to product positioning and market segmentation (Charalambous et al. 2001; Kiang et al. 2006). To the best of our knowledge, this is the first application of the self-organizing map to study patterns in international manufacturing strategies.

The chapter continues with a presentation of the data and the methods used. Then the results from the analysis, including the self-organizing map and feature planes are presented, and briefly analyzed. Finally the paper concludes with a summary and a discussion of the results.

2 Data and the research process

This chapter is based on data from the fourth International Manufacturing Strategy Survey (IMSS) project that was designed to explore and identify strategies, practices and performance of manufacturing firms around the world during 2005. The survey included 711 companies in 23 countries: Argentina, Brazil and Venezuela from South America; Canada and USA from North America; Belgium, Denmark, Estonia, Germany, Greece, Hungary, Ireland, Italy, Norway, Portugal, Sweden, The Netherlands and United Kingdom from Europe; China, Israel and Turkey from Asia; and also Australia and New Zealand. Independent, country-based, research teams performed surveys in their consecutive countries. The overall coordinator of the project is Politecnico di Milano, Italy.The primary method for data gathering was a questionnaire, which was distributed to the major business units in the ISIC 28-35 industrial sectors within each country. The questionnaire was translated from English to local languages and retranslated back to English, in order to make sure that the translation was accurate. The questionnaires were completed by operations-, manufacturing-, or technical managers of the companies. After data collection, a database for the entire worldwide study has been distributed to all contributing researchers and participating companies. The framework of the study is based on a manufacturing strategy perspective. This means that emphasis is placed on understanding the strategies and market priorities of the business units, the strategy's translation into manufacturing objectives, the manufacturing practices, and the areas of current and future manufacturing improvement activities. The questionnaire is divided into the following three sections:

A. Description, strategy and performance of the business unit. This section explores strategies, markets, primary modes of competition and cost structure data of the business unit.

B. Description, strategy and performance of the dominant activities of the plant. This section explores the manufacturing strategy, process design and manufacturing performance of the dominant activity.

C. Current manufacturing and supply chain practices, and past and planned improvement programs. This section explores the structure (facilities, technology, and degree of integration) and infrastructure (organization, planning and control systems, quality, and product development) and focuses on use and results from broad areas of activity, action programs, and improvements, such as IT, automation, quality, and empowerment. The original data includes 711 answered questionnaires (i.e. companies), with an average number of 31 questionnaires per participating country, with a minimum of 10 and a maximum of 82 per country. The response rate for questionnaires sent was 18% overall.

In order to reduce the number of variables, and to get a more reliable set of indicators, principal components analysis was applied to the IMSS data. Some of the original variables were, however, excluded from the analysis due to poor fit. After the analysis the number of variables that would be used to in generating the self-organizing map was reduced to 31. The research process is illustrated in Figure 1.

The questions identified through PCA are shown in Table 1. The first column shows the id code, the second shows the category, and the third column the topic of the question.

The SOM model was created using Viscovery SOMine 4.0, a user-friendly implementation of the SOM algorithm originally designed for customer segmentation tasks. Most of the data were likert scale (1-5) data, generally following a normal distribution. Therefore, very little preprocessing of the data was required, only a normalization by the variance was used. The size of the map used is dependent upon the purpose of the application; if clustering is desired, a small map is created, whereas if visualization is desired, a large map is created. A small map will force data into clusters according to similarity at the cost of a certain degree of accuracy, whereas a large map will sacrifice clustering ability for individual

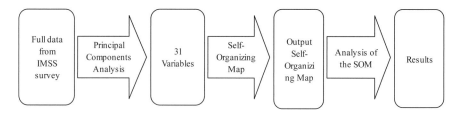

Figure 1 The research process in this study

data accuracy and detail. In this case our aim is to cluster the data, so we have opted for a smaller map with 200 neurons. A tension value of 0.5 was used. The tension value is a neighborhood range indicator, with low values producing more locally detailed maps, whereas higher values produce more general, coarser maps.

Table 1 The reduced battery of questions, identified using PCA

Id	Category	Topic
A5ad	Competitive strategy	Dependable deliveries
B3d	Cost structure	Proportion direct materials
B4d	Manufacturing strategy	Volume flexibility
B4p	Manufacturing strategy	Reduce procurement costs
B4q	Manufacturing strategy	Increase labor productivity
B4u	Manufacturing strategy	Increase employee satisfaction
B4v	Manufacturing strategy	Improve environmental performance
B6c	Manufacturing design	Proportion mass production
O11g	Organization of dominant activity	Continuous improvement program
PC6b	Process control actions	Process focus program
Q3a	Quality control actions	Quality improvement program
PD6f	Production design actions	Technological integration program
PD2e	Production design coordination	Job rotation, manufacturing - design
PD2b	Production design coordination	Formal meetings
PC1b	Planning and control	Lowest demand / month
SC13a	Flow of goods strategic customers	Share inventory level knowledge
SC13b	Flow of goods strategic customers	Share prod. planning and forecast knowledge
SC13f	Flow of goods strategic customers	Manage inventory at customer's site
SC13g	Flow of goods strategic customers	Collaborative planning
SC13h	Flow of goods strategic customers	Physical integration
SC15a	Key suppliers	Supply strategy assessment
T1c	Technologies	Automated loading/unloading
T1d	Technologies	Automated guided vehicles
T2a	Management support in ERP	Materials management
T2b	Management support in ERP	Production planning and control management.
T2c	Management support in ERP	Purchasing and supply management
T2d	Management support in ERP	Sales management
T2e	Management support in ERP	Distribution management
T2f	Management support in ERP	Accounting ad finance management
T2h	Management support in ERP	Project management
T2i	Management support in ERP	Product life cycle management

3 Results and analysis

Once the network was trained, a hierarchical clustering algorithm (Ward's method) was used to mathematically determine the clusters on the map. Four clusters were identified and labeled C1-C4. The final resulting self-organizing map, with the identified clusters, is shown in Figure 2.

In order to identify the actual characteristics of each cluster, the feature planes are used. Figures 3a and 3b show the feature planes of the final trained map. The feature planes illustrate the distribution of values for each individual variable, across the entire map. In full color, the highest values are illustrated by "warm" colors, such as red and orange, while the lowest values are illustrated by "cool" colors, such as dark blue. In this case, "H" has been used to illustrate areas of the map with high values, while "L" shows areas with low values. For example, we see that companies reporting high values in the question "proportion mass production" are located in the cluster on the left hand of the map, and that the same companies also report a high emphasis on increasing employee satisfaction.

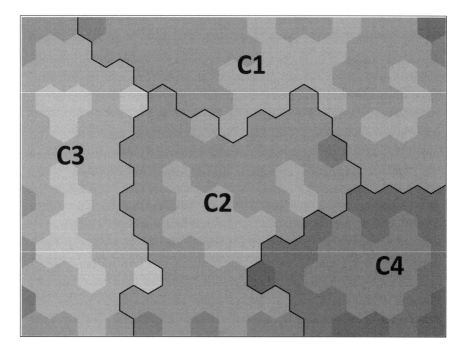

Figure 2 The final map with the four identified clusters

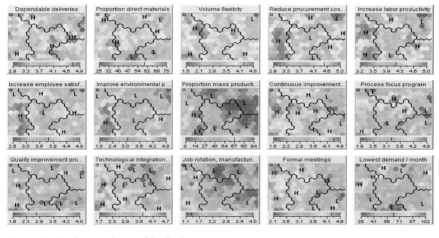

Figure 3a The feature planes of the final map

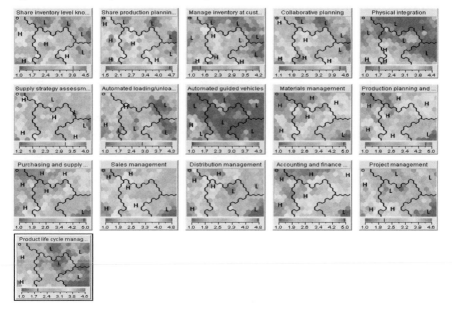

Figure 3b The feature planes of the final map (cont)

As was previously mentioned, four clusters of companies were identified. They will be presented in detail below:

Cluster 1: Low supply-chain integration

Cluster 1 (C1) is a mixed cluster, but it does have a number of identifying characteristics. Firstly, the cluster has a very low proportion of mass production. It also has a low focus on supply chain integration and cooperation. Management support in ERP-systems is strongly supported, but not for product life cycle or project management. Finally, the companies have a strong process focus. 56% of the companies in this cluster are privately-owned, but public companies account for

32% of the companies as well. The companies are medium sized compared to the others in the study. Cluster 1 is the largest cluster, with 30% of the records.

Countries with a large proportion of companies (>40%) in this cluster include Germany (~55%), Belgium, Sweden, and the UK. Countries with a low proportion of companies (<10%) in this cluster include Turkey.

Cluster 2: Integrated supply-chain companies

Cluster 2 (C2) is also a mixed cluster, but typical for these companies is their low focus on manufacturing strategy and high focus on supply chain integration. The companies in this cluster are also average sized, and consist of primarily privately owned companies (63%). This cluster also has the highest proportion of co-operative companies (5%).

Countries with a large proportion of companies (>40%) in this cluster include Ireland. Countries with a low proportion of companies (<10%) in this cluster include the UK.

Cluster 3: Mass production, high technology companies

Cluster 3 (C3) is a very production-oriented, high technology cluster. This is the only cluster with very high proportion of mass production. It is also a highly automated cluster, with strong ERP support for management, including support for project management and product life cycle management. This differentiates this cluster strongly from the others.

The companies have a clear focus on dependable deliveries as their competitive strategy. These companies have also reported a higher focus on all aspects of manufacturing strategy, significantly higher than in other clusters. Quality improvement and technology integration programs are also highly important in this cluster. Job rotation between design and manufacturing is common, as are formal meetings between the same. Finally, the companies also report high supply chain cooperation and integration. The companies in this cluster are on average the largest in the study, mostly privately-owned (58%).

Countries with a large proportion of companies (>40%) in this cluster include Turkey (~63%), Brazil (~62%), Venezuela (~50%), USA, and China. Countries with a low proportion of companies (<10%) in this cluster include Australia, Germany, and New Zealand.

Cluster 4: Production-oriented low-tech

This cluster (C4) is also production-oriented, but considerably less technology-oriented than cluster 3. This cluster reports a very low level of automation and low ERP support for management. Interestingly, this cluster differs from cluster 3 also in that direct costs account for a very small proportion of total costs. Cluster 4 is the smallest cluster with only 18% of the records. The companies in this cluster are on average much smaller than in the other clusters, and the majority are privately-owned (78%). Only 9% of companies in this cluster are publicly or institutionally owned. Countries with a large proportion of companies (>40%) in this cluster include New Zealand (50%), Hungary. Countries with a low proportion of companies (<10%) in this cluster include Brazil (0%), China, Ireland, Sweden, and Turkey.

Surveyed countries that exhibit uniform distribution across the four clusters (manufacturing strategy focus), 15-35% of companies in each cluster, include Argentina, Greece, Israel, Norway, and Portugal. The results per question are summarized in Tables 2a and 2b. The tables show the category and topic of the question, and the result per cluster according to the feature planes (Figures 4.3a and 4.3b). The results are displayed as follows: VL = very low; L = low; M = medium; H = high; and VH = very high. An empty cell means that no dominant value can be identified for the cluster, i.e. the results are mixed.

Table 2a The questions, their categories, and the results of the SOM clustering (VL = very low, L = low, M = medium, H = high, and VH = very high, and empty = non-defining)

Category	Topic	Cluster 1	Cluster 2	Cluster 3	Cluster 4
Competitive strategy	Dependable deliveries	-	M - VH	M - VH	M - VH
Cost structure	Proportion direct materials	-	-	M - VH	VL - M
Manufacturing strategy	Volume flexibility	-	M - VH	VH	VH
Manufacturing strategy	Reduce procurement costs	-	-	VH	M - VH
Manufacturing strategy	Increase labor productivity	-	-	VH	M - VH
Manufacturing strategy	Increase employee satisfaction	-	-	M - VH	-
Manufacturing strategy	Improve environmental performance	M	M	VH	M
Manufacturing design	Proportion mass production	L	L	M - VH	L
Organization of dominant activity	Continuous improvement program	-	M - VH	VH	L
Process control actions	Process focus program	-	-	-	-
Quality control actions	Quality improvement program	L - M	L - M	M - VH	L - M
Production design actions	Technological integration program	-	-	H - VH	-
Production design coordination	Job rotation, manufacturing - design	VL - M	VL - M	M - H	VL - M
Production design coordination	Formal meetings	-	-	H - VH	-
Planning and control	Lowest demand / month	-	-	-	-
Flow of goods strategic customers	Share inventory level knowledge	VL - M	M - VH	M - VH	M - VH

Table 2b The questions, their categories, and the results of the SOM clustering (VL = very low, L = low, M = medium, H = high, and VH = very high, and empty = non-defining)

Category	Topic	Cluster 1	Cluster 2	Cluster 3	Cluster 4
Flow of goods strategic customers	Share prod. planning and forecast knowledge	VL - M	M - VH	M - VH	M - VH
Flow of goods strategic customers	Manage inventory at customer's site	VL - L	M - VH	VL – H	VL - H
Flow of goods strategic customers	Collaborative planning	VL - M	M - VH	M - VH	VL - H
Flow of goods strategic customers	Physical integration	VL	-	-	VL
Key suppliers	Supply strategy assessment	M - H	M - H	M - VH	M - H
Technologies	Automated loading/unloading	L	L	M - VH	L
Technologies	Automated guided vehicles	VL	VL	VL – VH	VL
Management support in ERP	Materials management	VH	M - VH	VH	VL - M
Management support in ERP	Production planning and control management	VH	M - VH	VH	VL - M
Management support in ERP	Purchasing and supply management	VH	M - VH	VH	VL - M
Management support in ERP	Sales management	M - VH	M - VH	VH	VL - M
Management support in ERP	Distribution management	L - VH	L - VH	VH	VL - M
Management support in ERP	Accounting ad finance management	M - VH	M - VH	VH	VL - M
Management support in ERP	Project management	L - M	L - H	M - VH	VL - M
Management support in ERP	Product life cycle management	VL - M	VL - M	M - VH	VL

Figure 4 shows how companies from different countries divide up among the clusters.

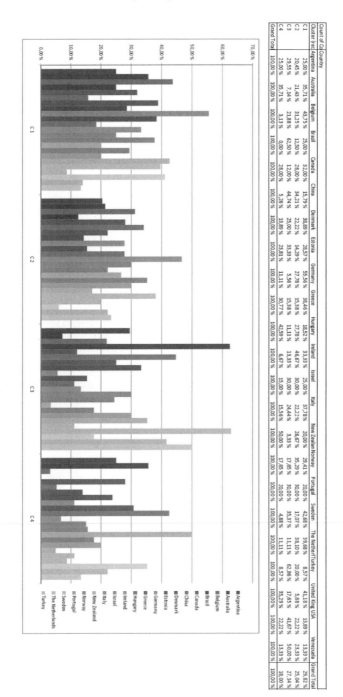

Figure 4 Companies from each country and how they are allocated among the clusters

4 Conclusions and summary

In this chapter we have performed an exploratory analysis of manufacturing strategies by using a self-organizing map. We have identified four clusters of companies that are differentiated by their (manufacturing) strategy focus in terms of mass-production, automation, use of ERP systems, and supply chain integration. The first cluster is an average cluster that contains companies that have a low degree of automation and supply chain integration. The second cluster contains companies that have a very high focus on integrated supply chain management. The third cluster is mass production oriented and has a high level of automation. In addition, the companies in this cluster have ERP systems providing advanced support for management, including project management and product life cycle development. The final cluster contains companies that are production-oriented as in cluster 3, but have a lower level of automation and ERP support for management.

It is, however, important to note that the number of participating companies per country is not very high, which is a limitation of this study. This limitation means that the results are not definitive; we cannot draw exclusive conclusions concerning strategies pursued by companies in different countries. However, the results are indicative and interesting, and access to this wide data is rarely available for analysis. The results on how companies in different countries are divided in these clusters are somewhat inconclusive, however, suggesting that there are significant differences between countries. Results in terms of some of the countries, e.g., Brazil and Turkey, are interesting and require further research – these are countries that seem to have a relatively high number of manufacturing companies relying on similar strategies. Looking at the strategic choices of the clusters against performance data for same companies would yield highly interesting results on the goodness of different strategies. This remains an issue for further research.

Acknowledgments The authors would like to acknowledge the financial support of the Academy of Finland (Domino, grant no. 104639).

References

Back B, Oosterom G, Sere K, van Wezel M. (1995) Intelligent information systems within business: bankruptcy predictions using neural networks. In: Doukidis G, Galliers R, Jelassi T, Krcmar H, Land F (eds) Proceedings of the Third European Conference on Information Systems ECIS '95, Athens, Greece, June 1-3, 1995:99-112

Back B, Sere K, Vanharanta H (1998) Managing complexity in large data bases using self-organizing maps. Account Manag Inform Tech 8:191-210

Charalambous C, Hadjinicola GC, Muller E (2001) Product positioning using principles from the self-organizing map. Lecture Notes In Computer Science, Vol. 2130: Proceedings of the International Conference on Artificial Neural Networks, Vienna, Austria. Springer-Verlag , London:457-463

Chen D-R, Chang R-F, Huang Y-L (2000) Breast Cancer Diagnosis Using Self-Organizing Map for Sonography. Ultrasound Med Biol 26(3):405-411

Costea A, Kloptchenko A, Back B (2004) Analyzing Economical Performance of Central-East-European Countries Using Neural Networks and Cluster Analysis. In: Proceedings of the Fifth International Symposium on Economic Informatics, May, Bucharest, Rumania. Editura Inforec, Bucharest:1006-1011

Eklund T, Back B, Vanharanta H, Visa A (2003). Using the self-organizing map as a visualization tool in financial benchmarking. Inform Visual 2(3):171-181

Frolich MT (2002) Techniques for improving response rate in OM surveys. J Oper Manag 20:53-62

Kasabov N, Deng D, Erzegovezi L, Fedrizzi M, Beber A (2000). Hybrid Intelligent Decision Support Systems for Risk Analysis and Prediction of Evolving Economic Clusters in Europe. In: Kasabov N (ed) Future Directions for Intelligent Information Systems and Information Sciences. Springer Verlag, Heidelberg

Kaski S, Kohonen T (1996) Exploratory Data Analysis by the Self-Organizing Map: Structures of Welfare and Poverty in the World. In: Neural Networks in Financial Engineering: Proceedings of the 3rd International Conference on Neural Networks in the Capital Markets, London, England October 1995. World Scientific, Singapore:498-507

Kiang MY, Hu MY, Fischer DM (2006). An extended self-organizing map network for market segmentation—a telecommunication example. Decis Support Syst 42(1):36-47

Kiviluoto K (1998) Predicting bankruptcies with the self-organizing map. Neurocomputing 21(1-3):191-201

Kohonen T (2001) Self-Organizing Maps. Springer-Verlag, Berlin

Kohonen T, Kaski S, Lagus K, Salojarvi J, Honkela J, Paatero V Saarela A (2000) Self organization of a massive document collection. IEEE Trans Neural Network 11(3):574-585

Lindberg P, Voss CA, Blackmon KL (1998) International manufacturing strategies: Context, content and change. Kluwer Academic Publishers, Dordrecht

Länsiluoto A, Eklund T, Back B, Vanharanta H, Visa A (2004) Industry Specific Cycles and Companies' Financial Performance - Comparison with Self-Organizing Maps. Benchmark Int J 11(4):267-286

Malhotra MK, Grover V (1998) An assessment of survey research in POM: from constructs to theory. J Oper Manag 16:407-425

Martin-del-Brio B, Serrano-Cinca C (1993) Self-organizing Neural Networks for the Analysis and Representation of Data: Some Financial Cases. Neural Comput Appl 1(2):193-206

Moattar-Husseini SM, Brien CO (2004) Strategic impications of manufacturing performance comparisons for newly industrialising countries. Int J Oper Prod Manag 24(11/12):1126-1148

Oja M, Kaski S, Kohonen T (2003) Bibliography of Self-Organizing Map (SOM) Papers: 1998-2001 Addendum. Neural Comput Surv 3:1-156

Rungtusanatham MJ, Choi TY, Hollingworth DG, Wu Z, Forza C (2003) Survey research in operations management: historical analyses. J Oper Manag 21:475-488

Vesanto J, Alhoniemi E (2000) Clustering of the Self-Organizing Map. IEEE Trans Neural Network 11(3):586-600

Visa A, Toivonen J, Bacb B, Vanharanta H (2000) Toward Text Understanding - Classification of Text Documents by Word Map. In: Dasarathy BV (ed) Proceedings of SPIE, Volume 4057, Data Mining and Knowledge Discovery: Theory, Tools, and Technology II:299–305

Yen RH, Sheu C (2004) Aligning ERP implementation with competitive priorities of manufacturing firms: An exploratory study. Int J Prod Econ 92(3):207-220

Chapter 5
The Term Innovation and its Front End –
Is There a Specific Asian View?

Alexander Brem

University of Erlangen-Nuremberg, GERMANY

Abstract Innovation is not just a very popular buzzword, but a very multi-faceted one as well. In this context, especially between different countries and continents, there are essential differences in terms and definitions of innovation and innovative activities, especially between Europe and Asia. Hence, before the background of globalized economies, a common understanding is needed for successful future intercultural projects and appropriate management. Especially in scientific research, a first step should be made in this direction. Therefore, a comprehensive view of the term innovation and its different interpretations is given.

1 Background

At present, innovation is one of the most popular buzzwords. There is no successful company that does not use this term in corporate communications and marketing. To date, there is still no common definition existing yet, especially within the continents and the corresponding different countries. Facing the variety of branches, industries and regions, in which companies are acting, not to mention the different individual characteristics and needs of the enterprises, this statement is not very surprising.

Taking a closer look on innovation management literature, there are different streams, differing mainly by region, especially the European and Asian perspectives are partly contradictive. There are even differences within certain countries. For example, Hauschildt mentions 18 different definitions of innovation (Hauschildt, 2004).

Due to the proceeding globalization of markets and companies, the current status needs to be updated, so that firms have a worldwide understanding of innovation and the activities that they can base their innovation management strategy on people who are working together in international projects, especially within Research and Development, need to have the same wording for their lasting collaboration. Otherwise these projects are often doomed to failure.

P.O. de Pablos, M.D. Lytras (eds.), *The China Information Technology Handbook*,
DOI: 10.1007/978-0-387-77743-6_5, © Springer Science+Business Media, LLC 2009

2 Innovation and innovativeness

2.1 Introduction and history

A company's competitiveness strongly depends on its innovativeness at the 'global frontier' (Porter and Stern 2001, p. 28), as innovation is not only an important factor for economic progress, but also an essential element in the competition of companies and nations in general (Beaver and Prince 2002). Innovativeness can be characterized by several attributes, Weber (2005) for instance defines an innovator as a company which:

- Searches and finds gaps,
- always looks for things to change or new things to do,
- has ideas that no one else has,
- does not give up too early,
- is ready to accept risks,
- sticks to ideas even against big resistance,
- takes chances that are futile to others.

Hence, corporate innovation management must play many different roles. The challenge is to manage the whole process from initial ideas to lasting realizations, which means to combine innovative and entrepreneurial tasks at the same time. Unfortunately, there is no common sense about how such processes and tasks shall look like, especially because innovation and entrepreneurship are still treated within different science streams.

Therefore, this chapter will give a review of relevant literature in both areas. One of the first and most famous definition of innovation can be traced to Joseph Schumpeters' forces of creative destruction (Schumpeter 1934):

- The introduction of a good or a significant improvement in the quality of an existing good.
- The introduction of a new method of production, i.e. an innovation in processes.
- The opening of a new market, in particular an export market in a new territory.
- The conquest of a new source of supply of raw materials or half-manufactured goods.
- The creation of a new type of industrial organization, i.e. an administrative innovation.

Therefore, all kinds of innovation include a specific level of newness, which is certainly concerned with novelty. Still, innovation is not simply invention: "Innovation incorporates both creation or discovery aspects, and diffusion or utilisation aspects" (Deakins and Freel 2006, p. 117), or, more theoretically, "innovation is commonly defined in terms of tangible entities that can be utilized by different people on different occasions, i.e. something is adoptable or diffusible" (Ford

1996, p. 1113). Pragmatic views of innovation define it as the successful implementation of creative ideas (Woodmann et al. 1993) or "as a process that provides added value and a degree of novelty to the organization and its suppliers and customers through the development of new procedures, solutions, products and services as well as new methods of commercialization" (McFadzean et al. 2005, p. 353).

2.2 The term innovation

The starting point for an innovation is mostly an invention (Utterback 1971) plus exploitation (Roberts 2007), but without successful commercialization, the invention will not become an innovation (Hauschildt and Salomo 2007; Gerpott 1999; Dewar and Dutton 1986; Martin 1994). Garcia and Calantone (2002) claim that innovation is a technology based opportunity of a new market or new service, while for example Glynn argues that any method different from traditional ones is already an innovation (Glynn 1996). As it is assumed that over 60% of economic growth is based on technological progress and not on improvements in labor productivity (Freeman and Soete 1997), it is not surprising that innovation is mostly seen as a certain kind of technological advance. In this context, the most common classification is the distinction between newness to the market and newness to the company (e.g. Cooper 1993; Hauschildt and Salomo 2007). Based on the evaluation of innovation studies, Tidd et al. (2005) state that "innovation is a process, not a single event, and needs to be managed as such", and that "the influences on the process can be manipulated to affect the outcome – that is, it can be managed" (p. 87). Thus, innovation management consists of all activities for the optimization of the whole innovation process (Olschowy 1990).

2.3 Innovation in small and big companies

In general, innovation is seen as a main vehicle for a new company to profitably enter a market and is a central force for driving competition among companies (Dosi et al. 1997). But is this true for small and big companies at the same time? In this context, Penrose (1959) states that a small company is not only a large company in miniature, so they are supposed to differ in their innovation activities as well (Voigt et al. 2003). Large companies are supposed to have a higher rate of innovativeness than smaller ones (e.g. Mowery and Rosenberg 1998), but this view was partly refuted, as small companies can be as successful in innovative activities as large corporations (e.g. Herbig et al. 1994; van Dijk et al. 1997; Koeller 1996; Schwalbach and Zimmerman 1991). This perspective is supported at the latest by the introduction of Christensen's 'Innovators Dilemma' (1997), according to which large companies have difficulties with abandoning well-established routines and practices, while smaller companies are much more flexible and adaptable. Therefore, they are supposed to be more innovative, especially when it comes to the creation of new industries. However, as far as technology diffusion and more process-oriented innovations are concerned, large companies are supposed to have an advantage, due to their financial resources and process know-how (Smith 2006; Teece 1986).

Still, innovativeness does not appear to be a major explanatory factor of successful innovation (Cohen 1995), as such factors can depend on other characteristics like a certain industry, not only on an optimum size of a company (Burton 1999). Even R&D is not only an 'undocked' special department for innovation anymore. Especially in large companies, R&D departments are increasingly forced to buy and sell all types of results from research activities, as the sole focus on 'producing' and buying patents is not sufficient anymore. Congruously, this part of the company also accounts for a certain business risk not only by selling and buying licences, researchers and small research companies or facilities, but by actively pushing internal and external venturing as well as spinning in and spinning out projects (Gibson 1981; Ortt and Smits 2006). Martin (1994) calls this 'interpreneurship' with the alternatives of technology acquisition and licensing, R&D consortia, strategic alliances combining complementary assets and between rivals. For these new roles, adequate human resources are needed (Brem, 2007).

2.4 Fuzzy Front End of Innovation

For further considerations, the understanding of the Front End of Innovation (FEI) plays an important role. Therefore, FEI will be defined and some recent approaches will be introduced.

The term '(fuzzy) front end' describes the earliest stage of an idea development and includes all time spent on an idea as well as activities focusing on strengthening this idea, prior to a first official discussion of an idea (Reid and Brentani, 2004). Wellsprings for ideas are both internal and external sources (von Hippel, 1988). In this context, the differences to the new product and process development are important to consider (see Table 1).

Furthermore, the terms (fuzzy) front end and front end innovation are synonymous. Following the argumentation of Koen et al. (2001) that fuzziness implies an innovation process phase consisting of unknowable and uncontrollable factors, solely the term front end innovation will be used in this paper. In this sense, this phase is partly analog to the introduced idea generation stage, but the focus on the front end is mainly on opportunity identification and analysis (Belliveau et al., 2004; Khurana and Rosenthal, 2002). Therefore, the front end is one of the greatest areas of weakness of the innovation process and fundamentally determines the later innovation success (Koen et al., 2001). So, the effective management of the front end results in a sustainable competitive (innovation) advantage. Surprisingly, there has been less research done on this issue so far (Kim and Wilemon, 2002).

Table 1 Front end innovation vs. new product and process development (Koen et al., 2001)

	Front end of innovation	New product and process development
Nature of work	Experimental, often chaotic, difficult to plan, Eureka moments	Structured, disciplined and goal-oriented with a project plan
Commerciali-zation date	Unpredictable	Definable
Funding	Variable; in the beginning phase, many projects may be 'bootlegged', while others will need funding to proceed	Budgeted
Revenue expectiations	Often uncertain, sometimes done with a great deal of speculation	Believable and with increasing certainty, analysis and documentation as the release date gets closer
Activity	Both individual and team in areas to minimize risk and optimize potential	Multi-functional product and/or process development teams

A flow-oriented approach, the so-called 'idea tunnel', which resulted from an older concept called 'development funnel' (Hayes et al., 1988), is the elementary basic model for front end considerations (see Figure 1).

Hence, there are two ways of gaining ideas: collecting ideas in the sense that the ideas are already present somehow, at least in the mind of a person or a group. Creating means a well thought-out generation of ideas through creativity methods. Consequently, creativity practice methods and techniques are needed to create a continuous spirit of creative evolution (Kelley and Littmann, 2005).

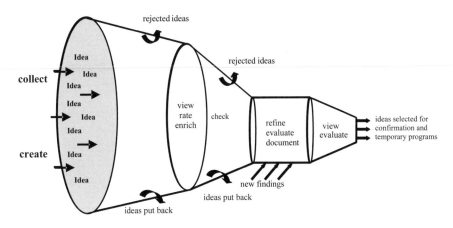

Figure 1 The idea tunnel (Deschamps et al., 1996)

Key elements for promoting corporate creativity are a motivating reward system, officially recognized creativity initatives, the encouragement of self-initiated activities as well as the allowance of redundancy (Stenmark, 2000).Nevertheless, several general requirements must be fulfilled in order to generate ideas that will be successful in the marketplace (Boeddrich, 2004):

- Considering the company's corporate strategy
- Obvious benefits for the ideas' target audience
- Systematically structured and conducted concept identification phase

Moreover, there are not only general, but also company-specific ramifications to consider which increase the complexity (Boeddrich, 2004). That is why there is always a dilemma between giving the front end a certain system and structure on the one hand and forcing creativity as well as implementing externals on the other hand.

Due to page restrictions, the following list of FEI models is not exhaustive, but gives an overview of existing approaches with different focuses.

The most popular one is the new concept development model from Koen et al. (2001), which is supposed to provide a common language for front end activities (see Figure 2).

The circular shape shows the flow, circulation, and iteration of ideas within the five core elements and the surrounding external influencing factors. A fundamental distinction is made between an opportunity and an idea:

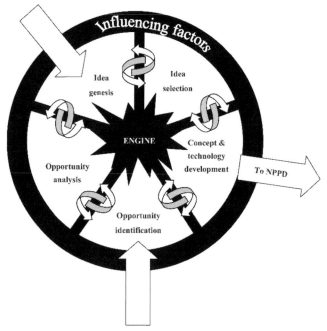

Figure 2 New concept development model (Koen et al., 2001)

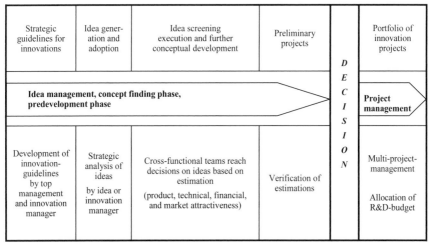

Strategic guidelines for innovations	Idea generation and adoption	Idea screening execution and further conceptual development	Preliminary projects		Portfolio of innovation projects

Figure 3 Front end model proposal (Boeddrich, 2004)

Thus, the opportunity identification and analysis precedes an (business) idea because these stages include an ongoing process of several information enrichment stages like market studies or scientific experiments. A formal business plan or project proposal finally indicates the changeover to the new product and process development.A proposal for a more process-oriented procedure is given from Boeddrich (2004) (see Figure 3).

In this framework, there is a specific differentiation between single process steps on the one hand and organizational responsibilities on the other hand.

He identified company-specific preconditions for the successful management of front end activities, confirmed by several other studies (Boeddrich, 2004):

- definition of company-specific idea categories,
- commitment to company-specific evaluation methods and selection criteria – especially with regard to K. O. criteria for approved projects,
- commitment to the owner of the idea management process,
- commitment to individuals or organizational units that promote innovation within the company,
- definition of creative scopes for the company,
- influence of the top management,
- number of stages and gates in the tailor-made idea management
- investigation of stakeholders in the structured front end and establishment of their participation.

A recent approach is from Sandmeier et al. (2004), who defined a very comprehensive process model and go explicitly into the topic market pull vs. technology push (see Figure 4).

Phase 1 focuses on the market and technology opportunities of a company. The central and iterative activities are the strategies and goals of an innovation.

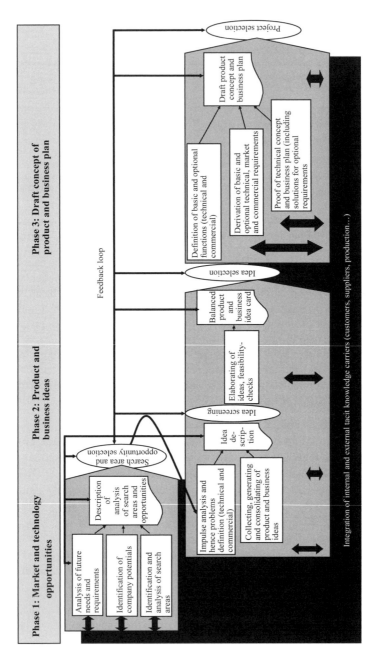

Figure 4 Integrated front end process model (Sandmeier et al., 2004)

Finally, there are one to two opportunities and search fields for the next stage. The next phase deals with the actual idea generation and evaluation with several sub-processes in order to result in the creation of balanced business and product cards. The final phase transfers the generated ideas into business plans and product concepts, which will be devolved to the product development phase. Moreover, role-specific responsibilities are assigned depending on the innovation development progress.

It can be summarized that the described models vary in terms of perception, resources considerations and detailing. They have in common that they are all based on empirical research, especially case studies. Hence, even across different companies, industries and strategies of product and process development, the front end innovation challenges and threats seem to be very similar. Still, more interbranch-based research is needed for further considerations.

3 Different views on the same issue

As stated, the definition of innovation is commonly based on any kind of (technological) invention with the accordant transfer of a new idea into a commercial product. In a broader sense, any method which differs from a traditional one can be called an innovation.

The European understanding of innovation focuses almost solely on the invention aspect combined with the factor of a successful market introduction. The common Asian view often differs in terms of the origin of the innovation. It is based on taking another, already existing technology or product, modifying it and introducing it to the market as well in research and concurrently in practice. Therefore it is not essential, where the original source of the innovation lies, the focus hereby is mostly on the successful commercialization of an idea (independent of certain trademark or property rights).

International conferences that deal with innovation, like ISMOT or ICMIT, often face views colliding with one another in topics such as open innovation or innovation process models.

As a good example, Chinese researchers are talking about 'indigenous innovation', which contains the following steps: (Xin-li 2005; Guo-jie 2005)

- Adopting the original innovation.
- Integration of the innovation into own innovative activities.
- Developing secondary innovation based on importing and absorbing foreign technologies.

Hence, indigenous innovation is seen as 'a process to explore potential market with in-house Research and Development activities and external knowledge acquisition' (Chen et al. 2006, p. 207).

Following this approach, innovation is not only based on an invention and the appropriate successful introduction into the market, but also on the adaptation of external technologies and their further development. This approach can `confuse` European researchers, without any valuation of the potential correctness of this way of thinking. Because this view of innovation implies - at least in technical way of thinking - that innovative activities can be completely based on external knowledge absorption, what is not within the scope of the common European terms of innovation.

As Chen et al. (2006) are stating, indigenous innovation is for them not just the key success factor for their researched case example (which was on the company Haier, one of the world's largest consumer product manufacturers), but a main goal of the Chinese innovation policy as well. So maybe the definition of indigenous innovation is an important dimension of innovation, which is currently just not included in recent innovation literature. Surprisingly, up to now there are no real scientific debates taking place on these topics, at least not in public.

4 Future directions

Consequently, to gain deeper insights into the various views of terms and definitions of innovation and innovative activities, a scientific debate is suggested where active talks and interdisciplinary discussions about theories, models and research results take place, especially before the background of different culture areas. Common definitions may not be a result of these first debates, but having a better understanding of the various views would be already a great benefit for all participating parties.

References

BEAVER, G. AND PRINCE, G., 2002. Innovation, Entrepreneurship and Competitive Advantage in the Entrepreneurial Venture. *Journal of Small Business and Enterprise Development*, 9 (1), 28–37.

BREM, A., 2007. *Make-or-Buy Entscheidungen im strategischen Technologiemanagement*. Saarbrücken: VDM.

BURTON, J. 1999. Innovation, Entrepreneurship and the Firm: A Post-Schumpeterian Approach. *International Journal of Technology Management*. 17 (1/2): 16-37.

GIBSON, J.E., 1981: *Managing Research and Development*. New York: John Wiley and Sons.

CHEN, J., JIN, X., HE, Y.-B., Yao, W., 2006. Jin, He, Yao. TIM based indigenous innovation: experiences from Haier Group. *2006 IEEE International Conference on Management of Innovation and Technology Proceedings*, pp. 207-210.

COHEN, W., 1995. Empirical Studies of Innovative Activities. In: P. STONEMAN, ed. *Handbook of the Economics of Innovation and Technological Change*. Oxford: Basil Blackwell, 182-264.

COOPER, R.G., 1993. *Winning at New Products: Accelerating the Process from Idea to Launch*. Reading, Mass: Addison Wesley.

CHRISTENSEN, C.M., 1997. *The Innovator's Dilemma: When New Technologies Cause Great Firms to Fail*. Boston: Harvard Business School Press.

DAEKINS, D. AND FREEL, M., 2006. *Entrepreneurship and Small Firms*. New York: McGraw-Hill.

DEWAR, R.D. AND DUTTON, J.E., 1986. The Adoption of Radical and Incremental Innovations: An Empirical Analysis. *Management Science*, 32 (11), 1422-1433.

DOSI, G., MALERBA, F., MARSILI, O. AND ORSENIGO, L., 1997. Industrial Structures and Dynamics: Evidence, Interpretations and Puzzles. *Industrial and Corporate Change*, 6, 3–24.

FORD, C.M., 1996. A Theory of Individual Creative Action in Multiple Social Domains. *Academy of Management Review*, 21 (4), 1112-1142.

FREEMAN, C. AND SOETE, L., 1997. *The Economics of Industrial Innovation*. London: Pinter.

GARCIA, R. AND CALANTONE, R., 2002. A Critical Look at Technological Innovation Typology and Innovativeness Terminology: A Literature Review. *Journal of Product Innovation Management*, 19 (2), 110-132.

GERPOTT, T.J., 1999. *Strategisches Technologie- und Innovationsmanagement*. Stuttgart: Schäffer-Poeschel.

GIBSON, J.E., 1981: *Managing Research and Development*. New York: John Wiley and Sons.

GLYNN, M.A., 1996. Innovative Genius: A Framework for Relating Individual and Organizational Intelligences to Innovation. *Academy of Management Review*, 21 (4), 1081-1111.

GUO-JIE, L., 2005: Indigenous innovation capability is the key tache for national competence, *Guangming Daily*, Feb. 24.

HAUSCHILDT, J. (2004). *Innovationsmanagement*. München: Vahlen.

HAUSCHILDT, J. AND SALOMO, S., 2007. *Innovationsmanagement*. München: Vahlen.

HERBIG, P., GOLDEN, E.J. AND DUNPHY, A., 1994. The Relationship of Structure to Entrepreneurial and Innovative Success. *Marketing Intelligence & Planning*, 12 (9), 37-48.

KOELLER, C.T., 1996. Union Membership, Market Structure, and the Innovation Output of Large and Small Firms. *Journal of Labor Research*, 17 (4), 683-99.

MARTIN, M.J.C., 1994. Managing Innovation and Entrepreneurship in Technology-based. New York: Wiley.

MCFADZEAN, E., O'LOUGHLIN, A. AND SHAW, E., 2005. Corporate Entrepreneurship and Innovation Part 1: The Missing Link. *European Journal of Innovation Management*, 8 (3), 350–372.

MOWERY, D.C. AND ROSENBERG, N., 1998. *Paths of innovation: Technological Change in 20th Century America*. Cambridge, MA.: Cambridge University Press.

OLSCHOWY, W., 1990. *Externe Einflußfaktoren im strategischen Innovationsmanagement: Auswirkungen externer Einflußgrößen auf den wirtschaftlichen Innovationserfolg sowie die unternehmerischen Anpassungsmaßnahmen*. Berlin: Erich Schmidt Verlag.

ORTT, J.R. AND SMITHS, R., 2006. Innovation Management: Different Approaches to Cope with the Same Trends. *International Journal of Technology Management*, 34 (3/4), 296-318.

PENROSE, E.T., 1959. *The Theory of the Growth of the Firm*. Oxford: Basil Blackwell.

PORTER, M.E. AND STERN, S., 2001. *Innovation*: Location matters. MIT Sloan Management Review, 42 (4), 28-36.

ROBERTS, E.B., 2007. Managing Invention and Innovation. *Research Technology Management*, 50 (1), 35-54.

SCHUMPETER, J.A., 1934. *The Theory of Economic Development*. Cambridge, MA: Harvard University Press.

SCHWALBACH, J. AND ZIMMERMAN, K.F., 1991. A Poisson Model of Patenting and Firm Structure in Germany. In: J.A. ZOLTAN AND D.B. AUDRETSCH, eds. *Innovation and Technological Change: An International Comparison*. Michigan: Ann Arbor University of Michigan Press, 109-120.

SMITH, D., 2006. *Exploring Innovation*. New York: McGraw-Hill.

TEECE, D.J., 1986. Profiting from Technological Innovation: Implications for Integration, Collaboration, Licensing and Public Policy. *Research Policy*, 15 , 285-305.

TIDD, J. BESSANT, J., & PAVITT, K. 2005. *Managing Innovation:* Integrating Technological, Managerial Organizational Change. New York: McGraw-Hill.

UTTERBACK, J.M., 1971. The Process of Technological Innovation Within the Firm. *Academy of Management Journal*, 14 (1), 75-88.

VAN DIJK, B., DEN HERTOG, R., MENKVELD, B. AND THURIK, R., 1997. Some New Evidence on the Determinants of Large and Small Firm Innovation. *Small Business Economics*, 9, 335-343.

VOIGT, K.-I., INGERFELD, M. AND WITTENBERG, V., 2003. Innovationen und Innovationscontrolling in jungen Unternehmen. In: A.-K. ACHLEITNER AND A. BASSEN, eds. *Controlling von jungen Unternehmen*. Stuttgart: Schäffer-Poeschel, 91-115.

WEBER, W.W., 2005. *Innovation durch Injunktion*. Göttingen: Sordon.

WOODMAN, R.W., SAWYER, J.E. AND GRIFFIN, R.W., 1993. Toward a Theory of Organizational Creativity. *Academy of Management Review*, 18 (2), 293-321.

XIN-LI, Z., 2005: Enhancing indigenous innovation capability is the key tache for changing economic development ways, *Science Time*, May 18.

Chapter 6
Beijing International IT R&D Hub

ZHAO Jing-Yuan

School of Management of Beijing Union University, CHINA

Abstract With the trend of globalization and internationalization of multinational enterprises R&D activities, more and more multinational enterprises transfer their R&D activities to Beijing. The paper focus on Beijing's location advantage to establish international IT R&D hub, explores the possibility to establish Beijing as international IT R&D Hub, analyzes Beijing international IT R&D hub's growth stages, including budding period, incubator period and development period. The paper proposes the strategy to establish Beijing international IT R&D Hub by means of building brand city, and discusses the model of Beijing brand city, business environment that is an important issue for building brand city, and the strategy of building brand city. Finally, the study analyzes the role and functions of government to establish R&D hub.

1 Introduction

With the advent of the knowledge economy, the R&D(Research and Development) , which products knowledge and turns knowledge into productivity, is more important than ever before. Along with the trend of economic globalization and increasingly fierce international competition, the organization forms of multinational enterprises' R&D have also greatly changed accordingly. In order to adapt to the complexities of the world market and the variety of products and consumer different preferences in different countries and also in order to fully make use of the existing scientific and technological resources, reduce the cost and risk in the R&D process of new product, some rather large multinational enterprises of the developed countries, on the basis of continuous improvement of the internationalization of the production, pay special attention to the optimal allocation of production factors. Developed countries have changed their traditional layout of R&D hub in their home countries and start to arrange R&D organizations on the global scale according to the comparative advantages of different countries in human resources, scientific and technological strength and the research infrastructure, as a result, the activities of the R&D of transnational corporations increasingly move to the direction of globalization. Traditionally, the R&D center of enterprise is based on the home country, but since 1980, enterprises' R&D gradually head for the world (Petrella 1989; Paoliz and Guerciui 1997; Patel and Pavitt 1998; OECD

P.O. de Pablos, M.D. Lytras (eds.), *The China Information Technology Handbook*,
DOI: 10.1007/978-0-387-77743-6_6, © Springer Science+Business Media, LLC 2009

1997; Guellec et al. 2001). At the same time, multinational enterprises' overseas R&D activities have been shifted to a two-way interactive model of technology search from the traditional one-way model of technology transfer.

Gassmann and Zedtwitz (1999) found that the R&D organizational structure of multinational enterprises has tended to be multi-level R&D network patterns, the R&D partnership formed among different R&D units can be engage in a two-way exchange of information and knowledge. Therefore, technology sourcing is not only the technology transfer, but also an important motive of enterprises' R&D internationalization (Paolize and Guercine 1997; Cantwell and Santangelo 1999). Most of the existing literatures claim that the R&D transfer is only the internationalization of developed countries' business operation function, although some literatures begin to realize that the internationalization of R&D has begun to involve other countries which is beyond the developed countries, (Amsden et al. 2001; Chen 2003; Chen 2004; Reddy 2000), very few literatures explore the internationalization of R&D from the perspective of developing countries. (Amsden et al. 2001). Along with this trend, An important issue related to this issues is not only whether multinational enterprises engaging in R&D in developing countries, more importantly, is with what kind of advantages of developing countries to attract multinational enterprises to set up R&D organization in local, the vast number of developing countries, including China, are trying to attract multinational enterprises to set up their R& D organization in their countries.

From a global point of view, the transfer of Multinational enterprises' R&D involves many fields, mainly in medicine, electronics and information, chemicals, automotive. For multinational enterprises, electronic information industry appears to be particularly conspicuous in their R&D investment in China. Chen (2003) according to the survey of multinational enterprises in mainland China, out of 58 of the 82 multinational enterprises is the IT (Information Technology) enterprises, of which 49 choose Beijing to set up R&D organizations. Beijing is in the special status in the process of building national R&D hub, how to take full advantage of the opportunity to improve the innovation ability of Beijing is an urgent subject to study.

In the traditional paradigm of R&D internationalization, technology transfer is basically a one-way, that is, product concept and technical knowledge based on the home country spread to external organizations, this process is known as export-oriented learning, and the new paradigm of R&D internationalization is the integration of the export-oriented learning and Internal-oriented economy, diversified Knowledge Center, the strong interaction of market and technology and the mutual transfer of technology in different areas are its characteristics (Liu 2005). The investment of R&D institutions in Beijing cover Beijing's R&D investment gap, at the same time, bring the latest technology in the world and effective methods of management on the talent and R&D to Beijing, and in addition greatly promote the formation of related knowledge networks in Beijing. It also play a vital role in terms of improving Beijing's efficiency of knowledge production and proliferation, enhancing local enterprises' R&D, and stimulating the development of information technology. How to make use of Beijing's advantages to attract overseas and domestic R&D to Beijing and turn Beijing into IT R&D center, enhance regional scientific and technological innovation capability is a significant practical issue.

2. Beijing's Location Advantage to Establish International IT R&D Hub

According to the study of Beijing Municipal Science and Technology Commission, Beijing has become a global transfer destination of R&D. In fact, Beijing Municipal Science and Technology Commission's data show that Beijing has already more than 2000 various types of R&D institutes with a certain scale, of which more than 1,000 have been set up by enterprises, more than 700 by universities and the government, more than 200 by private research institutes. More than 200 foreign investors have set up R&D institutions in Beijing, among which R&D of electronic information organizations are 100 accounting for 60% of the total number of foreign R&D institutions. Yu et al. (2004) found that by the end of 2002, multinational enterprises had at least set up 96 large R&D institutions in China, mainly concentrating in Beijing, Shanghai, Guangdong and JiangSu and other coastal cities, especially in Beijing and Shanghai. According to UN statistics, in 2004, from the volume point of view, foreign R&D institutes mainly locate in Beijing and Shanghai, more than 100 foreign R&D institutions separately, followed by Shenzhen, Guangzhou and Tianjin which have more than 50 foreign R&D institutes. Beijing has become the first place for multinational and domestic enterprise to set up R&D institutions.

Compared with other cities, Beijing has special advantages to become into R&D hub, as the capital with the most outstanding human resources, many universities and colleges, scientific research institutes, provides an effective safeguard for the development of R&D. As many foreign and domestic enterprises set up R&D organizations in Beijing, Beijing has become the exchange center of information and the distribution center of technology products. In the science and technology activities of the investment evaluation in 2004 and 2005, the index of science and technology activities inputs of Beijing listed on the first place of the whole country. Beijing, Shanghai, Shanxi, Guangdong, Liaoning, Tianjin, Jiangsu, Zhejiang are on the top eight, and also higher than that of the country's average level (national science and technology activities inputs index is 42.08 percent). And Beijing 2005 Technology activities input Index is increased 1.4 percentage points comparing to that of in 2004. This laid the foundation for Beijing to become R&D center. Beijing is on the top of environmental index of scientific and technological progress in 2004 and 2005 in China, increasing 2.26 percentage points in 2005 than in 2004. Beijing, Shanghai, Tianjin, Xinjiang, Jiangsu, Guangdong, Liaoning, Shanxi, Shandong, Zhejiang are top ten, and it is also higher than the national average (national science and technology advancement environmental index is 48.67 percent). According to R&D budget expenditure data, the R&D expenditures of Beijing in 2004 is RMB31.73 billion, ranking first in the country. In 2005, Beijing R&D expenditures is RMB38.21 billion, ranking first in the country, higher than the second one Shanghai, which is RMB17.37 billion.

The research project of Global IT R&D Transfer's Influence on Beijing and Beijing's Strategies analyzes multinational enterprises' IT R&D in China, claims that Beijing has the location advantage to become R&D transfer center. According to Zhao(2006), regarding the factor analysis of forming high-tech industrial cluster, combining with the motives for multinational enterprises' R&D transfer, we summarized that economic factor, knowledge spillover environment, human capital, the level of science and research, communications facilities, protection of intellectual property, foreign direct investment, business environment, and wage level are the main factors and may affect multinational enterprises' R&D investment in China. After screening and statistical analysis, we have concluded that R&D investment of multinational enterprises in China has a high degree of correlation with the effective utilization of each individual province's human resources, business environment, the actual use of foreign direct investment, science and technology level, and the level of intellectual property protection.

2.1. Human Capital

According to Zan (2004), the use of the host country's human capital is one of the motives to drive multinational enterprises to develop R&D globally. From the perspective of supply of economics, as senior R&D talent is relatively scarce, in order to obtain highly qualified personnel, multinational enterprises recruit top talent from overseas, especially from developing countries.

The purpose of some multinational enterprises setting up R&D institutions in China aimed mainly at China's abundant and cheap human resources. The so-called cheap is relative, compared with developed countries, China's human resources is cheaper, which led to the R&D organizations set by multinational enterprises mainly concentrated in human capital-intensive areas. The advantage of Beijing R&D talent is on the first place of China. There are 171 thousand R&D personnel in Beijing in 2005, ranking first in China by region (see Table 1).

Table 1 R&D Personnel by Region (2005) 1,000 Person-Years

Region	R&D personnel	Region	R&D personnel
Total	1364.8	-	-
Beijing	171.0	Shanghai	67.0
Tianjin	33.4	Jiangsu	128.0
Hebei	41.7	Zhejiang	80.1
Shanxi	27.4	Anhui	28.4
Inner Mongolia	13.5	Fujian	35.7
Liaoning	66.1	Jiangxi	22.1
Jilin	25.6	Shandong	91.1
Heilongjiang	44.2	Henan	51.2
Hubei	61.2	Yunnan	14.8
Hunan	38.0	Tibet	0.6
Guangdong	119.4	Shaanxi	53.7
Guangxi	17.9	Gansu	16.8
Hainan	1.2	Qinghai	2.6
Chongqing	24.6	Ningxia	4.0
Sichuan	66.4	Xinjiang	7.0
Guizhou	9.8	-	-

2.2 Business Environment

Multinational enterprises' R&D investment activities mainly located in the better area of business environment. Although the R&D products serves primarily for its own production, not necessarily to exchange technologies with local enterprises, but local business environment is the embodiment of the perfect degree of financial, institutional, cultural and taxation and other aspects, which provides good assurance for multinational enterprises' R&D activities. From the data analysis, Beijing's business environment is first place in 2006, followed by Shanghai, Tianjin. The regions with business environment in the forefront of the country, usually have more R&D institutions of multinational enterprises, which shows that the tax and the financial system in these regions is in the perfect condition to ensure the R&D activities of multinational enterprises to run smoothly.

2.3. Actual Scale of FDI Utilization

According to Mansfield (1979), Lall (1980) and Pearce (1989) research on the United States companies, the overseas subsidiary companies' production of multinational enterprises is the determinant factor for multinational enterprises to invest R&D overseas. Multinational enterprises' FDI flow will affect the investment of R&D, FDI is the most important factor for multinational enterprises' region choice for R&D investment overseas. Especially for developing countries, like China, the investment of multinational enterprises is to track the China's local market demand to meet the huge market demand, in order to meet market demand, R&D institutions need timely to know market trends, to develop the products to meet local demand by R&D activities.

In recent years, Beijing's actual scale of FDI utilization ranks nationwide in the top three, Guangzhou first, followed by Shanghai.

2.4. Standard of Science and Technology

Applicable R&D depends on the stock of basic research, the stock of local basic research directly determine the risk degree of applicable technologies' commercialization. And more, R&D activities will bring spillover, the effect of spillover depends on local people's learning and transforming ability (Lucas 2005). The regional level of science and technology, for multinational enterprises to set up R&D institutions, has enormous appeal. The data show that Beijing's level of science and technology is first place in the provinces.

2.5. Degree of Protecting Intellectual Property Right

Despite Ferrantino (1993) and Mansfield (1994) disputed in the issue that the protection of intellectual property right influenced a country's FDI flow, R&D activities' direct products is knowledge products, which need good policies to protect intellectual property right, the institutional factor for multinational enterprises' investment decision-making is an extremely important factor. R&D production's protection mainly dependent on the protection of private property right, especially the protection of intellectual property right for multinational enterprises to select investment regions is very important.

As the direct product of R&D activities is knowledge products, intellectual property right protection has great influence on the choice of multinational enterprises R&D investment location. Multinational enterprises will not set their critical R&D institutions in those regions where is lack of intellectual property right protection. However, there is no specific standard to measure the degree of intellectual property protection, we are using patent authorization number in every 10,000 people as a measure of the level of intellectual property protection standards, with a certain degree of subjective, for complex multinational enterprises' R&D activities, it needs to be carefully to draw the conclusions. Data show that Beijing ranked as the first in the provinces, followed by Shanghai.

By analyzing the location factors of multinational enterprises' R&D investment in china, it is Beijing' location advantage to attract multinational enterprises to move their R&D to Beijing, and Beijing' location advantage is the favorable condition for the growth of Beijing R&D hob. Similarly, location factors such as human capital, business environment, the level of science and technology and the degree of intellectual property protection, should be taken into consideration for domestic enterprises' transferring their R&D to the Beijing.

3 Growth Stage of Beijing International IT R&D Hub

Beijing international IT R&D hub is consisted of the enterprise organizations. According to Adizes' life cycle theory (2003), apart from a general sense of the common life cycle, Beijing international IT R&D hub as a cluster of high-tech industry organizations, has its own characteristics. The commercialization of R&D activities need experiencing three stages: stage of R&D, innovation and development stage and market development stage. R&D stage mainly carries out R&D activities on the basis of the ability of R&D personnel, and the second stage is innovative activities on the basis of acquired R&D results, and begin to introduce products to market. The market development stage mainly translate innovative results into products to market. According to high-tech industry's characteristics in various economic activities in the process of growth and development, the life cycle of Beijing international IT R&D hub is divided into three phases: budding period, incubator period, development period.

3.1. Budding Period

Budding period also can be seen as originality period, characterized by strong knowledge innovation, the core input element is intellectual and skills of science and technology personnel, fund input is low, generally account for only 5% to 10% of the total invested capital during incubator period. While the main risk of this stage is technology risk, which is very high level of risk.(Wang and Liu 2003). Looking at the history of Beijing international IT development, from 1980 to 1986, it can be considered as Beijing's budding period of IT hob. Beijing international IT R&D hub originated in the early 1980's "Zhongguancun Electronic Street." First, there was no policy to support, and even met the opposition of policy, until 1985, in the document of the CPC Central Committee's Decision on the Science and Technology Management System, the Central Committee decided to establish the National Natural Science Foundation and other science and technology funds, at the same time, open up more sources of funds, and encourage departments, enterprises and social groups to invest in science and technology. Thus, there are policies support on R&D funds and venture funds.

In budding period, Human resources mainly relies on a small number of science and technology personnel's intellectual support, they serve as both R&D personnel and business managers, the double identity, for science and technology personnel, who just down from technology posts, is a huge technical risk and management risk at the same time. In the budding period of Beijing international IT R&D hub is mainly formed by the so-called informal organizations, which is naturally formed group because of geographical relations, work relations, relations and friends.

Although the state issued policies to encourage R&D investments, but the state funds are mostly into state-owned units, research institutes, and so on, very little access to small technology enterprises, which assume great risks. And more, enterprises are mostly in simple production, have not formed their own brands, with low awareness, the market is mostly willing to spend more foreign exchange to import goods from abroad. the basic structure of Beijing international IT R&D hub in the budding period can be explained by Figure 1.

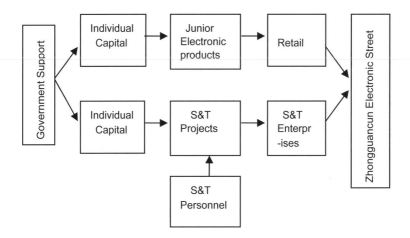

Figure 1 Basic Structure of Beijing R&D Hub in the Budding Period

3.2. Incubator Period

From 1986 1995, it can be considered as the incubator period of Beijing international IT R&D hub. Beijing IT industry, which center is Zhongguancun, has already a certain scale. In 1988, Beijing formally established China's first state-level high-tech industrial development zone. 1988's " Provisional Regulations of Beijing High Technology Industry Development Experimental Zone" explicitly set forth support policy for the scientific and technological enterprise, introducing various tax incentives and financial policies. Bank loans for scientific and technological enterprises gradual progressed under the support of governments, coupled with the relaxed financing channels, as well as the involvement of venture capital firms, created a new better situation for technology companies to get financial support.

To encourage academy personnel work in the part-time in technological enterprises, making technology conversion rate improved, the technical personnel in technological enterprises will not be restricted to communicate with abroad, a large number of university graduates, Chinese overseas students and foreign experts and scholars services in IT R&D, and greatly enhanced the level of science and technology(S&D). In the incubator period of Beijing international IT R&D hub, the R&D personnel for enterprises is very important, they pay great attention to negative aspects in their enterprises, and will is take core technology away to run business alone or rely on competitors when dissatisfied. At this stage, the govern mechanism of technological enterprises is human resources management, which mainly inspirits technical backbone personnel. Figure 2 is the basic structure.

3.3. Development Period

By 2000, Beijing's IT industry had developed to a relatively perfect state. From Zhongguancun trial zone to Zhongguancun Science and Technology Park, it

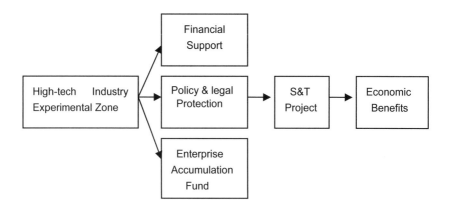

Figure 2 Basic Structure of Beijing R&D Hub in the Incubator Period

achieved leapfrog development. During this period, both the central authorities and local government in Beijing had issued relevant policies and instructions to encourage and promote the development of science and technology industry. The main characteristics of Beijing international IT R&D hub in the development period is that technological products had been accepted by the market, sales revenue and profits grew rapidly, the enterprises' cash flow could support the daily operations. The international competition for the talent was more intensive than before, especially IT industry, which center is software industry, the talents of developing countries were absorbed in a predatory way.

China bear the brunt of this trend. According to incomplete statistics, nearly 400,000 Chinese overseas students stay in the developed countries, while multinational enterprises in China had offered favorable wages to attract domestic talent and turned them into the local employees of foreign companies, the situation of brain drain became very serious. Faced with this situation, the government promulgated a series of policies to attract talent, together with enterprises incubator founded to support and encourage technology professionals to be entrepreneurs.

In the tide of internationalization, the multi-ply structure of Beijing international IT R&D hub had been formed. The pattern that IT industry is dominant had been broken. Haidian Park of Zhongguancun Science and Technology Park was an example, the income ratio of IT industry started to decline in 2004, new materials, optical and electrical machinery, environmental protection industry, energy-saving industry and the pharmaceutical industry developed rapidly, and industrial distribution tended to be more reasonable. The internal structure of IT industry also had been changed. Taking HaiDian Park of Zhongguancun Science and Technology Park as an example.

From the industrial added value, the proportion of computer unit decreased significantly, meanwhile, the proportion of software, communications and IC in market increased in 2002, the software industry had exceeded computer unit and was in a dominant position in terms of the electronics and information industry. Figure 3 is the basic structure of Beijing international IT R&D hub's development period.

It is worth noting that during this period, the Beijing international IT R&D hub emerged a new point of economic growth: information services. In 2004, production value of Beijing's IT service accounted for 7.4% of Beijing's GDP, ranking the second place of Beijing's tertiary industry, only after financial and insurance industry.

In 2004, there were 5,000 software and IT enterprises in Beijing, 3.7 times than that of in 2000, the average annual growth rate was 38%.

4 Strategy

The upgrade process of urban competitive power is a complex process to transform resources elements and add value. Building brand city is one of the ways to enhance urban competitive power. Brand city means the perfect integration of high-quality products, high-grade city and the high moral citizen, and achieve

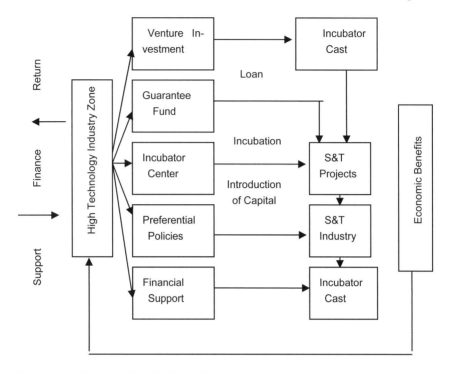

Figure 3 Basic Structure of Beijing R&D Hub in the Development Period

comprehensive, coordinated development of society. The study claim that building Beijing as a brand city is the strategic means for Beijing to become international IT R&D hub. The following is the discussion on brand city model and the strategy to build brand city.

4.1. Model of Brand City Building

Brand's connotation is from product or service trademarks with the high quality and famous name, to enterprises' marks reflecting the enterprises' culture and spirit, to city logo reflecting a urban or regional cultural and economical characteristics, has been continuously enriched and extended. The model driven by brand products is the model of establishing brand city. The model driven by brand products is that brand products lead the upgrading of the industrial chain as a whole, so that a number of brand industry groups in the city rise, driving brand city to build, at the same time, bring brand effect into play to build brand products by virtue of brand city. Figure 4 shows this model.

In China, Qingdao, Xiamen are built to be brand city driven by brand enterprises, Suzhou, Hangzhou develop the brand city driven by tourism brand. The brand city model of brand product-oriented is suitable for cities in the early growth period and development period, focusing on brand products to promote overall city to develop harmoniously and continually.

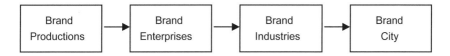

Figure 4 Model of Brand City Driven by Brand Products

Qingdao for example, in the process of brand city construction, the brand products became the pillar industry of Qingdao, bringing the secondary industry, the third industry to develop comprehensively, the interactive industrial chain was formed. Qingdao took use of the accumulated effect of brand products to attract more investment, a number of industry value chains were initially formed: relying on Haier, Hisense, to develop of electronic industry chain of home appliances, relying on Zhongshiyou, to develop petrochemical industry chain, relying on the Qingqi, Zhiwtai, Hercynian Bay base, to develop the automotive and locomotive container shipbuilding industry chain, relying on Qinggang, to develop of new materials and steel industrial chain, rely on Guofeng, to develop biopharmaceutical industrial chain. At the same time, promote small and medium enterprises industrial groups to develop, innovate supporting organization system, lengthen the production chain, to build brand city.

Furthermore, as international IT R&D hub, India makes full use of their software human resources advantage to develop software services and software export, the low-cost, high-quality software products enable India to become a world software processing base, has led to the brand city building driven by talent brand, and the brand city of Silicon Valley is driven by urban innovation.

4.2. Model of Beijing Brand City Building

Beijing's IT industry is in a leading position in China, the R&D investment is huge. The amount of R&D expenses and its percentage accounting in GDP in China are far ahead of other provinces and cities. This was largely attributed to the many universities and academies gathered in Beijing. In addition, Beijing, as the capital, its attractive power to human resources in terms of the economic and cultural advantages can not be underestimated, particularly to those talent who have received higher education. As China's first state-level high-tech industry development zone, Zhongguancun Science and Technology Park is the most intensive area, possessing Beijing technology, intelligence, talent and information resources, there are the park has Tsinghua University, Beijing University, and other 39 universities and institutes, the total number of college students is about 400,000, various types and levels of academy organizations are approximately 213, of which national engineering centers are 41, key laboratories 42, the state-level enterprise technical centers are 10. Zhongguancun annually produces thousands of the high level scientific and technological fruits. In 1999, Zhongguancun was named the highest experimental field of RMB per-mu yield. Excellent and low-cost human resources reduce R&D expenses, more attractive for enterprises.

After 20 years of development, Zhongguancun, as China's largest high-tech zone, has become the forefront of economic development and the typical representative of the high-tech zones in China. According to the study of Zhongguancun Science and Technology Park Management Committee and the Great Wall Enterprise Institute of Strategic Studies (2005), compared with the world several major science and technology parks, Zhongguancun Science and Technology Park mainly engages in R&D and services. The technical level of industry in the domestic is at advance stage, mainly focusing on the secondary technical R&D. The economic growth of Zhongguancun Science and Technology Park is fast, the income sales of Zhongguancun Science and Technology Park's IT industry is approximately 24.2 billion US dollars, software sales income is approximately 3.1 billion US dollars. From 2001 to 2004, Zhongguancun park patents' average growth rate is as high as 34.8%, 55.7 thousands people worked here, Bachelor accounting for 56%, Master accounting for 10.9%.In 2004, a total number of enterprises in Zhongguancun Park is 13,597, only inferior to Silicon Valley, but the world-class renowned large enterprises are scarcity. A great number of world-famous high-tech enterprises clusters in Silicon Valley, and even some high-tech enterprises are listed on the top of world. For example, Intel, Hewlett-Packard, Apple, Sun Microsystems, Cisco and Yahoo, and other world-renowned enterprises. In 2002, there are 39 enterprises in Silicon Valley, which sales income is over 1 billion US dollars. Therefore, in order to catch up with world-class IT R&D hub, Zhongguancun park must create world-class renowned enterprises.

Therefore, Beijing brand city can be built by building brand enterprises, by developing brand industries, and even by means of building Zhongguancun Park. See Figure 5.

4.3. A key Issue to Build Brand City—Business Environment

Generally, IT enterprises' final products are complex products, such complex products requires a large amount of products to support, according to modern industry logistics management theory(Johnson and Wood 1996), the high-tech IT enterprise need to survive in a good environment of intermediate industry supply. In fact, any enterprise has double identities in the market, relatively speaking, the enterprise is both producers and consumers, and needs to buy other enterprises' products as production inputs, also sales products to other enterprises. It is the input-output relationship of production that connects a number of enterprises to a chain of industry. The enterprises in the chain select to locate geographically close to each other to achieve the goal of cost-cutting. The value chain is all stages in the creation process of a commodity or service from raw material to finished

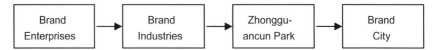

Figure 5 Model of Beijing Brand City

product, clearly associated with supply chain. The enterprise's activities of creating value are constituted by all stages from production to supply. The enterprise often only have a competitive advantage at some stage or area, which determines that enterprises need industry supply chain links between enterprises and technology transfer chain integration to realize the integration of value. The supply environment guarantee to reduce the transaction costs at least by the integration of freight, information acquirement.

In the deeper level, the trade promotes knowledge spillover, which is the essential element of industry cluster. Grossman and Helpman (1991) analyzed the issue of trade, and proposed the importance of knowledge spillover. The factor of trade influence knowledge spillover significantly.

With the development of modern transportation and communication technology, the freight accounts for a smaller and smaller proportion of goods cost. The position of the spatial distant related with freight has also fallen in a modern economy. In fact the transportation cost is only one factor of exchange costs, and exchange costs includes all resistances that affect products flow, such as, taxes, polities, systems, language, culture and so on.

The importance of business environment played an important role in Cambridge Industrial Park's dreariness. Saxenian (1994) reported that Cambridge Industrial Park passed through initial development and gradually decayed in the late 1980s of 20th century, the enterprises set up in the 1960s were still only a very small scale in the middle and end of 1980s. Athreye (2000) analyzed that the plight of Cambridge enterprises rooted in the British economic and political environment. Commerce environment had played an important role in the growth of Bangalore of India and Taiwan's Hsinchu of China. India established liaison offices and business center and other agencies overseas, and set up Indian National Association of Software and Services Companies (NASSCOM) and Electronics and Computer Software Export Promotion Council (ESC), focusing on the global market, providing expanded funding services for its member companies, grasping market opportunities by participating in trade exhibitions and overseas experts seminars.

To lower the venture, ESC had also established a broad world information network of counterpart organizations to improve member companies' ability and conditions of understanding international market. In India's Bangalore, the advanced communications infrastructure can link up the entire city's all IT buildings, which can link enterprises in the park to all corners of the world. Similarly, Taiwan successfully penetrated into the world's semiconductor market supply chain system by acceding to the largest semiconductor business association, leading Taiwan's semiconductor industry to become a global industry leader.

The importance of business environment in Guangdong Province of China plays an important role to develop science and technology industry. As Guangdong Province is located in the Zhujiang River Delta, in adjacent to Hong Kong, in the beginning of development of Hong Kong's high-tech industry, Hong Kong used cheap labor of Zhujiang River Delta to develop their own high-tech industry, and Hong Kong itself played a role of trade business center. Using of the trade advantage, Zhujiang River Delta began to develop imported materials processing industry, and then developed the processing industry and finally, large independent trade enterprises came into being. Shenzhen's Konka, a color TV enterprise, firstly processed zipper for Hong Kong enterprises, then it produced electronic watches, after further accumulation of capital, human capital had also been developed, Konka started to transform its product and today's situation is created. During the process of product transform, taking advantage of the high demand of domestic market for color television sets, and independent business activities played fundamental role.

4.4. Strategy of Establishing Brand City

The establishment of brand city is a huge project, involving economic, environment, social, and many other factors, thus, it is a long-term and dynamic process. Considering the condition of Beijing, we should focus on the following aspects.

4.4.1. Environment Building

In contemporary times, enterprises' operation and development are not only subject to their own conditions, but also constrained by external environmental factors. The environment construction can be divided into hard environment building and soft environment building .

Hard environment specifically refers to the local infrastructure construction, capital and human resources. For Beijing, the infrastructure is relatively perfect, the traffic is very convenient, the information network of traffic is highly developed. Beijing 2008 Olympic Games will greatly accelerate the pace of Beijing infrastructure construction, so as to effectively ease the current traffic jams, and other problems.

Fund is one of the very important factors for enterprises to develop. For Zhongguancun Park, the social capital is weak, lacking the foundation to cooperation and trust each other between enterprises, the collaborative network of specialized division of labor has not been formed yet. Perfect and effective venture investment mechanism will provide enterprises with abound capital to promote the development of enterprises, the important role of venture capital can be seen from the successful experience in the Silicon Valley. This paper will analysis the building of venture capital mechanism by using one chapter

Abundant human resources are a strong advantage for Beijing. Zhongguancun zone is not only one of the most intensive zone of human resources in Beijing, but also in the whole china, and even in the world. How to integrate these resources, and allow those R&D personnel to play important role is the direction to which the hard environment needs move. Learning from India's experience in terms of personnel training process, Zhongguancun must not only pay attention to the accumulation of expertise knowledge, but also to cultivate the spirit of unity and help. In addition, the software R&D needs international resources and information to support. To master English is a prerequisite skill. English can not be only a kind of language, a skill, but also it should be more suitable education mode for practical application.

The soft environment specifically refers to local policies, laws, and cultural environment. Policy environment is a key component of the soft environment, the good policy environment can promote the development of IT R&D hub. From the successful experiences of famous overseas IT hub and the development process of domestic IT R&D hub, it can be seen that the policy environment plays an indelible role. Beijing preferential taxation policy, the government investment policy, the R&D personnel policy attract deeply investors.

At present, China's overall legal environment still needs to be further promoted, Beijing is no exception. Building legal system is still at an early stage, enterprise development is lack of a sound system of laws and regulations to protect. For instance, the Zhongguancun Management Ordinance provides a set of rules, regulations and security system for enterprise development, but it still takes time to enrich, consummate and further improve the implementation of these rules. The work of the government in terms of improving the legal system and environment is a long way to go. With China's entrance to The World Trade Organization WTO, people constantly improve the concept of the law, the behave of government and enterprises is increasingly standardized, market mechanism is approaching healthiness, the environment of the law will be further improved.

Beijing, as the capital with long history and profound culture is lack of innovative cultural, the enterprise s' technological innovation vitality is inadequate, the core technology of independent R&D is scarcity, the mechanism and atmosphere to promote technological innovation is not enough. The innovation promoting the technological progress by progress is the source of R&D activities, a region possessing the innovational cultural in a large extent is determinate factor for the establishment of IT R&D hub. Therefore, one chapter will be tailed to analyses the building of innovational culture.

4.4.2. Venture Investment System Building

Beijing's venture capital mainly consists of state-owned assets management companies, stock companies, trust companies, large state-owned enterprise groups and banks, insurance companies and other institutions. Although Zhongguancun has set up a number of venture capital firms, the real behavior of venture investment is few.

In order to strengthen the building of venture investment structure, first, the perfect system of laws and regulations and the perfect financial credit market should be set up. This is the foundation of building venture investment system. Venture capital institutions would like to invest the enterprises with sound legal protection so that the enterprises can introduce venture investment. Credit is an indispensable condition. Secondly, the government pushes the development of venture capital through the publication of policies. The Beijing municipal government regulates that the growth of financial technology funds is not less than 20% annually, also the establishment of technological innovation funds is not less than RMB200 million. High-tech industry is supported to develop by marketing research, project exploitation and venture capital investment. Finally, through incentive tax system and other means to encourage local venture capital firms to establish, attract foreign venture capital firms and make Beijing not only rich in venture capital, but also can provide various economic and technical consulting services, therefore, the perfect venture investment system can be created.

4.4.3. Innovational Culture Building

We must first cultivate the innovational spirit of innovational talents in order to construct innovational culture. The innovational talents once generate good ideas, they will put them into use, being adventurous and not afraid of failure, thus, the growth of enterprises is not only promoted, but also speed the formation of innovational culture.

Secondly, the government should actively create an environment for innovation, and get the production and research cooperate closely, pay attention to the innovative culture of cooperation and communication, increase the investment into science and technology research, encourages technological innovation by policies, foster the development of key industries by measures such as government purchase, increase the intensity of supporting high-tech industry. The formation of culture can not be finished within one or two years with just one or two policies. It is a long and slow process. It will be very difficult to change the existing culture once it has been built. It has subtle effects on people's thoughts and behaviors. The culture building can not been finished in a short time, but its impact will be profound. In the long run, the cultural building is imperative.

Finally, it is necessary to build form the innovational mechanism is necessary, make use of venture investment system to support entrepreneur and innovation, and utilize stock options to encourage innovation. Stock options will get the interests of staff and the interests of enterprise interests together closely and greatly mobilizes the enthusiasm of the staff. Stock options create a large number of millionaires, which enables those innovational talents to involve into new innovative activities again and again. With the support of venture capital and the incentive of stock options, innovative talents play a role in the innovational environment and form new atmosphere, and in the end, to form innovative culture.

4.4.4. Other Aspects

In the process of building city brands, apart from the above aspects, the building of brand city is inseparable from shaping the city image. Singapore achieved "intelligent island" image by the implementation of "universal IT literacy activities", providing an environment support for Singapore to developing brand city. For Beijing, first of all, it is necessary to develop a good first impression, that is, transport, communications, telecommunications, sanitation, forestation, and other urban infrastructure, urban spatial layout, architectural features, and so on. These are the first what people are able to see and feel. To a certain extent, these first impressions are fully capable of making the investors to make investment decisions. First impression is the very important foundation.

Again, the improvement of public services, management level and efficiency is necessary. Government services, management level and efficiency are an important display window of urban image. The service standard of window industry, the rationality of various public affairs management agencies, all levels of government administration according to law, the quality of the government personnel, especially the quality of a small number of political figures, can be regarded as a second impression. The warm and thoughtful services of government, methodical management, efficient working, often make the investors feel at home, even dilute the negative impact left for the first time.

Finally, improving the citizen quality is necessary. The words and behavior, interpersonal relationships and social ethos, which are reflecting the city mental outlook, the public social values and moral character, social customs and so on, are the urban third impression, also the deepest level impression. On one hand, contacting with urban public can experience urban spirit, and more deeply into the community, experiencing urban spirit more deeply, the more real, on the other hand, the first impression and the second impression on the urban image are relatively volatile, temporary, and the third impression resulted from cultural accumulation with the relative stability and sustainability, often gives the most profound impression to people.

5 Role of Government

Governance is the public management model, which improve organizations and individuals in community to cooperate with each other. The individual needs to play a main role and tone with each other to keep good governance situation. In order to make Beijing grow into mature IT R&D hub, all relevant departments needs work together. Which main bodies is related with the establishment of IT R&D hub? How these main bodies deal with the opportunities and challenges in the new situation? These have become very important issues. Next, we will analyses each main body combining with the above discussion.

The government, as the market managers, plays a vital important role in the process of the establishment of IT R&D hub. Without the protection of relevant policies formulated by government, IT enterprises can not be set up, operated and developed smoothly in a healthy and orderly environment. The model of "enterprises play on the stage set up by government" is the vivid description of the role of government in this process. Every department of Beijing government should create a good investment, production and R&D environment for the development of IT enterprises, considering the characteristics of Beijing IT enterprises. Beijing government should do well in the following aspects in the process of establishing international IT R&D hub.

5.1. Further Improve the Law System

For making IT companies to operate in the perfect legal system, Beijing has promulgated a number of related laws and regulations. In June 1999 "Beijing's temporary regulations of encouraging the establishment of R&D institutions" was promulgated in Beijing. In September 2002, the Beijing municipal government completely amended the temporary regulations about encouraging the establishment of R&D institutions in Beijing and issued "Regulations of encouraging the establishment of R&D institutions in Beijing".The current law system makes a great contribution to the establishment of Beijing international IT R&D to a large extent. But the existing law system is till incomplete, with the growth of Beijing international IT R&D, it can not fully resolve the new problems under the new situation, particularly in relation to intellectual property rights and other foreign issues.

5.2. Strengthen the Supervision on Enterprises

Making use of the existing laws and regulations, relevant government departments should strengthen the functions of supervising and managing IT enterprises, so that Beijing's IT enterprises can develop in a healthy and orderly way, and create a market environment for fair competition.

5.3 Perfect Agency Service Organizations

Information consultation, asset assessment, foreign accounting audit, foreign lawyer offices, and other relevant agencies should be further established and improved. To further improve Beijing's agency service system. The government should play the role of guiding and supporting during the process of establishing system. The comparatively perfect agency organizations is a an important criterion to measure a perfect market.

5.4. Perfect the Service Mechanism for Enterprises

The government departments should simplify procedures to examine and approve, and improve service efficiency and service quality. The government service system of Beijing already has been developed to some extend, 18 districts, as well as Economy and Technology Development Zone, Zhongguancun Science and Technology Park have set up a "one-stop" office. According to the principle of "The one who approves the project will be in charge of the same project", the new approval model is joint approval and time limit control in the process of examination and approval. From January 2002, the government had launched "green channel for the approval of foreign investment project", processing foreign enterprises approval and registration formalities for free. However good mechanism needs to be seriously implemented. The Beijing Municipal government departments should further improve the potential ability of the existing service means to be a service government with willingness and spirit to help.

5.5. Further to Improve the Urban Infrastructure

Urban infrastructure will influence enterprises' decisions about setting up the production base and R&D institutions in the city, and will also influence technological personnel's choices to work here. In order to build a mature IT R&D hub, Beijing must improve the existing urban infrastructure (such as traffic road and transport facility, environment and sanitation, etc.).

5.6. Building Favorable Policies to Recruit and Retain Talent

The household registration system hampers enterprises to hire talent to a large extent, especially the household registration system is related closely to some problems, such as children's going to school. This will definitely weaken the existing advantage of Beijing in terms of the human resources if it can not be solved thoroughly. Currently, the situation of domestic competition for human resource is that the Yangtze River Delta" and "Zhujiang River Delta" attract the talent with high salaries and excellent living benefits. Beijing has the human resource reserve and backup due to the large number of universities and research institutions. If effective measures are not taken, the brain drain will become even more serious, the current talent advantage will be gradually weaken.

While solving the above problems, Beijing municipal government needs to set up the bridge between local IT companies and foreign multinational enterprises to attract more multinational enterprises to invest and cooperate in China. To establish mature international IT R&D hub, Beijing municipal government still need to solve many issues.

6 Conclusion

This paper focuses on the issue of establishing Beijing international IT R & D hub. The result reveals as following.

Beijing international IT R&D hub's growth stage includes budding period, incubator period and development period. From 1980 to 1986 can be considered as budding Beijing IT Center. Beijing international IT R&D hub originated in the early 1980's "Zhongguancun electronic street." From 1986 to 1995 can be regarded as the venture stage of Beijing international IT R&D hub. Beijing IT industry, which centers on Zhongguancun, has already been on a certain number of scale. By 2000, Beijing's IT industry has developed to a relatively perfect state. Zhongguancun achieves leapfrog development from testing zone to Zhongguancun Science and Technology Park.

The strategy of establishing Beijing international R&D hub is to build the brand city. The driven model of brand products is the model of establishing brand city. The establishment of Beijing city brand can be achieved by building brand enterprises, developing band products, and even by using Zhongguancun park to promote the brand city building. One of the important issues to build brand city is business that is significances for building band city.

The building of city brand is a huge project, involving economic, environmental, social and many other factors. For Beijing, the following aspects need to build e.g. environment building, venture investment system building and innovative culture building. Apart from the aspects mentioned above, the establishment of city brand cannot be achieved without the city image shape in the process of building brand city, as well as the standard and the efficiency of government service and management, and the improvement of citizen quality.

The government, as market managers plays an extremely important role in the process of establishing international IT R&D hob. IT enterprises cannot be set up, operated and developed in a healthy and orderly environment without assurance of governmental relevant policies formulated. The government should do the following aspects in the process of establishing international IT R&D hub: further improve the relevant laws and systems, strengthen supervision over enterprises, improve agencies' intermediary services, consummate the service mechanism for enterprises, and further develop the urban infrastructure construction, complete the talent policies.

References

Amsden A, Tschang T, Goto A (2001) Do foreign companies conduct R&D in developing countries. ADB Institute Working Paper 14, Tokyo Asian Development Bank Institute

Athreye S (2000) Agglomeration and growth: a study of the Cambridge hi-tech cluster. Preliminary draft-please comment 6: 1-48

Cantwell J, Santangelo G D (1999) The frontier of international technology networks: Sourcing abroad the most highly tacit capabilities. Information Economics and Policy 11: 01-123

Chen S H (2004) Taiwanese IT firms' offshore R&D in China and the connection with the global innovation network. Research Policy 33: 337-349.

Chen Y C (2003) Latecomer cities becoming new global innovation centers: case studies of multinational corporations' R&D centers in Shanghai and Beijing, paper presented at 2003 Annual Meeting of Association of American Geographers, March 6

Ferrantino M J (1993) The effect of intellectual property rights on international trade and investment. Weltwirschaftliches Archiv 129, 300-331

Gassmann O, Zedtwitz M(1999) New concepts and trends in international R&D organization. Research Policy 28:231-250

Grossman G M, Helpman E (1991) Innovation and growth in the global economy, MIT Press, Cambridge. Jonathan Eaton, Samuel Kortum (1993), International technology Diffusion, mimeo, Boston University

Guellec D, Bruno van Pottelsberghe, de la Potterie (2001) The internationalization of technology analyzed with patent data. Research Policy 30:1253-1266

Johnson J C, Wood D F (1996) Contemporary logistics, prentice hall upper saddle creek, New Jersey

Lall S(1980)The international allocation of research activity by U.S. multinationals. Oxford Bulletin of Economics and Statistics 41:313-331

Liu D X (2005) The modes and organizational coordination of R&D internationalization in MNCs. Science of Science and Management of S.& T. 3:10-14

Lucas B (2005) Economics of technological change and the natural environment: how effective are innovations as a remedy for resource scarcity? Ecological Economics 54(2 -3):148 -163

Mansfield E D, Teece D J, Romeo A (1979) Overseas research and development US-based firms. Economics 46: 187-196

Mansfield E (1994) Intellectual property protection, foreign direct Investment, and technology transfer. Discussion Paper 19, Washington DC: International Finance Corporation

OECD (1997) Facilitating International Technology Co-operation: Proceedings of the Seoul Conference. Organization for Economic Co-operation and Development, Paris

Paolize M, Guercini S (1997) R&D internationalization in the strategic behavior of the firm. Steep Discussion Paper No 39, Science Policy Research Unit, University of Sussex

Patel P Pavitt K (1998) National systems of innovation under strain: the internationalization of corporate R&D. SPRU Electronic Working Papers Series, 22, Science Policy Research Unit, University of Sussex

Pearce R D (1989) The Internationalization of Research and Development by Multinational Enterprises. Macmillan, London

Petrella R (1989) Globalization of technological innovation. Technology Analysis and Strategic Management 1 (4): 393-407

Reddy P (2000) Globalization of Corporate R&D: Implications for Innovation Systems in Host Countries. Routledge, London

Saxenian A (1994) Regional advantage. Harvard University Press, London

Wang X., Liu Y G (2003) Science and technology enterprises and the characteristics of the life cycle. Industrial Technology & Economy 22(4):79-80

Yu S Y, Wang X R, Shi W (2004) Country choice on multinationals R&D investment. Management World 1:46-54, 61

Zan B M (2003) Analysis on multinationals effect of R&D investment in China. World economy study 10:48-53

Zhao J Y (2006) Regional knowledge management and Beijing R&D center growth. Ph. D paper, Institute of Policy and Management Science, Chinese Academy of Sciences (CAS)

Chapter 7
Absorptive Capability, Local Innovation Networks, and International R&D Spillovers

An Empirical Study on the Chinese ICT Industry

Shouhua Wei[1,2], Xianjun Li[3] and Guisheng Wu[4]

[1] School of Business, Nanjing University, P. R. CHINA
[2] Center for the Yangtze River Delta's Economic and Social Development of Nanjing University, P. R. CHINA
[3] Department of Automitive Engineering, Tsinghua University, P. R. CHINA
[4] Research Center of Technological Innovation, Tsinghua University, P. R. CHINA

Abstract This chapter empirically explores the impact of different channels for both local innovation networks and international technology spillovers on the innovative performance of the Chinese information and communication technology (ICT) industry through analysis of panel data. Our findings indicate that the impact on innovation of ICT industry of international knowledge spillovers is about twice as much as that of local innovation networks. For the local innovation networks, we find that both local specialized and diversified economies have positive effects on knowledge spillovers, however, the positive effect of local academic spillover cannot be verified, which even shows a weakly negative effect. While for the international technology spillovers, we find that both export products and imported technologies have positive effects on technology spillovers, while the effect of FDI cannot be found. Our findings further suggest that regional ICT industry' s absorptive capability, which includes R&D effort and effective stock of knowledge, is a requisite for facilitating the spillovers of channel for both local innovation networks and international technology spillovers.

1 Introduction

It is widely accepted that the diffusion of the information and communication technologies (ICTs) has led to a substantial increase in the spread of knowledge due to the ICTs' capability of reducing the space and time barriers by the means of

P.O. de Pablos, M.D. Lytras (eds.), *The China Information Technology Handbook*,
DOI: 10.1007/978-0-387-77743-6_7, © Springer Science+Business Media, LLC 2009

transferring, collecting, and managing a great amount of information (Carbonara 2005). Indeed, convenient distant communications such as Internet, Email, and Mobile phone and so on do enable people to access information from all over the world in a few seconds. However, argue that all knowledge spreads immediately would be inexact in consideration of that it is now more than ever that the impact of tacit knowledge becomes evident (Marjolein 1996). Tacit knowledge is more difficult to spread by communicating over distance than contacting 'face to face', since it is usually embedded in particular location where economic activities present spatial agglomeration. Ample literature emphasizes the role of geographic agglomeration in technological innovation and economic development (Oakey 1985; Thomas 1985). Feldman and Florida (1994) pointed out innovations are more the product of the assembled resources, knowledge, and other inputs and capabilities that agglomerate in specific places than that of an individual firm, especially an isolated firm.

As far as information and communication technology (ICT) industry itself is concerned, it is an emerging industry in view of product life cycle, and it depends more on technical change than other industries, due to ICT goods, such as computers and communications equipments, being continuously getting cheaper than other goods. Therefore, as a herald of innovation and diffusion of technology and information, could ICT industry overcome the obstacles of geographic distance to innovate regardless of geographic 'milieux innovateur'? The 'milieux innovateur', according to Camagni (1989), is defined as a complex network of formal or informal relationships in a limited geographic area that enhances local innovative capability through synergistic and collective learning process, and in this paper we term it local innovation networks. The first purpose of the paper is aimed to explore the paradox phenomenon that geography still plays an important role in technological innovation due to convenient knowledge spillover, even though in technological frontier fields like ICT industry.

As a technology-follower, China has been sparing no effort, especially encouraged by information highway initiatives (IHI) in U.S.A in the middle of 1990s, to develop ICT industry to improve information infrastructure. ICT is viewed as a "pillar" industry in most regions and it has been a top priority of the government with tax subsidies or even free tax for new product development, and fiscal subsidies for R&D activities and so on. At the present time, the Chinese ICT industry has made great, even frog-leaping progress. However, there appears a large amount of variation in development of ICT industry among regions in China. ICT industry in the eastern coastal areas with high degree of openness shows greater growth rate than the national average level, while inland areas with low degree of openness are stagnant in their ICT industry. Therefore, the second purpose of this paper is to explore the extent to which the performance of innovation in the Chinese ICT industry at regional level is influenced by a variety of channels for international technology spillover, such as foreign direct investment (FDI), products export, and imported technologies.

Studies have shown the importance of external knowledge sources and utilization of networks in innovation process (Cohen and Levinthal 1990; Von Hippel 1998; Nonaka 1994) while some other studies suggest that the major part of innovation is also related to enterprise's internal departments in most industries (Oerlemans et al. 1998; Fritsch 2004; Love and Roper 2001). Similarly, a region may get more benefits if making effective use of both internal and external technological knowledge. And the former refers to local innovation networks and the latter is defined as international or interregional technology spillovers. As for the Chinese ICT sector, innovation depends not only on its domestic industrial networks but also on international technology spillovers. But which one plays a more important role in innovation? The third objective of this paper is to investigate the significance and magnitude of how technological innovation by geographic proximity and agglomeration, and how knowledge spillovers by international channels play a role in growth of the Chinese ICT industry at regional level.

Different from the existing literature that examines separately the impact of various elements of innovation, such as national innovative capability (Furman et al. 2002; Furman and Hayes 2004), local innovation networks (Camagni 1989; Jaffe 1989; Feldman and Florida 1994), and international channels for technology spillovers (Grossman and Helpman 1991; Coe and Helpman 1995; Liu and Buck 2007), the paper takes an eclectic approach and proposes an empirical model that combines a number of different explanations for innovative performance. Particularly, we expand the empirical model of source of innovation from geographic technological infrastructure created by Feldman and Florida (1994), the model of national innovative capability originated from Furman et al. (2002), and the model of innovative performance of the Chinese high-tech industry from both absorptive capability and international technology spillovers introduced by Liu and Buck (2007). And we take further steps by examining empirically the impact of a variety of internal and external factors. The internal factors depend mainly on local innovation networks, including interaction among academics, competitive firms, and the related suppliers and consumers in a region. The external factors involve in FDI, imported technology, and export-related learning. Thus, the contribution of the paper is an exploration of how the performance of innovation in high-tech industry is affected by both local innovation networks and international technology spillovers in a unified framework. The findings of this paper contribute to a better understanding of the spatio-temporal dynamics and dependent mechanism between internal and external factors and provide theoretical foundation and empirical evidence for policy makers and practitioners in China as well as in other developing countries.

The remainder of the chapter is structured as follows. The next section discusses the theoretical framework for this empirical study. Section 3 specifies the empirical model and introduces our data. The estimation and discussion of results are presented in Section 4. Section 5 concludes with policy implications.

2   Theoretical Background and Hypotheses

2.1 Theoretical Background

A variety of theoretical and empirical studies provide evidence that agglomeration of economic activities and knowledge spillover have a key effect on the performance of innovation and industrial development. On the basis of these studies, this paper focuses on the following three theories and related empirical models, namely new growth theory (Romer 1990; Furman et al. 2002), regional innovation system or local innovation networks (Camagni 1989; Lundvall 1992; Jaffe 1989; Feldman and Florida 1994), and international knowledge spillovers (Grossman and Helpman 1991; Coe and Helpman 1995; Liu and Buck 2007).

It is generally believed that there is an assumed linear relationship between investment in research and development (R&D), the creation of knowledge, the generation of innovation, and subsequent economic success. Especially, due to the contributions of Solow (1956) and Ambramovitz (1956) that emphasized the centrality of technological innovation in economic growth in the late 1980s, technological change are treated endogenously (furman et al. 2002). Romer's (1990) growth model articulates the economic foundation for technological progress by introducing an ideas sector for the economy, and according to this model, the producer of new ideas is a function of the number of ideas workers and the stock of ideas available to these researchers. If the level of R&D is increased, a corresponding increase in innovation and output should eventually follow. Furman et al. (2002) proposed a framework in which the determinants of national innovative capacity are based on three perspectives, namely ideas-driven growth theory, microeconomic models of national competitive advantage and industrial clusters, and national innovation system, and they highlighted the importance of the indigenous research effort and infrastructure to national innovative capacity.

However, the simple linear model linking R&D to general knowledge, from specific knowledge and innovation, has now been challenged. Malecki (1997) has shown that far from knowledge being simply linearly generated the process is characterized by an extensive range of feedback loops, circuits with dead ends and abandoned leads. And innovation studies have shifted from the single activity of R&D department to the networking process of interacting learning (Lundvall 1992; Von Hippel 1998). As a process of interacting learning, innovation is characterized by continuous internal and external feedbacks, which refer to internal R&D activities (knowledge stock, R&D personnel and R&D expenditure), as well as external co-operation with other firms (especially with customers and suppliers), knowledge providers (like universities and public research institutes), finance, training, and public administration. It is in this context that the concept of regional innovation system (RIS) has been introduced in contrast to earlier research that is based on technological change on a narrow definition of R&D, thereby ignoring the importance of other types of innovation inputs (Aslesen 2002).

In view of system approaches, innovation is considered to depend on not only learning capabilities in ideas sector or one's own R&D effort, but also capabilities of utilizing network interactions. There are two complementary theoretical explanations on the determinants of innovative performance from knowledge spillover. The first explanation focuses on how the related innovative actors enhance spillover effects by interacting. Innovation could be performed well if firms increasingly depend on their users, suppliers, universities and even competitors as initiators of source of new ideas (Cohen and Levinthal 1990; Von Hippel 1988; Nonaka 1994; Caloghirou et al. 2004). During the process of interacting, tacit knowledge that is considered to be embedded tightly with geographic proximity, often acts as a catalyzer and facilitates the interacting learning. Jaffe (1989) demonstrated the importance of geographically mediated commercial spillovers from university research and stated spillovers are facilitated by the geographic coincidence of universities and research labs within the state. Acs et al. (1992) later verified Jaffe's (1989) arguments and reinforced his findings by using the direct measure of the number of innovative products. Feldman and Florida (1994) confirmed that the geography of innovation is usually dependent on an area's technological infrastructure, which is related to the geographic concentrations of industrial R&D, university R&D, related industries, and business services. The second explanation emphasizes synergetic effects in a regional innovation milieu rather than specific process of interaction for spillover effects. Hoover (1937) distinguished between two types of external economies: localization economies and urbanization economies (Chinitz 1961; Hoover 1971; Isard et al. 1959; Aslesen 2002). Localization economies refer to externalities associating with the increase of total output in a particular industry, and in a dynamic context, these scale externalities are also called Marshall–Arrow–Romer (MAR) externalities (in reference to contributions of Arrow 1962; Marshall 1920; Romer 1990). Urbanization economies, on the other hand, occur where there is a diversified industrial base, such as extensive infrastructure and services, and in a dynamic context, these externalities are also called Jacobs' (1969) externalities.

The above-mentioned studies focus on within country or within region innovative infrastructure and industrial conditions without sufficiently considering international or interregional sources of technology spillovers. They emphasize on the role of R&D department activities and local innovation networks. But with the surging of knowledge-based economy and economic globalization, it is widely believed that knowledge originating in one country increasingly transcends national boundaries and contributes to productivity growth and technological progress in other countries (Grossman and Helpman 1991; Coe and Helpman 1995; Liu and Buck 2007). Coe and Helpman (1995) demonstrated that a country's productivity depends on its own R&D as well as the R&D efforts of its trade partners in a world with international trade in goods and services, foreign direct investment. And they also demonstrated that these spillover effects are stronger in countries with more openness. Liu and Buck (2007) empirically investigated the impact of different channels for international technology spillover on the innovation performance of Chinese high-tech industries, where these spillover channels includes imported technology, R&D activities of multinational enterprises (MNEs), and export-related learning on domestic innovation.

The paper employs an eclectic approach and proposes an empirical model that blends in a number of different explanations for innovative performance. In particular, we extend the empirical model of source of innovation supported by geographic technological infrastructure created by Feldman and Florida (1994), the model of national innovative capability originated by Furman et al. (2002), and the model of innovation performance affected by both absorptive capability and international technology spillovers to the Chinese high-tech industries coined by Liu and Buck (2007).

2.2 Hypotheses

As the above-analysis, we can make the following hypotheses based on the corresponding new growth theory, regional innovation system or local innovation networks, and international knowledge spillovers.

2.2.1 R&D Effort, Knowledge Stock and Absorptive Capability

According to Romer (1990) and Grossman and Helpman (1991), innovation feeds on knowledge that results from cumulative R&D experience on the one hand, and it contributes to the stock of knowledge on the other hand. Consequently the performance of innovation depends on its cumulative R&D effort and on its effective stock of knowledge, with the two being inter-related (Coe and Helpman 1995). In this view, new growth theory operates at a high level of abstraction, focusing on the economy-wide "knowledge stock" and the size of the R&D labor pool. Just as Furman et al. (2002) emphasized that domestic resources devoted to innovation have a general impact throughout an economy, Damijan et al. (2006) argued that internal efforts, such as domestic R&D activities at an industry/firm level may be important drivers of innovation. So general domestic innovative efforts and knowledge stock are also considered as important influences. In China, the promotion of domestic innovative activities in ICT industry has always been a top priority of the government with tremendous support. We focus on internal R&D efforts and take the knowledge stock as given. And we propose that,

H1: Innovation performance in the ICT industry is positively affected by the level of domestic firms' R&D activities in the sector in a region.

2.2.2 Geographic Coincidence between Academic and Industrial Technological Activities

The advantage of agglomeration for 'hi-tech' companies have traditionally been claimed by supporters of location theory on the basis of external economies of scale, i.e., access to R&D facilities, skilled labor force, research universities, and high levels of information (Kleinknecht and Poot 1992; Mustar 1997). In his classic work, Jaffe (1989) found a significant effect of university research on corporate patents, particularly in the areas of Drugs and Medical Technology, and Electronics, Optics, and Nuclear Technology. Later Acs et al. (1992) confirmed that university research does have a positive effect on the performance of innovation of firms in the light of product innovation. Whereas Markusen, Hall, and Glasmeier (1986) found that university R&D is negatively related to high-technology industry and employment. The experience indicates that agglomeration and technological externalities are potential factors in the early years of a 'hi-tech' complex, but on the other hand, once this early stage of agglomeration is over, the initial agglomeration of 'hi-tech' companies becomes less important (perez and Sanchez 2002). It is necessary to consider the spatio-temporal variation in analyzing technological complexes, so we propose that,

H2: Innovation performance in ICT industry is associated with the geographic coincidence between academic and industrial R&D activities in a region.

2.2.3 Local Innovation Networks among Enterprises

The emergence of institutional or informal networks, formed by clusters, groups or vertical associations of firms, appears to be one major feature of the contemporary industrial economy. Storper and Walker's (1989) theory of "geographic industrialization" captures the spatial nature of the process of technological change and industrial development. DeBresson and Amesse (1992) focused upon the concentrations of key resources and organizational networks where the role of agglomeration economies plays. These resources and networks are needed for investing cooperatively in the creation of new knowledge (R&D, design, engineering), and the external introduction of new knowledge through innovation acquisition, adaptation, and implementation (Belussi and Arcangeli, 1998). Since it is much easier to find network partners and get larger spillover effects in central metropolitan regions or in a industrial district, firms that are located in regions with high flows of both private and public or academic R&D are more likely to be innovative than firms located elsewhere. Some empirical studies further attempt to demonstrate which is more important for the localization or the urbanization of externalities. Whereas Glaeser et al. (1992) found that diversity raises firm growth in their study of US cities between 1956 and 1987, Henderson et al. (1995) showed that localization economies are important for urban growth between 1970 and 1987. This result would suggest that networks promote innovation and we should include a measure of networking as an explanatory variable on our study that,

H3: Innovation performance in ICT industry is positively correlated to local innovation networks in both Marshall–Arrow–Romer (MAR) externalities and Jacobs' externalities in a region.

2.2.4 Channels for International Knowledge Spillover

Inward FDI may affect local firms' innovation through knowledge spillovers involving various channels whereby one innovator learns from the research of others, without compensation (Branstetter, 2006). This may take place in a number of ways such as learning about the designs of new products and technology through interaction with foreign firms, human capital mobility or labor market turnover from multi-national enterprises (MNEs) to local firms, and the effect of demonstration through learning-by-doing or by observing the outputs of MNEs' R&D projects (Liu and Buck, 2007). But on the contrary, it has also been argued that inward FDI may negatively affect the productivity or innovative activity of local firms by monopolizing markets, drawing demand from local firms and substituting local suppliers with foreign ones (Aitken and Harrison 1999; Konings 2001; Liu and Buck 2007). So we mix these arguments and attempt to verify the impact of FDI on the Chinese ICT industry.

A large amount of literature has studied import-related international technological spillovers. Grossman and Helpman (1991) and Coe and Helpman (1995) identified a number of ways in which international R&D spillovers may affect domestic technological progress, as this source of international spillovers enables domestic researchers to access the ideas and technology developed by their foreign counterparts. Lumenga-Neso et al.(2005) empirically provided plenty of evidence that import-related R&D spillovers have a positive promotion in international technology transfer. More recently, Liu and Buck (2007) also demonstrated that imported technologies play a significant role in the innovative performance of the Chinese high-tech industries. We therefore propose a relationship between imports and innovation performance.

Besides FDI and imports, exports are also considered as a channel for technology spillovers. Learning-by-exporting can facilitate technology diffusion and transfer (Greenaway and Yu 2004). Exporting may lead to technology spillovers through two channels, including learning from foreign buyers, and adopting best-practice technology due to competitive international markets (Liu and Buck, 2007). Therefore, we propose the performance of innovation can benefit from learning-by-exporting as Liu and Buck (2007) did. Hence, we propose that,

H4: Innovation performance in ICT industry is associated with levels of FDI either positively or negatively.

H5: Innovation performance in ICT industry is positively associated with levels of imports of advanced technology and exporting activity in a region.

3 Methodology and data

3.1 Model

Following the aforementioned theoretic background and hypotheses, the performance of innovation in the Chinese ICT industry is considered a function of sources of R&D effort and technological spillovers including absorptive capacity, local innovation networks, and international R&D spillover (it is necessary to note that we view inter-regional R&D spillover equal to the international spillover as far as technology spillovers are concerned at regional level). The absorptive capability is knowledge stock, R&D personnel and expenditure in the Chinese ICT industry in a region at a given time. The local innovation networks include academic knowledge spillover and interactions among local enterprises under specialized or diversified innovation milieu. The international R&D spillover contains imported technology, exports and FDI. We build our theoretical model by combining the model of Furman et al (2002), the model of Feldman and Florida (1994), and the model of Liu and Buck (2007). Our model takes the following form:

$$Y_{i,t+1} = \delta_{i,t} (X_{i,t}^{NETW}, X_{i,t}^{FRD}) H_{i,t}^{A\lambda} A_{i,t}^{\phi} \tag{7.1}$$

where i denotes region or province in China, and t stands for year. $H_{i,t}^{A}$ is the total level of capital and labor resources devoted to ideas of the ICT economic sector. $A_{i,t}^{\phi}$ is the total stock of knowledge held by the ICT sector at time t, and $A_{i,t}^{\phi}$ is considered to drive future ideas production. The $X_{i,t}^{NETW}$ refers to the level of local innovation networks including knowledge spillover from local academics to ICT industry, and interaction among local enterprises under a localized and urbanized innovation milieu, or MAR dynamic externalities and Jacobs' dynamic externalities. The $X_{i,t}^{FRD}$ refers to the extent of the international knowledge spillover that affects ICT industry by means of FDI, imported technologies, and export products (learning by exporting). Under Eq.(7.1), we assume that the various elements of regional ICT industry are complementary in the sense that the marginal boost to innovation from increasing one factor is increasing in the level of all of the other factors. Based on this model and letting L denote the natural logarithm, our main specification takes the following form:

$$\begin{aligned} Ln(Y_{i,t}) &= \alpha + \delta_{netw} Ln(X_{i,t}^{NETW}) + \delta_{frd} Ln(X_{i,t}^{FRD}) \\ &+ \lambda Ln(H_{i,t}^{A}) + \phi Ln(A_{i,t}) + \varepsilon_{i,t} \end{aligned} \tag{7.2}$$

Conditions on a given level of R&D inputs (H^A), variation in the production of innovation (Y) reflects differences in R&D productivity across regions or time. For example, a positive δ_{netw} or δ_{frd} suggests that the productivity of R&D investment is increasing in the quality of the local innovation networks or international knowledge spillover. As Y measures the realized level of innovative output which is normally observed by delay, our empirical work imposes a one-year lag between the measure of innovative input and the observed innovative output, whereas Furman et al. (2002) employed a three-year lag.

The local innovation networks ($X_{i,t}^{NETW}$) measure the level of knowledge spillover and interacting innovation in local innovation milieu, including academic knowledge spillover to ICT industry (X^{ACAD}: ACAD R&D $_{i,t}$) in the region, interactions among enterprises in the same ICT industry in the region (X^{INDS}: SP(INDS) R&D $_{i,t}$), and interactions among enterprises in ICT industry and other industries in the region (X^{INDS}: DIV(INDS) R&D $_{i,t}$). Therefore, we classify the local innovation networks into three types. The first type is based on the theory of STI (Scientific and Technological Innovation) (Jaffe 1989; Acs et al. 1992; Jensen et al 2007), and we measure the interaction between academic R&D activities (including universities and public research institutes) and the ICT enterprises. Different from most developed countries with a market-oriented economy, the academic R&D actors in China involve in universities and public research institutes due to its transformation from a planning-oriented economy into a market-oriented economy. In other words, in China, university provides talents for society and basic research for public knowledge stock, while public research institutes focus on applied research that is closer to enterprises. So we combine university and public research institute' R&D activities into academic R&D activities, and use the sum of R&D expenditure from both university and public research institute as a proxy of the knowledge spillover from the academic (X^{ACAD}: ACAD R&D $_{i,t}$). The other two types of local innovation networks are based on the theory of DUI (Learning by doing, using, and interacting) (Lundvall 1992; Von Hippel, 1988; Jensen et al. 2007). And we postulate that the performance of innovation from DUI can be influenced by the degree of specialization (MAR externality) and the degree of diversity (Jacobs' externality) in the ICT sector in a region. In doing so, we should measure the degree of specialization and the degree of diversity in the ICT sector in a region. The specialization index we consider is the ratio of the share of the ICT sector in province to its average share across China as Batisse did (2002):

$$S_{s,p} = \frac{VA_{sp}/VA_p}{VA_{sn}/VA_n} \tag{7.3}$$

where VA_{sn} is the value added in ICT industry at the national level; VA_p is the total value added for province; and VA_n is the value added at the national level. If S is greater than 1, then province has a relatively high concentration of value added generated in ICT industry. Knowledge spillovers in the region are assumed to be greater when S is higher. And we define X^{INDS}: SP (INDS) R&D $_{i,t}$ as the product of $S_{s,p}$ and R&D expenditure in the ICT sector in a region:

$$X^{INDS}: SP(INDS)R\&D_{i,t} = INDS_{ICT(R\&D)} \bullet S_{s,p} \tag{7.4}$$

The index of diversity is the inverse of a normalized Herfindhal index of sectoral concentration as Ellison and Glaeser (1997) and Batisse (2002) did.

$$Div_{s,p} = \frac{1/\sum_{s'\neq s}^{S}(\dfrac{VA_{s'p}}{VA_p - VA_{sp}})^2}{1/\sum_{s'\neq s}^{S}(\dfrac{VS_{s'n}}{VA_n - VA_{sn}})^2} \tag{7.5}$$

where $VA_{s'p}$ is the value added in industrial sectors other that the one that is studied. A positive relationship between diversity and the sector's innovative performance in a given province supports Jacobs' theory. Batisse (2002) avers that this indicator represents the sectoral diversity faced by sectors in province; a high value of this index does not necessarily imply that the ICT sector is not concentrated in province. Therefore, we calculate X^{INDS}: DIV(INDS) R&D $_{i,t}$ as a product of $Div_{s,p}$ and R&D expenditure in the other sectors in a region as the following formula:

$$X^{INDS}: DIV(INDS)R\&D_{i,t} = INDS_{OTHER(R\&D)} \bullet Div_{s,p} \tag{7.6}$$

In addition, $X_{i,t}^{FRD}$ includes three variables, namely X^{FDI}: $FDI_{i,t}$, X^{EXP}:$EXP_{i,t}$, and X^{IMP}: $IMP_{i,t}$.

3.2 Data

To perform our proposed analysis, we must identify observable innovation measures and develop a dataset that tracks these measures across regions and over time. First of all, we need to define ICT industry. According to the classification of Information and Communication Technology Sector suggested by Ministry of Science and Technology, the Peoples' Republic of China, the ICT industry includes the two manufacturing industries of Manufacturing of Electronic and Telecommunication Equipments (METE) and Manufacturing of Computers and Office Equipments (MCOE). The former includes 7 sub-sectors at the three-digit level and the latter is composed of 1 sub-sector at the three-digit level. Appendix 7.A gives a brief description of the classification of ICT industry and basic information concerning the related code numbers of these sectors. Secondly, in view of the facts that more than 80% of all the innovative indicators in ICT industry such as value added, added value of new products, patents, R&D personnel, and R&D expenditure and so on comes from the METE industry, and that it is also difficult to acquire data both across regions and over years in the MCOE industry, we employ the METE industry as a proxy of ICT industry. Thirdly, all our empirical data are at the scale of province, and it has a large degree of aggregation. It is necessary to note that this census data has the common bias as in other census data: the provinces differ significantly in size; and the administrative boundaries do not necessarily reflect the true economic boundaries (of regions with similar economic characteristics). However, it is the only database available at regional scale in China.

To describe the relationship between measured innovative inputs and outputs in ICT industry at regional level, table 7.1 defines and provides sources for all variables; Table 7.2 and 7.3 report the means and standard deviations. All data are from China Statistical Yearbook on High Technology Industry, China Statistical Yearbook on Science and Technology, China Statistical Yearbook. As it has appeared that innovative inputs are spatially concentrated, Feldman and Florida (1994) confirmed the long-held notion that product innovations are concentrated in certain locations. In the next section, we will further explore the spatial distribution of innovative input and output in ICT industry across regions.

Table 7.1 Variables and definitions

Variable	Full variable name	Definition
Innovative output		
$I_{i,t+1}$: innovative new products	Industrial output value of new products in a region in year t+1.	Industrial output value of new products in ICT industry in a region in year T+1, 10 thousand Chinese Yuan, current price.
Quality of absorptive capability		
A: value added of ICT industry 1997$_{i,t}$	Value added of ICT industry in a region in 1997.	Value added of ICT industry in a region in 1997, 10 thousand Chinese Yuan, current price.
H^A: FTE R&D PERS$_{i,t}$	Aggregate personnel employed in R&D in ICT industry in a region.	Full time equivalent R&D personnel in ICT industry in a region.
H^A: R&D EXP$_{i,t}$	Aggregate expenditure on R&D in ICT industry in a region.	Total R&D expenditures in ICT industry in a region, 10 thousand of Chinese Yuan, current price.
Local Innovative Networks		
X^{ACAD}: ACAD R&D$_{i,t}$	Academic R&D expenditure in ICT industry in a region.	University and public institutes on R&D expenditures in a region, 10 thousand of Chinese Yuan, current price.
X^{INDS}: DIV(INDS) R&D$_{i,t}$	Spillover from the related firms or Jacobs' dynamic externalities.	All other industrial R&D expenditures in a region, 10 thousand of Chinese Yuan, current price.
X^{INDS}: SP(INDS) R&D$_{i,t}$	Spillover from the specialized firms or MAR dynamic externalities.	The product of LQ (location quotient of ICT industry) and R&D expenditures in ICT industry in a region, 10 thousand of Chinese Yuan, current price.
International or inter-regional R&D spillover		
X^{FDI}: FDI$_{i,t}$, Foreign direct investment	Foreign direct investment in a region.	Foreign direct investment in a region, 10 thousand Chinese Yuan, current price.
X^{EXP}: EXP$_{i,t}$, Export value in ICT industry.	Export output value added in ICT industry in a region.	Export output value added in ICT industry by a region, 10 thousand Chinese Yuan, current price.
X^{IMP}: IMP$_{i,t}$, Expenditure on technology import in ICT industry.	Expenditure on technology import outside the region in ICT industry in a region.	Expenditure on technology import in ICT industry in a region, 10 thousand Chinese Yuan, current price.

Notes: data of FDI and GDP from China Statistical Yearbook, data of R&D expenditure from university, institutes and industrial enterprises from China Statistical Yearbook on Science and Technology, and most other data from China Statistical Yearbook on High Technology Industry.

Table 7.2 Statistical descriptions of new products in ICT industry (1998-2005)(unit: 10,000 Yuan)

	1998	1999	2000	2001	2001	2003	2004	2005
Mean	343074.2	362423.2	578583.8	655829.3	747537.4	980194.2	1336252	1327544
Max	2580922	3386004	3400259	3849383	4883675	7361947	10718707	12181248
Min	186	156	149	145	136	126	132	112
SD	627374	728209	945567	1217273	1412283	1766652	2667542	2719496

SD denotes standard deviation.

Table 7.3 Statistical descriptions of main explanatory variables (1997–2004)

Variable	1997	1998	1999	2000	2001	2001	2003	2004	N
Absorptive capability									
Knowledge stock	242900 (424600)	290200 (522300)	374400 (709600)	490500 (913300)	541000 (969900)	646500 (1293800)	857400 (1881300)	1122000 (2519300)	240
FTE R&D	1006 (5573)	1020 (5730)	1033 (5898)	1229 (7083)	1651 (9655)	1675 (9886)	2102 (12283)	2078 (12051)	240
R&D expenditure	6224 (36141)	11552 (68495)	13474 (80877)	21995 (1295.88)	35168 (2123.32)	3746100 (22608100)	46439 (275888)	62733 (370977)	240
Local innovation networks									
Academic spillover	5715900 (16051600)	8059200 (17213400)	8367100 (19035100)	9311600 (18466000)	11126500 (20808000)	15191200 (26631100)	17780700 (31059800)	20002800 (34449300)	240
Diversity spillover	6684800 (7226500)	5414500 (4838300)	10715300 (10807300)	18151500 (18550400)	20231400 (20200700)	24417800 (25216000)	29679600 (30397200)	39263200 (42651500)	240
Specialized spillover	1326700 (4060700)	2612810 (8850400)	31374140 (11559700)	5376700 (16794200)	8604980 (28135000)	9778820 (35161800)	11529470 (43547200)	15355120 (58094500)	240
International knowledge spillover									
FDI	14967000 (23736100)	15096500 (24770600)	17646800 (26295100)	17490400 (28077800)	15455700 (25447100)	13453300 (23428700)	13311600 (23687400)	15099600 (24768600)	240
Export	3034000 (8512000)	3974000 (10873000)	5090000 (13677000)	7194000 (17549000)	8434000 (20505000)	10957000 (26387000)	14674000 (35662000)	24200000 (61543000)	240
Import	6604 (11142)	4683 (8751)	4587 (8887)	10412 (21998)	16317 (39763)	17959 (43014)	19871 (40397)	26788 (50979)	240

Sources: China Statistic Yearbook, China industrial Statistic Yearbook, China Statistic Yearbook on Science and Technology, China Statistic Yearbook on High-technology industry. (※) denotes standard deviation. And all values denote mean value

3.2.1 Dependent Variable

We use added value of new products rather than patents in ICT industry as the proxy of innovative output. As far as patent is concerned, it has some disadvantages. As Griliches notes succinctly, "not all inventions are patentable, not all inventions are patented, and the inventions that are patented differ greatly in 'quality', in the magnitude of inventive output associated with them (1990, p. 649)". Since the Chinese ICT industry is an emerging one in view of product life cycle theory, many inventions in ICT industry are not patented due to the changing market condition. We choose the added value of new products as the proxy of innovative output, and the innovative output provides a more direct measure of innovative activity than patent counts because each innovation is recorded subsequent to its introduction in the market. In general, the innovation dataset we choose is similar to what Acs and Audretsch (1987) used for the measure of innovative output. They measured the innovative activity as the number of innovations recorded in 1982 by the U.S. Small Business Administration from the leading technology, engineering, and trade journals in each manufacturing industry.

According to the data, the average added value of new products in ICT industry among regions has increased over time with 3430740 thousand Chinese Yuan in 1998 to 13275440 thousand Chinese Yuan in 2005, along with standard deviation of 6273740 and 27194960 respectively, which is about 2 times as much as the average (see table 7.2). That means there exists a large degree of variation among regions. To further describe the variation of spatial distribution, Fig. 7.1 compares the shares of added value of new products in the national total ICT industry in 2005, where rank in a decreasing order. And we find: (1) Guangdong province ranks the highest with a share of more than 30% in the national total, which is prominently higher than any other regions. This is caused by many factors including the developed industrialized level, economy of scale, the among highest degree of openness with large sum of FDI, export products, etc. (2) The share shows a descending pattern of east-middle-west areas in general. Almost all eastern coastal provincial areas such as Guangdong, Tianjin, Shanghai, Jiangsu, Fujian, Shandong, Beijing, Zhejiang and Liaoning rank high except for Hebei province. These areas are the most economically developed regions in China with high degree of openness. Most western inland provincial areas such as Qinhai, Neimenggu, Ningxia, and Guangxi rank low. These western areas are the economically less-developed regions in China along with low degree of openness. Most middle provincial areas with a developing economic state have the middle-level rank. And (3) some provinces with good scientific and technological infrastructure, like Shanghai, Jiangsu, Sichuan, Shaanxi, Chongqing and Hubei, rank relatively high, and it implies that innovative output of new products has positive relationship with local technological infrastructure.

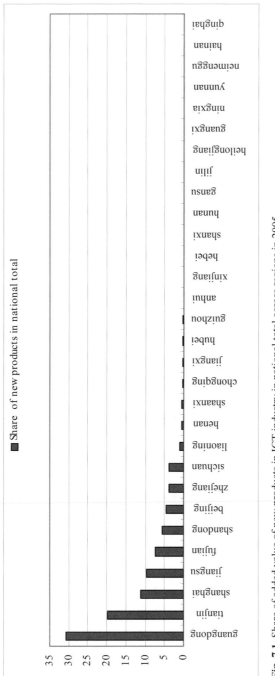

Fig. 7.1. Share of added value of new products in ICT industry in national total across regions in 2005
Source: China Statistic Yearbook on High-technology Industry (2006).

3.2.2 Independent Variables

To estimate the model, we need measures of a region's absorptive capability, local innovation networks, and international R&D spillover. For the absorptive capability and international R&D spillover, a number of relatively direct measures are available; however, direct measures of the local innovation networks are difficult to find in data. We attempt to address this challenge by employing intermediate measures or proxies that capture important economic outcomes.

3.2.2.1 The Absorptive Capability

The absorptive capability consists broadly of a region's knowledge stock, the overall level of human and capital resources devoted to innovative activity in ICT industry. Our analysis defines value added of new products of ICT industry as the measure for knowledge stock in a region at a given point in time (A). Value added of new products of ICT industry captures the ability of a region to translate its knowledge stock into a realized state of economic development, and so yields an aggregate control for a region's technological sophistication in the ICT field. Fig. 7.2 demonstrates the share of value added of new products in national total in the initial year of 1997 and 2004 respectively by ranking in a decreasing order of the share of 1997, and compares the changes of the share between 1997 and 2004. And we find: (1) some eastern coastal areas with large scale of economy, like Guangdong, Jinagsu, Shanghai, rank high in both 1997 and 2004, while most western inland areas with small scale of economy rank low in both 1997 and 2004, like Qinhai, Xinjiang, Ningxia. It may mean that knowledge stock in the ICT field has relationship with scale of economy in a region. (2) When comparing the changing shares between 1997 and 2004, there exists large difference among regions. Most of eastern coastal areas with good scientific and technological infrastructure, and high degree of openness, like Guangdong, Jinagsu, Tianjin, Shandong, Zhejiang show a positive increase. Whereas the areas with good scientific and technological infrastructure, but low degree of openness, like Sichuan, Shaanxi, Liaoning, Hubei, and etc show a negative increase. It may indicate that knowledge stock in the ICT field supported by the initial scientific and technological infrastructure is gradually diminishing while knowledge stock in the ICT field is more and more affected by the openness and scale of economy in a region.

We measure the level of capital and labor resources devoted to the knowledge creation and technical learning using each region's number of full-time-equivalent R&D personnel (FTE R&D) and expenditures on R&D (Chinese Yuan) in the ICT sector. We calculate shares of them in national total respectively. Fig. 7.3 compares shares of regional R&D personnel and R&D expenditures in national total among regions respectively, and ranks in a decreasing order by the share of

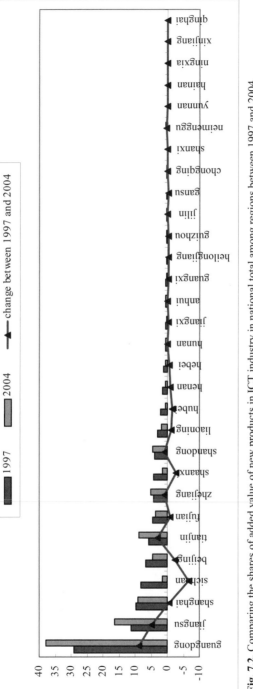

Fig. 7.2. Comparing the shares of added value of new products in ICT industry in national total among regions between 1997 and 2004

Source: China Statistic Yearbook on High-technology Industry (1998, 2005).

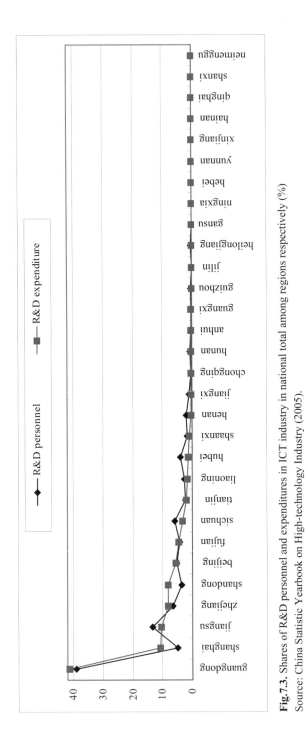

Fig.7.3. Shares of R&D personnel and expenditures in ICT industry in national total among regions respectively (%)

Source: China Statistic Yearbook on High-technology Industry (2005).

regional R&D expenditure. And we find: (1) it appears a descending pattern of east-middle-west areas. Eastern regions, like Guangdong, Shanghai, Jiangsu, Zhejiang, Shandong, Beijing and Fujian rank high, and middle regions, like Hubei, Hunan, Anhui, Jilin, Helongjiang and etc rank follow. Most western regions like Neimenggu, Qinghai, Ningxia and etc rank low, but some show the exception, like Sichun, Shaanxi and Chongqing, which rank relatively higher than their corresponding shares of innovative output. Perhaps it is related to the fact that lots of universities and public research institutes are located in these exceptional provinces. (2) Shares of R&D personnel and R&D expenditure in national total in most areas are far away from the average level, which means there exists a large degree of variation in spatial distribution. Guangdong in the Pearl River delta area ranks the highest with roughly 40% share of both R&D personnel and R&D expenditure respectively. Similarly, the three provincial areas in the Yangtze River Delta's area of Shanghai, Jiangsu, Zhejiang rank high, and the four provincial areas around Bohai Sea Rim areas of Beijing, Tianjin, Shandong and Liaoning also rank high. Then, some middle provinces such as Sichuan, Hubei, Shaanxi and Hunan rank relatively higher than their corresponding shares of value added of ICT industry. Most provinces in the west areas rank low with the shares of both R&D personnel and R&D expenditure. And (3) when comparing to the two cross-cutting elements of shares of R&D personnel and R&D expenditure, they show a roughly congruent spatial distribution, except Shanghai, Jinagsu, Beijing, Sichuan, Hubei and Henan. For those areas with comparatively less population, like Shanghai, Beijing and Tianjin, their shares of R&D personnel is lower than those of R&D expenditure, while those areas with comparatively more population, such as Jiangsu, Sichuan, Hubei and Hunan, their shares of R&D personnel are higher than their of R&D expenditure. The former has comparative advantage in R&D expenditure while the latter having comparative advantage in R&D personnel.

Finally, across the sample, the average value of both R&D personnel and R&D expenditure in the ICT sector has gradually increased over time (see table 7.3). As far as the values of standard deviation of them are concerned, they are about 5 times as much as that of the corresponding average value. That means there exists a large amount of variation among regions.

3.2.2.2 Local Innovation Networks

Now, we explore the spatial distribution of the three types of local innovation networks. Firstly, we combine university and public research institute' R&D activities into academic R&D activities, and use the sum of R&D expenditure from both university and public research institute as a proxy of the knowledge spillover from the academic (XACAD: ACAD R&D i,t). Then, we use the value of specialization index times R&D expenditure in the ICT sector in a region to measure the intensity of specialized innovation spillovers, and use the value of index of diversity times R&D expenditure in other sectors (except the ICT sector) in a region to measure the intensity of diversified innovation spillovers.

Fig. 7.4 compares the values of three types of local innovation networks, namely spillover intensity of diversity, specialization and academics, among regions in 2004, where rank in a decreasing order by the value of academic R&D expenditure. In comparison to the decreasing order of values of academic R&D expenditure, both the values of R&D expenditure of diversity and specialization show a huge variation among regions. The interaction intensity of specialized spillover is enlarged by the product of the specialization index and its R&D expenditure in the ICT sector, especially for those regions like Guangdong, Shanghai, Tianjin, Jinagsu and Beijing. While the interaction intensity of diversified spillover depends mainly on local other industrial R&D expenditure, so those areas with scale of economy, like Guangdong, Jiangsu, Shandong, Shanghai, Zhejiang and etc. have the high values. When comparing values of specialized spillover and diversified spillover, we can find the interaction intensity of specialized spillover is larger than that of diversified spillover in general.

3.2.2.3 International R&D spillovers

Now turning to the third explanatory variables, we postulate that the performance of innovation in ICT industry in a given province have a correlation with FDI, export products and imported technologies in ICT industry at home and abroad. Since opening policy implemented by the central government in the late 1970s, China has been among the largest host countries in FDI (including those coming from Hongkong, Taiwan and Macca areas) in the world. As far as its breakdown is concerned, the ICT sector is the largest sector in the total FDI volume, which accounts for 80% of the total volume of FDI, so we use a proxy of the total volume of FDI due to lack of breakdown data of the ICT sector at regional level. In addition to FDI, the export-oriented products have also made breakthrough due to policy supported by the central government. At the present time, a few cities, like Dongguan in Guangdong province, and Suzhou in Jiangsu province have been the key producer in ICT industry in both home and international market. There is a proverb 'a traffic jam in Dongguan or Suzhou would cause immediately a huge shock even a chaos in the international ICT market due to the lack of supplier of electronic or computer components'. The Chinese governments make great effort to attract FDI, export products, and import advanced technologies to upgrade technical levels.

Fig.7.5 gives a detailed description of spatial distribution of FDI, export products and imported technologies in ICT industry. FDI and export products show congruent spatial cluster with gross industrial output value of ICT industry. While imported technologies seem to have irregular distribution, with Beijing, Liaoning, Shanghai, Tianjin, and Jiangsu ranking high. Perhaps it depends on needs of local enterprises or support by local fiscal capability, and it is hard to explain the variation of spatial distribution. Table 3 shows that all the average values of FDI, export products, and imported technologies in ICT industry have gradually increased over time. As for the S.D. of them, they all are about 2-3 times as much as that of the corresponding average value, which is much smaller than other variables.

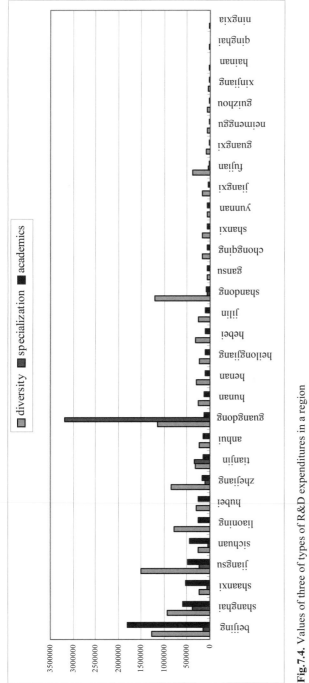

Fig. 7.4. Values of three of types of R&D expenditures in a region

Source: data calculated by authors, and basic data from China Statistic Yearbook on High-technology Industry (2005).

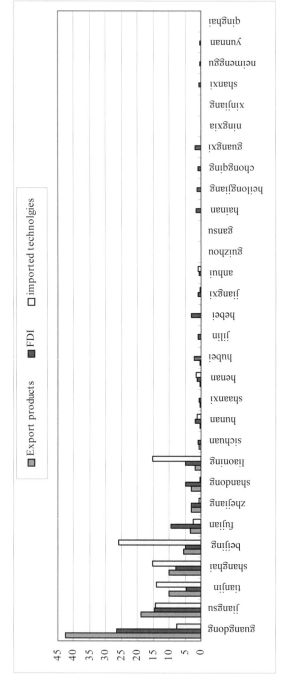

Fig.7.5. Shares of regional FDI, export products, and imported technologies in ICT industry in national total respectively (%)

Source: China Statistic Yearbook on High-technology Industry (2005).

4 Empirical Results

Our empirical results are presented in two parts. First, we present the paper's primary results, which evaluate the determinants of the performance of innovation in ICT industry with panel data. Second, we compare the significance of innovative performance affected by local innovation networks and international knowledge spillovers in ICT industry.

4.1 Determinants of the Performance of Innovation

Tables 7.4-5 present a broad range of results regarding the relationship between innovative output Y: I $_{i,t+1}$: innovative new products and the impact factors ($A_{i,t}, H_{i,t}^{A}, X_{i,t}^{NETW}, X_{i,t}^{FRD}$) that highlight the main relationships in the data as well as the source of variation underlying particular findings. Overall, we find a robust and relatively precise relationship between new products and impact factors: absorptive capability, local innovation networks, and international knowledge spillovers.

Table 7.4 evaluates a series of pairwise relationships between innovative output: added value of new products, and innovative inputs: added value of new products at previous year, R&D personnel, R&D expenditure, academic R&D expenditure, specialized knowledge spillovers of R&D expenditure, diversified knowledge spillovers of R&D expenditure, export products, FDI, and imported technologies. Since these measures are highly correlated with each other, it is useful to establish the unconditional relationship between each and innovative output. Individually, each measure explains between near two-thirds and 98% of the overall variation in innovative output. These results demonstrate that a large fraction of the variance in innovative output can be explained by single measure of impact factors.

Table 7.4 correlations between variables

	y	x1	x2	x3	x4	x5	x6	x7	x8	x9
Y	1.0000									
x1	0.8988	1.0000								
x2	0.8875	0.8393	1.0000							
x3	0.9047	0.8687	0.9126	1.0000						
x4	0.6975	0.7709	0.6902	0.7164	1.0000					
x5	0.9276	0.9456	0.9105	0.9624	0.7294	1.0000				
x6	0.7805	0.8283	0.7499	0.8054	0.8073	0.7740	1.0000			
x7	0.8880	0.9107	0.8193	0.8693	0.6869	0.9143	0.7590	1.0000		
x8	0.7372	0.8192	0.6936	0.6870	0.6053	0.7426	0.6696	0.8250	1.0000	
x9	0.8267	0.8615	0.8139	0.8330	0.7229	0.8606	0.7608	0.8264	0.7530	1.0000

Notes: Y: added value of new products, x1: added value of new products at previous year, x2: R&D personnel, x3: R&D expenditure, x4: academic R&D expenditure, x5: specialized knowledge spillovers of R&D expenditure, x6: diversified knowledge spillovers of R&D expenditure, x7: export products, x8: FDI, x9: imported technologies.

Table 7.5 Results of regressions

Y	Regression 5.1	Regression 5.2	Regression 5.3	Regression 5.4
	OLS with adjusted fixed effects, coefficients (standard errors)	OLS with adjusted fixed effects, coefficients (standard errors)	OLS with adjusted fixed effects, coefficients (standard errors)	OLS with adjusted fixed effects, coefficients (standard errors)
Constant	5.288743	5.527132	6.269239	6.222012
	(.3178147)	(1.061302)	(.7145151)	(1.300711)
x1	.4709433	.3574772	.3374367	.293303
	(.0529366)	(.1371711)	(.0729527)	(.1557331)
x2	.3876476	.3725246	.4043289	.3984423
	(.0849037)	(.0863731)	(.0837298)	(.0868399)
x3	.3439525	.1926795	.2452368	.1795011
	(.067358)	(.1490566)	(.0722331)	(.1486637)
x4		-.1034947		-.086287
		(.0660934)		(.0651933)
x5		.1612883		.0688273
		(.1375898)		(.1454062)
x6		.1321541		.1001382
		(.1296422)		(.1292766)
x7			.2115985	.2007181
			(.0551191)	(.0572822)
x8			-.0674746	-.0605996
			(.0659895)	(.0711772)
x9			.0053414	.0125584
			(.0464963)	(.0469161)
Obs.	240	240	240	240

Notes: Y, x1, x2, x3, x4, x5, x6, x7, x8, x9, ibid.

Table 7.5 begins with a specification similar to the model of the national innovative capability suggested by Furman et al. (2002). In the first regression (5.1),
we see that innovative new products are increasing in three variables suggested by
new or endogenous growth theory, knowledge stock: added value of new products
at the previous year, R&D effort: R&D personnel and R&D expenditure. Reg.
(5.1) shows that it is roughly equal for the coefficients as elasticity of the three variables, and it implies that an industry's existing level of technological sophistication and the level of inputs devoted to R&D play key roles in determining innovative output as suggested by proponents of endogenous growth theory.

We add the measures of $X_{i,t}^{NETW}$ including x4, x5, and x6 in Reg.(5.2) to explore how the local innovation networks play a role. By the results of Reg. 5.2, we
find: (1) the coefficients of two variables representing DUI, or MAR and Jacobs'
dynamic externalities are positive and roughly equal to each other. (2) The coeffi-

cient of the variable representing STI, or academic knowledge spillovers is slightly negative. (3) In addition, the coefficients of three variables representing absorptive capability all decrease to some extent, especially for the variables of knowledge stock and R&D expenditure. Similarly, we add the measures of $X_{i,t}^{FRD}$ including x7, x8, and x9 in (5.3) to explore how the international knowledge spillovers play a role. By the results of regression 5.3, we find: (1) the coefficients of two variables for export products and imported technologies are positive, whereas the coefficient of the variable for FDI is slightly negative. (2) As for the significance of elastic coefficients, export play have more impact to the performance of innovation than the other two channels of international knowledge spillovers, namely FDI, and imported technologies. (3) By the way, both the coefficients of two variables of knowledge stock and R&D expenditure representing absorptive capability decrease to some extent, while the coefficient of the variables for R&D personnel increases slightly.

Finally, we incorporate all the measures in (5.4) to explore to which extent the absorptive capability, the local innovation networks, and the international knowledge spillovers affect the performance of innovation. Regression 5.4 summarizes the results of the model tested on all the variables. And we find: (1) although the coefficients of the three variables for absorptive capability show a change to some extent, even two of them (knowledge stock and R&D expenditure) decreasing, it indicates that the absorptive capability has a prominent and stable impact on the performance of innovation comparing to all other variables. (2) As for the coefficients of the variables for the local innovation networks, they suggest that the local innovation networks have only a slight impact on the performance of innovation with an evident decreasing elastic coefficient. And (3) as for the coefficients of the variables for the international knowledge spillovers, it shows that the international knowledge spillovers keep a medial impact on the performance of innovation with two of them (export and FDI) almost not change and one of them (imported technologies) being even double.

4.2 Building Local Innovation Networks or Relying on International Spillovers?

Now, we discern the differentiated impact of the two categories of spillover effects comparing the elasticity of contribution of local innovation networks and international spillovers (see table 7.6). Firstly, we consider the sum of elasticity of absolute contribution according to regression 5.4, and find that the sum of the three variables for international knowledge spillovers with 0.152677 is nearly two times as much as that of local innovation networks with 0.082679. In terms of compared magnitude, other factors being constant, a 10% increase in international

Table 7.6 comparing elasticity of contribution of local innovation networks and international knowledge spillovers

Elasticity of absolute contribution				Elasticity of standard contribution			
X4	-0.086287	X7	0.2007181	X4	-0.05167	X7	0.225427
X5	0.0688273	X8	-0.0605996	X5	0.100178	X8	-0.03877
X6	0.1001382	X9	0.0125584	X6	0.0487	X9	0.012578
Sum	0.082679	Sum	0.152677	Sum	0.097212	Sum	0.199232

Notes: elasticity of absolute contribution is sourcing from Table 5 (Reg.5.4), while Elasticity of standard contribution is calculated by the following equation.

knowledge spillovers would increase new product added value by 1.53%, while only a 0.83% increase with a 10% increase in local innovation networks. Secondly, we compare the sum of elasticity of standard contribution, and also find that the sum of the three variables for the international knowledge spillovers with 0.199232 is two times more than that of the local innovation networks with 0.097212. In conclusion, we find that the performance of innovation in ICT industry at regional level is more affected by international knowledge spillovers than by local innovation networks.

5 Concluding Remarks

This study synergizes previous models on innovation and knowledge spillovers, and estimates the impact on innovative performance of absorptive capability, local innovation networks, and international knowledge spillovers in ICT industry at provincial level using panel data analysis. Our results suggest that the empirical determinants of the performance of innovation are:

1. Local absorptive capability is a fundamental and endogenous element for innovation just as the endogenous growth theory states. All the three of variables of knowledge stock, R&D personnel and expenditure have a positive and evident impact on the performance of innovation in ICT industry among regions. It is worth noting that R&D personnel play the most important role in innovation when all the variables are considered, while knowledge stock is the most important given only the three variables of local absorptive capability are considered alone. That's why Gangdong and Jiangsu with comparative advantage of human resources show better performance of innovation than other eastern coastal provinces with roughly equivalent R&D expenditure, close initial industrial conditions and similar degree of openness. In other words, to develop ICT industry at regional level, it requires local absorptive capability, especially human resources, and it is possible for those regions with comparative advantage of human resources do better in innovation and facilitate development of ICT industry.

2. Local innovation networks have a weak impact on the performance of innovation in consideration of both themselves observed alone and integrating all other factors. Surprisingly, it indicates that innovation in ICT industry in a region can hardly get support from local academic research in terms of the tiny but negative coefficient of the variable for local academic spillover. But it can well explain that some provinces like Shaanxi, Sichuan and Hubei with good academic infrastructure but lack of other supporting conditions for industrial development don't attain good performance of innovation, at least in ICT industry. In contrast, it shows both MAR dynamic externalities and Jacobs' dynamic externalities have some impact on the performance of innovation though they are not strong enough. It further implies innovation in ICT industry in a region is more relying on dynamic externalities of DUI than academic externalities of STI, when comparing the coefficients of the three variables of the local innovation networks.

3. International knowledge spillovers have a medial impact on the performance of innovation in consideration of the empirical results of both themselves observed alone and integrating all other factors. Interestingly, FDI do not promote innovation in the ICT sector due to its negative coefficient. Perhaps, it is derived from the aggregate effect of the data in the regional total volume, or it may also be due to that FDI hosted by China is more labor-intensive than knowledge-intensive. The other two variables of export products and imported technologies show positive impact on the performance of innovation. It suggests that both learning-by-exporting and importing do enhance domestic innovation with the effect of export products being larger.

4. The impact on innovation from the international knowledge spillovers is larger than that from the local innovation networks in terms of the sum coefficients of elasticity. It shows that the former is about two times as much as the latter when comparing the sum coefficients of elasticity of both absolute and standard contribution. Therefore, under the absorptive capability of a region being constant or effort in R&D activities being equivalent, it can acquire two times benefits from the international knowledge spillover as much as that from the local innovation networks. It can explain why some provinces like Fujian and Hainan with high degree of openness despite lack of enough academic support and scale of economies, have a good performance of innovation in ICT industry, and other provinces like Sichuan and Shaanxi with good academic support and enough scale of economies but low degree of openness, do not attain good performance of innovation in ICT industry.

Our findings generally suggest that the performance of innovation in the emerging technological area of the ICT sector depends on the synergetic effects from region's own R&D effort, local innovation networks, and international or inter-regional knowledge spillovers. The evidence confirms the arguments of new growth theory (Romer 1990; Grossman and Helpman 1991; and more others), local innovation networks (Feldman and Florida 1994) or industrial clusters (Porter

1990), and technology spillovers benefiting from a variety of international channels (Liu and Buck 2007).

The findings firmly support the current government's policy which aims at technology advancement through international sources of technology spillovers, and also suggest some further implications for policymakers. First, the government may need to foster innovation in the ICT or other high-technology sectors by allocating more resources to domestic R&D activities, particularly investing in R&D manpower. As shown in our research, local absorptive capability is a fundamental element for innovation, and it is indispensable to develop technological capabilities through one's own effort, especially R&D personnel. Second, it is necessary for a region to cultivate good industrial innovation milieu to develop ICT industry. One for best-practice is to develop industrial clusters in a region on the basis of specialized and diversified dynamic externalities. Third, a region may need to expand channels for international or inter-regional technology spillovers by attracting technology-intensive FDI, promoting export learning, and importing advanced technologies. Finally, it may be crucial for a region to make synergetic effects by taking advantage of both external and internal technological spillovers, and improving its own absorptive capability at the same time.

Acknowledgments This paper is Project (70673052/70672001) supported by National Natural Science Foundation of China, the Key Project of Ministry of Education of China (05JZDH0014), and the Project of Ministry of Education of China (07JC790047).

References

Acs Z J, Audretsch D B and Feldman M P (1992) Real effects of academic research: Comment. American Economic Review 81:363-367

Aitken B, Harrison A (1999) Do domestic firms benefit from foreign direct investment? Evidence from Venezuela. American Economic Review 89:605–618

Ambramovitz M (1956) Catching up, forging ahead and falling behind. Journal of Economic History 46:385–406

Arrow K (1962) The economic implications of learning by doing. Review of Economic Studies 29:155–173

Aslesen H W (2002) Innovative performance in the capital region of Norway. In: Acs Z J, Groot H L F and Nijkamp P (eds) The emergence of the knowledge economy. Springer-Verlag Berlin Heidelberg

Batisse C (2002) Dynamic externalities and local growth: A panel data analysis applied to Chinese provinces. China Economic Review 13:231-251

Belussi F, Arcangeli F (1998) A typology of networks: flexible and evolutionary firms. Research Policy 27:415-428

Branstetter L (2006) Is foreign direct investment a channel of knowledge spillovers? Evidence from Japan's FDI in the United States. Journal of International Economics 68:325–344

Caloghirou Y, Kastelli I, and Tsakanikas A (2004) Internet capabilities and external knowledge sources: complements or substitutes for innovative performance. Technovation 24:29-39

Camagni R P (1989) Cambiamento tecnologico, milieu locale e reti di imprese: una teoria dinamica dello spazio economico. Economia e Politica Industriale 64:209–236

Carbonara N (2005) Information and communication technology and geographical clusters: opportunities and spread. Technovation 25:213-222

Chinitz B (1961) Contrasts in agglomeration: New York and Pittsburg. American Economic Review 51:12-27

Coe D, Helpman E (1995) International R&D spillovers. European Economic Review 39:859–887

Cohen W, Levinthal A (1990) Absorptive capability: the new perspective learning and innovation. Administrative Science Quarterly 35:128–152

Damijan J P, Jaklic A, and Rojec M (2006) Do external knowledge spillovers induce firms' innovations? Evidence from Slovenia. University of Ljubljana LICOS Discussion Paper 156/2006

DeBresson C, Amesse F (1992) Networks of Innovators: A Review and Introduction to the Issues. Research Policy 20:363-380

Ellison G, Glaeser E L (1997) Geographic concentration in US manufacturing industries: a dartboard approach. Journal of Political Economy 105:889–927

Feldman M P, Florida R. (1994) The geographic sources of innovation: technological infrastructure and product innovation in the United States. Annals of the Association of American Geographers 84(2): 210-229

Florida R, Kenney M (1988) Venture Capital and Technological Innovation in the U.S. Research Policy 17: 119-137

Fritsch M (2004) R&D co-operation and efficiency of regional innovation activities. Cambridge Journal of Economics 28(6): 829-846

Furman J, Hayes R (2004) Catching up or standing still? National innovative productivity among 'follower' countries, Research Policy 33:1329–1354

Furman J, Porter M, and Stern S (2002) The determinants of national innovative capacity. Research Policy 31: 899–933

Glaeser E L, Kallal H D, Scheinkman J A, and Schleifer A (1992) Growth in cities. Journal of Political Economy 100:1126–1152

Greenaway D, and Yu Z (2004) Firm level interactions between exporting and productivity: Industry specific evidence. Research Paper Series No.1, Leverhulme Centre, Nottingham University

Griliches Z (1990) Patent statistics as economic indicators: a survey. Journal of Economic Literature 92:630–653

Grossman G, and Helpman E (1991) Innovation and Growth in the Global Economy. MIT Press, Cambridge, MA

Henderson V, Kuncoro A, and Turner M (1995) Industrial development in cities. Journal of Political Economy 103:1067–1090

Hoover E M (1937) The measurement of industrial location. Review of Economics and Statistics 17:162-171

Hoover E M (1971) An introduction to regional economics. Knopf, New York

Isard W, Schooler E W, and Vietorisz T (1959) Industrial complex analysis and regional development. Wiley, New York

Jacobs J (1969) The economy of cities. New York, Vintage

Jaffe A B (1989) Real effects of academic research. American Economic Review 79:957-970

Jensen M B, Johnson B, Lorenz E, and Lundvall B A (2007) Forms of knowledge and modes of innovation. Research Policy 36:680-693

Kleinknecht A, and Poot T (1992) Do regions matter for R&D? Regional Studies 26:221-232

Konings J (2001) The effect of foreign direct investment on domestic firms: evidence from firm level panel data in emerging economies. Economics of Transition 9:619-633

Liu X, Buck T (2007) Innovation performance and channels for international technology spillovers: Evidence from Chinese high-tech industries. Research Policy 36:1329–1354

Love J, Ropper S (2001) Location and network effects on innovation success: evidence for UK, German and Irish manufacturing plants. Research Policy 30:643-662

Lumenga-Neso O, Olarreaga M, and Schiff M (2005) On 'indirect' trade-related R&D spillovers. European Economic Review 49:1785–1798

Lundvall B A (1992) (Ed). National Systems of Innovation: Towards a Theory of Innovation and Interactive Learning, Pinter Publishers, London

Malecki E (1997) Technology and Economic Development: The Dynamics of Local, Regional and National Competitiveness, 2nd edition. London and Boston: Addison Wesley Longman

Marjolein C J (1996) Regional differences in technology: theory and empirics, Research Memoranda, Maastricht: MERIT, Maastricht Economic Research Institute on Innovation and Technology

Markusen A, Hall P, and Glasmeier A (1986) High Tech America: The What, How, Where and Why of sunrise Industries. Boston, Allen and Unwin

Marshall A (1920) Principles of economics. London, Macmillan

Mustar P (1997) How French academics create hi-tech companies: the conditions for success or failure. Science and Public Policy 24:37-43

Nonaka I (1994) A dynamic theory of organization knowledge creation. Organization Science 5:14-37

Oakey R (1985) High technology industries and agglomeration economies. In Hall P, Markusen A (eds) Silicon Landscapes. Boston, Allen and Unwin

Oerlemas L, Meeus M, and Boekema F (1998) Do networks matter for innovation? The usefulness of the economic network approach in analyzing innovation. Tijdschrift voor Econmische en Social Geografie 89:298-309

Perez M P, Sanchez M (2002) Innovation and Firm location in the Spanish medical instruments industry. In: Acs Z J, Groot H L F, and Nijkamp P (eds) The emergence of the knowledge economy. Springer-Verlag Berlin Heidelberg

Romer P (1990) Endogenous technological change. Journal of Political Economy 98:71–S102

Segal N, Quince R, and Wicksteed P (1985) The Cambridge phenomenon: the growth of a high-technology industry in a university town. Brand Brothers, Cambridge UK

Solow R M (1956) A contribution to the theory of economic growth. Quarterly Journal of Economics 70:65–94

Storper M, Walker R (1989) The Capitalist Imperative: Territory, Technology and Industrial Growth. Oxford, Basil Blackwell

Thomas M (1985) Regional economic development and the role of innovation and technological change. In: Thwaites A T, Oakey R P (eds) The Regional Economic Impact of Technological Change. New York, St. Martin's Press

Von Hippel (1988) The Sources of Innovation. New York, Oxford University Press

Appendix 7.A Selected Industries Representing the Chinese ICT Sector

Electronic and Telecommunication Equipments Manufacturing (ETEM)	SIC (40-404)	Sub-sector
	401	Manufacturing of communication equipment
	402	Manufacturing of radar and associated equipment
	403	Manufacturing of television and radio equipment and associated goods
	405	Manufacturing of parts of an electronic apparatus
	406	Manufacturing of electronic component
	407	Manufacturing of sound or video household appliance apparatus
	407	Manufacturing of other electronic apparatus
Computers and Office Equipments Manufacturing (COEM)	SIC (404+4154+4155)	
	4041	Manufacturing of integrated computer apparatus
	4042	Manufacturing of computer network equipment
	4043	Manufacturing of computer of peripheral apparatus
	4154+4155	Manufacturing of office machinery
ICT industry (including ETEM and COEM)		

Sources: "published format for sorting-out the statistical date of high technology industry", from China Statistics Yearbook on High Technology Industry, Beijing: China Statistics Press, 2006.

Chapter 8
Analyzing Growth of Mobile Telecommunication Services in China

Varadharajan Sridhar

Management Development Institute, Gurgaon, INDIA

Abstract Quick deployment and advancement in technologies have propelled the growth of mobile services in China. Since China contributes to about 20% of world's mobile subscriber base, it is important to study the factors that affect the growth of mobile telecom services. However, penetration of mobile services is not uniform across different regions of China. Though a number of cross-country studies exist, this is one of the first attempts to study the growth of mobile services across service areas of China. It is our objective to study what factors affect the growth of mobile services across different services areas of China. We model growth of mobile services using technology diffusion framework, incorporating other variables that impact growth. Our analysis of panel data using the model indicate that apart from traditional factors such as income and population, fixed line penetration seems to compliment growth of mobile services in China. The network effect also seems to be more prominent. Reasons for the above effects are discussed.

1 Introduction

China is the world's largest mobile communications market. The mobile subscriber base in China is 531.45 million as on October 2007 (ISI 2008). Total mobile revenue is around 400 Billion Yuan (US $ 52 Billion) for the year ending 2006. Government operators namely China Mobile and China Unicom provide mobile telecommunication services in China in 31 regions of the country. Table 1 gives the mobile subscriber base in China along with annual growth pattern and mobile density levels.

P.O. de Pablos, M.D. Lytras (eds.), *The China Information Technology Handbook*,   123
DOI: 10.1007/978-0-387-77743-6_8, © Springer Science+Business Media, LLC 2009

Table 1 Mobile Subscribers in China.

Year	Subscriber Base (in Million)	Mobile Density (per 100 people)	Annual Growth in Subscriber Base (%)
1992	0.1769	0.01	
1993	0.6393	0.05	261.39%
1994	1.5678	0.13	145.24%
1995	3.6294	0.29	131.50%
1996	6.8528	0.55	88.81%
1997	13.2329	1.06	93.10%
1998	23.8628	1.90	80.33%
1999	43.1940	3.42	81.01%
2000	82.7870	6.58	91.66%
2001	145.0040	11.03	75.15%
2002	205.9950	15.78	42.06%
2003	269.9530	21.41	31.05%
2004	334.8270	25.87	24.03%
2005	393.4100	30.68	17.50%
2006	443.5980	34.12	12.76%
2007 (Oct)	531.4500	40.20	

The growth of telecom subscriber base of both mobile and fixed Line in China is illustrated in Figure 1.

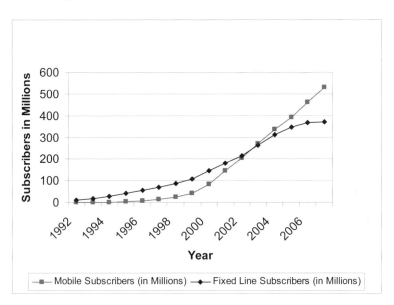

Figure 1 Telecom Subscriber Base in China

As is shown in Figure 1, the number of mobile subscriber base surpassed fixed line subscriber base in the year 2003 and continues to grow. On the other hand, the growth rate of fixed line subscriber base decreased and is currently at the inflexion point of saturation. Despite this substantial growth of mobile services, the penetration of mobile services is not uniform across different areas of China. Province wise mobile subscriber base in China is given in Table 2.

Qualitative narratives and descriptive statistics of the mobile sector for many countries are available from a variety of industry sources (e.g. PBC 2006, HKTU 2002). However, empirical studies of mobile market growth are much more limited in number (e.g. Sridhar 2006, Minges 1999). Though a number of cross country studies exist in literature that deal with growth of mobile services (Madden et al. 2004, Rouvinen 2006), research on mobile growth across different regions of countries are sparse. Sridhar (2007b) analyze the inter-regional growth of mobile services in India and indicate that competition is the main cause for subscriber growth. Developing models to explain the growth of mobile services across different regions, especially in the high growth market of China is critical for an in-depth understanding of the market. It is the objective of this paper to model growth of mobile services across different regions of China to better understand the mobile growth phenomenon.

2 Licensing of Mobile Services in China

Ministry of Post and Telecommunications (MPT) of the Chinese government was the monopoly mobile service provider in the country. In July 1994, the operational arm of MPT was renamed the China Telecommunications Corporation (China Telecom). China Unicom Ltd., a subsidiary of China United Telecommunications Corporation, was set up at the same time by the former Ministry of Electronics and Information to foster competition in the telecommunications industry. In May 2000, China Telecom was split into four separate entities, one of which was the lucrative mobile services, christened as China Mobile Communications Company (Loo, 2004). Currently China Mobile and China Unicom are the two licensed mobile operators in China in the 31 provinces. China mobile is the world's largest mobile phone company in terms of number of subscribers and has about 70% of market share in the country. The total subscriber base of China Mobile is about 369.34 million, more than the population of the US (China Mobile 2008). China Mobile provides Global Systems for Mobile (GSM) service in the country. China Unicom is the second largest mobile telecommunications network operator. China Unicom started its GSM services in 1995 and had about 160 million subscribers at the end of December 2007 (China Unicom 2007). In 2002, China Unicom started providing Code Division Multiple Access (CDMA) services and had a subscriber base of about 41 million as of July 2007. In both GSM and CDMA services, China Unicom accounts for about 30% of mobile subscriber base in the country.

Table 2 Province-wise Mobile Subscribers in China for the year 2005

Province	Subscriber Base (includes both GSM and CDMA) in millions	Population (in Millions)	Mobile Density (per 100 population)	Per Capita GDP in Chinese Yuan (in 1990 prices)
North				
Beijing	14.5945	15.3600	95.02	19260
Tianjin	5.0261	10.4253	48.21	15237
Hebei	17.8553	68.4400	26.09	6337
Shanxi	9.0618	33.5185	27.04	5357
Inner Mongolia	7.1233	23.8610	29.85	7013
North East				
Liaoning	13.5816	42.2000	32.18	8153
Jilin	9.1569	27.1500	33.73	5728
Heilongjiang	11.3233	38.1800	29.66	6201
East				
Shanghai	14.4416	17.7800	81.22	22118
Jiangsu	25.5004	74.6800	34.15	10530
Zhejiang	26.8634	48.9400	54.89	11796
Anhui	10.4691	61.1400	17.12	3777
Fujian	13.0230	35.3200	36.87	7990
Jiangxi	7.9836	43.0664	18.54	4047
Shandong	23.4732	92.3900	25.41	8610
South				
Henan	18.1497	93.7100	19.37	4854
Hubei	14.0126	57.0700	24.55	4908
Hunan	12.6622	63.2000	20.04	4426
Guangdong	64.0660	91.8500	69.75	10461
Guangxi	10.2107	46.5500	21.93	3761
Hainan	2.0387	8.2631	24.67	4651
South West				
Chongqing	9.4340	27.9700	33.73	4716
Sichuan	16.8973	82.0800	20.59	3865
Guizhou	5.0942	37.2500	13.68	2282
Yunnan	8.9884	44.4244	20.23	3358
Tibet	0.4694	2.7600	17.01	3910
North West				
Shaanxi	9.3810	37.1800	25.23	4247
Gansu	4.0844	25.9172	15.76	3206
Qinghai	1.3161	5.4250	24.26	4302
Ningxia	1.8108	5.9500	30.43	4376
Xinjiang	5.3130	20.0815	26.46	5571
Total	393.4058	1282.1300		

3 Factors Affecting Growth of Mobile Services

3.1 Income

Many researchers have studied the effect of income on telecom penetration. Researchers have argued that greater Gross Domestic Product (GDP) per capita signifies greater affordability which in turn increases demand for mobile telecommunication services (Jha and Majumdar 1999). In Madden et al. (2004) and Rouvinen (2006), per capita GDP is considered as one of the variables for studying mobile services growth. As indicated in table 2, there are wide variations in income levels across different provinces of China. We posit that income has a positive association with mobile subscription levels.

3.2 Population

Population is treated as a proxy for market size in Rouvinen (2006). In the study on changes in analogue and digital mobile user base population is taken as one of the variables in Liikanen et al. (2001). There are differences in population across the different service areas of China as shown in Tables 2. We hypothesise that population has a significant positive association with the mobile subscriber base.

3.3 Penetration of Fixed Lines

Fixed line penetration can capture the substitutability or complementarity apart from possible network and/or economies of scale efforts. In their work on mobile penetration Ahn and Lee (1999) indicate that apart from traditional economic variables, the fixed line penetration promotes diffusion process. For example, when cellular mobile service was introduced in China in 1992, there were already more than 11 million land line subscribers. Those who subscribed to the mobile services at that time derived a positive net utility as being able to talk to existing landline subscribers. In Rouvinen (2006), it is reported that fixed line penetration rate has significant positive association with mobile penetration. Since in China there are differences across regions in fixed line penetration we include this variable in our model and posit that fixed line penetration complements mobile penetration.

3.4 Network Effects

As more and more subscribe to mobile services, the utility of the system increases which results in marginal number of non-users subscribing to the system. This induces further growth and so on. However, when the population of potential subscribers is finite, the resulting pattern of growth tends to be S-shaped as shown in Gurbaxani (1990). A typical growth curve that has an S-shape has three distinct phases. In the initial stages, growth is less as subscribers are not fully informed and aware about the utility they derive by joining the system. However as the number of subscribers attains a "critical mass", the number of subscribers in the system is large enough for the growth process to become self-sustaining. Growth increases near exponentially in the second phase. The last stage indicates stability in growth as the saturation level of subscribers is reached.

There is also the diffusion of innovation theory which defines the process by which innovations such as cellular and Internet services are communicated through certain channels over time among members of the social system (Gurbaxani 1990). The adopter distribution over time is governed by the rate at which the innovation diffuses through a population. This theory also postulates that the total number of such innovation adopters as a function of time is expected to be an S-curve. Since in China the mobile services are in the second stage of exponential growth, we expect that subscriber base in previous periods have a strong positive association with the current subscriber base due to network externality effects.

There are critics of the S-curve growth pattern, prominent ones being those who proved that Internet growth is still exponential and the saturation point as predicted by previous researchers has been surpassed (Rai et al. 1998). Specifically, the S-curve theories ignore such external factors as government policies, technological advancements, and service innovations. As in Sridhar (2006), previous studies have pointed out that the saturation limit depends on a number of factors including growth in disposable income of potential subscribers, price of services, competition in the market place, price and availability of alternative communication channels, such as the Internet and regulatory policies regarding spectrum allocation and interconnection. In Madden et al. (2004), income and price were incorporated in a diffusion process framework to model growth of mobile telecom in the cross-country study. In Rouvinen (2006) an extensive model is built taking to account as many as 18 variables in a Gompertz model of growth.

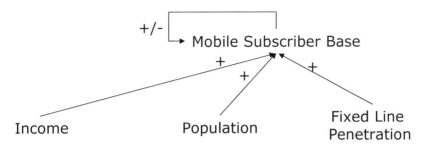

Figure 2 Causal Loop Diagram of Mobile Services Growth

We extend the model of Madden et al. (2004) and Rouvinen (2006) in our inter-region model of growth by taking in to account population, income and fixed line penetration in the Gompertz diffusion model. The hypothesized cause-effect relations are indicated in the causal-loop diagram shown in Figure 2. The relationship is positive (or negative) if a change in the causal factor produces a change in the same (or opposite) direction in mobile subscription.

3.5 Other Factors

There are many studies which quote competition as one of the main actors affecting penetration of mobile services (Sridhar 2007b). However, in China, the market for mobile services in China is split between the two state owned operators viz. China Mobile and China Unicom. The competition is not much and the overall market concentration as measured by Herfindahl-Hirschman Index (HHI) is about 0.55. Since there is a limited competition in mobile services and hence is not significant enough to be considered in the above model.

While both Madden et al. (2004) and Rouvinen (2006) take into account, price as being an important causal variable, we could not consider it in our model due to non availability of price data at the regional level for China. Since both China Mobile and China Unicom operate in all service areas, it is most likely that a uniform pricing strategy is used across the service areas as has been noted in countries such as India (Sridhar 2007). Hence the variation of price across regions is expected to be minimal.

4 Model for Analysing Mobile Penetration

Let $N_{i,t}$ be the number of mobile subscribers in service area i at time t. Over time it tends towards its equilibrium level $N^*_{i,t}$ along an S-shaped path. The Gompertz growth model specifies the rate of change as

$$\ln N_{i,t} - \ln N_{i,t-1} = \alpha \left(\ln N_{i,t}^{*} - \ln N_{i,t-1} \right) \tag{1}$$

where α is the speed of adjustment as illustrated in Sridhar (2006). Equation (1) describes the internal influence model as illustrated in Gurbaxani (1990). Augmenting equation (1) as in Madden et al. (2004) and Rouvinen (2006), with external factors mentioned in the previous section yields the following:

$$\ln N_{it} - \ln N_{it-1} = \alpha_0 + \alpha_1 \ln GDP_{it} + \alpha_2 \ln POP_{it} + \\ \alpha_3 \ln FL_{it} - \alpha_4 \ln N_{it-1} + \varepsilon_{it} \quad \forall i \in I, \forall t \in T \tag{2}$$

In equation (2) above, GDP refers to GDP per capita, POP indicates population, and FL denotes Fixed Line subscribers. A panel data set is constructed across 31 provinces of China for the period 1998-2005. Table 3 indicates the sources of data for the different variables.

Table 3 Sources of Data

Variable	Source of Data for China
Mobile Subscription	NBSC (2006)
Income	NBSC (2006); IMF (2007) for GDP deflators
Population	NBSC (2006)
Fixed Line Subscription	NBSC (2006)

5 Estimation and Analysis

Table 4 illustrates ANOVA results that show variation of the above variable values across different regions of China. ANOVA results indicate that there is indeed significant difference in the means of the above variables across the service areas.

Table 4 ANOVA Results of Different Variable Values Across Regions of China

Variable	China F(p)
Mobile Subscribers	6.845 (0.000)
Per Capita GDP	29.122 (0.000)
Population	928.867 (0.000)
Fixed Line Subscribers	13.697 (0.000)

Table 5 OLS Estimation of Growth Model

	Model Fit: N = 185; Adj-R^2 = 0.7600; F = 147.6270; sig = 0.000	
Variables	Coefficient	t-stat (sig)
Constant	-0.3040	1.9970 (0.0470)
Per Capita GDP	0.0510	2.1070 (0.0360)
Population	0.0880	2.4800 (0.0140)
Fixed Lines	0.2030	3.8660 (0.0000)
Subscribers $_{-1}$	-0.3340	-13.8910 (0.000)

Equation (2) is estimated using Ordinary Least Square regression procedure and the results are presented in Table 5.

Results indicate that along with the traditional factors such as population and income, fixed lines have a significant positive association with the growth of mobile subscriber base in China. The positive network effect is also significant.

6 Discussions

6.1 Effect of Fixed Lines

In China, until the last quarter of 2007, the fixed line subscriptions provided by the state owned China Telecom and China Netcom continued to grow despite the growth of mobile services. One important reason for this growth is attributed to the Xiaolingtong (also referred to as "a Little Smart", abbreviated as XLT) service based on Personal Handy-Phone System (PHS) technology provided by the incumbent fixed line service providers as pointed out in Yuan et al. (2006) and Sridhar (2007a). The XLT service was first introduced by China Telecom in November 2002 as a limited-mobility wireless technology that allowed subscribers to have mobile service at the price of landline (Table 6). China Netcom, the other fixed line operator subsequently introduced in its operating regions. Though the government officially restricted XLT to outlying cities and provinces, the service gained a strong national market foothold (PBC, 2006a). XLT is registered as fixed line service and by 2003, accounted for more than 40% of all fixed line subscriber additions in China (PBC 2006a). From its 1998 launch in Yuhang, a small city in Zhejiang province, XLT has spread to more than 600 cities nationwide with subscribers reaching about 91 million as of December 2006 (Yuan et al. 2006). Growth of XLT subscribers along with the mobile subscribers is shown in Figure 3. The positive correlation between XLT subscriptions and mobile subscriptions give support to our analysis that in China, fixed line complements mobile services.

Table 6 XLT Subscribers Across Different Regions

Province	XLT Subscribers
North	
Beijing	1.215
Tianjin	1.096
Hebei	3.254
Shanxi	1.694
Inner Mongolia	1.604
North East	
Liaoning	3.928
Jilin	1.754
Heilongjiang	2.998
East	
Shanghai	2.608
Jiangsu	10.32
Zhejiang	6.475
Anhui	2.197
Fujian	5.465
Jiangxi	1.926
Shandong	4.854
South	
Henan	4.463
Hubei	3.463
Hunan	2.623
Guangdong	9.867
Guangxi	1.984
Hainan	0.808
South West	
Chongqing	1.801
Sichuan	4.073
Guizhou	1.218
Yunnan	1.686
Tibet	0.405
North West	
Shaanxi	2.117
Gansu	2.252
Qinghai	0.396
Ningxia	0.41
Xinjiang	2.087
Total	91.127

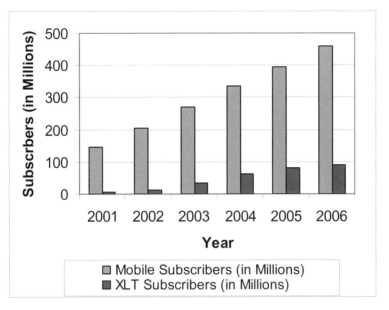

Figure 3 Growth of Mobile and XLT Subscribers

It is to be pointed out that even in India, the third largest mobile services market in the world, such a movement by the fixed line operators to provide limited mobile service started in 2001. However, due to the intervention by the regulator and the Indian government most of the fixed line operators migrated their licenses to provide full mobility services much like the other mobile operators (for detailed discussions on India's limited mobility case, refer to Sridhar 2007b). However, in China, the government turned a blind eye to the cheaper limited mobility services offered by the fixed line operators.

6.2 The Network Effect

The network effect indicated by the coefficient $\alpha_4 = -0.3340$ is significant for China[†]. This implies that every 1% increase in subscriber base yields about 0.33% increase in network subscription growth. Incidentally this elasticity is exactly the same as that calculated by Madden et al. (2004) in their global model of mobile telephony subscription. The strong positive network externality effect signals that mobile subscription growth is likely to continue in China in the years to come.

6.3 Income and Population Effects

The income and population have significant (at $p = 0.05$ level) positive effect on mobile subscription growth, as previous studies have shown. We argue below some of the factors that have contributed to this effect.

[†] Note the negative sign of α_4 in equation (2)

Pre-paid Subscription

Mobile communications market in China is largely prepaid. Pre-paid subscribers contribute to 81% of subscriber base for China Mobile. Though pre-paid users contribute to only about 37.6% of the subscriber base for China Unicom, the prepaid subscriber base continues to grow especially in its GSM business. These prepaid users are largely from low income group and yield lower levels of Average Revenue Per User (ARPU) (Sangwan and Pau 2005). The average ARPU for prepaid segment is about RMB 55 (US $ 7.36) compared to ARPU of RMB 216 (US $ 28.90) for the post-paid segment (PBC, 2008). It is pointed out by Zhang and Prybutok 2005) that prepaid subscriptions contributed to growth in mobile penetration.

Regulatory Levies

State imposed fee reductions and nil license fees charged by the government on mobile operations have resulted in low rental and usage charges. Sridhar (2007a) point out that a mere 3% service tax is levied on mobile services in China while in countries such as India, the total levies exceeds 30% of the revenue of mobile operators. The reduced levies in turn decrease usage charges and make mobile services more affordable.

Low Cost Handsets

Affordable mobile phones produced by domestic manufacturers have increased the levels of competition in mobile phone marketing China. Lower product packaging expectations of the Chinese consumers which often accounts for 40% and above of the normal mobile phone terminal prices further lowers the end product cost, giving local manufacturers an advantage over global brands (Sangwan and Pau 2005). Affordable mobile phones produced by domestic manufacturers have increased the levels of competition and consequent reduction in prices in the mobile phone markets.

Demographics of Mobile Users

It is estimated that 55% of mobile users in China are young working urban adults between the age of 25 and 35. For this market segment owning the mobile phones is a lifestyle symbol. Sangwan and Pau (2005) point out that mobile phones in China are an essential part of "San Da Jian" (the three big consumer items).

The above factors have reduced price of owning and using a mobile terminal which has become status symbol for most of the potential users. Thus more of the populace above a certain threshold of income are able to purchase mobile handsets and afford to use mobile services.

7 Conclusion and Future Research Directions

Mobile services are growing at near exponential rates in China. China is a large country and has wide disparities in demographics, and economics across regions as indicated in this paper. It is important to study the impact of different techno-economic variables on mobile services growth across regions of these countries so that regulatory policies could be formulated to sustain and improve the growth across regions of these two countries. This study is one of the first of its kind to analyze the inter-region growth of mobile services growth in China.

Results of the study indicate that the fixed lines compliment mobile services in China. Though further analysis is needed, the government's policy of allowing XLT services to be provided by the Fixed Line operators seems to have induced growth of mobile services with subscribers seeking these as complimentary services. Our results indicate that the network effect is still significant. Hence we can expect the growth of mobile services to continue in China in the years to come.

Though China adopted geographically oriented province-wise separation of service areas (unlike for example, in India where the service areas were conceived based on income levels and potential telecom revenues), the differences in demographics and economics across regions could have created non-uniform demand across the regions. It is assumed in this model that the demand is identical across different service areas or categories of service areas. Area specific intercepts using Fixed Effect Model or Random Effect Model shall be explored as presented in Madden et al. (2004) to analyze inter-service area variations closely.

The estimation and results are limited by the availability of data across service areas. Estimations are carried out using "exclude cases list-wise" option. Further improvements can be done to the estimation using the method presented in Rouvinen (2006) so that the robustness of estimation and hence the results can be improved.

It is pointed out in Madden, et al (2004) price is one of the variables that has significant effect on mobile subscriber growth. In our study we have not explicitrely modelled the effect of price. Though price variations across regions are not easily available and that they may be uniform across the regions due to pan-China coverage by both the operators, temporal variations in price can be used possibly in an instrumental variable framework to study these effects. It has to be noted that we model only the demand side of mobile services. As pointed out in Roller and Waverman (2001) and Sridhar and Sridhar (2007), economic development as indicated by per capita GDP and mobile penetration have dual causal relationship. For example it is demonstrated in Roller and Waverman (2001) and Sridhar and Sridhar (2007) how increase in income increases the demand for mobile services which in turn encourages operators to increase telecom investment using a set of supply-demand endogenous equations.

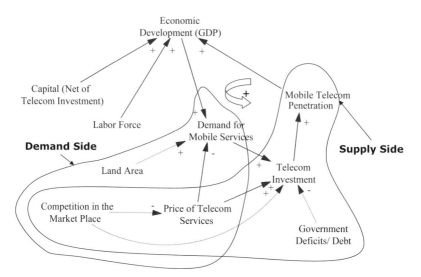

Figure 4 Causal Diagram that Incorporates Supply and Demand Side of Mobile Telecommunication Services

The causal diagram indicating the various cause-effect relationships is presented in Figure 4 (Sridhar and Sridhar 2006). Further research is needed to analyze such models that incorporate explicitly the dual causal effect between mobile penetration and economic development so that the effect of mobile penetration of economic development can be accurately estimated. Further it will be interesting to study the contrasts between China's mobile services growth and India's - the other fast going mobile growth markets in the world with markedly different market structure and regulation.

References

Ahn H, Lee M (1999) An econometric analysis of the demand for access to mobile telephone networks. Information Economics and Policy 11: 297-305.

China Mobile (2007) Subscriber Data for March 2007. http://www.chinamobileltd.com/. Accessed 10 January 2008

China Unicom (2007) Announcement in Respect of Statistics Data for the Month of March 2007. http://www.chinaunicom.com.hk/en/home/default.html Accessed 10 January 2008

Gurbaxani V (1990) Diffusion in Computing Networks: The Case of BITNET". Communications of the ACM 33:65-75.

Hong Kong telecommunications Users Group (HKTU) (2002) Asia Telecom Profiles http://www.hktug.org/newsltr/1999/may/pi_profile.html Accessed 10 May 2003

International Monetary Fund (IMF) (2007) World Economic Outlook Database. http://www.imf.org/external/pubs/ft/weo/2007/01/data/index.aspx Accessed 13 May 2007

International Telecommunications Union (ITU) (2005) Mobile Cellular Subscribers http://www.itu.int Accessed 1 October 2006

ISI Emerging Markets (ISI) (2008) Telecom Indstry Monthly Figures http://site.securities.com Accessed on 10 January 2008

Jha R, Majumdar SK (1999) A matter of connections: OECD telecommunications sector productivity and the role of cellular technology diffusion. Information Economics and Policy 11: 243-269

Liikanen J, Stoneman P, Toivanen, O (2001) Intergenerational effects in the diffusion of new Technology: The case of Mobile phones. Swedish School of Economics and Business Administration Working Papers 3.

Loo BPY (2004) Telecommunications Reforms in China: Towards an Analytical Framework. Telecommunications Policy 28:697-714

Madden G, Coble-Neal G, Dalzell BA (2004) Dynamic Model of Mobile Telephony Subscription Incorporating a Network Effect. Telecommunications Policy 28:133-144

Minges M (1999) Mobile cellular communications in the southern African region. Telecommunications Policy 23:585-593

National Bureau of Statistics China (NBSC) (2006) Yearly Data: Business Volume of Post and Telecommunications Services. http://www.stats.gov.cn/ english/statisticaldata/yearlydata/ Accessed 1 October 2006

Paul Budde Communications Pvt Ltd. (PBC) (2006) China – Mobile Market – Overview & Statistics http://site.securities.com Accessed on 10 January 2007

Paul Budde Communications Pvt Ltd. (PBC) (2008) China – Mobile Market – Overview & Statistics http://site.securities.com Accessed on 10 January 2007

Rai A, Ravichandran T, Samaddar S (1998) How to Anticipate the Internet's Global Diffusion. Communications of the ACM 41: 97-106

Roller LH, Waverman L (2001) Telecommunications infrastructure and economic development: A simultaneous approach. American Economic Review 91: 909-923

Rouvinen P (2006) Diffusion of Digital Mobile Telephony: Are Developing Countries Different? Telecommunications Policy 30: 46-63

Sangwan S, Pau L (2005) Diffusion of Mobile Terminals in China. European Management Journal 23: 674-681

Sridhar V (2006). Modeling the Growth of Mobile Telephony. Vision: The Journal of Business Perspective 10(3): 1-10

Sridhar V (2007a). Analyzing the Growth of Mobile Telecommunication Services Across Service Areas of China and India. In: Garg R, Jaiswal M (ed) Bridging Digital Divide Macmillan, New Delhi India

Sridhar V (2007b) Growth of mobile services across regions of India. Journal of Scientific & Industrial Research 66:281-289

Sridhar K, Sridhar V (2006) Telecommunications and Growth: Causal Model, Quantitative and Qualitative Evidence. Economic & Political Weekly 25:2611-2619

Sridhar K, Sridhar V (2007) Telecommunications Infrastructure and Economic Growth: Evidence from Developing Countries. Applied Econometrics and International Development 7(2): 37-56

Yuan X, Zheng W, Wang Y, Xu Z, Yang Q, Gao Y (2006) Xiaolingtong versus 3G in China: Which will be the winner? Telecommunications Policy 30:297-313

Zhang X, Prybutok VR (2005) How the Mobile Communications Markets Differ in China, the U.S., and Europe. Communications of the ACM 48(3): 111-115

Chapter 9
Virtual Worlds Success in Mainland

China Second Life vs. HiPiHi

Xi Zhang[1], Zhenjiao Chen[1], Doug Vogel[2], Zhongyun Zhou[1]

[1] USTC-CityU Joint Research Center, USTC Suzhou Institute for Advanced Study, P.R. CHINA
[2] Department of Information Systems, City University of Hong Kong, P.R. CHINA

Abstract The Chinese burgeoning Internet population will soon have an array of 3D virtual worlds in which to work and play. Second Life, a particularly well-known 3D virtual world, is also present in the Chinese market. However, Second Life faces some dilemmas in Mainland China; especially since its western model has not been widely accepted by Chinese users. It also faces a challenge from the Chinese local virtual world, HiPiHi. The many stories about the demise of foreign companies are a warning that the western Internet business may not succeed in China, although some local competitors may survive, such as Taobao in e-commerce and QQ in the instant message field. Which virtual worlds will succeed in China in the long run? This chapter compares the different strategies between Second Life and HiPiHi, and explores how these different strategies impact on user acceptance in the Chinese environment. Finally, we discuss how the emerging 3D virtual worlds are likely to develop in China.

1 Introduction

Due to increasing broadband Internet access, virtual worlds are rapidly emerging as an alternative means to the real world for communicating, collaborating, and organizing economic activity. In virtual worlds, people "co-inhabit" with millions of other people simultaneously [1]. They can interact with each other via computer-chat through their 3D virtual figures (avatars). In 2006, one virtual world, Second Life (www.secondlife.com), won great success and received global attention. By the end of December 2007, there were more than 11 million users registered in Second Life, and it is expected that this number will increase to 25 million in 2008. Many companies also have strong interests in conducting business in this platform. In Second Life more than 50 multinational organizations, such as IBM, Adidas, Dell and Vodafone, have established their "virtual stores." The report of

P.O. de Pablos, M.D. Lytras (eds.), *The China Information Technology Handbook*,   139
DOI: 10.1007/978-0-387-77743-6_9, © Springer Science+Business Media, LLC 2009

Gartner Group predicts that 80 percent of all active users and Fortune 500 enterprises will have an avatar or a presence in virtual worlds by 2012[‡].

As an important Internet business market with more than 210 million Internet population[§], China is getting into virtual worlds. Considering the over half a billion registered users of virtual communities and the popularity of 3D online games, it is believed that there will be even more Chinese users adopting virtual worlds. Several virtual worlds, such as Second Life, have announced their business plans in China. For example, Second Life is creating advertising boards and a virtual community for Chinese users and companies. However, even with the well laid out plan, Second Life has not yet met with success in the Chinese Market. One report of Qianjia shows that Chinese companies express weak interest in conducting business via this new platform[**]. The most critical reason is that few Chinese users are actually adopting Second Life for communication and real business. For example, in 2006, Shenzhen Development Bank (SDB) tried to open a "virtual bank" in Second Life, but they gave up after 2 months. They claimed that no one really accessed their virtual bank during this period. Based on the report of Qianjia, by the end of July 2007, there were only 4,544 Chinese users very active in Second Life, accounting for 0.92% of avatar count, as illustrated in Table 1. Most Chinese users registered their account in Second Life but rarely accessed it. The results show that Second Life has not replicated its successful model in western countries to the Chinese market. Thus, what will attract the acceptance of Chinese users to join the emerging technology, and what will increase corporate attention to virtual worlds in the Chinese Market.

Table 1 Top Countries by Active User Counts (adapted from qianjia.com)

Rank	Country	Active Avatar Count	% of Avatar Count	Total Hours	% of Total Hrs
1	United States	130928	26.45%	6,624,984.92	35.02%
2	Germany	45107	9.11%	2,192,576.15	11.59%
3	Brazil	36385	7.35%	733,757.62	3.88%
4	United Kingdom	35423	7.16%	1,242,005.38	6.57%
5	France	33792	6.83%	1,292,405.75	6.83%
6	Japan	27040	5.46%	947,155.55	5.01%
7	Italy	27035	5.46%	776,721.35	4.11%
8	Spain	21207	4.28%	754,272.75	3.99%
…	…	…	…	…	…
15	China	4544	0.92%	172,340.03	0.91%

[‡] Gartner Group, April 2007, http://www.gartner.com/it/page.jsp?id=503861

[§] China Internet Network Information Center, December 2007, http://www.cnnic.cn

[**] QianJia Second Life Insights, http://www.qianjia.com

Some comparisons of major players in the Internet business in China suggest that the platforms based on the "western model" may not easily succeed in China, although some local competitors will eventually succeed. For example, in the Chinese C2C market, eBay-China was defeated by a local competitor-TaoBao in 2006 [2]. In China, the external environment and user habits are vastly different compared to that of western counties. Chinese user adoption of virtual worlds is also influenced by their special environmental factors. As a western model based virtual world planning business operations in China, Second Life may also face challenges: 1) Government policy: For example, the Chinese government has not accepted virtual currency exchanges. This policy may reduce the usefulness of the "currency exchange system" of Second Life; 2) Hardware environment: The network environment in most places of China may not support high speed network requirements of Second Life; 3) Cultural barriers: The lack of awareness of culture differences between western users and Chinese users may lead to the high failure rate of foreign Internet business in China.

Obviously, foreign virtual worlds should adopt innovative strategies to impact on user acceptance behavior in China. In contrast to the "western model" of Second Life, Chinese local virtual worlds have developed some innovative solutions to suit the Chinese environments. In this regard, Second Life can learn from the role model of these major local competitors. An extremely well known Chinese virtual worlds is HiPiHi (www.hipihi.com), a Beijing-based 3D Virtual World founded in 2005. Currently with 40,000 registered users, HiPiHi is the biggest virtual world in China, focusing on the market of Chinese young people. It has provided some rather innovative strategies to suit the Chinese Internet environments and user culture, and received some very positive responses from users [3]. The emergence of HiPiHi has received attention and recognition from world famous enterprises, such as P&G, which have provided 3D advertising through the platform of HiPiHi. In November 2007, Intel-China became the first IT enterprise inhabitant in HiPiHi, and established an "Intel island" for initiating usage experience of their products[tt]. However, it is not at all clear which strategies of Second Life and HiPiHi are superior, and how these different strategies impact on user acceptance in the Chinese environment. To fill this gap, this chapter conducts an explorative study to compare the different IT strategies between HiPiHi and Second Life, and investigates the following research questions: 1) Which strategies are different between Second Life and HiPiHi? 2) How do these different strategies impact on user acceptance behavior in China? 3) Are there any other important strategies that should be promoted on which the two virtual worlds have not yet focused?

The remainder of the chapter is organized as follows. In section 2, we review the emergence of virtual worlds and introduce Second Life and HiPiHi. In section 3, we borrow the technology acceptance model (TAM) as a guideline for this study and provide our theoretical framework of comparison. In section 4 and 5, the research approach of comparison is introduced. These comparisons are supplemented with information gleaned from observations, logs from websites and

---

[tt]http://www.intel.com/cd/corporate/pressroom/apac/zho/date/2007/377304.htm

third party reports. Finally, we project how the emerging 3D virtual world is likely to develop in China.

2 Literature Review

2.1 The Emergence of Virtual Worlds

2.1.1 From Web 1.0 to Web 3.D

The Internet-based business has been through several stages so far. It started in the mid 1990s with a static presentation of content on web pages and the use of what is known as Web 1.0. This was followed by the introduction of social network technology, i.e., Weblogs, Wikis, and RSS feeds. Well known websites for these applications are Skype, Youtube, Myspace and Facebook. These technologies are also known as Web 2.0, providing people with new channels and more rich media in which to communicate and collaborate. Most recently, the emergence of 3D virtual worlds, now known as Web 3.D, has created a new stage of communication with an even higher level of interaction, complexity, and value creation. Web 3.D is the Internet-based virtual space, where people can create their own 3D 'virtual' personalities. One key feature of Web 3.D applications is the use of avatars, which can help address the lack of awareness. Unlike computer games, Web 3.D enables participants to construct their own personality (avatars) through which they interact with other people. People can design their own virtual characteristics and appearance including body proportions, facial features, clothing, and skin color. Millions of people with avatars, establish friendships, buy and sell virtual assets, and form large social networks.

Web 3.D has the potential of profoundly impacting the way people interact and conduct business, the best known example of which is Second Life. Figure 1 outlines the evolution over time from Web 1.0 to Web 3.D [4]; the figure shows the increased number of users from Web 1.0 to Web 2.0, and the projected even greater usage of Virtual Worlds by 2010.

2.1.2 Definition of Virtual World

There are many synonyms for virtual world, such as "Multi User Virtual Environment" [1], "Web 3.D" [5], and "3D World" [6]. In this study, we define virtual world as a computer-based simulated environment intended for its users to inhabit and interact via avatars. Virtual worlds are not just online 3D games, as there are no levels, no scores and there is no "game over." They exist in real time where individuals communicate, cooperate and collaborate with one other, like in real world. It can be assumed that the behavior of the users is very similar to real world behavior. In virtual worlds, users can build a business, establish a social club, marry a partner, and use virtual money to purchase property.

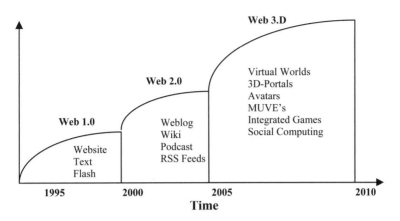

Figure 1 From Web 1.0 to Web 3.D (adapted from Hayes [4])

2.1.3 History of Virtual World

Virtual worlds are not a recent development. In 1978, the first 2D MUD (multi-user dungeon) was developed. Despite some early experiments in 1980s, the first 3D virtual world, "Alpha World," was introduced in 1995. It provided users with building tools to enable users to create required content [7]. A large number of users participated and exhibited great creativity. Unfortunately, neither social nor economic forces existed in this world to reward the creation and maintenance of large-scale and compelling content. The population waned and thus the business failed by 1999 [8].

In the early 2000s, some new virtual worlds emerged called "third generation of virtual worlds" [6]. In 2003, "Second Life" and "There" were launched; in 2007, "Multiverse" was launched [7]. Among these 3D Worlds, Second Life is the better known. Registrations in Second Life are growing rapidly, with the majority of members located in the US, Canada and the UK. Many companies have noted the business opportunities available on the site and have already set up residence in Second Life.

2.2 History of Second Life

Second Life was founded by Linden Lab in 2003. At first glance, Second Life seems strange as it has no predefined goals or objectives. Some people were concerned that it appeared to lack the challenges that provide positive feelings of accomplishment enjoyed from such a typical game environment. When it was first launched, it simulated several square kilometers, there were less than 1000 registered users, and it had no measurable economy. However, with the increased bandwidth and higher computing speed, the numbers of users grew very fast. Based on Linden Lab's research data from August 2006 and March 2007, the daily average residents online increased from 6,000 to 24,000 and total residence exploded from 450,000 to 4 million. By December 2007, there were almost 11 million inhabitants on Second Life. Forecasts using fitted second-degree polynomial trends project a daily average of 150,000 residents online and 25 million total residences in 2008. In 2007, the annual GDP of Second Life was equivalent to US$500 million.

2.3 History of HiPiHi

HiPiHi World was launched in July 2005 and is considered to be one the most famous virtual worlds in Mainland China. HiPiHi was founded by Hui Xu and Xinhua Lu, both Internet entrepreneurs with significant web experience. HiPiHi is pronounced as "HappyHi." There are 3 characters "i" in this word (the English equivalent of "i" would be "me") and with these three characters one can construct a community, society and virtual world. While most users in Mainland China treat HiPiHi as another 3D game, the founders aimed to build a complete 3D visual background to reflect the different environments of the real world. It provides users with a powerful creation engine and tools that allow users to create their own world step by step. Before the full public beta, they will invite around 10,000 users to be the original residents of the HiPiHi world.

After private tests and development for 14 month, in March 2007, HiPiHi provided its full public beta. From March 2007 to December 2007 it had five phases that reflect Chinese mythical events [9]. In the introduction of the English version, these phases also correspond to the Biblical story of God's creation of the world in 7 days[‡‡]. They are:

- Phase 1 (19 March 2007): In the beginning God created heaven and the earth: The tools for rendering the terrain, hills, fields, terraces, water, flora, etc., are introduced.
- Phase 2 (22 April 2007): God created Adam and Eve and the human race using the image of Himself: The tools for creating more detailed avatars are introduced.
- Phase 3 (25 June 2007): God created all earthly things: The tools for creating all sorts of objects are introduced.
- Phase 4 (August 2007): The Mirage: The economic system and social system are established.
- Phase 5 (Fall 2007): The formal version was opened to public. By December 2007, HiPiHi already had almost 40,000 users.

[‡‡] "What is HiPiHi", http://www.hipihi.com/index_english.html

3. Theoretical Background:

3.1 Technology Acceptance Model (TAM)

In this study, we focus on Chinese users' acceptance of Virtual World. We first incorporate core constructs of the Technology Acceptance Model (TAM) as our guiding theory. TAM was developed by Davis [10], based on the Theory of Reasoned Action (TRA) and illustrated in Figure 2.

In the model of Davis [10], there are two core constructs influencing users' technology acceptance behavior: perceived usefulness (PU) and perceived ease of use (PEOU). As the best known theory in information systems, TAM has been used extensively for understanding user acceptance of different information technology, e.g., groupware acceptance [11], online shopping [12, 13], online games adoption [14], enterprise systems adoption [15], and mobile games acceptance [16]. Despite the extensive uses of TAM, recently researchers suggest that the two dimensions are too narrow and shine light on only a part of technology acceptance and use. Further, they believe that more factors from other aspects (such as emotional reactions and social factors) should be included to explain acceptance more consistently and comprehensively [17, 18]. Thus, some new factors have been proposed to better explain the acceptance of IT applications. For example, Venkatesh et al. [19] who proposed TAM2 include, a new factor with subject norms (SN), which is the degree of individual perceptions of external pressures when performing the behavior. TAM2 is widely adopted in studies of social network software. In the online entertainment field, some researchers have also proposed "perceived enjoyment" (PEN) of playing as the intrinsic motivation of user acceptance [14, 16]. Based on the definition of virtual world, it provides a virtual society in which people can work and play. It has the characteristics of social network software and online entertainment. Thus, we propose our general model of user acceptance of virtual worlds, as illustrated in Figure 3.

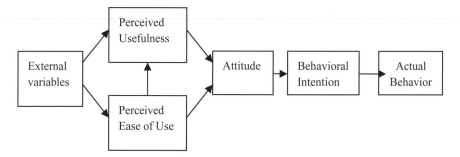

Figure 2 Technology Acceptance Model [10]

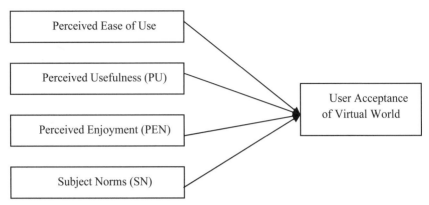

Figure 3 Determinants of Users Acceptance of Virtual World

Based on this model, there are four dimensions of user acceptance of virtual worlds. We develop measures for each dimension.

A. **Perceived Ease of Use (PEOU):** PEOU is "the extent to which a person believes that using a particular technology will enhance job performance" [10]. The following three measures are factors affecting levels of PEOU based on literature [10]. PEOU is measured by the extent to which these factors are present or not.

Skillfulness:	Whether it is easy for users to become skillful as using Second Life (or HiPiHi).
Quickness:	Whether it is quick for users to learn to use Second Life (or HiPiHi) to interact.
Learning:	Whether learning to use Second Life (or HiPiHi) is easy for users.

B. **Perceived Usefulness (PU):** PU is "the degree to which a person believes that using the system will be free from effort" [10]. The following measures are factors affecting levels of PU based on the literature (e.g. Davis 1989). PU is measured by the extent to which these factors are present or not.

Efficiency:	Whether users enhance work efficiency by using Second Life (or HiPiHi). For example, whether users could reduce cost by doing business via the platform.
Effectiveness:	Whether Second Life (or HiPiHi) enhances user effectiveness or performance. For example, whether they can earn real money in it.

C. **Perceived Enjoyment (PEN):** PEN is the extent to which the activity in question is perceived to be enjoyable, apart from any performance consequences or utilitarian considerations [13]. The following three measures are factors affecting levels of PEN based on the literature [20]. PEN is measured by the extent to which these factors are present or not.

Enjoyable:	Whether users find using Second Life (or HiPiHi) to be enjoyable.
Pleasant:	Whether the actual process of using Second Life (or HiPiHi) is pleasant.
Fun:	Whether users have fun using Second Life (or HiPiHi).

D. **Subject Norms (SN):** SN is the degree of individual perception of external pressures that one should perform the behavior [19]. The following two measures are factors affecting levels of SN based on the literature [19]. SN is measured by the extent to which these factors are present or not.

Influencing People:	Whether people who influence user behavior believe they can use Second Life (or HiPiHi).
Important People:	Whether people who are important to users think that they can use Second Life (or HiPiHi).

3.2 Strategies of Virtual Worlds

There are several strategies which virtual worlds can provide to attract user acceptance. The story of Second Life provide three innovative strategies for success since it: 1) creates a new 3D technology platform to support virtual communication (technology solution), 2) promotes innovative "free creation" game model (game model); and 3) provides "Linden dollar exchange system" (business model). However, when Second Life is applied to China, these strategies should be adapted to suit the Chinese environment. Moreover, the CEO of HiPiHi also claimed that the culture of virtual worlds should be proactively promoted to suit the local Chinese culture. In this regard, how to promote a culture of virtual worlds to suit Chinese users' personal values becomes a critical strategy. Thus, we consider comparing four types of strategies of virtual worlds as following:

A. **Technology Solution (TS):** The TS strategy is how Second Life (or HiPiHi) develops technology approach and solutions to suit Chinese network or hardware environment. There are four sub-strategies of TS:

Interface:	By which user adopts to play and communicate with others.
Network:	The network requirement to run the game smoothly.
User Hardware:	The hardware (e.g., CPU) requirements of user to run the game.
Server Requirement:	The number of servers is required to support one million on-line users in the same time.

B.   Business Model (BM): The BM strategy is how Second Life (or HiPiHi) supports virtual business in the game. There are at least two sub-strategies of BM:

Virtual Property Policy:	How Second Life (or HiPiHi) protects virtual property.
Exchange System:	How users exchange their virtual currencies in the game.

C.   Game Model (GM): The GM strategy is how to support users to work and play in Second Life (or HiPiHi). There are three sub-strategies of GM:

Social Network:	How the game promotes social networks among the users.
Creation Model:	How much complexity for users to create virtual products.
Task Orientation:	How much freedom for users playing in the game.

D.   Virtual World Culture (VWC): VWC strategy is how Second Life (or HiPiHi) promotes virtual culture in the game to suit the Chinese environment and users' personal values. There are at least two sub-strategies of VWC:

Virtual Society Rules:	How Second Life (or HiPiHi) develops its social rules.
Extent of Virtuality:	How Second Life (or HiPiHi) promotes the spirit of virtual worlds. How much the extent of virtuality of the platform? Is it for pure entertainment or mixed with work?

4 Research Approach

In this research, we investigated how the four strategies of virtual worlds (technology solution, business model, game model and virtual world culture) impacted on four determinants of user acceptance behavior (perceived of ease of use, perceived usefulness, perceived enjoyment and subject norms) in the Chinese environment. A world renowned virtual world (Second Life) and a local competitor (HiPiHi) were chosen in order to compare their strategies and possible impacts on user behaviors. The comparison was supported by secondary data collected from a variety of sources: 1) direct observations in Second Life and HiPiHi for nearly three months from September to December 2007; 2) Records of user comments from two well known online forums of Second Life (www.d2life.net) and HiPiHi (forums.hipihi.com); 3) Linden research white paper [21]; and 4) reports from third party research groups regarding Chinese virtual worlds market (e.g., blog.zhaoke.com). The theoretical framework of comparison is illustrated in Figure 4.

In our comparison analysis, we use the form of matrices to present the information systematically to the reader, and enable the identification of coding procedures to reduce information of categories [22].

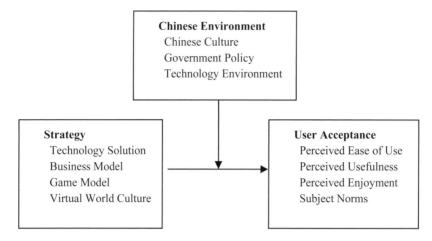

Figure 4 Theoretical Framework of Comparison

The stage of the coding process is shown as following:

- Read text recorded from observation and logs
- Divide text into segments of information
- Code Segments
- Refine codes
- Collapse codes into themes

For ease of recording the comparison results, we designed a coding scheme to guide the coding process, as illustrated in Table 2. The comparison results are displayed in matrices and charts.

Table 2 Classification for Coding of Comparison

Construct/Concept	Code	Measure	Sub-Code
1. Perceived Ease of Use	PEOU	Skillfulness	PEOU-SKI-XX
		Quickness	PEOU-QUI-XX
		Learning	PEOU-LEA-XX
2. Perceived Usefulness	PU	Effectiveness	PU-EFE-XX
		Efficiency	PU-EFI-XX
3. Perceived Enjoyment	PEN	Enjoyable	PEN-ENJ-XX
		Pleasant	PEN-PLE-XX
		Fun	PEN-FUN-XX
4. Subject Norms	SN	Influencing People	SN-INP-XX
		Important People	SN-IMP-XX

XX=Related Strategies (Technology Solution, Business Model, Game Model and Virtual World Culture)

5 Comparison between Second Life and HiPiHi:

5.1 Technology Solution (TS) Comparison

5.1.1 Interface

Second Life:
   The interface is the important media in human computer interaction. People can operate avatars, create new buildings and communicate with others via the interface. Based on comments from online forums regarding interface, there are two core considerations about the interface of Second Life: Language and complexity. First, the interface of Second Life is difficult for Chinese users to _learn_. Second Life has multi-language versions of interface. It has also developed a Chinese version of interface which can be downloaded from the website. However, the mixed version with different languages may cause problems for users to learn. For example, in the version of "Secondlife1.13.3.x", there are many Japanese words in the Chinese interface. These bugs negatively impact on Chinese users' understanding of functions. Second, Second Life has at least 10 categories with 5-6 functions in each category. Without Chinese language guidelines, the complex interface may lead to difficulties for Chinese users to become _skillful_, that is, it takes several hours to become skillful. One user in "d2life" complained that "_I downloaded Second Life and accessed it; however I find there are too many windows in the interface. I don't know how to use some basic functions to let my avatars run_".

HiPiHi:
   Contrary to the complex interface of Second Life, HiPiHi's interface is easier to learn and use. First, HiPiHi only has two languages: Chinese and English. The HiPiHi support team also provides a Chinese version of guidelines to new users with which people can _learn_ to use the functions more easily. Also, HiPiHi reduces the number of categories on the interface to help beginners to become _skillful_ more quickly. Based on observation, the simple style of interface may save users' time, and enhance the perception of ease of use.

5.1.2 Network

Second Life:
   Another challenge of Second Life in China is network speed. Both Second Life and HiPiHi are 3D virtual worlds that require high speed network to support running the game smoothly. One attractive function of Second Life is its voice chatting system, which can support users chatting with each other. Second Life believes that the system will bring rich media to users to communicate more _quickly_. However, based on the technology report of Linden Lab, the lowest requirement

of network speed is 300Kbps for running Second Life[§§]. With the increasing bandwidth, the increased network speed of USA to 2Mbps supports using Second Life for *quick* communication. However, the network environment in Mainland China may not support Second Life very well. First, the average network speed in Mainland China of 512Kbps may not support the higher application of Second Life, such as virtual conference. Second, the network in Mainland China is divided into two parts which belong to different companies: Telecom and CNC Net. The bottleneck between these two networks may lead to decreased communication between users in different networks. In this network environment, people may not adopt the voice chatting system due to the low voice quality.

HiPiHi:

HiPiHi provides the technology solution for adapting the special Chinese network environment. For example, based on the report of internal tests, the average network requirements for running HiPiHi is only 100Kbps, which can be supported in most parts of China. Considering the lower speed of communication between the two networks, HiPiHi provides two groups servers in different networks. If users complain about low speed, they can help users to change their virtual lands to other networks. At this time, HiPiHi can only support chatting by text which may reduce the *quickness* for users to interact. HiPiHi has also announced their plan to develop a voice chatting system in the near future. With an innovative technology solution for the Chinese network environment, it may enhance the user communicating more *quickly* in the long run.

5.1.3 User Hardware:

Both Second Life and HiPiHi have high requirements of hardware. Users must pay more for the CPU, memory and Video Card. Compared to some web 2.0 applications (e.g., MSN, weblog), virtual worlds cost users more for hardware investment. Based on the observation from the online forums, some Chinese users complain about the *higher cost* of hardware.

5.1.4 Server Requirement

Second Life:

According to the Fittkau & Maass' report[***], the bottleneck of Second Life development is a higher technology solution for servers. Based on the technology solution of Second Life, one server can only support 64 acre virtual lands. At the end of November 2006, Second Life had provided more than 3,000 servers to support millions of online users in 800 square kilometers (about two-thirds of Hong Kong). If Second Life wants to increase the number of users in Mainland China, it

---

[§§] Linden Lab Research, http://www.secondlife.com/whatis
[***] Fittkau&Maass's Second Life Report, http://www.handelsblatt.com

has to apply more servers. The increased costs will lead to the *higher prices for service* (e.g., virtual lands) to Chinese users.

HiPiHi:

As the newly launched virtual world, HiPiHi has advantages in technology solutions. The advanced technology solution for servers can reduce the cost of servers, and reduce user cost. At the end of December 2007, HiPiHi had no more than 100 servers to support online users and even then it had the potential ability to support many more users. Based on observation, the cost of servers distributed to each user can be accepted by users. The comparison results are summarized in Table 3. For example, "(PEOU-LEA)-" under "Second Life" indicates that the "Interface" strategy of Second Life may have a negative impact on the dimension "learning (QUI)" of user "perceived ease of use(PEOU)" in the Chinese environment.

Table 3 Comparison Results of TS Impact

		Second Life	HiPiHi
	Interface	(PEOU-LEA)-	(PEOU-LEA)+
		(PEOU-SKI)-	(PEOU-SKI)+
Technology Solution (TS)	Network	(PEOU-QUI)-	(PEOU-QUI)+
	User Hardware	(PU-EFI)-	(PU-EFI)-
	Server Requirement	(PU-EFI)-	(PU-EFI)+

5.2 Business Model (BM) Comparison

5.2.1 Virtual Property Policy

One characteristic of virtual worlds is that users can freely create intellectual products. Both Second Life and HiPiHi have provided policies to ensure users to have full rights to their intellectual property with their virtual product. Thus, users have another way of enhancing their properties. Based on several reports of virtual worlds, e.g. [9], the rights of virtual property will positively impact on the users' *perception of effectiveness* on using virtual worlds.

5.2.2 Exchange System

Second Life:

Can virtual properties be exchanged for real money? The most attractive selling point of Second Life is its "exchange system" between virtual currency (Linden dollar) and real money (e.g., US dollars). In USA, 20 Linden dollars can be exchanged for 1 US dollar legally through the exchange system in Second Life. This exchange system ensures that the users can work, conduct business and earn real money through this new platform. For example, Anshe Chung became the first real millionaire in Second Life. She registered a company in Second Life (http://www.anshechung.com). In this virtual world she buys virtual land, designs buildings and sells them for higher prices. The legend of Anshe Chung has received global attention. More and more people register in Second Life with the dream of becoming the second Anshe Chung. However, the same business model may not be copied in Mainland China due to the government policy. The application of Second Life in China faces the challenge that its exchange system is illegal in China. The finance market of China has not fully opened, and the central government is concerned that the free exchange of virtual currency may destroy the real finance market in Mainland China. Recently, the central government provided a formal notice forbidding the exchange between virtual currency and real money. This is a challenge to Second Life since it is difficult to attract people to use this platform *without opportunities to earn real money*.

HiPiHI:

As the local competitor who is more familiar with Chinese policy, the HiPiHi's business model may give some guidelines to Second Life. The management team of HiPiHi designed a more *flexible business model* to fit the Chinese policy. Currently, HiPiHi does not promote illegal exchanges between virtual currency and RMB. Alternatively, it provides point cards of small denominations. Users can exchange virtual properties with lower prices to these point cards legally. Then, HiPiHi also cooperates with some C2C platforms (e.g., Paypal and TaoBao) to support exchanges with higher prices in the next stage. Finally, with the release of the government's policy, HiPiHi will establish the exchange system as in Second Life to support freely exchange. This flexible business model has step by step support for the user requirements of conducting business in different stages. The comparison results are summarized in Table 4.

Table 4 Comparison Results of BM Impact

		Second Life	HiPiHi
Business Model (BM)	Virtual Property Policy	(PU-EFE)+	(PU-EFE)+
	Exchange System	(PU-EFE)-	(PU-EFE)+

5.3 Game Model (GM) Comparison

5.3.1 Social Network

Second Life:

From 2003 to 2007, Second Life took almost five years to establish its society. Currently, millions of people live in Second Life. Most inhabitants are separated by distance, and they can "teleport" to different places when they want to join in a conference and communicate with others. However, the society of Chinese people tends to develop slowly in this "separated living" style. Based on Hofstede's cultural dimension theory, Chinese people are more collectivistic, while western people are more individualistic [23]. Many Chinese users complain that the first place they lived was desolate and there were no other Chinese people online. Even if there is a "Chinese Town" in Second Life; it may be rare for people to visit it if there are no valuable social events in it.

HiPiHi:

Contrary to the living style where people live separately, HiPiHi promotes a "centralized society." It opens living regions step by step. At first, people live together in a small region, and then as the population grows, HiPiHi will open other regions. In this way, people can establish their social network and interact with others more *efficiently*. Based on observation, from September to December 2007, the society in HiPiHi increased rapidly. For example, inhabitants have taken several parties in the society. It is believed that the "centralized" model may help the society of Chinese users to gain critical mass.

5.3.2 Creation Model

Second Life:

Second Life promotes "free creation." Linden Lab developed four creation systems: 3D product design, figure design, land edit, and higher language coding system-LSL (Linden Script Language). With the LSL, people can design the most amazing things that they can imagine. Thus, some people call Second Life a "dream land" where people can *enjoy* a different life. Users can find new figures every time they access it. However, it requires *longer time to learn* to use LSL. Especially for Chinese people who cannot read English materials, it is more difficult for them to use LSL to design 3D products.

HiPiHi:

HiPiHi has more focus on easy creation. It provides essential modules and colors which are easy to *learn* and in which to become *skillful*. Users can learn to use it to create their buildings, figures and clothes very easily and quickly. However, as the population increases, more and more similar buildings and figures exist in the HiPiHi. Sometimes, you can meet people with the same face or the same clothes; people can also be talking at the same time. The potential challenge of HiPiHi is that it *may not hold people's interest* in the long run. How to ensure that the personalities of users are the important issue in the development of HiPiHi remains a question.

5.3.3 Task Orientation

Second Life:

In the development of Second Life, users' early creation leads to more and more user registrations. Second Life promotes free creation and individualism. Thus, there are few guidelines and tasks to teach new users how to work and play in this world. However, in China, the fact is that "requirements" lead to creation. As the report of Qianjia[2] indicates, many companies have established virtual stores in Second Life and then encourage people to visit them. Most Chinese users register in Second Life for advertising. However, when they access the virtual world, they lose their way and do not know what they should do next. Many people complain that shopping in the virtual stores of Second Life is *inefficient*.

HiPiHi:

HiPiHi, to some extent, adopts successful experience of some 3D online games (e.g., World of War). It provides a detailed guideline to the world. When new users arrive in the central place, there is NPC to provide guidelines to play. HiPiHi even cooperates with some companies to provide some tasks to users. For example, users may be given a task of visiting an Intel virtual store to see several advertisements, after which they will be paid with point cards. In the first stage of HiPiHi, providing tasks to train users can help them to obtain *real benefits* and enhance their *efficiency* to use the platform. The comparison results are summarized in Table 5.

Table 5 Comparison Results of GM Impact

		Second Life	HiPiHi
	Social Network	(PU-EFI)-	(PU-EFI)+
		(PEN)+	(PEN)-
Game Model (GM)	Creation Model	(PEOU-LEA)-	(PEOU-LEA)+
		(PEOU-SKI)-	(PEOU-SKI)+
	Task Orientation	(PU-EFI)-	(PU-EFI)+
			(PU-EFE)+

5.4 Virtual World Culture (VWC) Comparison

5.4.1 Virtual Society Rules

Second Life:

In Second Life, the society role is somewhat loose. Nowadays, the top two industries in Second Life are gambling and sex. Millions of users spend a lot of time on gambling and virtual sex. However, these two industries are illegal in Mainland China. If Second Life (China) does not provide some rules to limit Chinese users to visit these two industries, it may be prohibited by the *government*. Moreover, the *parents* who have direct influence on young users may view Second Life as a risqué game and forbid their children to access this game.

HiPiHi:

HiPiHi is now inviting users and experts in different fields to help them design the rules. For example, in HiPiHi, users are encouraged to use polite words. These rules can help HiPiHi obtain the appreciation from the *government*.

5.4.2 Extent of Virtuality

Inhabitants in Second Life establish their own culture, e.g., special language in communication. However, the social culture of Second Life (China) and HiPiHi are ambiguous now. The only one we have observed is that both platforms emphasize the business application in the Chinese market, except for entertainment. It is too early to observe the cultural differences and how their culture impacts on user behavior. The comparison results are summarized in Table 6.

Table 6 Comparison Results of VWC Impact

		Second Life	HiPiHi
Virtual World Culture(VWC)	Virtual Society Rules	(SN-INP)- (SN-IMP)-	(SN-INP)+
	Extent of Virtuality	N/E	N/E

Note: N/E is non significant findings from comparison

6. Discussion

There are several reasons why Second Life is so successful in the world. It is believed that Second Life has at least 3 characteristics: 1) convergence of social networking and content creation, 2) immersive networked 3D environment, and 3) inclusion of elementary economic principles [24]. According to the CEO of Linden Lab, the success of Second Life is due to the fact that it offers a set of capabilities or strategies which 1) provide different ways superior to the real world, 2) provide tools that enable people to create new things, 3) allow residents to own intellectual property rights to their creations and sell them[†††].

[†††] Interview to Philip Rosedale, .Net Magazine, 2 August 2007, http://www.netmag.co.uk/zine/discover-interview/philip-rosedale

At first glance, HiPiHi is very similar to Second Life, such as the 3D graphics interface. However, it is believed that HiPiHi is not just a copycat of Second Life. The virtual world is not just a 3D environment, but a complicated social system including the property policy, financial policy, social culture, etc. As a virtual world born in China, the developers hope HiPiHi can suit the Chinese environment and embrace Chinese culture.

Unlike the "western model" of Second Life, HiPiHi claims that it focuses on the "eastern model" of user behavior and provides some strategies accordingly. For example, HiPiHi management team is very experienced in the Chinese market, and claims that the "business models similar to those employed by 2D sites can also be applied in 3D" [3]. The income of HiPiHi users includes: selling land, advertising boards, and a range of branded products incorporated within the world; however, users must share part of their income with HiPiHi. At the same time, the market is taking HiPiHi seriously. In the test period, they had been approached by the marketing departments of many foreign and Chinese companies looking to become involved. From August 2007 to December 2007, the company closed investments involving companies and individuals from the United States, Japan and Singapore for almost $10 million, and there may be further rounds in the future.

Are there some differences in the strategies of HiPiHi and Second Life? Which strategies actually enable Chinese users to accept Virtual Worlds? And, which Virtual World will succeed in the long run in the Chinese market? In section 5, we compared the different strategies between these two cases, and investigated how these strategies impact on Chinese user acceptance of Virtual Worlds. The comparison of different strategies is illustrated in Table 7.

Table 7 Different Strategies between Second Life and HiPiHi

	Second Life	HiPiHi
Technology Solution(TS)	1. Multi-language Version 2. Complex Functions 3. Higher Requirement of network speed and number of servers	1. Chinese Version 2. Simple Functions 3. Low requirement of network speed and servers
Business Model (BM)	1. Virtual Currency Exchange System	1. More flexible exchanging strategy
Game Model (GM)	1. Separating inhabits 2. Higher freedom of creation system (LSL) 3. Rare tasks	1. Centralizing inhabits 2. Simple creation system 3. Providing tasks to new users
Virtual World Culture(VWC)	1. Higher freedom in society rules	1. Forbidding sex and gamble

In technology solution, Second Life may face some problems in its application in China. First, the complex interface may reduce the Chinese users' perception of ease of use. Second, its high requirements of hardware and servers may increase the cost of Chinese users who adopt this platform. The most serious problem is that the Chinese network speed cannot support Second Life smoothly. Considering these bottlenecks, Second Life (China) may learn from HiPiHi who has applied some innovation technology solutions to solve problems.

In the business model, Second Life should be aware that the Chinese government forbids exchanges between virtual currency and RMB. With this policy environment, there may be a reduced users' perception of usefulness on this platform without a legal exchange system unless. HiPiHi provides a better way by providing a flexible business model where users use point cards and adopt a third party C2C platform to exchange their virtual properties.

In the Game model, Second Life promotes "individualism" and "free creation," while HiPiHi encourages "collectivism" and "task orientation." Based on the observation, the impact of the two strategies on user acceptance is like "double-edge swords". First, the high freedom of the creation system of Second Life enhances the users' enjoyment, while the rare guidelines may reduce the efficiency of using this platform for work and play. Second, the simple systems and task orientation of HiPiHi ensure the efficiency of users, but a too simple creation system may reduce users' interest in the long run. In the Chinese environment, the game model should be adapted to better balance the "efficiency" and "freedom."

In the virtual world culture, the strategies of both virtual worlds are currently ambiguous. In fact, the greatest challenge to the Chinese virtual world is how to promote a culture to fit the Chinese local culture. Another case regarding the success of Habbo (a 2D virtual world) may give us some enlightenment. Compared to 3D virtual worlds, Habbo has many disadvantages, for example, users cannot create tools freely. However, it was very popular in 2007. One of the factors to success is that Habbo emphasizes the virtuality and entertainment, but focuses on business application immediately. The spirit of Habbo fits the local culture of China. At least at this time, most Chinese people would like to access virtual space for "pure entertainment" and try to separate work and play significantly. There are many more studies that should be conducted to investigate the relationship between the virtual world culture and Chinese local environment, for example, how to define the 3D virtual world spirit to better fit Chinese culture.

Despite some significant findings from observation, the limitation of this study is that is lacks empirical evidence, because the two virtual worlds have conducted business in China for only a short time. As the development of 3D virtual worlds in China continues, empirical studies should be applied, and a more rigorous model of user acceptance of virtual world in China should be integrated.

7. Conclusion

In this research, we compared different strategies between Second Life and HiPiHi to investigate how these strategies potentially impact on user acceptance behavior, and sought to find which strategies would better suit the Chinese environment. Based on the reviews and comparison, there are three bottlenecks of Second Life in China: 1) High requirement of network speed, 2) illegal exchange system, and 3) game model without task orientation. As the local virtual world, HiPiHi may have a good approach to solving these problems. However, HiPiHi also faces bottlenecks, such as a too simple creation system reducing users' interest in the long run. At the current phase, both platforms have similar problems in that their society culture and spirit are ambiguous. The clear definition of local culture, such as how to balance "virtuality" and "reality", should receive more attention from Chinese virtual worlds.

References

[1] Fetscherin, M.Lattemann, C. (2007) User Acceptance of Virtual Worlds: An Explorative Study about Second Life Second Life Research Team. www.secondliferesearch.blogspot.com. Accessed 10 January 2008

[2] Ou, X.Davison, R. (2007) IM in C2C Markets: A Translucent Technology Designed to Facilitate Interactions. Proceedings of Twenty Eighth International Conference on Information Systems, Montreal, 2007

[3] Allen, D. (2007) New Virtual Worlds to Conquer in China. Asia Times

[4] Hayes, G. (2006) From Web 1.0 to Web 3.D. http://blog.kunzelnick.de/category/second-life/. Accessed 10 January 2008

[5] Baker, S. (2007) Web 3.0. BusinessWeek October 24:

[6] Terdiman, D. (2006) A Brief History of the Virtual World. CNET News.com November 9:

[7] Bainbridge, E. G. (2007) History of Virtual Worlds. http://www.avatarplanet.com/ history.php. Accessed 10 Jan 2008

[8] Ondrejka, C. (2005) Changing Realities: User Creation, Communication, and Innovation in Digitial Worlds Linden Lab.

[9] Zhu, M. (2007) Hipihi is opening the Door of 3D Experience. New Economics (in China)

[10] Davis, F. D. (1989) Perceived Usefulness, Perceived Ease of Use, and User Acceptance of Information Technology. MIS Quarterly 13: 319-340

[11] Lou, H., Luo, W., Strong, D. (2000) Perceived Critical Mass Effect on Groupware Acceptance. European Journal of Information Systems 9: 91-103

[12] Gefen, D., Karahanna, E., Straub, D. (2003) Trust and TAM in Online Shopping: An Integrated Model. MIS Quarterly 27: 51-90

[13] Koufaris, M. (2002) Applying the Technology Acceptance Model and Flow Theory to Online Consumer Behavior. Information Systems Research 13: 205-223

[14] Hsu, C. L.Lu, H. P. (2004) Why DO People Play On-line Games? An Extended TAM with Social Influences and Flow Experience. Informaton & Management 41: 853-868

[15] Hwang, Y. (2005) Investigating Enterprise Systems Adoption: Uncertainty Avoidance, Intrinsic Motivation, and the Technology Acceptance Model. European Journal of Information Systems 14: 150-161

[16] Ha, I., Yoon, Y., Choi, M. (2007) Determinants of Adoption of Mobile Games Under Mobile Broadband Wirelesss Access Environment. Information & Management 44: 276-286

[17] Legris, P., Ingham, J., Collerette, P. (2003) Why do People Use Information Technology? A Critical Review of the Technology Acceptance Model. Information & Management 40: 191-204

[18] Szajna, B. (1996) Empirical Evaluation of the Revised Technology Acceptance Model. Management Science 42: 85-92

[19] Venkatesh, V.Morris, M. (2000) Why Don't Men Ever Stop to Ask for Directions? Gender, Social Influence, and Their Role in Technology Acceptance and User Behavior. MIS Quarterly 24: 115-139

[20] Venkatesh, V., Morris, M. G., Davis, G. B., et al. (2003) User Acceptance of Informaiton Technology: Toward a Unified View. MIS Quarterly 27: 425-478

[21] LindenResearch (2006) What is Second Life? Secondlife.com. http://secondlife.com/whatis/. Accessed 10 January 2008

[22] Tesch, R. (1990) Qualitative Research: Analysis Types and Software Tools. Falmer, New York

[23] Hofstede, G. (1980) Culture's Consequences: International Difference in Work-related Values. Sage, Beverly Hills, CA

[24] Eliens, A., Feldberg, F., Konijn, E., et al. (2007) VU@Second Life- Creating a Virtual Community of Leaners. 1-8

Chapter 10
The Role of China in Requirements Research

Alan M. Davis[1] **and Ann M. Hickey**[1]

[1] College of Business, University of Colorado, USA

Abstract China was the first country to create gunpowder, the seismograph, the magnetic compass, steel, paper, and the suspension bridge. Yet in the twentieth century, China seemed to take a back seat to the West regarding the invention and exploitations of information technology (IT). This paper shows how China's role in one area within IT, namely requirements engineering (RE), is dramatically increasing in the past 15 years, and in fact, China has become one of the world's leaders in this area of research. This paper carefully examines the demographics of the entire corpus of RE publications and shows the roles played by authors from China. It discovers that although the demographics of RE research in Asia are very similar to the rest of the world, wide differences exist between individual Asian nations. Specifically, China's rate of growth in RE publication production far exceeds any other Asian country.

1 Introduction

In the third century B.C., the Chinese discovered the magnetic compass. In the second century B.C., the Chinese discovered that the introduction of oxygen into an iron blast furnace removed carbon from the iron and produced a super-hard material called steel. During the following 800 years, they invented the suspension bridge, a design still used today extensively; paper, which was used as clothing prior to its subsequent discovery (by the Chinese) as a writing medium; the seismograph, which they used to predict and record earthquakes; and, of course, gunpowder. In the thirteenth century, the Chinese were the first to use rockets. This incredibly inventive history was followed by relative quiescence. As computers were developed and applied in the West, China seemed to take a back seat, content to use time-tested techniques for science, agriculture, finance, transportation, and communication.

Only in the past 10-20 years has China rejuvenated its natural ability to invent. And part of that rejuvenation has been applied to exploitation and invention in the area of information technology (IT). This paper traces the role that China has played in the authorship of publications in one area of IT, namely, requirements

P.O. de Pablos, M.D. Lytras (eds.), *The China Information Technology Handbook*,   161
DOI: 10.1007/978-0-387-77743-6_10, © Springer Science+Business Media, LLC 2009

engineering (RE). Quality performance of requirements engineering is a prerequisite to effective exploitation of IT. Taking a leadership role in RE research and publication could foreshadow China's excellence in the performance of RE, which in turn could energize its IT industry.

Requirements engineering (aka requirements management [0] aka RE) comprises the set of disciplines involved with determining, analyzing, pruning, documenting, and validating the desires, wants, and needs of customers and users of an information system (IS), as well as the external behaviors of a solution system. If requirements engineering is performed poorly, or not at all, the likelihood is high that the resulting IS will fail to satisfy the needs of the intended customers and users. The fact that over half the IS built today fail to satisfy these needs [0] provides evidence that we are likely performing requirements engineering poorly. Given this common understanding, it is of no surprise that requirements engineering has become a major research area within academia, corporations, and governments. Countries that discover how to best perform RE will likely become the IT leaders of the future.

Since 1963, approximately 4,500 English-language books, journal articles, and conferences papers have been written to address the problems associated with RE 0]. Although publications in the more general disciplines of information systems [0-0] and software engineering [0-0] have been extensively studied, none have focused on national contributions. Only two publication studies have been performed within the sub-domain of IT called requirements engineering. The first was by Gervasi, et al. [0], where the authors carefully analyzed the publication trends in one long-running conference using lexical analysis; they provided no data on national trends. The second was by Davis, et al.0], where the authors performed demographic analysis of all RE publications between 1963 and 2006 for the world in aggregate, but focused neither on China nor Asia.

The goals of this chapter are:

- To show the contributions made by China to the RE publication corpus.
- To contrast the rate of RE publication growth within China in comparison to other countries.
- To contrast the average number of authors per publication in China and other Asian countries in contrast to the rest of the world.
- To contrast the degree of collaboration across countries and across organizations for Asian countries and the rest of the world.
- To show the contributions made by various continents, in general, and Asia, specifically, to RE publications.
- To contrast the rate of requirements engineering publication growth within Asia in comparison to the rest of the world.
- To highlight the top RE publication producing organizations in China, in Asia, and in the world.

This investigation is particularly interesting because requirements are traditionally written in natural language. Since many Asian countries use non-Roman characters for language representation, much non-Asian research in RE could be inapplicable to Asia. This would seem to imply that Asian countries would need to do their own unique natural language RE research. While this provides a unique research opportunity for Asian researchers, it may also prove to be a negative - at least in terms of recognition by the broader RE research community - if this research is only viewed of interest to local researchers and published in Asian-language journals. This highlights a critical issue for many Asian researchers. English appears to be the most widespread language used for presentation of IT research results. Since this paper addresses only English-language publications, it can be used by Asian researchers to track how their own research compares to that produced in English.

2 Research Method

Our research method is a quantitative meta-analysis (aka a descriptive literature review) 0] of RE publications from 1963 through 2007. The database of 4,559 publications used in this study derives from a series of events spanning 17 years [0]:

- *Original Paper Compilation.* In 1989, one of the authors compiled an extensive bibliography of requirements-related material for eventual publication in [0].
- *Updated Paper Compilation.* In 1992, that same author updated the extensive bibliography for publication in [0].
- *On-Line Availability.* Between 1992 and 1996, the authors continued to collect such references and commencing in 1996, posted them on-line at a site that came to be known as REQBIB [0]. That website has been publicly available since early 1996. It has received over 48,000 hits since that time.
- *Use of Online Databases.* Since 2001, we have been conducting regular online searches of IEEE Xplore, the ACM Digital Library, ScienceDirect, Kluwer Online, Engineering Village 2, Wiley Interscience, and SpringerLink to search for papers whose keywords, abstracts or titles contained any combination of the words "requirement," "specification," "prototype," "analysis," "scenario," "conceptual modeling," "enterprise modeling," and "use case." The titles and abstracts of the resulting list of papers were examined manually to determine relevance, and added to REQBIB as appropriate.
- *Use of Search Engines.* Since 2001, we have been conducting regular searches for "software" and any combination of the aforementioned keywords using Yahoo and Google search engines. When these searches uncovered publications that were relevant (based on titles only), they were added to REQBIB.
- *Incorporation of Visitor Feedback.* The website has always invited visitors to send us emails identifying any missing publications. Although such emails arrived weekly in the late 1990's, it has now become a mere trickle.
- *Internal Closure.* The lists of references contained within approximately 50% of the publications were examined manually for items not contained in the database. When new items were detected, they were added to the database. We

stopped after examining 50% of them because we were no longer detecting new entries, i.e., we had reached saturation.

- *Conversion to Database.* In late 2004, the REQBIB html file was translated automatically into an Access database, and from that point on, continued maintenance was conducted in parallel on both the html file (for public access) and the Access database (for our ongoing research). Although some requirements-related internal reports appear in REQBIB, these were omitted from the Access database.
- *Database Augmentation.* We also augmented the database derived from REQBIB with more complete information for analysis, including:
    - o Actual names (family name and given name initial) of all authors were added (REQBIB had included only the lead author's name when there were three or more authors).
    - o Affiliations of authors were determined by examining on-line and/or paper versions of all publications, and were entered manually. Note that this resulted in organizational affiliations of the authors at the time of publication, not at the current time.

The resulting database includes [0]:

- 4,559 RE publications spanning the years from 1963 through 2007. We determined the complete list of authors for 4,555, or 99.9%, of them.
- 5,153 unique authors of RE publications
- 9,292 unique assignments of authors to publications. We determined the affiliations of 8,963, or 96.5%, of the author-publication pairs.

Although we make no claims concerning 100% completeness of our database, we believe that it is (a) the largest ever collected for RE, and (b) complete enough to make the data analysis trends accurate.

After collecting this data, we proceeded to classify all publications into two categories:

- *Journal.* All peer-reviewed, traditional academic journals and magazines. Explicitly excluded are auxiliary articles from these journals, such as guest editor introductions, book reviews, etc.
- *Other.* All other papers, books, and book chapters, such as conference/workshop papers, trade press articles, auxiliary articles form peer-reviewed journals, and so on.
- and affiliations of all authors into three categories:
- *Academic.* Any university or college.
- *Industrial.* Any for-profit or not-for-profit company as well as their associated research facilities. Any consultant or consulting company.
- *Government.* Any federal, state, or city government.
- We also recorded the countries in which all such affiliations were located. Microsoft Access queries were written to extract the data in a consistent and repeatable manner. The results of these queries were then imported into Microsoft Excel in order to facilitate the creation of the graphs and tables shown in this paper.

3 Results for All RE Publications

3.1 General RE Publication Trends

A total of 4,559 publications were identified by our study. The earliest occurred in 1963 and the latest included in this study in 2007. Figure 1 shows how dramatic the growth of interest has been over this span of 45 years, with approximately half of them in just the past 6 years. Approximately 24% of the items were published in journals. 460 conferences and over 250 journals were represented. The most common venues for publication, in decreasing order, were IEEE's *International Conferences/Symposia on Requirements Engineering* (11.3%), INCOSE's *Annual Conference on Systems Engineering* (5.5%), Springer's *Requirements Engineering Journal* (4.0%), *The Requirements Engineering Workshop: Foundations for Software Quality* (REFSQ; 2.9%; this is the venue studied in the aforementioned study by Gervasi, et al. [0]), *IEEE Software* (2.5%), *IEEE Transactions on Software Engineering* (2.1%), IEEE's *Computer Software and Applications Conference* (COMPSAC; 2.1%), IEEE's *International Conference on Software Engineering* (1.9%), ACM *Software Engineering Notes* (1.5%), Butterworth's *Information and Software Technology* (1.4%), IEEE's *Hawaii International Conference on System Sciences* (1.2%), and Elsevier's *Journal of Systems and Software* (1.2%).

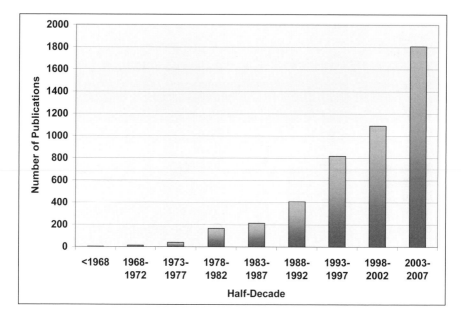

Figure 1 Quantity of Publications in Domain of Requirements Engineering

3.2 China's Role vs. World

Of the 4,559 publications, 2% originated from China. Although not remarkable by itself (after all, China represents 21% of the world's population), its rate of growth in the past few years has been phenomenal. To better understand this, let us examine the distribution of RE publications by country, followed by the rates of growth of RE publications by country.

Table 1a shows the top 20 RE producing countries of the world as of the end of 2007. China ranks #12, but is second to just one other Asian country, namely Japan, which has produced almost twice as many as China. However, let us examine RE production in these same 20 countries as of just 10 years ago, as shown in Table 1b. Here the trends become more evident. Notice than Japan's percentage contribution fell from 3.4% to 2.8%, while China's percentage contribution has risen from 0.8% to 2.0%.

Of these 20 countries, the largest rates of growth of RE publications appear in Finland, Spain, India, Australia, and China, in that order. The largest declines appear in USA, Israel, Japan, UK, and Norway.

Table 1 (a) Top 20 Requirements Engineering Publication-Producing Countries 1963-2007. (b) Year 1963-1997 Output for Same Countries Shown in (a)

USA	40.5%	USA	56.4%
UK	15.6%	UK	15.9%
Canada	7.2%	Canada	4.2%
Germany	6.3%	Germany	4.2%
Australia	4.0%	Australia	1.4%
Spain	3.3%	Spain	0.5%
Italy	3.1%	Italy	2.1%
Japan	2.8%	Japan	3.4%
France	2.7%	France	1.7%
Sweden	2.6%	Sweden	1.5%
Netherlands	2.4%	Netherlands	1.0%
China	2.0%	China	0.8%
Brazil	2.0%	Brazil	1.3%
Austria	1.7%	Austria	0.7%
Belgium	1.6%	Belgium	1.3%
Israel	1.2%	Israel	1.5%
Finland	1.1%	Finland	0.1%
S. Korea	1.1%	S. Korea	0.5%
India	1.0%	India	0.3%
Norway	0.9%	Norway	0.9%

3.3 China's Role vs. Other Asian Countries

Of the 4,559 RE publications, 372 were written by individuals from 10 Asian countries. To no surprise considering Table 1a, Figure 2 shows the leaders are Japan, China, and South Korea. In this and all subsequent figures, we have included Hong Kong and Macau within China's data to reflect their current status, even though they were protectorates of UK and Portugal during most of the period of this study.

Japan is clearly in the lead, but its production is slowing while China's is increasing. If the trend in the past decade continues, China will pass Japan in total RE publication production in just a decade. To see how Asian countries are producing RE publications as a function of time, Figure 3 shows the five leading Asian countries annual production of RE publications. Japan was obviously the Asian leader in RE in the early 1990's and did not return to this leadership role until the early 2000's. Since the early 2000's, China, India, and South Korea have made incredible gains on Japan. In fact, China has now passed Japan in RE publication production, not a huge surprise considering the fact that China's R&D expenditures surpassed Japan's in 2006 [0]. Meanwhile, India has passed Japan and South Korea; its rate of growth in R&D expenditures is considerably higher than South Korea's although their actual R&D expenditures for 2006 are fairly close [0]. To examine the relative rates of growth for these five Asian countries in more detail, we performed two additional analyses:

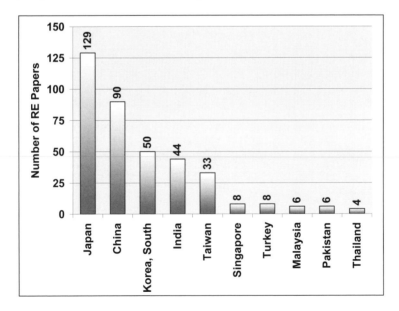

Figure 2 Relative Production of Requirements Engineering Publications by Asian Countries 1963-2007

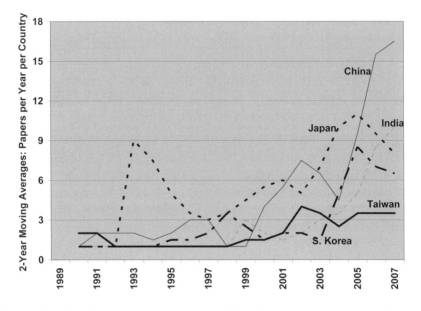

Figure 3 Two-Year Moving Averages for Quantity of RE Publications by 5 Leading Asian Countries

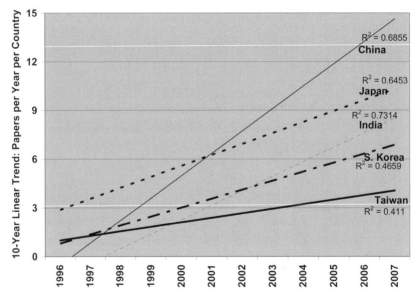

Figure 4 Ten-Year Linear Trend for Quantity of RE Publications by 5 Leading Asian Countries

- A linear regression on the actual annual RE production data for the decade in question. This analysis, shown in Figure 4 along with the R^2 values, shows that China has surpassed Japan, and India appears to have passed South Korea, but the R^2 values are too low to be conclusive (at least relative to the South Korea and Taiwan trends).

- A comparison of RE publication and the nation's gross domestic product (GDP), as shown in Figure 5. To aid in visual analysis, we have included diagonal lines corresponding to 80, 40, and 20 RE publications per US$1T GDP. This graph shows the leaders as Taiwan, South Korea, and Singapore, followed closely by Japan. The wide distribution on this graph demonstrates that RE publication is not just a function of economic prosperity, although it may be a leading indicator of economic prosperity.

The average number of authors per paper across the entire database of 4,559 papers is 2.3. That is, for the average paper, 2+ individuals co-author the paper. For Asia, the average number of authors per paper increases to 2.8, roughly a third higher than the international average. It might be interesting to see if this is uniform across all Asian countries or whether it is true for only some Asian countries. The columns of Figure 7 (which use the left y-axis) show how this number varies among all Asian countries involved in writing articles in RE. The line graph (which uses the right y-axis) shows the number of papers involved; thus the authorship data for Turkey and Thailand, though outliers, are not significant due to their low paper volume. However, the figure does show significant differences between China (2.96), South Korea (2.9) and Japan (2.88) vs. Taiwan (2.45) and India (2.23), which are more similar to the rest of the world.

- A comparison of RE publication and the nation's GDP per capita. Now, China and India become the major leaders, but this is not a surprise considering their large populations. See Figure 6. To aid in visual analysis, we have included diagonal lines corresponding to 8, 4, 2, and 1 RE publications per US$1T GDP per capita.

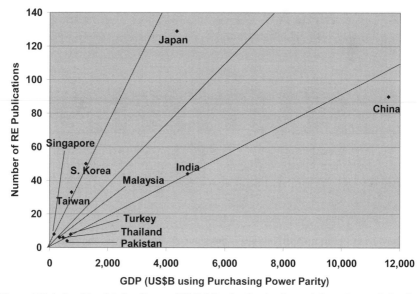

Figure 5 Relationship of Asian Country RE Publication Production and Gross Domestic Product

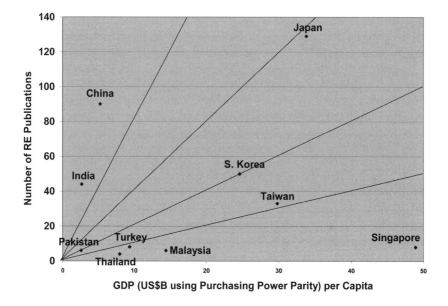

Figure 6 Relationship of Asian Country RE Publication Production and GDP per Capita

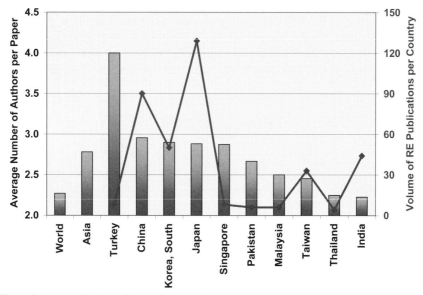

Figure 7 Average Number of Co-Authors per Paper Among Asian Countries

Note that the column for Asia (i.e., the second column from the left) is not just the weighted average of all the columns to its right because some papers are co-authored by multiple countries within Asia and thus contribute to the average number of authors in multiple countries.

On average, 71% of all papers worldwide have at least one author from academe. In Asia, 84% of all papers have at least one author from academe. The columns of Figure 8 (which use the left y-axis) show how this percent varies from Asian country to Asian country. As before, the line graph (which uses the right y-axis) shows the volume of papers involved. Note that the figure shows significant differences between Taiwan (100%), China (94%), and South Korea (92%), where academe dominants RE publication (and possibly RE research as a whole), vs. Japan (64%) and India (48%) where RE productivity clearly extends beyond academe. This phenomenon could be attributed to the historic lack of capitalism in Chinese, which would encourage and reward R&D investment by corporations. It also could reflect the strategy of the Chinese government to make major investments in universities since 2002, including the creation of at least 35 new schools of software [0].

Worldwide, on average, 34% of all papers have at least one author from industry. Asia as a whole exhibits almost the same, 31%. But Figure 9 shows a tremendous range from Asian country to Asian country, e.g., only 7% of the papers from China have at least one author from industry while over half the papers from Japan and India have at least one author from industry, demonstrating the strong tradition of industry participation in Japan and India which may just be starting in China.

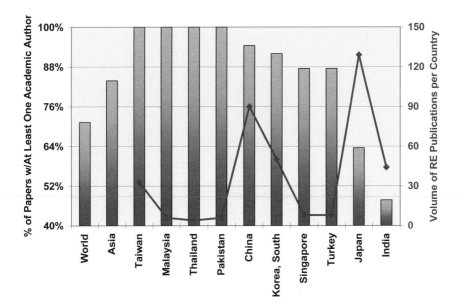

Figure 8 Percent of Papers Authored by at Least One Academic

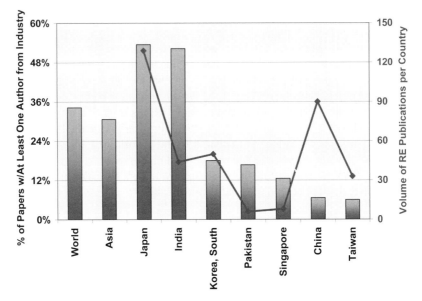

Figure 9 Percent of Papers Authored by at Least One Individual from Industry

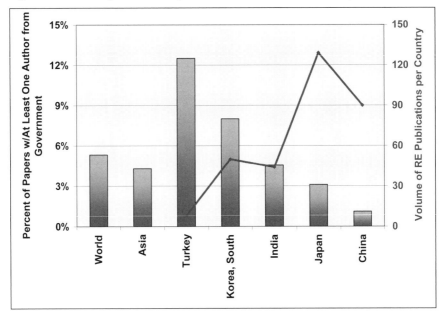

Figure 10 Percent of Papers Authored by at Least One Individual from Government

Worldwide, on average, only 5% of all papers have at least one author from government. In Asia 4% of all papers have at least one author from government. Figure 10 shows how this percent varies significantly among the four Asian countries that have government authors; China (1%), Japan (3%), India (5%) and South Korea (8%). Overall, it is clear that RE publication in China is currently dominated by academe, while in Japan and India there is strong collaboration between academe and industry with some government participation, while in South Korea the limited collaboration that does occur is with government organizations.

In examining the entire database of RE publications, we find that 29% of all papers have been co-authored by a team of authors that represent multiple organizations. In Asia, this number is much higher, at 40%. To better understand the types of collaboration occurring in Asia, we proceeded to analyze the degrees of International, non-academic, and other collaboration for individual Asian countries, as follows:

- We define *international collaboration* as a paper co-authored by a team from multiple countries. For the entire world, only 9.7% of RE papers fall into this category. In this study, we found that Asian-authored papers are much more likely (16.1%) to have co-authors from multiple countries (see first two columns of Figure 11). We also found remarkable differences among the Asian nations (See remaining columns of Figure 11). Thailand, Malaysia, and Turkey each has a very small number of papers, so the percents are somewhat exaggerated. However, look at the degree of international collaboration for India and China vs. the other Asian countries as well as the entire world. Specifically, Chinese-authored and Indian-authored papers are twice as likely to include authors from other countries. So much for China's isolationist tendencies of the middle to late 20th century. Only Taiwan researchers have a rate of international collaboration lower than the world average.

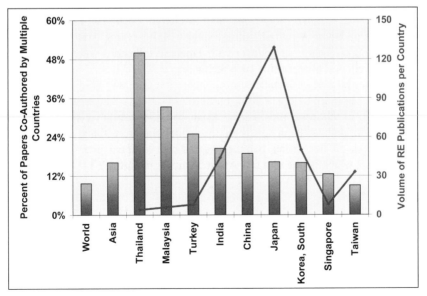

Figure 11 Degree of International Collaboration by Country

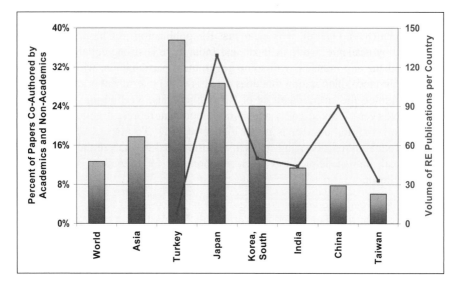

Figure 12 Degree of Non-Academic Collaboration by Country

- We define *non-academic collaboration* as a paper co-authored by academics *and* at least one other author from either industry or government. Once again, we found remarkable differences among the Asian nations (See Figure 12). Look at how different this kind of collaboration is in Japan (29%) vs. China (8%)! Research into technology transfer [0] indicates that such transfer is eased when researchers and businesses cooperate on joint applied research efforts. The fact that Chinese industries and academic organizations are not co-authoring papers may inhibit Chinese industries benefiting from technological breakthroughs. This is in contrast with Japanese industries which may have a higher likelihood of absorbing such technology.
- Finally, we plotted *all* instances of collaboration (i.e., any case where a paper was authored by individuals from multiple institutions). The result is shown in Figure 13. In this case, most of the Asian countries are fairly similar, and all surpass world data. High levels of this collaboration without corresponding high values on the earlier two figures indicate national inter-university co-authorship, which is true of a few Asian countries including China.

3.4 Continental Trends

North America traditionally held a commanding position in the world of RE publication, reaching a peak of around 70% of all RE publications by 1980. Yet, since 1980, its position has been eroded slowly every decade until now, when it contributes just 35%.

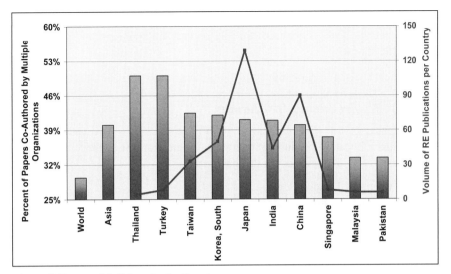

Figure 13 Degree of Collaboration by Country

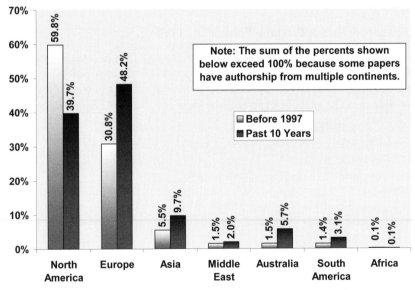

Figure 14 Cumulative RE Publications by Continent: 1963-1997 vs. 1998-2007

Most of that erosion has been caused by growing European and Asian interest in requirements engineering, their contributions growing from virtually none in the early 1970's to a present day contribution of over 52%. However, growing interest in Australia and South America has also contributed to the North American erosion. This trend can be seen more dramatically when we look at the change in total distribution of all RE publications published in 1963-1997 vs. 1998-2007. As shown in Figure 14, the running rate of North America has decreased 34% (i.e., (39.7-59.8)/59.8) in 10 years, while Australia, South America, Asia, Europe, and the Middle East have increased 280%, 121%, 76%, 56%, and 33%, respectively. However, of the three continents with the biggest RE research records, Asia is growing the fastest.

3.5 Top RE Producing Institutions

The top RE publication producing institutions in the world (i.e., those accounting for 1% or more of all papers in the database) are:

1. City University, London (UK) -- 2.4%
2. University of Toronto (Canada) -- 2.1%
3. Lancaster University (UK) -- 1.3%
4. University of Manchester (UK) -- 1.2%
5. Univ of Colorado at Col Springs (USA) -- 1.1%
6. University of Calgary (Canada) -- 1.1%
7. Fraunhofer (Germany) – 1.0%
8. Imperial College in London (UK) -- 1.0%
9. AT&T (USA) -- 1.0%
10. University of Paris 1, Pantheon-Sorbonnes – 1.0%

The fact that these 10 organizations account for just 13% of total RE publication output indicates the widespread nature of interest in the field. Meanwhile, all institutions in Asia that have produced 1% or more of the papers with at least one author with an Asian affiliation (percent shown is out of the 372 Asian papers):

1. Univ. of Ritsumeikan (Japan) – 4.6%
2. Chinese Academy of Science, AMSS (China) – 3.8%
3. NTT (Japan) – 3.8%
4. Tokyo Institute of Technology (Japan) – 3.8%
5. Sogang Univ. (South Korea) – 3.5%
6. Univ. of Beijing (China) – 3.5%
7. National Central Univ. (Taiwan) – 2.7%
8. Shinshu Univ. (Japan) – 2.7%
9. Toshiba (Japan) – 2.7%
10. Univ. of Tokyo (Japan) – 2.7%
11. Infosys Technologies Ltd (India) – 2.4%
12. KAIST (South Korea) – 2.4%
13. National Chiao Tung Univ. (Taiwan) – 2.4%
14. Kyoto Univ. (Japan) – 2.2%
15. City Univ. of Hong Kong (HK, China) – 1.9%
16. Hitachi (Japan) – 1.9%
17. United Nations Univ. (Macau, China) – 1.9%
18. Wuhan Univ. (China) – 1.9%
19. Mitsubishi (Japan) – 1.6%

20.Univ. of Tsukuba (Japan) – 1.6%
21.Fujitsu (Japan) – 1.3%
22.National Univ. (Singapore) – 1.3%
23.Philips (India) – 1.3%
24.Soongsil University (South Korea) -- 1.3%
25.Tata Consulting (India) – 1.3%
26.Tsinghua University (China) – 1.3%
27.Univ. of Macau (Macau, China) – 1.3%
28.Hong Kong University of Technology – 1.1%
29.Keio Univ. (Japan) – 1.1%
30.NEC (Japan) – 1.1%

Note that of these thirty, 13 are from Japan, 8 from China, 3 are from each of South Korea and India, 2 are from Taiwan and 1 is from Singapore.

4 Results for RE *Journal* Publications

Because journal publications are so highly regarded in academic circles, we repeated some of our analyses for journals only.

4.1 General RE Journal Publication Trends

Worldwide, 1,098 journal articles have been written that address RE-related topics. The earliest occurred in 1963 and the latest in this study is in 2007. Like Figure 1, Figure 15 shows steady growth of interest in this discipline, in this case for journal publications only.

4.2 China's Role vs. World

Of the 1,098 journal papers written in the field of RE, authors from China again account for approximately 2%. As in the case of publication in general, China's rate of growth of journal production has been spectacular. Table 2a shows all countries that account for 1% or more of all RE journal publications as of the end of 2007. As in the earlier case of Table 1, it is interesting is to see how the Table 2a countries have changed their level of activity with respect to RE journal publication over the past decade. Table 2b shows these same 20 countries along with their total cumulative RE publication as of 1997. Once again, some remarkable trends emerge. China ranks #13 in RE journal paper production, second only to Japan within Asia. Unlike the case of general RE paper production, Japan's output of journal papers is increasing (from 2.0% to 2.6%), while China's output is growing even more dramatically (from .7% to 1.9%).

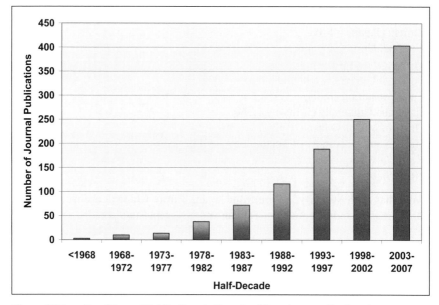

Figure 15 Quantity of Journal Publications in Domain of Requirements Engineering

Table 2 (a) Top 20 Requirements Engineering Journal Publication-Producing Countries 1963-2007. (b) Year 1963-1997 Journal Output for Same Countries Shown in (a)

USA	41.8%	USA	58.5%
UK	18.8%	UK	16.7%
Canada	7.1%	Canada	5.0%
Germany	5.2%	Germany	4.3%
Australia	3.8%	Australia	0.9%
Italy	3.2%	Italy	2.0%
Spain	3.0%	Spain	0.5%
Netherlands	2.6%	Netherlands	1.1%
Japan	2.6%	Japan	2.0%
Sweden	2.6%	Sweden	0.9%
France	2.3%	France	1.4%
Israel	2.0%	Israel	2.7%
China	1.9%	China	0.7%
Korea, South	1.8%	Korea, South	0.2%
Taiwan	1.8%	Taiwan	0.5%
Brazil	1.6%	Brazil	1.1%
Austria	1.5%	Austria	0.5%
Belgium	1.5%	Belgium	1.4%
Denmark	1.5%	Denmark	1.6%
India	1.1%	India	0.7%

4.3 China's Role vs. Other Asian Countries

Of the 1,098 RE journal publications, 111 were written by individuals from 9 Asian countries. To no surprise considering Table 2a, Figure 16 shows the leaders are Japan, China, South Korea, Taiwan, and India. Notice that South Korea's output is growing more dramatically than either of its Asian neighbors (from .2% to 1.8%). To see this more clearly, Figure 17 shows three-year moving averages for the five leading Asian countries annual production of RE journal publications.

The average number of authors per journal article across the entire database is 2.4. For Asia, the average number of authors per journal article is higher, 2.9, the same as for RE publications in general. Figure 18 shows how this varies among all Asian countries involved in writing journal articles in RE ranging from highs of 3.15 and 3.1 for South Korea and China, respectively, to a low of 2.17 for India (ignoring the low volume producers). These results are almost identical to RE papers in general.

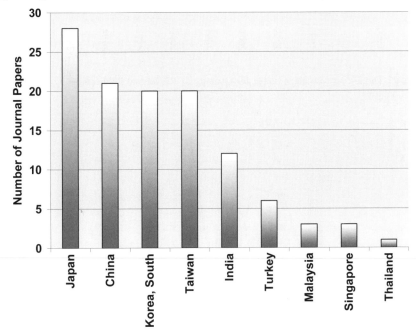

Figure 16 Relative Production of RE Journal Publications by Asian Countries 1963-2007

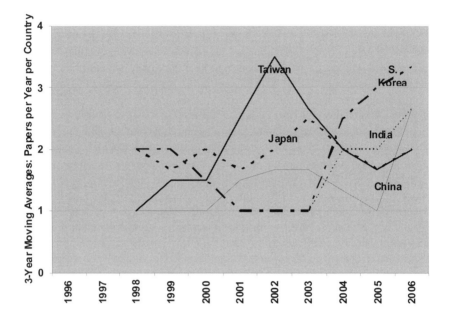

Figure 17 Three-Year Moving Average for Quantity of RE Journal Publications by 5 Leading Asian Countries

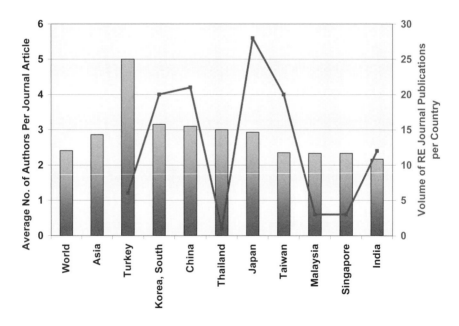

Figure 18 Average Number of Co-Authors per Journal Article Among Asian Countries

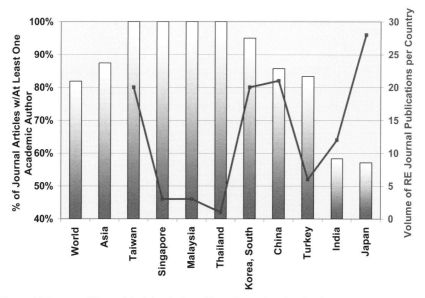

Figure 19 Percent of Journal Articles Authored by at Least One Academic

Worldwide, on the average, 82% of all journal papers have at least one author from academia. This is higher in Asia, with 87%. Figure 19 shows how this percent varies from Asian country to Asian country. Once again, significant differences exist among the major contributors, with Taiwan at 100% and Japan and India below 60%! This reinforces our earlier observations concerning RE publications in general.

Worldwide, on the average, 28% of all journal articles have at least one author from industry. This is almost identical in Asia, where 29% of all journal papers have at least one author from industry. Figure 20 shows how this percent varies from Asian country to Asian country. To no surprise given Japan's and India's relatively low academic participation (as shown in Figure 19), their industrial participation is much higher than in other Asian countries. This is in sharp contrast to Taiwan where only 5% are authored by people from industry. China's percent at 14% is well below average for Asia as well as the world.

Next, we analyzed the database of RE journal papers to see if collaboration in Asian-authored journal articles is any different than collaboration in RE journal articles as a whole. Figure 21 shows the same data as Figure 11, but includes journal articles only. In both cases, China and India experience the most international collaboration.

We also wanted to examine if collaboration in general is any different when we consider just journals. Figure 22 shows the same data as Figure 13, but limits the data to only journal articles. First note that collaboration is more common on journals than on RE publications in general. For example, Figure 13 shows that worldwide and Asia-wide collaboration is at 29% and 40% respectively, but

Figure 22 shows that for journals specifically, worldwide and Asia-wide collaboration increases to 38% and 55%, respectively. Meanwhile, within Asian countries, large differences also appear, e.g., China increases from 40% to 67%, India increases from 41% to 58%, and Japan increases from 41% to 50%. Perhaps the huge changes can be explained by the fact that if a group of researchers all reside in the same country, they may be more likely to publish in a journal in their national language. When collaboration extends to multiple countries, papers may be more likely to appear in English-language journals, the subject of this research study.

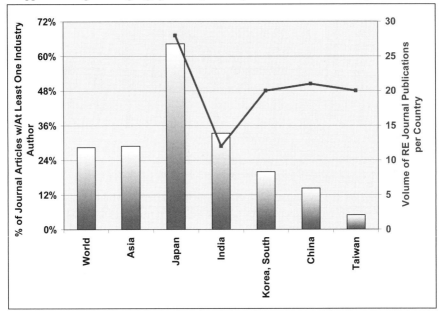

Figure 20 Percent of Journal Articles Authored by at Least One Individual from Industry

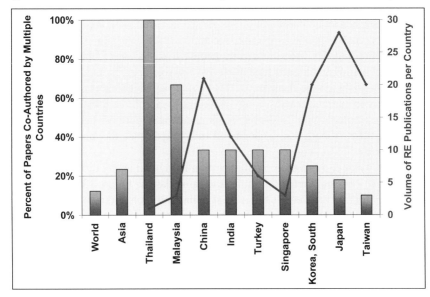

Figure 21 Percent of Journal Articles Authored by Individuals from Multiple Countries

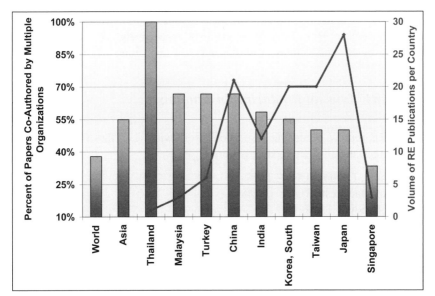

Figure 22 Percent of Journal Articles Authored by Individuals from Multiple Organizations

4.4 Continental Trends

Figure 23 is identical to Figure 14 except that it is limited to just journal publications. In this figure, we see the same general trends, i.e., that North America is decreasing its share to the benefit of all other continents. In this case, the running rate of North America's journal production has decreased 39% ((37.9-62.5)/62.5) in 5

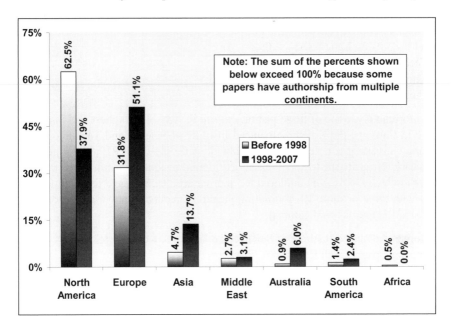

Figure 23 Cumulative RE Journal Publications by Continent: 1963-1997 vs. 1998-2007

years, while Australia, Asia, South America, Europe, and the Middle East have increased by 567%, 191%, 71%, 61%, and 15%, respectively. This says that in the area of prestigious publications, Australia and Asia are making major inroads.

4.5 Top RE Journal Producing Institutions

The top RE journal producing institutions worldwide (i.e., those accounting for 1% or more of all RE journal papers) are:

1. City Univ., London (UK) – 2.6%
2. Univ. of Manchester (UK) – 2.1%
3. AT&T (USA) – 1.5%
4. Univ. of Colorado at Col Springs (USA) – 1.5%
5. Univ. of Minnesota, Minneapolis (USA) – 1.5%
6. Univ. of Toronto (Canada) – 1.5%
7. Univ. of Maryland, College Park (USA) – 1.4%
8. Georgia State University (USA) – 1.3%
9. Univ. of Southern California (USA) – 1.3%
10. Brunel University (UK) – 1.2%
11. Lancaster Univ. (UK) – 1.2%
12. Naval Research Laboratory (USA) – 1.2%
13. Univ. of Calgary (Canada) – 1.2%
14. Naval Postgraduate School (USA) -- 1.1%
15. Univ. of Aachen – RWTH (Germany) – 1.1%
16. Catholic Univ. Rio de Janeiro (Brazil) – 1.0%
17. Fraunhofer (Germany) – 1.0%
18. George Mason University (USA) – 1.0%
19. Imperial College (UK) – 1.0%
20. Jet Propulsion Lab (USA) – 1.0%
21. Technion (Israel) – 1.0%
22. Univ. of Paris 1 (France) – 1.0%
23. Univ. Politecnica Madrid (Spain) – 1.0%

Unfortunately, none of these institutions are in Asia. The highest ranking Asia-based institutions, the Korean Advanced Institute of Science and Technology and Sogang University, are tie for 35th worldwide with .6% of all RE journal publications each. Here are the top Asia-based RE journal-producing institutions (because of the low volume of Asia-authored RE journal articles, we have listed all institutions with three or more RE journal publications; percents shown are percents of all Asian RE journal publications):

1. Korean Advanced Institute of Science and Tech. (S. Korea) – 6.3%
2. Sogang Univ. (South Korea) – 6.3%
3. National Central Univ. (Taiwan) – 5.4%
4. NTT (Japan) – 5.4%
5. Chinese Acad of Sci, AMSS (China) – 4.5%
6. City Univ. (Hong Kong, China) – 3.6%

7. National Chiao Tung Univ. (Taiwan) – 3.6%
8. Univ. of Tokyo (Japan) – 3.6%
9. Fu-Jen Catholic Univ. (Taiwan) – 2.7%
10. Galatasaray University (Turkey) – 2.7%
11. National Univ. (Singapore) – 2.7%
12. Toshiba (Japan) – 2.7%
13. Tsinghua University (China) – 2.7%
14. Univ. of Ritsumeikan (Japan) – 2.7%
15. Wuhan Univ. (China) – 2.7%

Note that 4 out of these fifteen are from China, 4 are from Japan (and surprisingly two of these are corporations, not universities), 3 are from Taiwan, 2 are from South Korea, and 1 is from each of Singapore and Turkey.

5 Limitations

The results reported in this paper exhibit some limitations:

- First and foremost, this experiment has considered only English-language publications. This could be a very serious limitation because many Asian countries have their own prestigious research journals, and hold their own national conferences, many of which address key issues in software engineering. This is particularly true in China. The results reported in this paper may be skewed especially because industry-based authors may be more likely to publish in domestic local-language conferences. We would encourage colleagues in China to expand this research by including publications written in Mandarin, Wu, Min and Cantonese.
- The mechanism we used to gather papers for this study (as described in Sect 2) has the potential to eliminate some RE papers from the study. For example, in some cases, we used just the titles and abstracts to determine of the paper addressed a RE-related subject. It is possible that poorly written abstracts or abstracts that use terminology that we are not familiar with could relegate the paper to dismissal rather than consideration.
- The mechanism we described at the beginning of this paper for populating our database achieves closure among all publications using certain terms in their titles and abstracts. However, it is possible that another "world" of RE research exists that (a) does not use any of the terms listed in Section 2 and (b) is not referenced by any of the items in the current database. As new search terms are suggested to us, we regularly run additional searches to see how many more papers are added to the database. For example, we recently searched for the expressions "conceptual modeling" and "enterprise modeling" (these were not in our original list of search terms), and found that these searches added less than 1% additional publications to our database, and no changes to the results given in the paper. By doing these regular follow-on searches and finding so few additional items, we are also validating our methodology.
- Modest authors may have visited the REQBIB website, recognized that their publications were not represented, but failed to contact us about the omission. We believe that this is not a serious limitation because we have relied on so many other sources of data.

6 Conclusions and Contributions

It is well recognized that performing quality requirements engineering is a prerequisite to effective IT development. Thus, RE research may be a leading indicator of future success in the IT industry. If this is the case, then China's meteoritic success in RE research may bode well for their leadership role in IT in the next decade. As far as we know, this is the first time that anybody has attempted to understand the differences between continental and national contributions to the field of requirements engineering in general, and China specifically. It is the first time that anybody has attempted to understand authorship characteristics and demographics China, Asian countries and the rest of the world.

Some interesting observations emerge from the study:

Concerning English-language RE publications in general,

- Japan is the national leader within Asia in total RE publication output. However, China's and India's rates of production have exceeded Japan's in the past decade and they will pass Japan in total production soon. See Figures 3 and 4.

- Papers with Asia-affiliated authors tend to have more authors than the general population. For China, this is even more so. See Figure 7.

- Papers with Asia-affiliated authors are more likely to have academic authors than the general population (84% vs. 71%; see first two columns of Figure 8). In China, this rises to 94%. This indicates limited involvement by Chinese industry in RE publication. This could also mean that Chinese industry is (a) conducting IT research but not publishing results, or (b) not conducting IT research, in which case they could fall behind other countries in the globalization of IT. This is not the case in all of Asia; in Japan and India, for example, academic authors are less likely to appear on the byline than for the general world population (see last two columns of Figure 8). To no surprise, the opposite is true for authors with industrial affiliations. Thus, Asia-affiliated authors are slightly less likely to have industrial authors than the general world population (31% vs. 34%; see first two columns of Figure 9). This is especially the case with China where only 7% of papers are authored by industry.

- Although industry tends not to be involved in RE publication, general collaboration is far more common in Asia than in other parts of the world. Asian-authored papers are more likely to have co-authors from multiple countries (16% vs. 10%; see first two columns of Figure 11), and Chinese authors are even more (19%) likely to co-author with nationals of other countries. Furthermore, Japanese- and South Korean-authored papers are *twice* as likely to include authors from both academia and non-academia than other countries (29% and 24%, respectively, vs. 13%, as shown in Figure 12), whereas China is almost *half* as likely (8%).

- Asia has made significant strides relative to other continents during the past decade. Ten years ago, authors with Asian affiliations accounted for just 5.5% of the total RE publication base. By 2007, they accounted for almost 10% (that is a huge increase in its position relative to the other continents in just 10 years!). See Figure 14.

- Of the top thirty RE-producing institutions in Asia, 43% are in Japan, 27% are from China, 10% are from each of South Korea and India, 7% are from Taiwan, and 3% are from Singapore.

Concerning RE journal publications specifically

- Japan is the national leader in RE journal paper output within Asia. However, China and South Korea are close behind and gaining.
- Journal papers with Asia-affiliated authors are slightly more likely to have academic authors as the general population (87% vs. 82%; see first two columns of Figure 19). However, this is not the case with Taiwan, where academic authors are much *more* likely to appear on the byline than for the general world population; nor is it the case with Japan and India, where academic authors are much *less* likely to appear on the byline than for the general world population (see last two columns of Figure 19). China's record is close to world averages. To no surprise, the opposite is true for authors with industrial affiliations (see Figure 20). Thus, Taiwanese-authored papers (5%) are much *less* likely to have industrial authors than the general world population (28%); and Japanese-authored papers (64%) are much *more* likely to have industrial authors than the general world population.
- In Asia, journal articles are twice as likely (23% vs. 12%) to include authors from multiple countries as the rest of the world (see Figure 21). China is even more likely (33%).
- Asia has made significant strides relative to other continents during the past decade. Ten years ago authors with Asian affiliations accounted for just 4.7% of the RE journal publications. By 2006, they accounted for 13.7% (that is a huge increase in its position relative to the other continents in just 10 years!). See Figure 23.

In the future, it might be interesting to investigate the relationship, if any, between

- Conducting RE research and improved RE practices in industry, by country and/or region.
- Improved RE practices in industry and economic prosperity, by country and/or region. Figures 5 and 6 begin to show some preliminary results.

If such correlations exist, then RE publication trends could be used as a leading indicator of future economic prosperity.

Acknowledgments The authors would like to acknowledge the contributions made by Oscar Dieste, Natalia Juristo and Ana Moreno. Al Davis acknowledges partial sponsorship by the Spanish Ministry of Education Grant SAB2005-0041.

References

Davis A (2005) Just enough requirements management. Dorset House, NY

The Standish Group (1990) The Chaos Report. www.standishgroup.com

Davis A, Hickey A, Dieste O, Juristo N, Moreno A (2007) A quantitative assessment of requirements engineering publications – 1963-2006. In: Proc working conference on requirements engineering: foundation for software quality. Springer-Verlag, Berlin

Athey S, Plotnicki J (2000) An evaluation of research productivity in academic IT. Comm AIS 3:1-20

Grover V, Segars A, Simon A (1999) An assessment of institutional research productivity in MIS. Database 23:25-29

Im K, Kim K, Kim J (1996) An assessment of individual and institutional research productivity in MIS. Decision Line 31:8-12

Huang HH, Hsu J (2005) An evaluation of publication productivity in information systems: 1999 to 2003. Comm AIS 15:555-564

Farhoomand A, Drury D (1999) A historiographical examination of information systems. Comm AIS 1:Article 19

Lending D, Wetherbe J (1992) Update on MIS research: A profile of leading journals and U.S. universities. Database, 23:5-11

Vessey I, Ramesh V, Glass R (2002) Research in information systems: An empirical study of diversity in the discipline and its journals. JMIS 19:129-174

Vogel D, Wetherbe J (1984) MIS research: A profile of leading journals and universities. DataBase 16:3-14

Glass R, Vessey I, Ramesh V (2002) Research in software engineering: An analysis of the literature. Information Software Technology 44:491-506

Glass R, Chen T (2005) An assessment of systems and software engineering scholars and institutions (1999-2003). J Systems Software 76:91-97

Gervasi V, Kamsties E, Regnell B, Ben Achour-Salinesi C (2004) Ten years of REFSQ: A quantitative analysis. In: Proc 10th international workshop on requirements engineering: foundation for software quality (REFSQ '04)

King W, He J (2005) Understanding the role and methods of meta-analysis in IS research. Comm AIS 16:665-686

Davis A (1990) Software requirements: analysis and specification. Prentice Hall, Upper Saddle River, NJ

Davis A (1993) Software requirements: objects, functions and states. Prentice Hall, Upper Saddle River, NJ

http://web.uccs.edu/adavis/reqbib. Accessed 25 March 2007

Belew B (2006) China will overtake Japan in R&D spending. www.PanAsianBiz.com. Accessed 4 Dec 2006

China Daily (2006) China overtaking Japan in R&D spending. www.chinadaily.com. Accessed 5 Dec 2006

Yang F (2006) Development of software engineering: Co-operative efforts from academia, government and industry, keynote address. In: Proc 28th IEEE international conference on software engineering. IEEE Computer Society Press, Los Alamitos, CA

Potts C (1993) Software engineering research revisited. IEEE Software 10:19-28

Chapter 11
Cultural Characteristics and Effective Business in China

Maria Fernanda Pargana Ilhéu

ISEG/UTL, PORTUGAL

Abstract For firms in the international market the cultural characteristics of host country societies, where their managers are going to deal and work, must be learned, absorbed and adopted. A person's perception of market needs is framed by his or her own cultural experience. More than factual knowledge of Chinese culture the interpretative knowledge is very important and difficult, since it comes from a matrix of philosophic, religion and political explanations which are completely different of the western one. Chinese "guanxi", emphasizes personal trust building, the use of social bonds in dealing with partners, competitors and clients in general good personal networks, is a critical success factor for business performance in China. For instance in technology transfer and equipment sales, special financial help, and barter emerged as more important factors in building customer relationships. Chinese culture emphasizes diffused relationships; as a result the Chinese tend not to separate business from interpersonal relationships. Although Chinese pattern of buying is each time more focused in buying the very best, the latest technology and the most well known brand, maintaining an effective "guanxi" relation with decision makers helps to enhance business performance.

1 The Importance of Cultural Environment in International Business

Socio-cultural values are a major aspect of firm's environment (Begley and Tan, 2001). Societies have collective cognitive styles, which affect perception, behavior, thinking patterns and business practices which characterize their national cultures. National culture, that has become an important concept, in international business literature Roath *et al.,* (2002) refers to deeply set of values, that are common to the members of a nation and constitutes a system of shared norms, values and priorities, a code of expected behaviors in that society.

These shared beliefs are learned since childhood through family example, school education programs and social gathering (Sirmon and Lane, 2004), *"culture*

P.O. de Pablos, M.D. Lytras (eds.), *The China Information Technology Handbook*,   189
DOI: 10.1007/978-0-387-77743-6_11, © Springer Science+Business Media, LLC 2009

includes both conscious and unconscious values, ideas attitudes and symbols that shape human behavior and pass from generation to generation" (Bradley, 2002, p.89). Our values and attitudes help to determine what we think is good or bad, right or wrong, what to buy or buy not, what is important and what is desirable, and they are interrelated with some aspects of culture, like religious creeds and beliefs. The literature on "*business ethics shows extensive proof of the influence of nationality on values that is feelings of right or wrong*" (Hofstede *et al.*, 2002, p.787).

Religion is a main string of culture, understanding religion, means examining our deepest convictions. Language has been described as a cultural mirror that affects the content and nature of the culture, because language is not only a communication tool, but also a code of ideas.

Material culture, the material things that people create and use is very much related to aesthetics and has various important implications in market trends and marketing offers, such design in Italy, glamour and fashion in France, technology in Germany, Zen style in Japan (Bradley, 2002).

Social scientists define national culture as "*patterns of thinking, feeling and acting rooted in common values and conventions of society*" (Nakata and Sivakumar, 2001, p.257). According with their findings, national culture influences marketing activities including international marketing strategy, market entry decision, innovation and product development approach. For instance Hofstede (1991) refer, that 50% of differences in management attitudes, believes and values are explained by national cultures.

Hofstede (1980), define culture as a collective mental program that people have in common and identified four initial widely used dimensions of countries culture characteristics:

1. "*Individualism versus collectivism*" (IDV), the value of individual's identity and rights, compared with those of the group, cultures high in collectivism are group oriented. Members of more collectivist cultures tend to protect one another more and threat out-group members more harshly than do individualistic cultures. The relational emphasis in collectivist societies justifies for instance strong network ties between businesses and customers (Nakata and Sivakumar, 2001). Network forms of organization, have been developed, most exclusively, in the so-called collective social and economic cultures, and China is a good example of it (Kao, 1993, Fukuyama, 1995, Achrol, 1997, Yeung, 1997, Ritcher, 1999).

2. "*Uncertainty avoidance*"(UAI), which basically measures tolerance for risk, cultures with high uncertainty avoidance tends to seek ways to create closed protective ways to control their environments. To reduce uncertainty SMEs engage in coalition activities such as alliance formation (Steensma *et al.*, 2000).

3. "*Masculinity versus femininity*"(MAS), high masculinity cultures favor material achievements; femininity cultures value quality of life and relationships.

4. "*Power distance*"(PDI), indicates the tolerance for social hierarchy and class structures, high power distance cultures, exhibit class and power differences by

position on the hierarchies and social standing that tend to close themselves to outsiders.

Hofstede (1991) mention a fifth dimension found in a Pan-Asian study, the Confucian dynamic or long-term orientation (LTO), the positive pole of this dimension, represents values such as thrift, persistence, loyalty and are oriented for the future where the negative end represents conservativeness, tradition and are oriented by the past. How far this dimensions affect international market strategy and how cultural distance might affect the business relationship between firms of different countries are important issues on this research. Without being exhaustive some observations can be done to enlighten the how national culture dimensions affects international marketing strategies.

The research of Nakata and Sivakumar (2001) shows, that in a individualist culture, marketing strategy focus the satisfaction of buyers through product and service's novelty, variety, functional and transactional aspects, aiming at individual gratification where in collectivist societies such as China, marketing strategies, emphasizing group membership and affiliated benefits are more successful.

Collectivist societies developed the value of "face" with origins in Chinese culture, is the value that better predicts behavior and conduct business negotiations in East Asia, but can be considered a universal value. Theory of face provides a model to connect socio-cultural dimensions to individual decision making, face is defined as "the evaluation of self based on internal and external (to individual) judgments concerning a person's adherence to moral rules of conduct and position within a given society", (Begley and Tan 2001, p.538).

Nakata and Sivakumar (2001) findings, also refer that higher uncertainty avoidance has been associated with the preference for management style based on hardware control systems, such as detailed planning and accounting audits, and transactions are normally made under written contracts embedded in law systems, which rule even the most simple acts, while lower uncertainty avoidance communities are more at ease with the unknown and have a management style based on software human relationship, based on trust and non written commitments being also more flexible and empirically linked to higher levels of innovation.

In power distance societies with great inequality among members, is expected different special privileges and symbols of status for those in higher social and hierarchical positions, marketing interpretation is to differentiate clients giving more privileges to the more acquainted, creating closed clubs, admission cards for same and so on. In higher power distance countries like China, Japan, Taiwan, "customers who are acquainces, even only by referral, are typically given more privileges such as price discounts" (Nakata and Sivakumar, 2001, p.260).

Also some of the most prestigious brands are originated or have their best markets in countries with high power distance such as Italy, Germany, France, Japan, and Hong Kong. In lower distance countries equality comes in the approach of marketing with uniformed offers in quality, benefits and value, not surprising that the mass merchandisers such as Wal-Mart, Ikea, McDonald's have their origins in these kinds of countries, like USA, Sweden.

In societies lower in masculinity that focus on caring for others, improving the quality of life, avoiding self-recognition, people are more emotional and marketing benefits from developing human centered relationships, friendship and affiliation prevalence to achievement can be observed in decision making, where in high masculinity societies, the rational responding to firms marketing efforts is made by cognitive evaluation of product attributes and value expectations.

Consumption and business may be directly related to national culture, for instance achievement and success and the material symbols of success, such as status purchases, are much more important in societies higher in masculinity (Bradley, 2002).

Societies high in Confucian dynamic, or long-term orientation, such as the Japanese and the Chinese, incorporate the long-term view into many aspects of business from building suppliers networks, to corporate financing, in these kind of societies decisions needs time to take, since nobody is in a hurry and all perspectives have to be considered, several levels of the hierarchy listen until a consensus is build, these obliged to long negotiations. With long-term orientation societies of East Asia countries, are more likely to emphasize education and training, work with persistence and patiently wait for long-term reward, their attitude also favor long-term rather than short-term relationship (Li et al., 2001).

For Bradley (1991) the main work of international marketing is to answer to local culture and to interlink the business with its contextual environment "strategic success depends on an understanding of the culture and competitors in the foreign markets, and the possession of positive perceptions within the firm" (Bradley, 2002, p.170). For firms in the international market the cultural characteristics of host country societies, where their managers are going to deal and work, must be learned, absorbed and adopted.

A person's perception of market needs is framed by his or her own cultural experience (Keegan and Green, 2000). Our own culture determine the way we understand other cultures, because we have to interpret other cultures signals in terms of our system of values, our creeds and beliefs what constitutes our Self-Reference Criterion (Bradley, 2002).

As mentioned by Cateora (1993, p.15), "The primary obstacle to success in the international marketing is a person's Self-Reference Criterion (SRC), in making decisions" the cultural references, past experience, information and knowledge affects, the capacity of the decision maker of seeing a foreign market characteristics in its true light. There is a normal spontaneously trend to react and act, without thinking on the basis of our own culture, which is often different from the foreign country culture and so often the decision don't produce the expected feedback.

It is very difficult to understand and deal with SRC because as per Cateora (1993), it is like an "iceberg" only the least part of it is visible, and the most important part of it, the base, cannot be seen, so is crucial to recognize its existence and try to act carefully using a cross cultural attitude, and be aware of the need to be sensitive to cultural differences is a must, if a firm wants to be successful in foreign markets. A lesson that SRC teaches is that a "vital critical skill of the global marketer is unbiased perception, the ability to see what so is in a culture",

(Keegan and Green, 2000, p.149). Forgetting this, can be a powerful negative force in international business, and lead to failure.

Convergence of cultures is nowadays widely verified in people's behavior and practices regarding global products and brands, but these "rather manifestations of culture are sometimes mistaken for all there is; the deeper, underlying level of values, which determine the meaning for people of their practices, is over-looked" (Hofstede, 1991, p.181). Globalization forces, modern communication services, facilities of transportation and international education, can reduce cultural difference (Hofstede et al., 2002). But although the world is moving ever closer to becoming a "global village", is not completely there yet (Dow, 2000). Thus even with the referred convergence, cultural distance continues to be an important issue to take into consideration when defining marketing strategy, entry modes decisions or business management in international markets.

1.2 Cultural Distance

Cultures differ widely in the extent to which unspoken, unformulated and inexplicit rules govern, how information is handled, and how people interact and are related to each other. For a foreign the facility of understanding and communicate in a culture is inversely related to the importance that culture places on "silent language" and "hidden dimensions" (Bradley, 2002, p.102). For example, China and Japan are high in these dimensions and Germany and US are low.

Cultural distance encompasses differences in religion, language, material culture, work ethics, social structure ideology and values, between the home country and the host country (Ekeledo and Sivakumar, 1998). Although there are other forms of measurement, literature shows the preference of academics for trying to explain cultural variety and distance through the utilization of Hofstede's (1980, 1991) dimensions.

Cultural distance is considered to influence firms desire to reduce the level of uncertainty by using various control mechanisms, the firms level of uncertainty is related with the degree of unfamiliarity, and with the business and law practices of the host country. For instance cultural distance influences the firm's view that a contract is a control mechanism and a way to manage the relationship, "the greater the cultural difference between the home countries of the manufacturer and its foreign distributor, the more likely the manufacturer will need to emphasize the legal dimension of relational governance" (Roath et al., 2002, p.10). High degree of cultural distance may lead the firm to insist upon a more formal contract structure.

When US firms set up their foreign distribution subsidiaries "they preferred joint ventures over integrated modes of distribution in the more cultural distant markets such as Japan and South-east Asia" (Brouthers & Brouthers, 2001, p.179).

The relationship between cultural distance and ownership is far from certain, empirical evidence is ambiguous and even contradictory, Brouthers & Brouthers (2001) and Shenkar (2001) cite studies, where no relationship were found,

between cultural distance and full ownership modes of entry preference. But Er-
ramili et al. (2002, p. 229), therefore refer than when cultural distance is high the
firms "actually prefer to internalize", to control resources transfer and to protect
their competitive advantages.

International marketing decisions should take into consideration cultural studies, as how the cultural environment of a country are receptive to foreigners and
new marketing offers, the impact of that particular environment has in operational
management and strategic decisions formulation. Hofstede (2004) give us insights
into other cultures and allow us to formulate a cross-cultural analysis between cultural dimensions of home and host countries.

Complex, intangible, culture has been difficult to conceptualize and scale, measuring difference between cultures presents a great challenge by obtaining standardized measures is possible to tangibilize cultural distance and utilize it as a tool
to bypass culture complexities, and define marketing and entry mode strategies
(Shenkar, 2001). If this information is well understood and applied properly, the
level of uncertainty and risk can be reduced and more successful results can be obtained. Two examples of culture differences can be seen in Figure 1.

It may be argued that Hoftstede´s dimensions do not reflect current values since
they are based on data collected thirty years ago, but national culture changes are
very slow and Hofstede indexes are still the most comprehensive set of value
measures available, and this framework is each time more used by conceptual and
empirical studies, *"Hofstede is the third most cited author (the first two being John
Dunning and Michael Porter) in international business studies between 1989 and
1993"* (Sivakumar and Nakata, 2001, p.556).

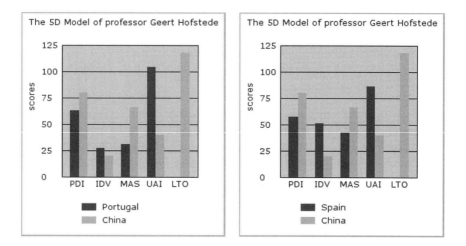

Figure 1 Cross-Cultural Analysis of Portugal and Spain vs. China
Source: Hofstede, 2004.
PDI-Power Distance Index, IDV-Individualism Index, MAS-Masculinity Index,
UAI-Uncertainty Index, LT0 -Long-Term Orientation.
Note: LTO measure only exists for some countries

With this framework, several hypotheses can be tested like the role of power distance and uncertainty avoidance on entry mode decisions or uncertainty avoidance and long-term orientation on the joint-ventures failures rate or the individualism index with the propensity of forming networks, or the cultural distance with the performance of joint ventures.

Luo (1999) found the performance of foreign joint ventures in China to be negatively associated with cultural distance between partners. Research on western joint-ventures in China, suggests that it is difficult for westerns to understand and handle the differences in time horizon with their Chinese partners (China is the country with highest score in long-term orientation), yet handle such differences is a pre-requisite for successful cooperation, since different time perspectives lead to cultural clashes (Barkema and Vermeulen, 1997).

Researchers generally agree that alliances between culturally similar partners have higher possibility of success than alliances between culturally distant partners, Pothukuchi, *et al.* (2002, p.245), refer that *"cultural incompatibility may cost more than strategic incompability in organizational alliances"*, and *"cultural compatibility between partners is the most important factor in the endurance of a global alliance"* (Skarmeas *et al.*, 2002, p. 763).

But also numerous studies found that firms are more likely to enter through joint-ventures than wholly-owned enterprises when cultural distance between home country and host country is high, *"the benefits of having a partner with knowledge of local networks, consumer preferences, institutional framework, and so on apparently outweigh the (potential) hazards of having to deal with a partner with a different cultural background"* (Barkema and Vermeulen, 1997, p.850).

Related to cultural distance is psychological distance, identified as *"factors preventing or disturbing the flows of information between firm and market"* (Dow, 2000, p. 52). These factors can explain the lack of direct communication with existing and potential buyers, or the lack of access to general market information. Hofstede doesn't deal with differences in language, religion, education, political and legal systems or level of industrial development, which are most often referred to justify psychological distance, but these are difficult to measure dimensions.

In a globalized world, where firms turn more international, *"managers and representatives with intercultural disposition can play a key role in establishing, developing and maintaining inter-firm relations that cross national boundaries"* (Skarmeas *et al.*, 2002, p.772) contribute to long term relationships commitment in international market. Also from an international management standpoint firms may find the investment of resources in cultural training programs, an important issue in its internationalization process.

Brouthers & Brouthers (2000, p.91) suggest that the *"cultural context helps to define profit potential and/or the risks associated with a specific market entry"*, they consider cultural context broader than national context including investment risks associated with different host country cultural, legal, political, economic, systems as well as market attractiveness. Cultural distance takes into consideration not only geographical distance and physical characteristics but also economic and cultural differences (Bradley, 2002).

1.3 Interpersonal Relations and Negotiation Strategies

Fu et al. (2004, p.284), refer that the "effectiveness of global managers depends on their ability to exercise influence in culturally mixed interpersonal networks". They identified 16 tactics to influence interpersonal relations which they grouped into 3 categories; persuasive, assertive and relationship based. The persuasive strategy to influence managerial behaviors includes rational persuasion (based on logical arguments), inspirational appeal (appealing to target's values and ideals), and consultation (appealing to target's participation). The assertive strategy consists of persistence (repeated insistence with the target to perform), pressure (using demands and threats), and upward appeal (seeking higher authority support). The relationship-based strategy includes personal appeal (asking personal favors), informal engagement (utilizing non work environments), socializing (involving the target socially before making requests), and giving gifts and exchanging (giving the target something in exchange for help).

In their research these strategies were related with national cultures dimension and they concluded that in cultures with high uncertainty avoidance managers perceived assertive influence strategy, such as seeking for help from high authorities to be more effective than relying on persuasive strategy. For instance they refer that managers in China rated assertive tactics such as coalition and upward appeal, higher, whereas managers in lower uncertainty avoidance cultures like US prefer persuasive strategy. In other hand, people with long-term orientation cultures, may be more likely to emphasize relationships with others in the workplace and use these relationships to influence them. They mention that in China high in this cultural dimension, managers prefer relationship-oriented tactics such as giving gifts and personal appeals, whereas in short-term oriented cultures, like US, prefer persuasive tactics such as rational persuasion and consultation.

In a generic level of analysis the world can be divided into basic types of cultures, "eastern" versus "western", the first being characterized by high power distance, collectivism, femininity and long-term orientation dimensions, and the second by low power distance, individualism, masculinity and short-term dimensions, but as seen before each national culture is a specific case, and in east and west countries, there are cultures which are a mixed of these general classifications. Other important distinction is that eastern countries are "high-context" cultures and western countries are "low-context" cultures, this means that the social context of transactions has higher importance in eastern cultures (Malhotra et al., 1998).

Bradley (2002), refer that there are important differences between Chinese and Western views of relationships, in the West successful transactions lead to good relations, in China if a relationship is well build then transitions will follow. A special relationship "Guanxi" governs the exchange of favors, it involves a long-term relationship of mutual exchange, based on trust which forms bonds between people, namely between buyers and sellers, manufacturers and distributors, government officials and private entrepreneurs, favoring networks and long-term alliances.

Fu et al. (2004), suggests that in cultures high in collectivism such as Japan and China managers were more likely to make appeals to the desire of people to be accepted by others, using relationship-based strategies, whereas managers in individualistic cultures like US were more likely to use persuasive strategies. But collectivism is also linked to the assertive strategy because is also associate with great hierarchy in interpersonal relationship and assertion is well accepted in hierarchical systems.

Fu and Yukl (2000) found that Chinese managers rated coalition formation, upward appeal, giving gifts/favors and personal appeals as more effective and rational persuasion, consultation as less effective as do US managers, they refer that these preferences were consistent with Chinese culture dimensions of high collectivism, high uncertainty avoidance and long-term orientation and the US cultural dimensions of low collectivism, low uncertainty avoidance and short-term orientation.

The roles of people in society and their social ranks in society are also important influences in non manifest communication, "social classes, the family, positions of men and women, group behavior and age groups are interpreted differently within different cultures" as well as social mobility and class structures (Bradley, 2002, p. 100).

These findings are important for managers to have knowledge of the influence strategies that are effective across cultures, but also to understand the negotiations strategies that are relevant to specific cultures.

Cultural factors has also an important role in shaping marketing environment namely in influencing consumer behavior, lifestyles and consumption patterns (Malhotra et al., 1998).

Cultural understanding of host country and adjustment to its business practices has the ability to transform "cross-border economic transactions into enduring relationships embedded in a social context" (Skarmeas et al., 2002, p. 772).

2 Consequences of Chinese Cultural Characteristics in Business Strategy in China

"To do effective business in China you must be willing to adjust to Chinese - style commerce, rather than waiting for the Chinese to suddenly adopt western practices just because we think they should" (Engholm, 1994, p32).

In China values are imposed socially and through tradition, since they have never been driven by religion. The Chinese do not have an officially religion, but a lot of religions and philosophies are practice there from Taoism, Buddhism, Islamism,

Catholicism and Protestantism. But their philosophic base is Confucianism, which served as the foundation of Chinese education for some 2000 years and is applied to politics, ethnic and power relationship, being they family, professional, academic or business (Graham and Lam, 2003).

Also the Taoism the most popular religion, influences the Chinese personal behavior, according with the philosopher Lao Tsu, the contemporary of Confucius who provide the inspiration for Taoism, the key to life is to find the Tao (the way), between two forces the yin (the feminine) and the yang (the masculine), the middle ground, the compromise. Both Lao Tsu and Confucius were more concerned about finding the way, than the truth, these moral values have consequences in the negotiating style of Chinese, which "*are more concerned with the means than the end, with the process more than the goal*" (Graham and Lam, 2003, p.84).

The Islamism counts with 20 million people and practically is confined to Xinjiang province. The Christians and Protestants are about 4 and 13 million persons; the Buddhism imported from India, has a lot of adherents and is a rare example of success of foreign influences.

Cultural Chinese value model shows a man-to-himself orientation, the value abasement, in which modesty and self effacement is held high and a confrontational approach to various situations as when saying "*no*" is avoided. Rather than saying no outright, Chinese business people are more likely to change the subject, ask other questions, turn silent or responding by "*using ambiguous and vaguely positive expressions with subtle negative implications*" (Graham and Lam, 2003, p.86).

Chinese usually do not impose them, they are shy and they don't like to make a target of themselves, by high profile exposure. Living always under autarchic systems they know by ancestrally experience that the best way to avoid problems is that nobody notice them, and they try to get things on their favor by negotiation, in consequence they have developed remarkable negotiation skills, this is a consensual opinion among all the foreigners living in China or negotiating with Chinese (Graham and Lam, 2003).

Chinese like to negotiate, and they are ready for any type of negotiation with patience, ability and slyness, which make long negotiations, an important part of daily business, giving the impression that they do not care for time and efforts invested. Another important fact deriving from this cultural dimension is that "*Chinese prefer to resolve disputes and disagreements by personal contacts and negotiations rather then through judiciary system*" (Ho, 2001, p. 80).

In fact as mention before they normally utilize soft relationship tactics such as socializing, giving gifts, using personal appeals, informal engagement and exchanging, although when necessary they don't reject assertive strategies such as coalition and upward appeal (Fu and Yukl, 2000). They cultivate the sympathy of foreigner's negotiators for their cause and at some time they manipulate the personal relations and the feelings of friendship and group obligations.

It is important to remember the Chinese people's wariness of foreigners which they have learned to fear and to be protected from, due to the country's long and violent history, with attacks and invasions from all points of the world, on this account Graham and Lam (2003, p.85) say that *"the Chinese trust only two things: their families and their bank account"*.

Also China's sense of pride plays a role in how the Chinese deal today with foreign business people and countries. The way westerners do business and international standards of business are of little concern to the majority of Chinese business people.

The pride of the Chinese has some times the form of cultural elitism, offending outsider's moral and contributing to isolate China. As referred by Ho (2001) the general attitude of the Chinese towards the foreigners is a mix of respect, distrust and distance, basically because they suspicious them, and they don't know how to treat them as equals. This fact can be explained by the reason, that historically China was considered by the Chinese as the *"Middle kingdom"*, the *"Central Empire"*, the center of the World, surrounded by the barbarian people, which were politically and culturally lorded by the Chinese, justifying their feeling of superiority and sense of pride, so even today the Chinese person feels a deep sense of national and cultural pride.

The Chinese family is the base of social organization, and one root of Chinese ethnocentrism. The family transmits the majority of emotional and cultural values, and the Chinese person counts with the solidarity of the family, during all his life. Yau (1994, p.67) affirm *"As for an individual, the family is a source which constantly diffuses cultural influences on him throughout his whole life"*. For Chinese the family is in the center of the inner circle, which is the complex web of its social relationships. This inner circle is enlarged first with close relatives then with distant relatives, heart friends, persons from the place were they are born and so it is takes the organization of a clan.

As seen, Chinese national cultural is high in collectivism dimension, and this nature is reflected in the Chinese family and kinship system, which means *"continuous and long-lasting human ties which do not have clearly defined boundaries"* (Yau, 1994, p.75).

Chinese regard family and kinship, as a basis for relating with others and their primary concern is to protect their private kinship interests. As a consequence of this relational orientation dimension of Yau (1994, p.76), Chinese are group oriented and *"when making decisions, a Chinese individual should always take into account other members of the family"*.

So, an important cultural characteristic is that most Chinese, whether they are from Macao, Hong Kong, Taiwan on Mainland, tend to be group oriented, identifying themselves strongly with the group they belong to, be it family, clan, enterprise or ethnic group.

Another important aspect of the relational orientation dimension is the decision making process, Yau (1994, p.72) refer *"Chinese have a strong respect for authority. They are prone to trust totally without questioning"*. The reason for this behavior is in the Confucius's five cardinal relations, which rules the relations between; sovereign and minister, father and son, husband and wife, old and young, and between friends, except for the last, all the relationships were taught to be strictly hierarchical and the ruled were counseled to pay obedience and loyalty to the ruler (Graham and Lam, 2003).

These relations have served effectively to control social behavior and they were transplanted from the classic Chinese organization as described above to the hierarchy of communist system, which took power since 1st October 1949.

As a marketing consequence for this respect for authority (Yau, 1994), findings were that Chinese consumers tend to respond more to reference group leaders, being them family elders, political leaders, and enterprise leaders than to advertising. Also on decision making process is important to understand that classic Chinese always respect the decision of the father in the family, so to have a decision done by a son or daughter, the father has to be convinced first.

Another consequence is that Chinese consumers tend to have higher brand loyalty than their counterparts in West countries (Yau, 1994, p.78), "*Chinese consumers, often endeavor to conform to group norms and therefore have a high tendency to purchase the brand or product which members of the group recommend*" and "*if a reference group has established a product as the normative, Chinese consumers are not likely to deviate from the accepted product on their own*".

Also according to Eckhardt and Houston (2002), brands have historically been used for social purposes in China, because of decentralization and ambiguous class divisions, there was a constant rise and fall of family wealth and position and this necessitate the use of material symbols to mark status, the social function of brands is still paramount today because Chinese consumers use brand names as a tool to build social relationships.

McGuiness *et al.* (1991) findings were that Chinese culture tends to rank everything hierarchically so that is highly desirable to buy what is at the top, as a consequence perceived product quality had the most influence on preferences, price may not be that important in the final decision. Also promotional and service activities had the major influence on customer relationship ratings, since these activities generate interaction between suppliers and customers.

Considering the changing consumption values in today's Chinese market and the existence of different consumer segments in terms of different consumption values, marketers should be sensitive to different consumption needs, in particular, product designing, pricing, branding, packaging and positioning strategies should be based on an understanding of the characteristics of the target market, for instance "*when targeting today's young Chinese consumer who has strong hedonic values, marketers should focus on symbolic or expressive meanings of a product or brand, emphasize the emotional or fantastical experience of consumption, appeal to the consumer's desire for exploration, novelty and innovation in promotion messages*" (Wang *et al.*,2000, p.182).

Another important aspect of Chinese cultural characteristics is their pictographic language, because in Chinese written language, is a picture than sequences of words; Chinese thinking tends toward a more holistic processing of information. This codified language which foreigners cannot read, also shows the Chinese protection and distrust of foreigners.

The Chinese children are better at seeing the big picture while the western have are more at ease when describing details, as a consequence the Chinese think in terms of the whole, while Westerns think sequentially by parts, breaking up complex negotiation tasks into series of small issues: price, delivery, quantity, product details and the so forth, while Chinese negotiators tend to skip the details, talk about this issues as a whole as orientation principles and leaving details to be settled during operational routines (Graham and Lam, 2003). On negotiation grounds the Chinese try always to establish its own rules, forcing the foreigners to accept generic principles, which they constantly remind during negotiations.

Other important relational dimension of Yau (1994) is time, which is divided in past-time orientation and continuity. The important to refer in past-time orientation is the respect Chinese have for their past and their history, the respect for their ancestors, which are worshiped in the altars build in their own homes which is a way to say that they live with them for ever and the obligation to pass forward everything they have received from their parents, namely the cultural values.

Yau (1994, p.79) refer the Chinese proverb "among the three unfilial duties, to have no heir is the greatest". So the obligation of Chinese to have heirs and to prepare them as best as possible, providing the best education, to carry well their duties and to fulfill the hopes that parents and ancestors have not yet accomplished.

The other orientation of time is continuity, the Chinese believe, that interrelations with objects and others are continue, could hardly be broken and are processed in circle. One of the characteristics of Chinese culture is a high value in long-term orientation dimension (Hofstede, 1991, 2004) as a consequence the time a negotiation takes doesn't matter, they are very patient and one of their most used tactics is to let times pression to play against foreigner negotiator.

Some of Chinese cultural characteristics are so important to understand Chinese behavior and negotiating style that should be detailed.

2.1 "Guanxi" (Personal Connections)

An important relational culture dimension is "Guanxi" (Ho, 2001, p.80) explains that, "the term literally means relationship, social relations in general or a specific social relation between individuals in particular".

Chadee and Zhang (2000) refer that within the business context "Guanxi" can be approached in several ways: a) the use of close friends and associates (network) as intermediaries in assisting in business negotiations and activities; b) socializing with the propose of developing business connections; c) developing a high degree of mutual trust between business partners and d) using government officials to bypass or facilitate legal and administrative hurdles which is called a back door practice.

"Guanxi"; loosely translated as "connections" in PRC "are compared with relationship market as it has emerged on the West" (Ambler et al., 1999 p.75). Relationship marketing in the West refers to the process of establishing, maintaining and enhancing inter-organizational relationships with customers and other stake-holders (Chadee and Zhang, 2000), but it is not rooted in cultural values as the Chinese "Guanxi" is.

Chinese place a premium on individuals social appraise within their group of friends, relatives and close associates. Good "Guanxi" depends on a strict system of reciprocity or what Chinese call "hui bao" (Graham and Lam, 2003). They give and expect favors and the business deal may depend on how this reality is accepted in non business ways, is the base of "Guanxi" system, which is a web of obligations, which carries expectations that include favors to be returned. Although the word is relatively new, the concept is rooted in Confucianism, "the self is always a relational self" a man only exists in a social context and those outside the network are barely seen as existing at all (Ambler et al., 1999, p. 76)

Within the business context, "Guanxi" can be classified as one important intangible barrier in doing business in China, Chadee and Zhang (2000, p.133) consider it so important, that it can be compared to a "second currency" which permeates the economic sphere and constitutes a "key and ´secret´ to corporate success in China".

In Chinese cultural model, the flexibility in interpersonal relations comes from the principle of "doing favors" which signifies one's honor to another. Favors done for others are often considered to be termed "social investments" (Yau, 1994, p. 73) they are almost always remembered and returned, though not right away, long-term reciprocity is a cornerstone of good "Guanxi", ignoring reciprocity in China is not just bad manners it is immoral (Graham and Lam, 2003).

As seen before "Guanxi" involves a long-term relationship and is based on trust and trust has been found to have a positive effect on export performance and for Chinese business people is more important than any signed contract, in this context is very important for having a successful business relationship (Ambler et al., 1999, Graham and Lam, 2003).

Accordingly with Ho (2001, p.80), "The marketing implications of the concept of `Guanxi` are that exchange between the sellers and buyers often is based on social relations rather than rights and privilege". As a corollary, one of the implications of "Guanxi" is the need to develop an image of good corporate citizen.

Chinese place high importance on personal friendship existing prior to doing business, they are a critical precondition to effective business, their results show that "personal friendship appear to have significant influence in its first three years but business issues such as product quality and cooperation than take over" (Ambler et al., 1999, p.84). Their findings confirm that "Guanxi" have a positive impact on performance of ventures in China, so it can be said that they concluded that "Guanxi" is essential on development of business with China; this is the dimension of interdependence of Yau (1994).

Also Chadee and Zhang, (2000) shows that "Guanxi" significantly facilitate trade partnering, business negotiating and problem solving and generally contribute positively to the overall performance of firms.

But some have argued although "Guanxi" can be very helpful, particularly the relationships with government is not enough to guarantee success in Chinese market, officials change position, fall out of favors or simply promise more than they can deliver, and there is no substitute for good understanding of the market, and producing a competitive product (Lieberthal and Lieberthal 2003).

On the practical side the experience shows that "Guanxi" is no longer enough to provide competitive edge (McKinsey, 2004) and is becoming less and less important; as China moves to a market economy and the legislation is more transparent (InterChina Consulting 2004, p.18), refers "Government officials might believe they are still very important, but the practice is quite different". They advise that better than "having Guanxi" what is more important is the ability to "build Guanxi" with local authorities, local customers, local tax offices, and this ability is not so different of what is required in many Western countries, by using the right people foreigners companies can as well do it as do Chinese companies.

Anyway in technology transfer and equipment sales, special financial help, and barter emerged as more important factors in building customer relationships (McGuiness et al., 1991). Chinese culture emphasizes diffused relationships; as a result the Chinese tend not to separate business from interpersonal relationships. Generally, successful technology transfer is accompanied by healthy personal relationships and effective coordination interactions (Lin and Germain, 1999).

Moreover, Sin et al. (2000) findings validate the long term belief that relationship marketing similar to Chinese "Guanxi", which emphasizes personal trust building, the use of social bonds in dealing with partners, competitors and clients in general good personal networks, is a critical success factor for business performance in China and firm's degree of customer orientation is positively associated with sales growth and the overall performance in China.

Foreign firms can gain an edge over their competitors in Chinese market, by building and maintaining their own "Guanxi" network, because it constitutes an important marketing tool, (Chadee and Zhang, 2000), since "Guanxi" related variables, such as sales force, marketing and credit-granting have been found to be significantly and positively related to firm's performance (Luo, 1997).

People who understand the importance and meaning of "Guanxi", such as Chinese from Hong Kong, Macao, Taiwan and Singapore are generally more successful in China. Foreign investors and companies willing to export to China "can gain edge over their competitors in Chinese market by building and maintaining their own `Guanxi` network, because `Guanxi` constitutes an effective and efficient marketing tool" (Chadee and Zhang, 2000, p.133).

2.1.1 Overseas Chinese Network

Overseas nationals, the so-called Diaspora, have been a special important subset of foreign investors in countries such as China, (Ojah and Monplaisir, 2003).

Huntington (1999, p.197) refer, that *"The government consider mainland China the mother country of a Chinese civilization, in relation to which all the Chinese communities should be oriented"* and *"to the Chinese government the Chinese Di-*

aspora even when citizens of any other country, are members of the Chinese community and in a certain extend subjects to the Chinese government"

The Chinese government to call upon the patriotic feelings of their Chinese compatriots living overseas, to participate on the development of Mainland China with trade cooperation, investment and to teach China the entrepreneurial spirit and introduce efficient management has utilized this vision.

For many generations, emigrant Chinese entrepreneurs have been operating in a network of family and clan, laying foundations for stronger links among business, across national borders. Chinese owned businesses in East Asia, USA, Canada, Australia and Europe and are increasingly becoming part of what is called the Chinese Commonwealth, not based in any country; their commonwealth is primarily a network of entrepreneurial relationships. For Chinese, network has always been a very important part of their culture, following Confucianism's belief in the individual's inability to survive by him (Chu, 1996).

Different activities, different dimensions, this Chinese Commonwealth consists of many individual companies spread around the world, that share a common culture, *"Overseas Chinese is an empire of 55 million people interlaced by systems of guilds, benevolent societies, tongs, triads, kongsi, and name-and-place associations, which individually and together supply the personal connections and financial linkages that make the Overseas Chinese such a potent force. It is an empire without borders, national government or flag"* (Seagrave, 1995, p.2).

Anwar (1996) affirm, that from these 55 millions Overseas Chinese around 50.3 million live in East Asia and comprise heterogeneous groups based on many dialects and sub dialects; of course this correspond to many subcultures, diverse occupation styles and entrepreneurial specialization.

The Chinese Diaspora is emerging as the main force behind the sizzling growth of the Pacific Rim economies, in the studies of Chinese business; network has been viewed as one of the key factors contributing to the enormous success of Chinese business in Hong Kong and other Asian countries (Chu, 1996). Members of Chinese Diaspora dominate trade and investment in every East Asian country except Korea and Japan. They possess not only the biggest reservoir of capital but also actual political connections and the best practical information for surviving in different markets such as China, Indonesia, Vietnam, Malaysia, and Singapore. Start with values, regardless of where they live on how rich they are the Overseas Chinese shares an abiding belief in hard work, value of trust, role of strong family ties, frugality, emphasis on higher education, integrity, long-term planning and entrepreneurial abilities.

For the Overseas Chinese these attributes aren't relics from their culture's past but compelling rules to live by. According to Anwar (1996, p.813) the success of the Overseas Chinese is due to *"a propensity for hard work, good connections, and an ability to keep business expenses low"*. The explanation for this is given by some academics that stress the teachings of Confucius to the ancient Chinese philosopher who exalted the virtues of family and clan solidarity and education.

But Confucius legacy also had a downside, in this hierarchical vision of society merchants ranked at the very bottom, which helps to explain why China created few notable businessmen in Mainland China itself even before Mao Zedong communist revolution. The success of the Overseas Chinese is the result of bad times in China itself. The Chinese who left the mother country had to struggle and that became a culture of its own, passed on from father to son through each generation. Because we have no social security, the Overseas Chinese habit is to save a lot and make a lot of friends.

Overseas Chinese rose only when they reach foreign countries, and this in not merely a recent phenomenon mostly concentrated on post-communist revolution. In fact the biggest wave of migration came at the high tide of European colonialism in the last century, when Chinese run away from famine and plague and streamed into Southeast Asia as poor peasants and coolie laborers. Many who started, as workers at western-owned rubber plantations and tin mines later become small merchants, by the times the colonialists departed from places such Indonesia and Malaysia, after the Second World War, the Chinese were the most experienced local businessmen left.

The uncertainties and risks raised by their life as immigrants have reinforced the Overseas Chinese penchant for a guarded controlling style of doing business. Most of their enterprises even multibillion-dollar public companies are family affairs, ruled by a patriarch who makes all key decisions. Major deals are done, only with people he knows and trusts. Just about every Chinese business proprietor is a hand´s on entrepreneur.

One benefit of such culture is speed and the Overseas Chinese smell profits quickly and make decisions even quicker. They are pragmatic not legalistic. Another advantage is patience, with both ownership and management firmly in the hands of a single family, Overseas Chinese companies are often more willing and certainly more able than widely held public corporations to take a long view of their investment.

Above all, business intelligence and capital flows across the Overseas Chinese community because its members are superb networks. The foundation of this persuasive network is *"Guanxi"*, personal connections, *"cross-shareholding, family connections and a system of intricate business practices based upon achieving economies of scale and putting stronger emphasis on dealing with other Chinese firms"* (Anwar, 1996, p. 812).

Anwar (1996) refer three successful forms of capitalism in Asia-Pacific: Japanese, South Korean and Overseas Chinese Network whose business activities with their worldwide operations resemble Western MNCs and helps to drive the economies of fast-growing countries of Asia including China. These networks are characterized by small and medium size business units, normally family owned, most often they have centralized structures in terms of authority and power, they are conscious on costs running their businesses with tight control of inventory, they link up with other ethnic Chinese businesses and networks and they concentrate on sectors like, land and property development, banking, engineering/construction, textiles/fiber, finance, consumer electronics, food, computers/semiconductors and chemicals.

In total, including investment from Overseas Chinese leaving in USA, Australia and Europe, nearly 80% of unbound FDI in the 1980´s come from Chinese Diaspora; the flood of non Chinese FDI began only in 1990´s, in other words China's development might have been very different had there not been the strong patriotic sense of millions of Chinese leaving overseas, many of whom pooled their capital, technology and access to export markets with cheap Chinese labor force to produce China's export boom (Ojah and Monplaisir, 2003).

The attraction China exercises on these investors is not a surprise, since the common Chinese culture, language and close geographically distance greatly reduces the costs of doing business in China for them. Historically *"networks are essential to foreign-Chinese success in China"*, attributes such as *"Guanxi"*, familiarity and knowledge of the Chinese culture and language together with cheaper land and labor, explains the success of this formula (Anwar, 1996, p. 814).

It is important to refer that Chinese influence is not limited to the Greater China it is extended to countries where Chinese have predominance in business. In fact Chinese make up 10% of Thailand population, and owned 90% of all investments in the commercial sector, 90% of all investments is the industry sector and 50% of all investments in the banking and finance sector, in Indonesia they make 4% of population and they dominate 70% to 75% of private domestic capital, in Malaysia they account for 37% of population and they control between 55% to 60% of the economy, in Singapore, Chinese make up 80% of the population and they control the economy, in Philippines 3% control 70% of the economy.

Chinese are also making a presence in Canada, in Vancouver 20% of population is already Chinese, in California, luxurious residential areas are being reshaped with Chinese culture landscape, and on London Stock Exchange and business area their presence is well noticed. *"In the west the least understood Asian phenomenon is the role of the Overseas Chinese who live outside the mainland of China, not only in Taiwan, Hong Kong and Singapore, but also those in Indonesia, the Philippine, Malaysia, Thailand and in Vancouver and Los Angeles and London. The most successful entrepreneurs in the world they are the force that will catapult Asia to economic dominance"* (Naisbitt, 1995, pp.xi and xii).

An important business strategy to foreigners to enter Chinese market is *"to team up and create partnerships with Overseas Chinese companies"* (Anwar, 1996, p. 814). Firms particularly the small size ones are particularly keen on *"utilizing relational linkages to establish themselves in Southeast Asia and China, where the ethnic Chinese population serves as an interface for networking"* (Chen & Chen, 1998, p. 463). For instance many small and medium-size firms from Taiwan which are known to be weak organizations linked by strong networks (Redding, 1996) established themselves in Southeast Asia and China, because Chinese business community serves as an interface assisting to link up.

2.2 "Zhongjian Ren"- The Intermediary

As mentioned in China, suspicion and distrust characterize negotiations with strangers and so trust must be earned or transmitted via the "*Guanxi*" of business associates which pass along its trusted links to other partners, those links can be hometown, family, school or previous business ties.

As seen in Chinese context, trust is very important for doing business, as a consequence in China a crucial step in the phase of negotiation, is to identify the personal links which can be useful in approaching the Chinese negotiators, which can make the foreigners negotiators trustfully, this trust can be built on long-term negotiations, but this links can also be earned, by finding a talented Chinese which can be contracted or associated to the venture and bring with him all the necessary "*Guanxi*" making the intermediation of the negotiation (Graham and Lam, 2003).

The go-between is indispensable in the negotiation, only a native Chinese speaker can understand, which is behind the moods, body language, intonations, facial expressions that the Chinese negotiators show during the negotiations sessions, it will be interpreter not so much of words as of cultures, and because is has good links with both sides he can understand what are the objectives and problems over the table and settle differences bringing harmony to the negotiations.

2.3 "Mien-tsu"- Face or Social Capital

In the relational orientation model of Yau (1994), an important dimension in the interpersonal relations among and with the Chinese is the concept of "*Face*" which is divided in two types, "*Lien and Mien-tsu*". "*Lien*" represents the confidence of society in the integrity of ego's moral characteristics; the lost of it, turns the individual into a marginal in the community.

Face or "*Mien-tsu*", on the other hand, stands for the kind of prestige that is related with reputation, achieved through prestige in life got from success and ostentation (Yau, 1994), it defines a persons place in his social network, and it is the most important measure of social worth (Graham and Lam, 2003).

The amount of "*Mien-tsu*" a person has is a function of its social status and it varies according with the group with which he interacts and is its social capital. The Chinese are always under a strong pressure to meet the expectations of the group they interact, to maintain their "*Mien-tsu*" and to reciprocate a due regard to the "*Mien-tsu*" of the others (Yau, 1994).

Sources of "*Face*" can be wealth, intelligence, attractiveness, skills, position and good "*Guanxi*" itself. Chinese think of "*Face*", in quantitative terms and like money can be earned, lost, given or taken away (Graham and Lam, 2003). To cause others to loose it is the most aggressive offence that can be done to a Chinese and will not be forgotten ever. As mention before collectivist societies tend to give high value to "*Face*".

The more traditional the Chinese are, the more they will judge themselves in terms of how much or how little respect they expect from others - that is their level of "*Face*". One's face it is something to prize and to protect, commercial relationship with high-level decision-makers cannot be made or maintained by those of low status, those without "*Face*".

The Chinese deals with others on a reciprocal basis, and due to high distance power dimension, (Hofstede, 1991, 2004) respect to the Chinese obliges to clarify and differentiate their status ranking. Egalitarian - minded westerner often forget that Chinese culture, places high priority on recognizing this, and that behaving should be in accordance with a person's social standing. In business a western insensibility to shades of status gradation can have disastrous results.

The concept of "*Face*", can affect marketing variables, by encourage Chinese to buy only products with a well-known brand or reputation, the ranking of everything by hierarchy make highly desirable to buy what is in the top (McGuiness *et al.,* 1991).

3 Conclusions

More than factual knowledge of Chinese culture, the interpretative knowledge is very important and difficult, since it comes from a matrix of philosophic, religion and political explanations, which are completely different of the western one, so the Self Reference Criterion methodology should be employed if ones want to successfully get into Chinese market.

The typical Chinese businessperson, gains influence and power through affiliation rather than independent action, unconnected individuals are powerless, especially in the realm of business. Chinese are team players, tightly networked being very difficult to a Westerner to break into a Chinese commercial group. Until recently business in China was a personal in-group activity largely closed to strangers.

It is important to use a Chinese liaison at the first approach to introduce the foreigners into the appropriate business groups. Even so, door will not open quickly but perseverance and socializing with the Chinese, which can after knowing the person bring him into their business community, can eventually give the foreigners same change of being accepted.

One should keep in mind that the success of a foreign company, depends on the business group in China that have accepted him as a member, and to gain membership in a group the foreigners has to find the nature of the commonality, since people can share political, family, regional and language bonds, and must observe its social customs and commercial rules. An immense business power is embodied in complex Chinese business networks throughout the Asia Pacific Rim. They possess not only the biggest reservoir of capital, but also actual political connections and the best practical information for surviving in different markets such as China, Indonesia, Vietnam, Malaysia, Taiwan and Singapore. Above all, business intelligence and capital flows across the Overseas Chinese community, because its members are superb networks. Acceptance in a Chinese group is a long term process, Chinese culture is long term oriented, trust is a key word in this process and the fidelity of the foreigner is going be at prove.

In fact trust is very important for doing business, as a consequence in China a crucial step in the phase of negotiation, is to identify the personal links which can be useful in approaching the Chinese negotiators, which can make the foreigners negotiators trustfully, this trust can be built on long-term negotiations, but this links can also be earned, by finding a talented Chinese which can be contracted or associated to the venture and bring with him all the necessary "*Guanxi*" making the intermediation of the negotiation.

The foundation of this persuasive network is "*Guanxi*", personal connections. "*Guanxi*" involves a long-term relationship and is based on trust and trust has been found to have a positive effect on export performance, and for Chinese business people is more important than any signed contract, in this context is very important for having a successful business relationship.

An important business strategy to foreigners to enter Chinese market is to create partnerships with Overseas Chinese companies, which gives them "*Guanxi*", and business intermediation. Firms particularly the small size ones, are particularly keen on their networks to establish themselves in Southeast Asia and China.

Relationship marketing similar to Chinese "*Guanxi*", which emphasizes personal trust building, the use of social bonds in dealing with partners, competitors and clients in general good personal networks, is a critical success factor for business performance in China and firm's degree of customer orientation is positively associated with sales growth and the overall performance in China. For instance in technology transfer and equipment sales, special financial help, and barter emerged as more important factors in building customer relationships. Chinese culture emphasizes diffused relationships; as a result the Chinese tend not to separate business from interpersonal relationships. Generally, successful technology transfer is accompanied by healthy personal relationships and effective coordination interactions.

Culturally Chinese have a strong respect for authority, and as a marketing consequence Chinese consumers tend to respond more to reference group leaders, being them family elders, political leaders, and enterprise leaders than to advertising. Another consequence is that Chinese consumers tend to have higher brand loyalty than their counterparts in West countries, and have a high tendency to purchase the brand or product, which members of the group recommend, and if its reference group has established a product *as* the normative, Chinese consumers will not *deviate* their buying decision from the accepted product.

Brands have historically been used for social purposes in China, because of decentralization and ambiguous class divisions, there was a constant rise and fall of family wealth and position, and this necessitate the use of material symbols to mark status, the social function of brands is still paramount today because Chinese consumers use brand names as a tool to build social relationships.

Chinese culture tends to rank everything hierarchically, so that is highly desirable to buy what is at the top, as a consequence perceived product quality had the most influence on preferences, price may not be that important in the final decision. Also promotional and service activities had the major influence on customer relationship ratings, since these activities generate interaction between suppliers and customers. Also the concept of "Face", can affect marketing variables, by encourage Chinese to buy only products with a well-known brand or reputation, the ranking of everything by hierarchy make highly desirable to buy what is in the top.

References

Achrol, Ravi S. (1997), Changes in the Theory of Inter Organizational Relations in Marketing: Toward a Network Paradigm, Journal of the Academy of Marketing Science, Vol. 25 (1), pp.56 -71.

Ambler, Tim, Chris Styles and Wang Xiucun (1999), The Effect of Channel Relationships and Guanxi on the Performance of Inter-province Export Ventures in the People's Republic of China, Research in Marketing, 16, pp.75-87.

Anwar, Syred Tariq (1996), Overseas Chinese Business Networks in Asia, Journal of International Business Studies, 27, 4, pp.811-815.

Barkema, Harry G and Freek Vermeulen (1997), What Differences in the Cultural Backgrounds of Partners are Detrimental for International Joint-Ventures?, Journal of International Business Studies, 28(4), pp.845-864.

Begley, Thomas M. and Wee-Liang Tan (2001), The Socio-Cultural Environment for Entrepreneurship: A comparison Between East Asian and Anglo-Saxon Countries, Journal of International Business Studies, Vol. 32, N° 3, pp.537-553.

Bradley, Frank (1991), International Marketing Strategy, Prentice Hall, London.

Bradley, Frank (2002), International Marketing Strategy 4th, FT Prentice Hall.

Brouthers, Keith D. & Lance Eliot Brouthers (2000), Acquisition or Greenfield Strat-up? Institutional, Cultural and Transaction Cost Influences, Strategic Management Journal, 21(1), pp.89-97.

Brouthers, Keith D. & Lance Eliot Brouthers (2001), Explaining the National Cultural Distance Paradox, Journal of International Business Studies, Vol.32, N° 1, pp.177-189.

Cateora, Philip R. (1993), International Marketing 8th, International Student Edition, Series in Marketing, Irwin, Boston.

Chadee, Doren D. and Benjamin Y. Zhang (2000), The Impact of Guanxi on Export Performance: A Study of New Zealand Firms Exporting to China, Journal of Global Marketing, Vol.14, N° 1,2, pp.129-149.

Chen, Homin & Tain-Jy Chen (1998), Network Linkages and Location Choice in Foreign Direct Investment, Journal of International Business Studies, Vol.29, N° 3, pp.445-468.

Chu, Priscilla (1996), Social Network Models of Overseas Chinese Entrepreneurship: The Experience in Hong Kong and Canada, Canadian Journal of Administrative Science, Vol. 13, N° 4, pp.358-365.

Dow, Douglas (2000), A Note on Psychological Distance and Export Marketing Selection, Journal of International Marketing, Vol. 8, N° 1, pp.51-64.

Eckhardt, Giana M. and Michael J. Houston (2002), Cultural Paradoxes Reflected in Brand Meaning: McDonald's in Shanghai, China, Journal of International Marketing, Vol.10, N° 2, pp.68-82.

Ekeledo, Ikechi and K., Sivakumar (1998), Foreign Market Entry Mode, Choice of Service Firms: A Contingency Perspective, Journal of Academy of Marketing Science, Vol. 26, N° 4, pp.274-292.

Engholm, Christopher (1994), Doing Business in Asia's Booming "China Triangle", New Jersey: Prentice Hall, Inc.

Erramilli, M. Krishna, Sanjeev Agarwal, Chekitan S. Dev (2002), Choice between Non-Equity Modes: An Organizational Capability Perspective, Journal of International Business Studies, Vol.33, N° 2, pp.223-242.

Fu, P.P. and G. Yukl (2000), Perceived Effectiveness of Influence Tactics in the United States and China, Leathership Quarterly, 11(2), pp.251-266.

Fu, P.P., J. Kennedy, J. Tata, G. Yukl, M.H. Bond, T. Peng, E. S. Srinivas, J.P. Howell, L. Prieto, P. Koopman, J.J. Boonstra, S. Pasa, M. Lacassagne, H. Higashide and A.Cheosakul (2004), The Impact of Societal Cultural Values and Individual Social Beliefs on the Perceived Effectiveness of Managerial Influence Strategies a Meso Approach, Journal of International Business Studies, Vol.35, N° 4, pp.284-305.

Fukuyama, F.(1995), Trust, New York: Free Press.

Graham, John L. and N. Mark Lam (2003), The Chinese Negotiation, Harvard Business Review, Vol. 81 (10), pp.82-91.

Ho, Suk-Ching (2001), Executive Insights: Growing Consumer Power in China. Some Lessons for Managers, Journal of International Marketing, Vol. 9, N°1, pp.64-83.

Hofsted, G. (1980), Culture's Consequences, Sage Publications.

Hofsted, G. (1991), Cultures, Organizations: Software of the Mind, London, McGraw-Hill.

Hofsted, G., Cheryl A.Van Deusen, Carolyu B. Mueller, Thomas A. Charles (2002), What Goals Do Business Leaders Pursue? A Study in Fifteen Countries, Journal of International Business Studies, Vol. 33, N° 4, pp.785-803.

Hofsted, G. (2004), www.geert-hofstede.com

Huntington, S. (1999), O Choque de Civilizações, Gradiva.

InterChina Consulting (2004), Opportunities in the Chinese Market, pp.4-54.

Kao, John (1993), The Worldwide Web of Chinese Business, Harvard Business Review, March-April, pp.24-36.

Keegan, W. and M. Green (2000), Global Marketing 2nd, Prentice-Hall, New Jersey.

Li, Ji, Kevin Lam and Gongming Qian (2001), Does Culture Affect Behavior and Performance of Firms? The Case of Joint-Venture in China, Journal of International Business Studies, Vol. 32, N° 1, pp. 115-131.

Lieberthal, K. and G. Lieberthal (2003), The Great Transition, Harvard Business Review, Vol. 81 (10), pp.71-81.

Lin, Xiaohua and Richard Germain (1999), Predicting International Joint-Venture Interaction Frequency in US-Chinese Ventures, Journal of International Marketing, Vol.7, N° 2, pp.5-23.

Luo, Yadong (1997), Guanxi and Performance of Foreign-invested Enterprises in China: An Empirical Inquiry, Management International Review, 37 (1), pp.51-70.

Luo, Yadong (1999), Time-Based Experience and International Expansion: The Case of an Emerging Economy, Journal of Management Studies, 36, pp.505-534.

Malhotra, Naresh K., James Agarwal and Imad Baalbaki (1998), Heterogeneity of Regional Trading Blocs and Global Marketing Strategies, A Multicultural Perspective, International Marketing Review, Vol. 15, N°6, pp.476-506.

McGuiness, Norman, Nigel Campbell and James Leontiades (1991), Selling Machinery to China: Chinese Perceptions of Strategies and Relationships, Journal of International Business Studies, Second Quarter, pp.187-207.

McKinseyQuarterly, 2004, China Today, Special Edition.

Naisbitt, John (1995), Megatrends Asia: The Eight Asian Megatrends That Are Changing the World, London: Nicholars Brealey Publishing Limited.

Nakata, Cheryl and K. Sivakumar (2001), Instituting the Marketing Concept in a Multinational Setting: The Role of National Culture, Journal of the Academy of Marketing Science, Vol. 29, N° 3, pp.255-275.

Ojah, K. and L. Monplaisir (2003), Investors´ Valuation of Global Product Design and Development, Journal of International Business Studies, 34, pp.457-472.

Pothukuchi, V., F. Damanpour, J. Choi, C.C. Chen and S. H. Park (2002), National and Organizational Culture Differences and International Joint Venture Performance, Journal of International Business Studies, 33, pp.243-265.

Redding, S. Gordon (1990), The Spirit of Chinese Capitalism, Ed. Clegg Stewart R., New York: Walter de Gruyter.

Richter, Frank-Jürgen (1999), Business Networks in Asia, Promises, Doubts and Perspectives, Westport, Quorum Books.

Roath, A.S., S.R. Miller and S.T. Cavusgil (2002), A Conceptual Framework of Relational Governance in Foreign Distributor Relationships, International Business Review, 11, pp.1-16.

Seagrave, Sterling (1995), Lords of the Rim: The Invisible Empire of the Overseas Chinese, London: Bantam Press.

Sin, Leo Y. M, Alan C. B. Tse, Oliver H. M. Yau, Jenny S. Y. Lee, Raymond Chow and Lorett B. Y. Lau (2000), Market Orientation and Business Performance: An Empirical Study in Mainland China, Journal of Global Marketing, Vol.14, (3), pp.5-29.

Sirmon, David G. and Peter J. Lane (2004), A Model of Cultural Differences and International Alliance Performance, Journal of International Business Studies, 35, pp.306-309.

Sivakumar, K. and Cheryl Nakata (2001), The Stampede toward Hofstede's Framework: Avoiding the Sample Design Pit in Cross-Cultural Research, Journal of International Business Studies, Vol.32, N° 3, pp.555-574.

Skarmeas Dionisis, Constantine S. Katsikeas and Bodo B. Schlegelmilch (2002), Divers of Commitment and its Impact on Performace in Cross-Cultural Buyer-Seller Relationships: The Importers Perpective, Journal of International Business Studies, Vol.33, N° 4, pp.757-783.

Skenkar, Oded (2001), Cultural Distance Revisited: Towards a More Rigorous Conceptualization and Measurement of Cultural Differences, Journal of International Business Studies, Vol. 32, N° 3, pp.519-535.

Steensma, H.Kevin, Louis Marino, K.Mark Weaver and Pat H. Dickson (2000), The Influence of National Culture on the Formation of Technology Alliances by Entrepreneurial Firms, Academy of Management Journal, Vol. 43, N° 5, pp.951-973.

Wang, Chen-Lu, Zhen-Xiong Chen, Allan K.K. Chan and Zong-Cheng Zheng (2000), The Influence of Hedonic Values on Consumer Behaviors: An Empirical Investigation in China, Journal of Global Marketing, Vol. 14, N° 1/2, pp.169-183.

Yau, Oliver, H.M. (1994), Consumer Behavior in China, Customer Satisfaction and Cultural Values, Routledge.

Yeung, H. Wai-Chung (1997), Transnational Corporations from Asian Developing countries: Their Characteristics and Competitive Edge, in: Strategic Management, in a Global Economy, Wortzel, H.V. and L. H. Wortzel, John Wiley and Sons, Inc., pp.22-45.

Chapter 12
The Impact of IT on Organizational Forms

Liang-Hung Lin

National Kaohsiung University of Applied Sciences,Taiwan, P.R. CHINA

Abstract This chapter describes how information technology enables new organizational forms, and presents famous cases in the Taiwanese electronics companies.

1 Information

Information technology is viewed as an crucial tool in the management of organizational design and development since the adoption of technologies can foster organizational changes in structure and strategy. Due to the development of advanced information technologies, the increased uncertainty for technologies has caused the pressures for organizations to refine their operation process, marketing process, and even working process. From the perspective of organizational management, IT increases information sharing by diminishing transaction cost of information exchange. The advanced IT tools, such as internet, intranet, and world wide web, have facilitated communication in working groups and organizations. Previous studies have examined the IT impact on organizational structure. This chapter wishes to describe how IT enables new organizational forms, and present famous cases in the Taiwanese electronics companies.

2 IT-enabled structural variables

Structure, as the blueprint for activities, includes the table of organization covering departments, positions, and programs. Three affective contextual variables exist, including environment, technology, and size that allow organizations to

generate different types of structures. From this perspective, information technologies are not merely changes of organizational environment, but also are an
important technology for a firm, particularly for information and e-business related industries. Managers can use information technologies to develop IT-
enabled design variables that can help in designing suitable structures to manage
strategy/environment fit. Scholars reported useful IT-enabled design variables for
designing new structures to facilitate corporate coordination and inter-
organizational communication among organizations. These variables include:

1. virtual components, which can create virtual departments via electronic data
   exchange and inter-organizational delivery system (For example, if some firms
   wish their parts suppliers to replace the inventory, they may ask the suppliers to
   offer parts on demand or at the last minute by using electronic mail and express
   delivery);
2. electronic linking, by using electronic mail and telecommunication technologies;
3. technological leveling, which can refine the organizational hierarchy by using
   electronic communication tools;
4. mass customization technology;
5. Internet, intranet, and extranet; and
6. technological matrixing, which forms matrix structures by electronic mail, fax,
   and telecommunication technologies.

Organizations must modify their structure continuously when the environment
changes more rapidly than before. Facing keen competition, firms should maintain
and improve competitive advantage by developing collaborative strategies such as
joint venture, strategic alliance, and vertical integration. Accordingly, some organizational activities must be separated and become the business of the collaborative
partners, indicating changing of operational processes for both parties. From this
perspective, organizations should adopt the appropriate competitive strategy and at
least one modified structure to respond to these considerations. According to information technologies, organizations have addressed and implemented numerous
innovative structures. Vertically integrated electronic and virtual organizations recently have been identified as the most representative and innovative of these new
structures in the information related industries. Vertically integrated electronic organization and virtual organization can be considered the general application of
IT-enabled design variables and traditional design variables.

3 The e-enabled vertically integrated organizations

From an organizational adaptation perspective, restructuring refers to increase the efficiency and effectiveness of management through significant changes in organizational structure, often accompanied by downsizing. In the information age, many organizations have recommended numerous new structures to face the keen competition in the rapidly changing environment. For example, Apple Computer adopted a new and informal hierarchy in the 1990s when the organization moved from a traditional structure to an e-enabled process-based structure. To reduce operational costs, forms can establish functional departments that do not actually exist in the firms. Outside suppliers supply virtual components to firms by using electronic data interchange (EDI) and overnight delivery system. FedEx's eShipping system is an example for the application of virtual component organization. Large OEM/ODM electronics firms in Taiwan thus combine the implications of virtual components and vertical integration and set up e-enabled vertically integrated organizations in their restructuring practices. Based on the interorganizational control and coordination, this restructuring has properties of flexibility and reducing manufacturing cost that reduces the risk and uncertainty of technological change.

Guided by the corporate vision that electronics products should be an integral part in every office and every home, Foxconn Technology Group has become the leading provider of joint R&D, manufacturing, and service in the global communication, consumer electronics, and computer industries (3C). Through the corporate strategy of "total cost advantages", Foxconn becomes the largest company in Taiwan, and also the largest exporter in Greater China. By positioning itself as a service provider rather than a manufacturer, Foxconn adopts eCMMS (see Fig. 1 and 2) business model to integrate its various operation processes and outsider suppliers. Foxconn's eCMMS symbolizes e-enabled components, modules, moves, and service that contain the vertically integrated one stop shopping model through solutions of molding, tooling, mechanical and electronic parts, modules, system assemblies, design, development, manufacturing, maintenance, logistics, and after-sale services. The flexibility and low-cost advantage come from fast molding and assemblies through combining module design and component manufacturing. Furthermore, eCMMS can be extended to mechanical modules, electrical modules, system assemblies and testing in the global 3C industries. In addition to purchase components or modules, customers can ask Foxconn to assemble final products. Coping with keen competition, eCMMS also include joint design and joint development functions in order to reduce time to mass production. Suppliers (backward) or distributors (forward) in the global 3C industries are all potential customers of Foxconn. This e-enabled vertical integration business model facilitates low cost and high quality advantages for the largest electronic manufacturing service provider in Taiwan.

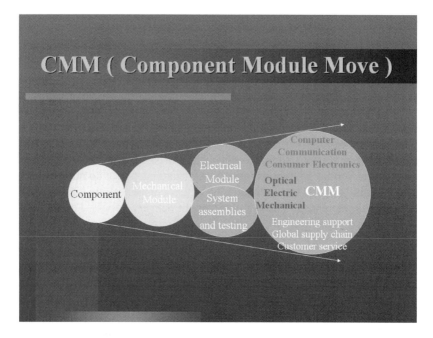

Figure 1 Traditional CMM (Component Module Move) Model

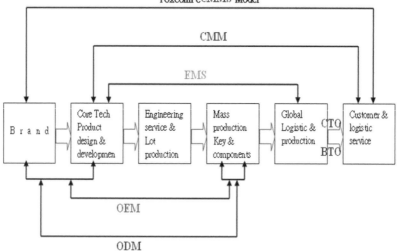

Figure 2 CMM and eCMMS Models

4 Virtual organization

The virtual organization is considered a rapidly respondent organization of marketing orientation and satisfying customer need designed to orient itself to the market and satisfy customer needs. Scholars addressed that within this structure members are organized in distinct geographical spaces and in different times, from managerial to operating levels, to accomplish organizational tasks. The characteristics of this structure are flexible, indicating the capability to adapt to the environment, fluid communication, the capability to discover potential consumer needs, and virtuality, which controls the breaking of formal structure. Virtual structure is limited in two respects: the lack of physical flow and equipment, and incomplete knowledge transportation. Meanwhile, virtual organization has three advantages:

- dependence on federation;
- spatial and temporal independence; and
- flexibility.

Taiwan Semiconductor Manufacturing Company (TSMC), the largest Taiwanese IC firm, is a representative and innovative example of virtual organization. The establishment of TSMC in 1987 represented the beginning of the semiconductor foundry industry. TSMC reported annual sales of over four U.S. billion in 2002, and employs over 15,000 professional workers worldwide. Facing an unstable environment and fierce global competition, in 1996 TSMC decided to integrate traditional business-to-business communication tools, such as letters, faxes, express deliveries, telephone calls, and meetings, and implemented its virtual foundry. The virtual foundry is a suite of web-based applications that provide customers real time information on wafer design, engineering, and logistics. The virtual foundry allows customers to monitor key information through online access to electronic supply chain management (SCM), such as purchase orders, wafer in progress (WIP) reports, and so on. Introducing the virtual foundry, TSMC said that the system would allow its customers to immediately understand the situation of wafer fabrication, assembly and testing. All information is updated from once every three days to three times a day. The Virtual Foundry of TSMC includes three major e-services: SMC-Online, TSMC-YES, and TSMC-Direct. According to internet and intranet, TSMC-Online (see Fig. 3) allows customers to handle their production process via sharing information such as technology standards and MPS. TSMC-YES system (see Fig. 4) allows customers to reduce their product's error rate via on line test system. TSMC-Direct system (see Fig. 5) tries to establish the workflow to workflow integration between TSMC and its customers.

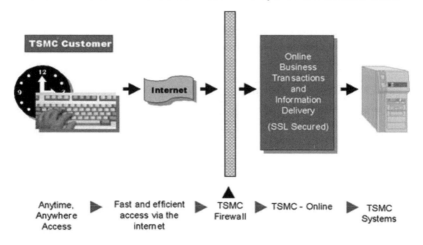

Figure 3 TSMC-Online system

Source: TSMC website: http://www.tsmc.com.tw

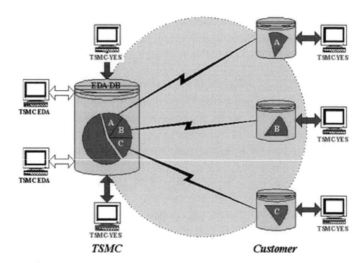

Figure 4 TSMC-YES system

Source: TSMC website: http://www.tsmc.com.tw

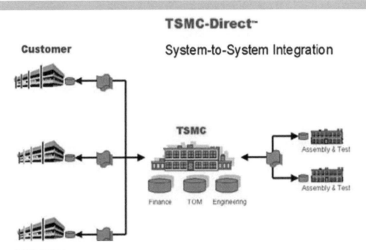

Figure 5 TSMC-Direct system

Source: TSMC website: http://www.tsmc.com.tw

5 Discussion

Various structural innovations have rapidly and widely been adopted and diffused in the Taiwanese electronic industry. This chapter has two major implications. First, most firms apply information technologies as a base for structural design in response to the dynamic global environment. As a powerful media of communication, IT-enabled structures also raise the possibility of diverse business-to-business electronic commerce and intra-organizational collaboration among firms in different industries. Facing fierce competition, new organizational structures must be continuously addressed and improved due to adaptation to environmental change. Second, information technologies can enhance various organizational improvements such as increasing performance, reducing paper works, and enhancing working flexibility. It is clear that IT can increase communication effectiveness among individual, teams, and organizations. In the information age, IT strengthens a shift from the so called command and control firms into the IT and information based organizations. New forms of IT-enabled organizations should be particularly emphasized in both manufacturing and service industries.

Chapter 13
Intellectual Capital and Competitive Advantage in the Globalization Context

An Empirical Analysis of creative industries in China

Ru-Yan Hong[1] **and Xiao-Bo Wu**[1]

[1] College of Management, Zhejiang University, Zhejiang, P.R. CHINA

Abstract This chapter is to investigate and to test empirically the association between a firm's intellectual capital (IC) and its competitive advantage in the globalization context. This study first identified IC sub-components as drivers believed to be important in enhancing competitive advantage on the basis of the in-depth interviews with firms. Next, the study's insights are combined with those available in the relevant literatures to have developed the hypotheses. These hypotheses are examined using data collected from 168 Chinese creative enterprises by means of "on-site" survey. Finally, the conclusion comes out with a discussion of managerial implications and suggestions for future research. After definitions are clearly developed for leading elements of IC, results from statistical analysis revealed that sub-components of IC have almost positive direct relationships with a firm's competitive advantage. These findings are consistent with resource-based view propositions in the IC literature indicating that intellectual capital is a valuable, non-substitutable, and inimitable strategic resource and with similar propositions in knowledge-based theory concerning knowledge-based resources and capabilities. However, control variables including external environment and firm size have significantly negative relationships with a company's competitive advantage. These results suggest that an effort to enhance firm's competitiveness by investing in IC is important in the globalization context.This research helps not only managers investigate and identify pertinent IC configurations but also directors pay careful attention to managing organizational "soft assets" - IC to obtain sustainable competitive advantage in the fast and furious international competition.The authors believe that most knowledge development efforts in IC and CIs have focused on Western economies and companies; considering its size, rapid growth rate, and market reforms, China has emerged as an important new context for CIs development; current understanding of the factors associated with IC management successes in China remains limited. So this paper addresses this knowledge gap, proposes a clear study framework and uses mixed methods for CIs in china to guide future research.

P.O. de Pablos, M.D. Lytras (eds.), *The China Information Technology Handbook*,   221
DOI: 10.1007/978-0-387-77743-6_13, © Springer Science+Business Media, LLC 2009

1 Introduction

In the globalization context China is now positioning its creative industries (CIs) as priorities for strategic growth. The CIs characterized by the generation and exploitation of intellectual property such as advertising, architecture, design, art, crafts, fashion, software and computer games make up an increasingly important element of economic competitiveness in china. According to relative literature, competitive advantage and superior performance of a organization or nation largely originate from their "soft assets"-intellectual capital (IC)-based on knowledge, expertise, experience, culture and so on (Bontis,2003; Stewart, 1994; Edvinsson, 2002; Teece, 2000; McGaughey, 2002). Many researchers claim that IC is the most valuable asset and the super strong weapon in the knowledge-based economy. This is particularly so in the intellect-intensive CIs. That is to say, intellectual capital (IC) is at the heart of CIs.

Unfortunately, IC has drawn widespread attention throughout Europe and the United States with its claim that it can uncover hidden resources of the firm (Blair and Wallman, 2001). As a result, knowledge development efforts in this important domain have centralized mainly on firms in those developed countries for about score years, limiting understanding of the factors influencing firms success in emerging and transitional economies (Liyanage et al., 2002). While the size of such economies may account for this relative lack of research attention, China stands out as an exception for four reasons. First of all , with China's rapid economic growth, and with a growth rate of gross domestic product (GDP) that far exceeds that of other developed countries, China ranks as one of the world's most important economies (Child and Tse, 2001). Secondly, China has a very different political, economic, social, and cultural environment to that of Western countries, presenting a unique trade environment (Boisot and Child, 1988; Hofstede and Bond, 1988; Lau et al., 2002). Thirdly, with the rapid development of information technology and the acceleration of urbanization, emphasis on the consumption of cultural and creative products has increased dramatically. Last but not least, market- oriented economic reforms and entry into the WTO have opened up Chinese markets. As a consequence, many foreign firms, frequently in alliances with Chinese partners or independently, now are exploiting many projects around China.

This study therefore focuses on the CIs in developing nation, China. The goal of the research is to identify and to test empirically significant factors associated with organizational competitive advantage in Chinese creative enterprises. In accomplishing this, a multi-methods approach is adopted due to the limited literature concerning IC and CIs in China. Hence the present study first identify IC factors as drivers believed to be important in enhancing competitive capabilities in concrete context on the basis of the in-depth interviews with firms' members. Next, the study's fieldwork insights are combined with those available in the resource-based view of firm (RBV), knowledge management theory, and IC literature to develop hypotheses linking competitive advantage and IC including human capital (HC), structural capital (SC), intellectual property capital (IPC) and relationship capital (RC). And then, the statistical analysis is used to examine empirically these hypotheses through using data collected from 168 Chinese creative firms by means of "on-site" survey. Finally, we conclude with a discussion of managerial implications and suggestions for future research.

The present study makes two contributions to knowledge in this important field. For one thing, factors and interrelationships important in understanding firm success in Chinese CIs are identified and are verified empirically. This research's empirical results provide new insights into how IC and competitive advantage are connected in the dynamical transitional context of Chinese markets. For another thing, more widely, the IC is identified as a crucial core resource related with competitive advantage under complex business conditions. This supports largely untested resource-based view (RBV) and IC theory propositions as to the potential value of firms' core resources in enabling organizations to behave in ways that allow them to successfully adjust to their environment and improve firm's global competitiveness.

2 Theory Development and Research Hypotheses

With the emphasis on knowledge, the notion of IC has been facilitated by the general understanding of the meaning of intangibles in some countries notably America and Europe (Hayek, 1945; Machlup, 1962; Sveiby 1986). However, as presented by recent literature reviews on the topic (Canibano et al., 2000; Petty and Guthrie, 2000), the main-stream discussions about the increasing importance of IC or intangibles such as goodwill and dedication within the organizations appeared during the 1980s. Some researchers generally viewed IC as non-monetary sources of probable future economic profits, lacking financial substance that may or may not be sold separately from other corporate assets (Sveiby, 1986; Itami, 1987). However, most contributions emerged during the 1990s in a variety of fields (Chaminade and Roberts, 2002) such as identifying (Johanson et al., 2001a, 2001b), accounting (Roberts, 1999; Can˜ibano et al., 2000), management (Sveiby, 1990; Bontis, 1996, 1999; Meritum, 2002). As indicated by Petty and Guthrie (2000), the study focus ranges from the need to better understand intellectual capital (Brooking, 1996; Stewart, 1991; Sullivan, 1998, 2000), and adopt a common accepted classification (Roberts, 2000) to a range of different methods and tools such as the balanced scorecard (Kaplan and Norton, 1992, 1996), the intangible asset monitor (Sveiby, 1997), the Skandia navigator (Edvinsson and Malone, 1997) and value chain scoreboard (Lev, 2001) to visualize and measure and to create standards for management and reporting IC.

Simultaneously, different initiatives have been undertaken by a variety of international actors and institutions, such as the OECD, the European Union, Mill Valley Group, Intellectual Capital Management Gathering, entrepreneurial and industry associations as well as by individual firms and researchers (Can˜ibano and Sa´nchez, 2003). Especially, the mobilization by the international organizations has moved in phase with a large number of initiatives in the business sector, both at industry (Roberts and Berthling-Hansen, 2000) and at firm level. In this special issue various researches and policy interests have been triggered. During the past two decades, the concept of intellectual capital has had time to develop in specific pockets of experimentation, generating specific interpretations and operationalizations. For example, chief knowledge officers (CKO) position and IC departments have been established to manage their IC in some companies such as Skandia AFS, Dow Chemical, Ernst & Young, Xerox, IBM and Lotus. Up to now, the literatures in relation to IC and multiform experiments in the management and reporting of intellectual capital continue to be found. Unfortunately, although they realize the potentially important role of IC in today's turbulent environments, the concept and classification of IC still remains a "black box" around which there is much conceptual fuzziness and overlap among intangibles, IC and intellectual property and is little operationalization and measurement. Thus, there is still a need for a common theoretical framework as well as a lack of tools and models to help firms develop their own customized system for the IC management.

Therefore, to enable the systemic study of IC mature, it is imperative to introduce a greater clarity about their content domain, conceptualization, and operationalization in Chinese context. In fields of relatively undeveloped inquiry, the use of qualitative in-depth interviews is a proper start for developing research propositions (Zaltman, 1997). Twenty-three in-depth interviews were conducted with managers by way of on-the-spot inquiry in 18 different enterprises in East China's Zhejiang Province, Shanghai City and Jiangsu Province. Of course, these analyzed were non-randomly selected. They shared a characteristic of no previous experience but, at minimum, had a strong interest in the topic. They comprised two state-owned companies, six share-holding firms, three joint ventures, and seven private enterprises. The interviewees included eight directors, six project managers; five design consultants; three chief financial officer; two chief information officer; and two staff employees in different sectors of CIs. While position titles varied, all interviewees held positions with responsibility for development of creative organization. Most interviews were typically lasted one to three hours. Open-ended questions were used focusing on major issues with regard to firm competitive advantage such as the following: (1) How do directors and managers in this firm think about what results in high-speed growth and favorable competitive position? and (2) What are the internal and external factors in your company that seem to impact creative products or services success and failure? All interviews were recorded and subsequently were compiled.

The fieldwork data suggested four particular domains relevant to understanding creative enterprises success in China. First, directors and managers identified firm value consistent with agents of the concept of HC (Stewart, 1997; Bontis,1998; Davenport, 1999) as being important determinants of company success. For example, one director commented that Generally, the growth of creative firms primarily depend on creative and professional talents. Individual creativity, skill, talent and competence are the sources of corporation value. With rapid change of business environment and market demand, different firm can show different adaptability to market because of different status of HC investment and talent pool. Facing the uncertain environment, the firm with abundant talents can timely grasp market opportunities, make new development strategy, develop new products and technologies, guide and create new market demand, and accordingly take up advantageous competitive position. Conversely, the firms with scarce talents may often miss the boat due to the absence of innovation capability. One project manager in architecture design firms indicated that in our company designers play an important role in project design. Because human is sciential carrier, the realization of the value of knowledge and originality must depend on human behaviors. The more one person learns and knows, the better his competence and performance are. The fieldwork therefore shows that Chinese creative enterprises view HC regarding knowledge, experience, skills and talents as being core determinants of business success.

This fieldwork insight is broadly consistent with the IC literature and RBV of the firm that consider HC possessed by personnel such as knowledge, experience, know-how and ideas frequently exists in the hidden and uncoded form and doesn't leech on to organization (Edvinsson and Sullivan, 1996; Stewart, 1997). Because it has a long-term accumulation process and causal ambiguity, which render competitors difficult to imitate (Lippman and Rumelt, 1982; Reed and DeFillippi 1990). Sustainable competitive advantage just derives from firm specific combinations of knowledge-based resources that are valuable, tacit and difficult to imitate (Amit and Shoemaker, 1993; Nonaka and Takeuchi, 1995; Nonaka and Teece, 2001). Consistent with the present study's fieldwork insights, HC is identified in the literature as an organizational core resource that can create firm value. From this perspective, HC is viewed as an important knowledge- based asset that is rare, inimitable and insubstitutable. Further, we discriminated two kinds of HC in Chinese creative enterprises including HC with responsibility for management decision making and HC with responsibility for decision of execution. The former mainly embodys entrepreneurship such as entrepreneur quality and capability of management and innovation which behaves obviously in the phase of startup or reform of firms (Pena, 2002). The latter primarily includes knowledge, know–how and innovation abilities acquired by employees by means of normal education, vocational training, learning by doing and earning by using in practice through. Both together construct the most important footstone of creating company value, playing a crucial part in gaining competitive advantage. Hence, the following research proposition is proposed:

H1(1): A firm's entrepreneurship is associated positively with its competitive advantage.

H1(2): A firm's employee competence is related positively with its competitive advantage.

Second, managers in the present study's fieldwork also identified essentials of the SC within their firm as being elements in determining firm competitiveness.

For example, one design consultor described that organizational environment such as company culture, MIS, regulations and systems is very significant for creative teams. Motivating mechanism influences the speed and the quality of a creative project. Staff should be happy to go to work. Indeed, a positive working environment is very important to mutually share knowledge and experience. You cannot force people together. For instance, if employees feel nice about their organization, then they will trust each other, support each other and work together with pleasure. One chief information officer pointed out that harmonious internal environment as being "basic establishment" or "knowledge platform" provides firm support for motivating employees to bring their utmost potential and creativity into play. Then cooperating happily with each other will accelerate translation from uncoded tacit knowledge of individual brain into coded explicit knowledge possessed by corporation. This collective know-how embed in the organization and further reside within the organizational routines or rules. The fieldwork interviews showed that SC is the backbone and infrastructure of an organization (Burr and Girardi,2002) and can render new claim be applied and value be repetitively created as well as expand HC value and attemper corporation resources to support new claim (Stewart, 1997).

These insights concerning SC have not only been a focus of attention in IC literature, but also consistent with notions of knowledge-based theory that consider companies as somewhat sticky bundles of knowledge resources. Organizational design should involve attention to organization structures, systems and routines which allow knowledge sharing and achieve this knowledge integration within communities of practice (Grant, 1991, 1996). Because routines and recipes are a potential source of organizational stability and of adaptability (Feldman and Rafaeli, 2002). Thus, in a sense, SC is structural tacit knowledge containing in the organization itself (Sveiby, 1996). It natively belongs to organization and have the features of integrativity and untransferability, so anyone in firm can not absolutely hold its ownership and control rights (Stewart, 1997; Edvinsson and Sullivan, 1996). Consequently, On the basis of investigation and literatures, SC is defined as a complete set of organizational capabilities and knowledge systems consisting of organizational strategies, policies and process and so on (Dzinkowski, 2000). In this context SC is further divided into process-oriented SC concerning procedures and rules in work and coupling SC concerning structure, culture and mechanisms (Bassi, 1999; Swart, 2006). These structural know-how can ensure effective operation of the organization (Brooking, 1996; Stewart, 1997; Sullivan, 2000). Apparently, consistent with the present study's fieldwork insights highlighting the important role of a supportive organizational climate and routines in the globalization context, IC literature and knowledge-based theory indicates that SC can constitute an important source of sustainable competitive advantage (Barney,1991; Grant, 1996). This suggests that:

H2(1): A firm's process-oriented SC is associated positively with its competitive advantage.
H2(2): A firm's coupling SC is related positively with its competitive advantage.

Third, directors and design consultors in this research's on-the-spot inquiry identified elements of intellectual property capital (IPC) such as copyright, patent and business secret (Brooking, 1996; Sullivan, 2000) as being crucial factors in creating firm competitive advantages. For example, one design consultor indicated that creative design is greatly creatively intellectual work. Each design and consultation completed by designers who apply special theories, skills and experience always agglomerate their wisdom and innovation spirits. If creative enterprises can view intellectual property as a kind of specific capital form, it will realize an important aim—superior profits and competitive advantages in the near future. Indeed, many firms often erect barriers to competitor imitation by utilizing IPC such as patents and technology secrets to get the upper hand or transfer intellectual property to gain considerable transfer fee and further increase corporation value. One director argued that actually intellectual property should be a kind of right capital and especial knowledge capital protected by law. With the entry into WTO and increasingly furious market competition, struggle for intellectual property protection in Chinese CIs is becoming more urgent. In such context, nation and creative enterprises should prescribe original and innovative productions as legally protected properties such as copyright and patent right, which can not only encourage employees to innovate but help firm make technological progress and strengthen competitive power. The fieldwork therefore suggests that Chinese creative firms view IPC as being important determinants of enhancing competitive advantage.

This fieldwork insight is generally consistent with the IC literature and knowledge management theory that views IPC as coded knowledge or special knowledge that presents physical form and might translate into profits (Sullivan, 2000). IPC such as patent, copyright, trademark, expertise, trade-secret is intellectual fruits protected by law (Brooking, 1996; Sullivan, 2000; Roos et al, 1998). Accordant with the present study's fieldwork insights, IPC is identified in the literature as firm resources that can abstract value. From this aspect, IPC is viewed as a greatly valuable intellectual asset in Chinese CIs. That is to say, IPC protected by law can not only ensure their innovation fruits and design freedoms but also avoid lawsuits so as to actualize legal monopoly for their intellectual productions (Sullivan, 2000).

H3(1): A firm's IPC is associated positively with its competitive advantages.

Fourth, many interviewees commonly identified RC such as formal and informal relation networks in the internal and external organizations (Bourdieu, 1980; Coleman, 1988; Saint-Onge, 1996) as being important determinants in obtaining priority and improving company competitiveness. For instance, one project manager indicated that it is very important for Chinese creative firms influenced deeply by relationship culture to manage social relationship. To a large extent, good ties and mutual trust between customer and enterprise can reduce transaction costs such as search and information costs and bargaining and decision costs. Moreover, nicer social relationship makes communication stronger between customers and firm so as to some clients become not only benefitors and diffusers in the process of firm innovation but also key cooperators and informants in the course of firm exalting market competitive position. One chief financial officer believed that social networks plays a vital role in business activities and making profits. For example, good relationship networks often can render company obtain invaluable information, capture opportunities that make business bring the dying back to life, take rare resources and projects of low risk and high yield, and consequently make the best use of the advantages and bypass the disadvantages and remain invincible in furious global competition. The fieldwork therefore shows that RC is seen as significant determinants of creative enterprises success. It provides access to resources (Nahapiet and Ghoshal, 1998) and sets the context within which other forms of capital interact. The more RC a company has the more efficient its transaction and the more productive it is (Bothwell, 1997).

This fieldwork insight is widely accordant with the social capital theory and IC literature that considers RC is a kind of knowledge and abilities that an actor can benefit from social networks (Granovetter, 1985; Coleman, 1988). These networks including endowed relationship and acquired network ties have been based on mutual confidence, trust and cooperation between among people and firms (Nahapie and Ghoshal, 1998; Ronald, 2001). Thus, according to present literatures, combining with this study's fieldwork, we identified two levels of RC, involving RC's dense tightness and wide extent (Cohen and Fields, 1999; Fukayama, 1995). The former presents directly long-term intercourse and mutually deep cooperation, faithful companionship, high trust and knowledge sharing between creative firm and other actors and so on (Leana and van Buren, 1999; Saint-Onge, 1996; Burt, 1992). The latter presents directly and indirectly wide connections with other actors such as supplier, competitors, agencies, governments, research institutions (Roos et al, 1998; Edvinesson, 1997), which can also accelerate resource flow, especially tacit knowledge transfer (Nonaka and Takeuchi, 1995). From this perspective, to invest and accumulate RC as being an important knowledge-based resource can enhance firm's competitiveness and performance (Bourdieu, 1980; Stewart, 1997). This suggests that:

H4(1): A firm's dense tightness of RC is associated positively with its competitive advantage.

H4(2): A firm's wide extent of RC is related positively with its competitive advantage.

3 Research Method

3.1 Data Collection

To test the hypotheses, data were collected via a questionnaire survey of creative enterprises in the east China's Zhejiang province, Shanghai city and Jiangsu province. To maximize the generalizability of this study's findings, a multi-industry sample was selected. A purposive sampling plan was developed to ensure representation of a wide variety of CIs, resulting in a eight industry-sector research design comprising (1) computer software and games; (2) architecture design; (3) advertising; (4) fashion design; (6)cosplay; (7) new media; and (8) music publishing. Using a range of government sources and commercial directories, enterprises were sampled that were engaged in the design and sale of creative products and services and where individuals or groups with responsibility for creative products or services could be identified. This resulted in a sample of 200 enterprises that included state-owned companies, share-holding firms, joint ventures, and private enterprises. A senior-level manager at each firm was contacted initially by telephone or interview to elicit participation and to identify the most knowledgeable informant, and 187 firms agreed to participate.

To conquer the difficulties of low response rate and high costs of survey research in China, an "administered on-site" method was used to collect questionnaires (e.g., Snow and Thomas, 1994). Questionnaires were administered to vice presidents, project managers, technical executive, senior designers, chief R&D officers and so on. Questionnaires were administered in either one-on-one interview formats or were administered by key individuals who supervised their completion by the designated respondents within each firm. In all, 168 useable surveys were completed, representing a 90% response rate. As a result, the respondents' mean job tenure (6.3 years) and familiarity with their areas (3.87 on a five-point scale) suggest that this study's key informants had significant experience in their firms on which to draw in providing data. Moreover, subsequent visits to the participating firms to verify questionable responses and verification of details with neutral observers supplemented the data collection. When available, internal company reports and archives were consulted for verification and revision.

3.2 Measures

The measures in this study included different elements of the IC constructs hypothesized to influence competitive advantage. Measures of all constructs consisted of five-point Likert-type scaled questions.

The dependent variable of the present study is competitive advantage. Competitive advantage is the core of organizational performance in competitive market (Porter, 1985), Consistent with previous studies, this research used a perceptual measure of competitive advantage. Drawing on insights from qualitative fieldwork, respondents were asked to assess their firm's competitive position relative to its competitors in terms of gross output value, retained profit, return on investment, customer satisfaction, company's member satisfaction, market share, and new market exploitation over the past three years using a five-point Likert scales with anchors from 1= "low" to 5= "high". Compared with average level within respective industry sector, competitive advantage was measured twofold: (1) actual profitability, i.e., financial performance (3 items) and (2) growth potential, i.e., non-financial performance (4 items). Adaptations of existing scales were used to measure competitive advantage (Kaplan and Norton, 1996; Firer and Williams, 2003).

Independent variable is IC. The study first established the IC structure through a thorough literature review and specific fieldwork. Considering that the IC configuration of the CIs may be squarely different from other industries, repetitive revision and verification was conducted in order to reach a more satisfactory content validity of the measurement instrument. Eventually, the operational definitions for these variables were modified from the prior studies (Saint-Onge, 1996; Stewart ,1997; Barathi, 2007). Respondents were asked to assess the degree to which the statements in the IC scales with thirty-four items described the practices in their firm using a five-point Likert scale with anchor labels from 1= "strongly disagree" to 5= "strongly agree". Included in the independent variables were measures related to human capita including employee competence (5 items) and entrepreneurship (5 items), structural capital including process-oriented SC (4 items) and coupling SC (4 items), IPC (5 items), and RC including dense tightness of RC (6 items) and wide extent of RC (5 items).

Control variables include four aspects. To control for the potential impact of other common variables on competitive position of the creative firms, collected data on firm size (number of employees), firm age (years of operation), competitive environment (macro- environment and task- environment) and tangible assets (financial assets and real assets) as control variables were included in the regression model (Murphy et al., 1996; Steven, 2003).

3.3 Unidimensionality, Scale Validity, and Reliability

To obtain unidimensionality, the interitem correlations were calculated and item-to-total correlations were corrected for each item, taking one scale at a time. Items for which these correlations were not significant (p<.01) were eliminated. Principal-axis factoring explored the unidimensionality of each purified scale using an eigenvalue of 1.0 and factor loadings of 0.25 as the cut-off points (Steenkamp and Van Trijp 1991). Computing reliability coefficients explored the reliability of each purified, unidimensional scale. When the coefficient alpha was smaller than .7, the item with the lowest item-to-total correlation was removed until meeting the .7 level.

The internal consistency and convergent validity of the scales was investigated by performing a series of confirmatory factor analyses (CFA) at the first-order and second-order level. Values of .7 for composite reliability and .5 for average extracted variance were used as indicators of the internal consistency of the scales (Bagozzi and Yi, 1988). The criterion of all factor loadings being significant (p<.05) was used as indicator of convergent validity (Bagozzi et al. 1991). The results of the factor analysis, summarized in Table 1, indicate that nearly all of the reliabilities Cronbach's coefficient alphas exceed the .70 threshold level for acceptable reliability and that the majority of the values for average extracted variance exceed the threshold level of .50. Convergent validity is indicated by the fact that in each model the items load significantly on the corresponding latent construct.

Table 1 Means, Standard Deviations, Reliability Coefficients, Average Variance Extracted, and Interconstruct Correlations

Variables	Items	Mean	Std. Dev	AVE	CRC	Correlations								
						Y1	Y2	X1	X2	X3	X4	X5	X6	X7
Y1. Actual profitability (Financial performance)	4	3.72	0.70	0.68	0.75	-								
Y2. Growth potential (Non-financial performance)	3	3.57	0.72	0.57	0.74	0.00	-							
X1. Employee competence	5	3.73	0.73	0.68	0.88	.58***	.45***	-						
X2. Entrepreneurship	5	3.68	0.69	0.60	0.83	.37***	.35**	0.00	-					
X3. Process-oriented SC	4	3.59	0.75	0.64	0.80	.44***	.37**	.38*	.27*	-				
X4. Coupling SC	4	3.61	0.78	0.60	0.76	.48**	.45**	.53*	.33*	0.00	-			
X5. IPC	5	3.25	0.79	0.61	0.84	.63***	.56***	.52**	.49*	.47**	.53*	-		
X6. Dense tightness of RC	6	3.63	0.77	0.61	0.86	.33*	.36**	.41**	.22**	.36*	.34**	.37**	-	
X7. Wide extent of RC	5	3.28	0.80	0.62	0.84	.35**	.39***	.36*	.37**	.22*	.48**	.49*	0.00	-

Notes: n=168; *p<0.1; **p<0.05; ***p<0.01. AEV: Average extracted variance. CRC: Composite reliability coefficients

Table 2 Summary of Regression Results for Competitive Advantage (Actual Profitability and Growth Potential)

Dependents Variables	Independents Variable										
	X1 Employee competence	X2 Entrepreneurship	X3 Process-oriented SC	X4 Coupling SC	X5 IPC	X6 Dense tightness of RC	X7 Wide extent of RC	X8 Firm age	X9 Environment	X10 Firm size	X11 Tangible assets
Y1. Actual profitability (Financial performance)	$.206^{**}$	$.103$	$.083$	$.093$	$.283^{***}$	$.165^{**}$	$.127^{*}$	$.081$	$-.018$	$-.133^{*}$	$.007$
	(2.521)	(1.343)	$(.977)$	(1.211)	(3.228)	(2.141)	(1.783)	$(.999)$	$(-.267)$	(-2.178)	$(.100)$

$F=11.57^{***}$, $R^2=0.449$, Adj. $R^2=0.410$, S.E.$= 0.59751$, DW$=1.997$

Dependents Variables	X1	X2	X3	X4	X5	X6	X7	X8	X9	X10	X11
Y2. Growth potential (Non-financial performance)	$.374^{***}$	$.213^{***}$	$.160^{**}$	$.097$	$.269^{***}$	$.069$	$-.065$	$-.016$	$-.150^{*}$	$-.006$	$.038$
	$(4.492)-$	(2.887)	(2.108)	(1.334)	(3.114)	(1.155)	$(-.939)$	$(-.282)$	(-1.721)	$(-.117)$	$(.658)$

$F=17.76^{***}$, $R^2=0.556$, Adj. $R^2=0.525$, S.E.$=0.56851$, DW$=1.906$

Note: $n=168$, $^{*}p<0.1$, $^{**}p<0.05$, $^{***}p<0.01$.

In the table 2, the values of 1.997 and 1.906 for DW statistic indicated that there were no serial correlation in the regression models. To test for multi-collinearity in all regressions, the variance inflation factors and tolerances were calculated. All the values were within the normal range (VIF<2.0, tolerance>0.5), thus suggesting that multi-collinearity was not a serious problem (Hair et al., 1998). Moreover, the results of collinearity diagnoses showed that multi-collinearity didn't exist because the values for condition index were less than 15 threshold level and eigenvalues did't exeed 0 limit (Tacq, 1997). Simultaneously, according to residual statistic results and 3-σprinciple of probability, the maximum of standardized residual absolute values below 3 indicated that there were no singular data in the sample, and the regression models didn't exist heteroscedasticity via judging from the residual scatter charts. Obviously, all regressions exhibit good statistic characteristics.

4.1 The Relationship between Human Capital and Organizational Competitive Advantage

The findings support H1(1) and H1(2), as employee competence has positive significant relationship with actual profitability (b=.206, p<.05) and growth potential (b=.374, p<.01). Entrepreneurship has positive significant relationship with growth potential (b=.213, p<.01). This findings are consistent with the studies suggesting that human capital as being the important source of creativity and hard core of IC structure improve competitiveness of creative enterprises and accelerate their innovative commercialization (Sullivan, 2000; Mohan and Mark, 2005).

4.2 The Relationship between Structure Capital and Corporation Competitive Advantage

Consistent with H2(2), process-oriented SC is related positively to the growth potential (b=.16, p<.05). Thus, the present study's finding supports partially past research arguing that structure capital as organizational "infrastructure" or "knowledge platform" is antecedent of the efficiency and effectiveness in the process of creating company value (Edvinsson and Sullivan, 1996). However, coupling SC has no significant direct relationship with competitive advantage. An explanation may be that this study, in contrast to previous studies, controls for the mediating role of other variables in the relationship between SC and competitive advantage (Barathi, 2007).

4.3 The Relationship between Intellectual Property Capital and Organizational Competitive Advantage

The results provide support for H3, as intellectual property capital has a positive and significant relationship with actual profitability (b=.283, p<.01) and growth potential (b=.269, p<.01). Consistent with past research, this finding reveals the importance of intellectual property capital to obtain sustainable competitive advantage (Brooking, 1996; Sullivan, 2000; Sveiby, 1997).

4.4 The Relationship between Relationship Capital and Company Competitive Advantage

In support of H4(1), H4(1), dense tightness of RC (b=.165, p<0.05) and wide extent of RC (b=.127, p<0.1) have significant and positive relationships only with actual profitability. Thus, this finding is consistent partly with the authors' theoretical expectations and with empirical results as reported by, for instance, Sant-Onge(1996), Stewart(1997), and Pena (2002). Again, an explanation may be that this study controls for the mediating role of other variances in the relationship between RC and growth potential (Barathi, 2007).

4.5 The Relationship between Firm Age, Environment, Firm size, Tangible Assets and Competitive Advantage in Creative Enterprises

Firm age and tangible assets have no significant direct relationship with competitive advantage. Negatively significant relationship (b=-.150, p<0.1) between environment and growth potential indicates that to a large extent dynamic and furious competitive environment restricts Chinese creative firms to improve higher competitive position and management performance. Similarly, firm size has a significant and negative relationship (b=-.133, p<0.1) with growth potential, indicating that to blindly pursue "large and comprehensive" management pattern is not rational choice for Chinese creative enterprises.

5 Managerial Implications

The present study accomplished its research purpose by depicting two aspects of competitive advantage, by illustrating their relationships with IC configurations. There are several implications for theoretical knowledge concerning firms' competitive advantage.

First, the connotation of IC factors may be more comprehensive to the stand-alone IC constructs in illustrating its relationship to competitive advantage. It provides more details about what the IC factors contain. Moreover, the important role played by organizational IC configurations in determining a firm's competitive position in the CIs is identified and supported empirically, which in turn explains significant variance in creative product or services success in Chinese creative firms. Therefore, given the size and growing importance of the Chinese market to both Western firms and the global economy, this provides important insights for both researchers and managers. In one respect, the identification of resource or capability as an important driver of competitive advantage in China suggests some similarity between drivers of company success in China and Western countries. However, knowledge-based IC is not a very key factor that previously has been identified explicitly as an important driver of competitive advantage in a rapid development context in China.

Second, this study's results indicate the human capital including employee competence and entrepreneurship of the firm is significant in determining market competitive position and company long-term development. As far as employee competence are concerned, more often than not firms with this type of IC configuration have good company's image, brand and goodwill in market because employees can provide creative products and services needed by customers through applying ideas, experience, knowledge and skills. Moreover, entrepreneurship containing many entrepreneur capacities, such as innovation and adventuring spirit, efficiency and sincerity is radical driver of enterprise reform and growth. This conclusion can be supported by previous studies (Edvinsson, 1997; Roos, 1998; Sullivan, 2000), which show that human capital is the footstone and source of competitiveness. Researches also have found that human capital is an important strategic resource for firms and act as an excellent entry barrier to ward off competitors, especially technology-intensive creative firms, to achieve a competitive advantage (Duysters et al, 2000; Barney, 1991). Thus, manager should pay more attention to investment in human capital and cultivation of innovative capability by improving organizational systems.

Third, this research's fieldwork interviews and its empirical results demonstrate the importance of the structural capital of the firm in explaining how firms' engage in organizational behaviors that enable them to achieve superior competitive status. This conclusion can be supported by Pena (2002) empirical examination, which shows that structural capital significantly impact on the growth and performance of the new-built enterprises. Studies also suggest that structural capital can provide good organizational climate for supporting personnel to bring novel ideas into play and apply technology and knowledge, to quickly adapt to ever-changing environment and to successfully plan and implement strategy (Pena, 2002; Steven, 2003). Hence, managers should be especially concerned about a just and fair salary system and perfect and rational incentive mechanism, should take great care to foster knowledge-sharing culture and encourage managerially and technologically innovation and should make efforts to implement total quality management system and reliable information management system so as to enhance firm products or services quality, decline the management cost and improve competitive performance.

Fourth, the present study's findings reveal the significance of the intellectual property capital of the firm in illustrating how firms' engage in intellectual property generating and exploiting that enable them to achieve superior actual profitability and growth potential. While IC literatures posit that intellectual property capital is a potentially important firm resource and act as an excellent entry barrier to ward off competitors (Brooking, 1996; Sullivan, 2000), there have been few empirical attempts to examine this proposition. The present research identifies and examines empirically the intellectual property capital variable as an important antecedent of firms' competitive advantage attainment in globalization context. Thus, managers in practice should take new technologies, ideas and patents of their company into high consideration. This will also lead to insights into how to protect and develop intellectual property capital.

Fifth, RC based on trust and cooperation is also an important IC configuration needed by competitive advantage creation. Indeed, value form existing in relationship networks - dense tightness and wide extent of RC - are utmost attractive and almost convulsing. Some studies also suggest that under many conditions, RC including organizational internal and external societal network assets can help company reduce cost, increase degree of differentiation and strengthen key customers' reliability (Edvinsson, 1997; Sullivan, 2000; Roland and Goran, 2007). From a value point of view, the extent to which a company is capable of creating reciprocal value with customers, suppliers, partners and even employees depends on the extent to which it can construct more intimate adherence and commutative loyalty than their rivals. RC is, in effect, the linchpin of a business relationship, and as such it is the cement keeping the joined rocks of a partnership secure even when storms occur or others try to split the joined rocks. Therefore, if firms can earnestly build and run those different kinds and layers of RC, firms' investment returns and outstanding achievements will greatly be improved.

In summary, these findings are expected, based on an empirical study of 168 creative enterprises in Chinese CIs, to help managers and researchers better understand the key elements - IC leading to firm success and the importance of IC for competitive advantages. Therefore, in practical efforts managers should pay careful attention to identifying organizational "soft assets" - IC factors and reinforcing IC investment and management.

6 Limitations and Directions for Future Research

This study was conducted within the context of the Chinese CIs. Hence, several limitations should be addressed in future research. First, while it was ensured that creative firms from a number of different areas and sectors were included in this study's sample, the time and resource requirements for collecting valid survey data in China necessarily limited the sample size. While this research represents an important step in identifying IC factors associated with obtaining competitive advantage in Chinese CIs, additional research is required to enhance confidence in the generalizability of these findings. That is to say, although the results of this study show relatively strong relationships between almost all predictor variables and competitive advantage, any claim as to the generalization of the findings to other contexts or industry segments should be made with caution.

Second, in this study, data were used with the assumption that IC factors influence competitive advantage obtainment; however, competitive advantage may reversely influence IC configurations. According to the new surge of strategic thinking, sustainable competitive advantages can be secured through rearranging and using capabilities embedded in processes and through continually reshaping the portfolio of assets (Hafeez, et al, 2002; Teece, et al, 1997). Therefore, the competitive advantage may impact the establishment and construction of firm IC.

Third, cross-sectional data are relied upon in testing the hypotheses. Importantly, this means that the direction of the relationship between IC factors and competitive advantage cannot completely be ascertained empirically. There is, therefore, a reliance on theory-driven arguments from IC theory supported by fieldwork insights in specifying the causal relationships in this study's hypotheses. To validate the causal chain hypothesized in this study requires multitrait-multimethod research design, longitudinal data collection and time-series analyses.

Fourth, the data on dependent variables, independent variables and control variables were collected on same style scales using the key informant approach, which may have caused common method bias. While careful attention was given to identifying appropriate informants and ensuring key informant quality, and while no indication of common methods problems was found, the potential still exists for respondent bias to affect the observed relationships (Phillips, 1981). In this study, the analysis indicated that the responses of the several informants in each respondent creative firm were not significantly different, suggesting that respondent bias may not be a significant problem in the data. Nevertheless, collecting data from multiple informants to minimize potential response bias would enhance confidence in the present results or future research. Of course, locating additional competent informants willing to provide survey information is challenging.

Above and beyond these limitations, the empirical results show that the role of IC in obtaining competitive advantage efforts should be a focus for future research. While this fieldwork led to a focus specifically on the CIs and only focused on two groups of constructs—IC configurations and competitive advantage, this is only one of a number of different dimensions of IC management. Future researchers should further examine the role of other dimensions of IC identified in management theory, such as IC identification and impact on creative product development processes and organizational performance in different area contexts and industry segments.

References

Amit, R. and Shoemaker, P. (1993), "Strategic assets and organizational rent," Strategic Management Journal, Vol. 14, No. 1, pp. 33-46.
Bagozzi, R. P., and Yi, Y. (1988), "On the evaluation of structural equation models", Academy of Marketing Science, Vol. 16, No. 1, pp. 76-94.
Bagozzi, R. P., Yi, Youjae and Phillips, Lynn W. (1991), "Assessing construct validity in organizational research", Administrative Science, Quarterly, Vol. 36, No. 3, pp. 421-458.
Barathi Kamath G, (2007), "Intellectual capital performance of the Indian banking sector", Journal of Intellectual Capital, Vol. 8, No. 1, pp. 96-123.
Barney, J. (1991), "Firm resources and sustained competitive advantage", Journal of Management, Vol. 17 No.1, pp.99-129.
Blair, M.M. and Wallman S.M.H. (2001), "Unseen wealth: report of the brookings task force on intangibles", Brookings Institution Press, Washington D.C.
Boisot, M.H., and Child, J. (1988), "The iron law of fiefs: bureaucratic failure and the problem of governance in the Chinese economic reforms", Administrative Science Quarterly, 33, 507-527.
Bontis, N.(1996), "There's a price on your head: Managing intellectual capital strategically", Business Quarterly. Summer, pp. 41-47.
Bontis, N.(1998), "Intellectual Capital: An exploratory study that develops measures and models", Management Decision, Vol. 36, No. 2, pp. 63-76.
Bontis, N. (1999), "Managing organizational knowledge by diagnosing intellectual capital: framing and advancing the state of the field", International Journal of Technology Management, Vol.18, Nos. 5/6/7/8, pp. 433-462.
Bontis, N. (2003), "National intellectual capital index: the benchmarking of Arab countries", Journal of Intellectual Capital, Vol. 5, No. 1, pp. 13-39.
Bothwell, R. (1997), "Indicators of a healthy civil society", in Burbridge, J. (Eds),Beyond Prince and Merchant: Citizen Participation and the Rise of Civil Society, Pact Publications, New York, NY, pp. 2492-262.
Bourdieu, P. (1980), "Le capital social: notes provisoires", Actes de recherches de sciences sociales, Vol. 31, pp. 2-3.
Brooking, A. (1996), "Intellectual Capital", London: International Thomson Business Press.
Burr, R. and Girardi, A. (2002), "Intellectual capital: more than the interaction of competence × commitment", Australian Journal of Management, Special Issue, Vol. 27 pp.77-87.
Burt, G. (1992), "Structural Holes", Harvard University Press, Cambridge, MA.
Can˜ibano, L., Garcı́a-Ayuso, M. and Sa´nchez, M. P. (2000), "Accounting for intangibles: a literature review", Journal of Accounting Literature, Vol. 19, pp. 102-130.
Can˜ibano, L. and Sa´nchez, M.P. (2003), "Measurement, management and reporting on intangibles: state-of-the-art", paper presented at the American Accounting Association 2003 Annual Meeting, Honolulu, HI, August 3-6.

Chaminade, C. and Roberts, H. (2002), Social capital as a mechanism. connecting knowledge within and across firms, paper presented at the third European Conference on Organizational Knowledge, Learning and Capabilities, Athens, Greece, April.

Child, J. and Tse, David K. (2001), "China's transition and the implications for international business", Journal of International Business Studies, Vol. 32, No. 1, pp. 8-21.

Cohen, S.S. and Fields, G. (1999), "Social capital and capital gains in Silicon Valley", California Management Review, Vol. 41, No.2, pp. 108-30.

Coleman,J.S.(1988), "Social capital in the creation of human capital", American Journal of Sociology, Vol.94, pp. 95-120.

Davenport, T. (1999), "Human capital", Jossey-Bass, San Francisco, CA.

Dzinkowski, R. (2000), "The measurement and management of intellectual capital: an introduction", Management Accounting, No. February, pp. 32-36.

Duysters, G. and Hagedoorn, J. (2000). Core Competencies and Company Performance in the Worldwide Computer Industry. Journal of High Technology Management Research, Vol. 11, No. 1, pp. 75-91.

Edvinsson, L. (1997), "Developing intellectual capital at Skandia", Long Range Planning, Vol. 30, No. 3, pp. 266-373.

Edvinsson, L. (2002), "Corporate longitude"e, Bookhouse Publishing, Stockholm.

Edvinsson, L. and Malone, M. (1997), "Intellectual capital: realizing your company's true value by finding its hidden brainpower. New York: HarperCollins.

Edvinsson, L. and Sullivan P. (1996), "Developing a model for managing intellectual capital", European Management Journal, 1996, Vol. 14, No. 4, pp. 56-68.

Feldman, M. S. and Rafaeli, A. (2002), "Organizational routines as sources of connections and understandings", Journal of Management Studies, Vol. 39, pp. 309-331.

Firer, S. and Williams, S. M. (2003), "Intellectual capital and traditional measures of corporate performance", Journal of Intellectual Capital, Vol. 4, No. 3, pp. 348-360.

Fukayama, F. (1995), "Trust: the social virtues and the creation of prosperity", Free Press, New York, NY.

Granovetter, M. (1985), "Economic action and social structure: the problem of embeddedness", American Journal of Sociology, Vol. 91 No.3, pp.481-510.

Grant, R. M., (1991), "The resource-based theory of competitive advantage: Implications for strategy formulation", California Management Review, Vol. 33, No. 3, pp. 114-135.

Grant, R. M. (1996), "Toward a knowledge-based theory of the firm", Strategic Management Journal, Vol. 17, No. 4, pp. 109-122.

Hafeez, K., Zhang, Y. B. and Malak, N. (2002), "Core competence for sustainable competitive advantage: A structured methodology for identifying core competence. IEEE Transactions on Engineering Management, Vol. 49, No. 1, pp. 28-35.

Hair, J. F., Anderson, R. E., Tatham, R. L., and Black, W. C. (1998), "Multivariate data analysis (5th ed.)", Upper Saddle River, NJ: Prentice-Hall.

Hayek, F. A. (1945), "The use of knowledge in society", American Economic Review, Vol. 35, pp. 519-530.

Hofstede, G. and Bond, M.H. (1988). "The Confucius connection: From cultural roots to economic growth", Organizational Dynamism, Vol. 6, pp. 4-21.

Itami, H., & Roehl, T.W., (1987), "Mobilizing Invisible Assets", Harvard University Press, Cambridge, Mass.

Johanson, U., Mårtensson, M. and Skoog, M. (2001a), "Measuring to understand intangible performance drivers", European Accounting Review, Vol. 10, No. 3, pp. 1-31.

Johanson, U., Mårtensson, M. and Skoog, M. (2001b), "Mobilizing change through the management control of intangibles", Accounting, Organizations and Society, Vol. 26, No. 7/8, pp. 715-733.

Kaplan, R. S. and Norton D. P. (1992), "The balanced scorecard: measures that drives performance", Boston: Harvard Business Review, Vol. 70, No. 1, pp. 71-79.

Kaplan, R. S. and Norton, D. P. (1996) "The balanced scorecard: translating strategy into action", Boston: Harvard Business School Press.

Lau, Chung Ming, Tse, David K. and Zhou, Nan (2002), "Institutional Forces and Organizational Culture in China: Effects on Change Schemas, Firm Commitment, and Job Satisfaction", Journal of International Business Studies, Vol. 33, No. 3, pp. 533–550.

Leana, C.R. and van Buren, H.J. (1999), "Organizational social capital and employment practices", Academy of Management Review, Vol. 24, No.3, pp. 538-55.

Lev, B. (2001), "Intangible Assets: Management, Measurement and Reporting", The Brooking Institution, Washington, DC.

Lippman, S. A. and Rumelt R. P. (1982), "Uncertain imitability: An analysis of interfirm differences in efficiency under competition", The Bell Journal of Economics, 13(2), Autumn, pp. 418-438.

Liyanage, S., Johanson, U. and Hansson, B. (2002), "Management of knowledge and intellectual capital", Editorial in Special Issue of Singapore Management Review, Vol. 24, No. 3, pp. 1-6.

Machlup, F. (1962), "The production and distribution of knowledge in the United States," Princeton University Press.

McGaughey, S.L. (2002), "Strategic interventions in intellectual asset flows", Academy of Management Review, Vol. 27, No. 2, pp. 248-274.

Meritum, (2002), "Guidelines for managing and reporting on intangibles (Intellectual Capital Report)", Madrid: Fundacion Airtel.

Mohan, S. and Mark, A. Y. (2005), "The influence of intellectual capital on the types of innovative capabilities", Academy of Management Journal, Vol. 48, No. 3, pp. 450-463.

Murphy, G. B., Trailer, J. W. and Hill, R. C. (1996), "Measuring performance in entrepreneurship research", Journal of Business Research, Vol. 36, No. 1, pp. 15-23.

Nahapiet, J. and Ghoshal, S. (1998), "Social capital, intellectual capital and the organization advantage", Academy of Management Review, Vol. 23, No.2, pp. 242-66.

Nonaka, I. and Takeuchi, H. (1995), "The knowledge-creating company: How Japanese companies create the dynamics of innovation, Oxford University Press.

Nonaka, I. and Teece, D.(eds), (2001), "Managing industrial knowledge: creation, transfer and utilization", Sage Publications.

Pena, I. (2002), "Intellectual capital and business start-up success", Journal of Intellectual Capital, Vol. 3, No. 2, pp. 180- 198.

Petty, R. and Guthrie, J. (2000), "Capital Literature Review: Measurement, Reporting and Management," Journal of Intellectual Capital, Vol. 1 No. 2, p.155-176.

Phillips, L. W. (1981), "Assessing measure error in key informant reports: A methodological note on organizational analysis in marketing", Journal of Marketing Research, Vol.18, No. 4, pp. 395-415.

Porter, M. E., 1985, Competitive advantage: creating and sustaining superior performance, Free Press, New York.

Reed, R. and DeFillippi, R.J. (1990), "Causal ambiguity, barriers to imitation, and sustainable competitive advantage", Academy of Management Review, Vol.15, No.1, pp. 88-102.

Roberts, H. (1999), "The bottom line of competence based management: Management accounting, control, and performance measurement", Working paper, Norwegian School of Management, Oslo.

Roberts, H. (2000), "Classification of intellectual capital", in Grojer, J.E., Stolowy, H. (Eds),Classification of Intangibles, Groupe HEC, Jouy-en-Josas, pp.197-205.

Roberts, H. and Berthling-Hansen, (2000), "Ready for Intellectual Capital? A multiple case study of 25 firms in the Norwegian graphical, newspaper and magazine industries", Paper presented to the 23d Annual Congress of the European Accounting Association, March 2000, Munchen, Germany.

Roland, B. and Groan, R. (2007), "The importance of intellectual capital reporting: Evidence and implications", Journal of Intellectual Capital, Vol. 8, No. 1, pp.7-51.

Roos, J., Roos G., Edvinsson, L. and Dragonetti, N. C. (1998), "Intellectual Capital: Navigating in the New Business Landscape", New York: New York University Press.

Saint-Onge, H. (1996), "Tacit knowledge: the key to the strategic alignment of intellectual capital", Strategy & Leadership, Vol. 2, No.March-April, pp.10-14.

Snow, C. C. and Thomas, J. B. (1994), "Field research methods in strategic management: Contributions to theory building and testing", Journal of Management Studies, Vol. 3, No. 4, pp. 457-480.

Steenkamp, J.E.M. and van Trijp, H.C.M. (1991), "The use of LISREL in validating marketing constructs", International Journal of Research in Marketing, Vol. 8, pp. 283-299.

Stewart, T. A. (1991), "Brainpower: how intellectual capital is becoming America's most valuable asset", Fortune, 3 June, pp.44–60.

Stewart, T. .A. (1994), "Your company's most valuable asset: Intellectual capital", Fortune, New York, October 3, pp.28-33.

Stewart, T. .A. (1997), "Intellectual capital: The new wealth of organizations", Doubleday, New York, NY.

Sullivan, P.H. (1998), "profiting from intellectual capital: extracting value from innovation", New York: John Wiley & sons, Inc.

Sullivan, P.H. (2000), "Value-driven intellectual capital: How to convert intangible corporate assets into market value", New York: John Wiley&Sons, Inc.

Sveiby, K.E. (1986), "The know-how company", Kunskapsföretaget, Liber: Malmö.

Sveiby, K.E (1990), "Kunskapsledning (Knowledge Management)", Ledarskap Stockholm.

Sveiby, K.E. (1997), "The new organizational wealth: managing and measuring knowledge based assets, Berrett-Koehler Publishers, San Francisco, CA.

Swart, J. (2006), "Intellectual capital: Disentangling an enigmatic concept", Journal of Intellectual Capital, Vol. 7, No. 2, pp. 136-159 .

Tacq, J. (1997), "Multivariate analysis techniques in social science research: from problem to analysis", London: Sage Pub.

Teece, D. J. (2000), "Managing intellectual capital: organizational, strategic and policy dimensions", Oxford University Press.

Teece, D.J., Pisano, G. and Shuen, A. (1997), "Dynamic capabilities and strategic management", Strategic Management Journal Vol.18, No. 7, pp. 509-533.

Zaltman, Gerald (1997). Rethinking Market Research: Putting People Back In. Journal of Marketing Research, Vol. 34, No. 4, pp. 424–437.

Chapter 14
The Innovest Ratings of Chinese Organizations:

A Benchmarked Analysis

Edward J. Lusk, CPA, Ph.D.

Professor of Accounting, State University of New York (SUNY), College at Plattsburgh, School of Business and Economics, USA and Emeritus, Department of Statistics, the Wharton School, University of Pennsylvania: Philadelphia, USA

Abstract We selected performance relationships of 14 Chinese companies listed on the Hong Kong and Shanghai Stock Exchanges and compared them to three benchmarked comparison groups, all of which were rated by Innovest iRatings. Twelve of 14 Chinese organizations were given the lowest Innovest rating that would usually constitute a clear "Sell/Do Not Buy" market signal. These Chinese companies were compared to industry- and size-matched non-Chinese firms which were organised into three category groupings: top-, average-, and low-ranked based upon their Innovest iRatings. We compared the Chinese organizations to these three benchmarked groups on the following three measures: the firm's period beta (β) from the one-factor capital asset pricing model (CAPM), market capitalization (MCAP), and net operating income (NOI). We found no support for the low ratings given to the Chinese companies by Innovest, in that the performance profiles of these Chinese firms on MCAP and NOI were not statistically significantly different from any of the benchmarked firm groupings. Further, with respect to β, we found strong support for upside and downside--that is, symmetric volatility, counter to the downside and limited-upside volatility suggested by the low Innovest iRatings ratings.

1 Introduction

The Chinese economy is one of the fastest growing in the world with an average annual growth of approximately 9% per year over the last 13 years. Such rapid growth identifies China as an economic power playing an ever-more-important

P.O. de Pablos, M.D. Lytras (eds.), *The China Information Technology Handbook*, 243
DOI: 10.1007/978-0-387-77743-6_14, © Springer Science+Business Media, LLC 2009

role in the global economy. Its growth in the past 10 years is largely the result of China's political stability; relaxation of state controls on the economy, in particular regarding the massive state-owned enterprise (SOE) system; and policies encouraging free-market competition and foreign investment (Economist 2006). These features have been the pre-conditions for the maturation of the Chinese economy, which now benefits from extensive partnering, venturing, and establishment of supply-chain links with China.

To maintain such growth, attention will have to be given to further relaxation of state ownership, development of a consistently applied legal framework, and assurance of sustainable growth for the economic actors. To further cultivate such controlled growth, it seems that China will continue to move away from the SOE system and establish a more diverse market base of traded organizations. (*Shanghai Daily* 2007)

One result of the maturing Chinese markets will be an increase in the number of analysts, such as Innovest Strategic Value Advisors, rating Chinese organizations. Such ratings offer important information that investors often use in allocating their resources (Barber et al. 2006). This is the point of departure for our study. The unique question that we wish to address is: What is the predictive validity of the Innovest ratings of Chinese organizations compared to a benchmarked group of similar companies with respect to their financial and market performance? We are in effect asking about the validity of the Innovest ratings as resource investment signals.

2 Our Study

The Market and Financial Performance Measures

We have selected three basic financial performance measures:

1. **Beta**, denoted by **ß**, a performance measure of the capital asset pricing model (CAPM), which is a measure of the variation of the company's stock relative to the overall expected return on the market (Sharpe 1964). ß is a risk measure of the organization relative to the market, assuming that covariation relative to variation of return proxies for risk. If ß is greater (*less*) than 1, the company has more (*less*) risk than the market—that is, relative return variation. Therefore, because ß is the slope of the one-factor regression model of the company's returns as they relate to market returns, ß is simply the return regression multiplier.

2. The market value or **market capitalization** of the organization, denoted as **MCAP**. This measure is calculated as the number of shares of stock outstanding multiplied by the market price of the stock at the end of the fiscal year.
3. The annual reported **net income** for the firm's ordinary/normal operations, denoted as net operating income (**NOI**).

These three measures are the standard information often used to profile a traded company (Arnold 2005). Controlling for relative size, as was done for our sampling, the first two measures, ß and MCAP, are theoretically and in practice independent measures of performance. The reported net operating income (NOI) is, of course, positively associated with market capitalization. This means that on average, the higher the net income, the higher the market value of the organization. We will use these relationships to test for the representativeness, or the generalizability, of our results. Specifically, we expect to find (1) a positive association between the NOI and the MCAP, and (2) that ß will be independent from both NOI and the MCAP. If we do observe such relationships, we will have confidence in the generalizability of our results.

For each of the companies in our sample, we downloaded the following information from the OSIRIS (Bureau Van Dijk) database on August 11th 2007:

- Market capitalization (MCAP) for the years 2004, 2005, 2006
- Net operating income (NOI) for the years 2004, 2005, 2006
- CAPM ß calculated for 1 month, 3 months and 1 year

For these three variables, averages were used in the analysis due to power considerations.

The Corporate Rating Model

Consider now the scoring of the sampled organizations. The category measure of a company was an aggregate measure developed by Innovest Strategic Value Advisors (www.Innovestgroup.com), a group that rates organizations based upon the following components: *Stakeholder Capital, Human Capital, Strategic Governance,* and *Environment*. Each of these rubric components is further subdivided into a number of supporting sub-components. For example, *Stakeholder Capital* includes assessment of Customer Relationships and Alliance Partners; for *Environment,* Board and Executive Oversight and Eco-Efficiency are considered. Based upon an extensive investigation considering about 120 variables, a rating selected from the following seven rubrics is given to the organization. These rubric descriptors are paraphrased from Innovest iRatings (2007) following:

AAA is given to a company with minimal, well-identified environmental/social risks and liabilities, and with a strong ability to meet any losses that might materialize. Such a company is extremely well-positioned to handle any foreseeable tightening of regulatory requirements and is strongly positioned strategically to capitalize on environmentally/socially driven profit opportunities.

AA characterizes a company with well-identified environmental/social risks and liabilities, for which it would be able to meet most losses that might materialize. This position is unlikely to be impaired by any foreseeable tightening of regulatory requirements. The company is strategically well-positioned to productively take advantage of environmentally/socially driven profit opportunities.

A, as a rating, indicates that the company has large but well-identified environmental/social risks and liabilities, with sufficient financial and managerial strength to absorb all but exceptional risks. Further, it is able to finance any currently proposed regulatory requirements, and the company has above-average positioning with respect to profit opportunities.

BBB is given to a company with strong managerial capability, but where environmental/social risks and liabilities are a potential source of loss, though not on any material scale. The company has an average level of positioning vis-à-vis profit opportunities.

BB attaches to a company with good managerial capability, but where environmental/social risks and liabilities are a potential source of material loss. They have a below-average level of strategic positioning.

B indicates that the company has environmental/social risks and liabilities, the nature and magnitude of which create a strong likelihood of material losses in both profitability and competitive position. This B rating suggests significantly below-average strategic positioning regarding the company's ability to capitalize on environmentally/socially-driven profit opportunities.

CCC, the lowest of the ratings, is given to a company when there are significant doubts about management's ability to handle its environmental/social risks and liabilities, and where these risks and liabilities are likely to create a serious loss. Also, the company has a well-below-average ability to capitalize on environmentally/socially-driven profit opportunities.

Innovest Strategic Value Advisors has been rating organizations for more than a decade, and is a well-recognized and reputable organization. (Whittaker 2000, Willis 2003, and Derwall et al. 2005) Innovest is also unique in providing extensive ratings of both Chinese and non-Chinese companies within industry groups. Additionally, as the Innovest scoring rationale is applied to an individual firm, considering its institutional framework, the rating also has the desirable feature of being an enterprise-stakeholder saliency map across institutional frameworks (Williamson 1996).

Sample Selection. We selected all Chinese companies rated as of August 10th 2007 in the Innovest iRatings database. These 14 organizations are listed alphabetically in Table 1 following:

Table 1 The sampled Chinese organizations and their Innovest ratings

Aluminum Corporation Of China Limited	BBB
Bank Of China Limited	CCC
Bank Of Communications Co. Ltd	CCC
China Construction Bank Corporation	CCC
China Cosco Holdings Company Limited	CCC
China Life Insurance Company Limited	CCC
China Shipping Development Co Ltd	CCC
China Telecom Corporation Limited	B
Huaneng Power International,Inc.	CCC
Nine Dragons Paper (Holdings) Limited	CCC
Petrochina Company Limited	CCC
Ping Insurance Company Of China Limited	CCC
Shanghai Electric Group Company Limited	CCC
Sinopec Shanghai Petrochemical Co., Ltd.	CCC

3 Analysis and Results

Let us first consider validation of the sample that we collected by testing the following hypotheses:

Validating Hypothesis 1 (*VH1*): market capitalization (MCAP) and net operating income (NOI) will be positively associated.

Validating Hypothesis 2 (*VH2*): β will not exhibit association with MCAP nor with NOI.

These hypotheses are the standard expectations, both theoretically and in practice, that have characterized well-functioning markets since the inception of the CAPM (Arnold 2005).

We will report the usual Pearson correlation coefficients; and for purposes of robustness, we will note the Spearman non-parametric measure of correlation (Sall et al. 2005). The conservative two-tailed p-values will also be reported, with a false-positive error cut-off 0.05 to be used as our indicator of statistical significance.

In testing the above validating hypotheses, we find that the correlation of MCAP with NOI is 82%, with a p-value of less than 0.001, thus rationalizing rejection of the null of no association in support of VH1. As for VH2, the association of β with MCAP and NOI are 5% and 9% respectively; both p-values of which are greater than 0.5, providing no evidence for the rejection of the nulls in support of VH2. The Spearman tests result in identical inferences.

Discussion. These results suggest that our data follows the usual and expected relationships, and thus rationalizes the generalizability of our study results as a non-biased reflection of the underlying factors driving the relationships for our four samples.

4 The Benchmarking Results

To develop the benchmarking, we ordered the companies in the Innovest iRatings database from most highly rated to lowest rated, and then took 10 firms each from: the top-rated organizations (TRO), the average-rated organizations (ARO), the low-rated organizations (LRO), as well as all of the Chinese companies (n=14). Before examining these relative performance statistics on our three measures, we will present the correspondence of the Innovest ratings to the three category groupings that we have created as discussed above. This information appears in Table 2, where we have noted the percentages of those organizations in the respective median categories. For example, 100% of the 10 companies in the top-scored group were ranked by Innovest as AAA, and 86 % (12/14) of the Chinese organizations were rated CCC.

Table 2 Ratings of the Innovest-classified firms

Scored Firms	TRO (100%)	ARO (100%)	LRO (100%)	Chinese Firms (86%)
Innovest Rating	AAA	BBB & BB	CCC	CCC

These percentages are expected and indicate that the identification of the top-, average-, and low-ranked organizations indeed follow the Innovest assessment. This is important to the benchmarking of the Chinese organizations because it could be the case that the Innovest scoring did not provide good discrimination. For example, if Innovest had rated most all of the organizations as AAA, then the benchmark comparison of the ordered median groupings would have been biased on the high side. Table 2 indicates that the Innovest scoring developed distinct and reflective ordered categories that are useful in benchmarking.

The Benchmarked Comparisons

Recall that the Chinese organizations are compared to the benchmarked groups based upon three criteria: β, market capitalization (MCAP) and net operating income (NOI). This information is presented in Table 3. We have conducted the usual one-way Analysis of Variance (ANOVA) tests, and the overall Wilcoxon Rank Sum Test p-values will also be reported as a test for robustness.

Table 3 The Average Variable Information Classified by Group

Scored Firms	TRO	ARO	LRO	Chinese Firms
Beta (β)	0.96	0.90	0.91	1.30
MCAP (in millions)	24.2	22.5	10.5	16.8
NOI (in millions)	2.9	1.9	0.8	2.5

Beta (β), the measure of relative volatility. Here the overall ANOVA p-value is 0.02, with a Wilcoxon p-value of 0.04. The only 95% confidence interval that does not contain 1.0 is for the Chinese firms. A β of 1.0 is the *market* benchmark, indicating that the company has the same return volatility/risk as does the market. The fact that the value of β for the Chinese organizations is greater than 1.0 suggests that the Chinese companies have higher volatility than does the market, while the firms in the other three benchmarked categories are similar to the market in terms of volatility. Usually, β values greater than 1.0 are less desirable than lower β values in that higher β values indicate higher risk as defined in the CAPM. In this case, the Chinese organizations have a higher return multiplier than the market, meaning that if the expected market return increases by 2%, then the expected return of the Chinese companies will increase by 2.6%--that is, 2% times 1.3. However, the same is true for the downside. If the expected market return falls by 2%, then the expected return for the Chinese organizations will decrease by 2.6%.

Market capitalization of the organization (MCAP). Here we find that there are no statistically significant differences among the Chinese organizations compared to the three groups of companies that we are using as our benchmarks. The ANOVA and Wilcoxon overall p-values were both greater than 0.5. This indicates that all of the companies in the four groups noted in Table 3 are, on average, more similar than different respecting market capitalization.

Net operating income (NOI): The related statistic. There is also no statistically significant difference in financial performance as measured by net operating income. This is not surprising because there were no MCAP differences among the Chinese companies and the benchmarked organizations, and MCAP and NOI are highly correlated.

5 Discussion and implications

Our benchmarked analysis indicates that the Chinese organizations rated CCC, the lowest Innovest rating, do not differ from the companies in the three benchmarked categories regarding market capitalization and operating net income. This is a surprising result! When we first collected ratings information from Innovest and saw that most of the Chinese organizations were rated CCC, we took these ratings to mean that these companies present *significant* doubts about management's ability to handle environmental/social risks and liabilities, and that these risks and liabilities were *likely* to create *serious losses*. In other words, at best one could only hope for these Chinese firms to maintain their return positions, but in all likelihood they would be in jeopardy of collapsing under the weight of their managerial incompetence, or due to their precarious economic positioning. However, such a characterization does not seem to be borne out by our analysis. These Chinese firms, both in market capitalization and net income, are not different than the AAA-rated companies.

A further question about the CCC rating is raised by the fact that β for the Chinese organizations is the only relative volatility index which is statistically greater than 1.0, meaning that the Chinese firms exhibit more volatility relative to the market on the upside *and* on the downside. This is inconsistent with a rating of CCC, which suggests jeopardy only on the downside. The relatively high β is more consistent with the recent information provided by *Asia Pulse*, where it is noted that both the Shanghai and Shenzhen stock exchanges are now entering more mature phases. Both have moved away from emerging market status and are doing very well in meeting the return expectations for both the SOE sector (which constitutes 60 percent of the market capitalization) and the private sector (*Asia Pulse* 2007).

In summary, our analysis raises questions about the meaning and validity of Innovest's ratings of Chinese organizations. Rather than the precipitous positioning and eventual downward slide suggested by the Innovest ratings, we see viable and competitive Chinese companies. One final note: as of November 3rd 2007, all of these organizations are still being traded on their respective exchanges.

Acknowledgments The authors wish to thank Professors Kameliia Petrova and Karyn Neuhauser, SUNY: Plattsburgh, NY USA for their careful reading and helpful suggestions. Also, we wish to thank Ms. Ellen Slack of the Lippincott Library of the Wharton School, University of Pennsylvania, for her expert editorial assistance.

References

Arnold G (2005) Handbook of corporate finance: A business companion to financial market, decision and techniques, 2nd edition. Prentice-Hall, New Jersey

Asia Pulse (June 18 2007) China's bull-run may be back despite recent bear-hug. Via Factiva docs.html?pc=CN&pub_id=ASIAPULSEHK&sv=EMIS Accessed October 2007

Barber B, Lehavy R, McNichols M, et al (2006) Buys, holds, and sells: The distribution of investment banks' stock ratings and the implications for the profitability of analysts' recommendations. J Account & Economics 41:87-117

The Economist. (March 25 2006) Balancing act: A survey of China [Special Section]. 378, 8470: 3-20

Derwall J, Guenster N, Bauer R, et al (2005) The eco-efficiency premium puzzle. Financial Analysts J 61:51-63

Innovest iRatings http://www.innovestgroup.com/ Accessed October 2007

OSIRIS BVD Suite. http://wrds.wharton.upenn.edu/demo/bvd/osiris.shtml Accessed October 2007

Sall J, Lehman A, Creighton L (2005) JMP Start Statistics--Version 5, 2nd edn. Duxbury Press, Belmont, CA

Shanghai Daily, (15 June 2007). Only 80 to 100 SOEs to remain by 2008. Via Factiva docs.html?pc=CN&pub_id=SHDAILYDAILY&sv=EMIS Accessed October 2007

Sharpe W (1964) Capital asset prices: A theory of market equilibrium under conditions of risk. J Finance 19:425-442

Whittaker M (2000) Global climate change: Uncovering hidden investment risk and opportunity. The Geneva Papers on Risk and Insurance 25:619-628

Williamson O (1996) The mechanisms of governance. Oxford, New York

Willis A (2003) The role of the global reporting initiative's sustainability reporting guidelines in the social screening of investments. J Bus Ethics 43:233-237

Chapter 15
Language-divides and Global Inequalities:

Problems and Solution

Pak Hung Mo

Hong Kong Baptist University, School of Business, Department of Economics, HONG KONG (SAR), P.R. CHINA

Abstract In the enlightening article written by Thompson (1977), he perceived that our economy has reached another saturation point in the information age. A potential quantum jump in economic evolution that can bring us to a much higher levels of wealth creation is available. However, this potential is inhibited by a fundamental linguistic constraint. He suggests that a possible solution to the constraint is the creation of a global ideographic writing system. In this paper, we will discuss the problems created by the language divide, analyze the differences, costs and benefits of the phonetic and logographic writing systems, and then we suggest a framework with examples for the development of natural logographs in order to tap the potential huge benefits provided by the information and communication technology.

Dedication This paper is dedicated to Charles K. Bliss, the inventor of Blissymbolics, a enthusiastic and committed believer of a global universal symbolism. He was motivated by the sufferings caused by phonographic writing systems. He wrote: ' The inventor ... was born in the Babel of old Austria, where 20 nationalities hated each other, mainly because they spoke and thought in different languages.' (Bliss, 1965, p. 10) 'My hopes rest with the librarians of mankind, with my future readers, and ultimately with the ethical power working in the brain cells of all human beings. May they overcome the dangers of words in all languages, before more millions of men, women and children will die because of words.' (Bliss, 1965, p. 825). It is the luck and the honor of this author who happens to be in the position of being able to contribute from a new perspective and to accomplish this important mission for the humankind.

P.O. de Pablos, M.D. Lytras (eds.), *The China Information Technology Handbook*,   253
DOI: 10.1007/978-0-387-77743-6_15, © Springer Science+Business Media, LLC 2009

1 Introduction

In this chapter, we review the language barrier hindering the potential revolution in transnational development made possible by the advances in information and communication technology (ICT). A system of natural logographs (NL) is then proposed to solve the problem. Language and economic variables influence one another in several ways. The demand for communication is a derived demand of the potential gains from the division of labor and trade. The linguistic characteristic of a speech community is therefore affected by its extent of the division of labor. The residents in a self-contained geographic region tend to be monolingualists. Those near the boundary of several speech communities tend to be bi- or multi- lingualists and those reside in a trading center are usually multilingualists. The need for communications determines the linguistic characteristics of speech communities. The demand for a market language depends on the extent of the potential division of labor that in turn depends on the transportation, communication and trading possibilities. The economic strengths of different languages determine the selection of a market language which depends on the economic strengths of its speakers.

On the other hand, speeches are substantial barriers to communication and therefore to the potential gains from trade. Different speeches and phonographs prohibit alien speech communities from inter-exchanges. These alienations in communication hinder the formation of a large cultural and trading community that shares similar beliefs, information, technologies, knowledge and the gains from division of labor. The alienations also cause frequent political and economic conflicts among different speech communities. Language is an essential economic as well as the social foundation for the development and prosperity across different speech communities.

In reviewing the events in the world history, similar questions appear in my mind again and again. Why did Europe integrate and disintegrate while China has been basically unified culturally and politically for thousands of years? Similarly, why did Soviet Union integrate and then disintegrate? How can the hatred between the Arabian and Latin speech communities last for thousands of years while thousands of ethnic speech communities in China can basically coexist and trade in harmony? At this stage, hard evidences seem difficult to be established for resolving the puzzles. Our conjecture is that the different writing system has played an essential role on the evolutions in these different parts of the globe.[1] Writing system is an essential social infrastructure which determines the level of communication barriers between different speech communities. Low communication barriers promote cooperative activities among different speech communities and vice versa. The adverse effects of the communication barriers between speech commu-

---

[1] Related discussions can be found in American Council of Learned Societies (1942); Bliss (1965), Gernet (1972) and Mo (2004, 2007). As will be discussed, logographic writing systems have unifying effects while phonographic writing systems have diverging effects among speech communities.

nities become more and more apparent when the ICT is increasingly governing the evolution process of our economies. (For instance, Warschauer, 2003). The potential benefits promised by ICT will never be fully realized unless the linguistic barriers can be removed. (Thompson, 1977, 1983)

The author has to admit that he has very limited knowledge on linguistic literatures and problems years ago. It is his luck that makes this paper possible: being educated and grown up in a country using a logographic writing system for thousands of years while having chance to be trained as an economist in profession in a great country using a phonographic writing system and read the inspiring papers written by Thompson (1977), Marschak (1968) and Chen (1996). The existence of this paper itself illustrates the inspiring power of cross-cultural interactions under a pluralistic environment. It is the product of an innovative comparison and mix of the ideas, characteristics and information embodied in different cultures. We fully understand that our proposal of introducing a universal natural logograph might irritate most if not all members of different speech communities in the world. Language has long been the 'nationalism' issue which is as sensitive as color and race. This very sentiment has made language a long-lasting barrier for the development of humankind. In this paper, we want to draw the attention of the world community about the benefits of our proposed design that might realize the dreams of many visionary scholars including Gottfried Wilhelm Leibniz, Bliss (1965) and Thompson (1977). As suggested in World Employment Report 2001, the information and communication revolution is a steerable revolution and we have the potential to influence its directions. The new information and communication technologies can both enhance and threaten the quality of our lives, livelihoods and institutions. Our challenge is to capture their potential benefits and minimize their risks through appropriate policies and institutions at the national and international levels.

The rest of the paper is organized as follows. The next section discusses the opportunities and risks associated with the ICT revolution. It is followed by a analysis of the characteristics of different writing systems with an introduction and discussion on the NL. The basic symbols with examples and the corresponding keyboard design about the NL are attached in the Appendix. The last section concludes.

2 The Problems Generated by the ICT

The advances of ICT have generated enormous opportunities for the advances of human race. They give learners direct access to vast bodies of knowledge, as well as tools to analyze and search for desirable information and knowledge. Digital networks and portals of education enrich and sometimes replace conventional educational processes, providing cheap access to a diversity of information, allowing interactivity and individualized learning experiences on a scale never previously possible. The decline in transaction, coordination and monitoring costs also lead to an increased efficiency of intra-firm networks as well as substantial cost-savings associated with inter-firm network. Since the ICT provides real time coordination, information and learning at negligible costs, companies and nations that can harness the benefits can substantially raise their productivity. Many scholars have envisioned a quantum jump in the world economy. However, the rosy world of the ICT era has no signs to be emerging in the near future while the global instabilities, inequalities and conflicts generated by increasingly intimate contacts among different speech communities become increasingly acute. It becomes obvious that some essential barriers have to be removed before the potential gains from the ICT can be fully realized. The digital divide created by the ICT is attributed to two barriers: the technology and linguistic.

The international organizations such as the World Bank and the United Nations have expressed serious concern that poorer societies lacking technological investments will drift farther behind their wired rivals in the global marketplace, whereas advanced industrialized societies will surge even farther ahead due to dramatic productivity gains from the utilization of ICT. (Norris, 2001; Warschauer, 2003) There are many plausible reasons why the emerging ICT era may reinforce disparities between individuals and nations. As investment in ICT has the capacity to boost productivity, advanced economies that are at the front of the technological revolution may even further ahead. Those falling behind may lose their jobs due to automation and disintermediation. ICT enables routine tasks to be digitally instructed and automated. The low skill labors are therefore replaced. The reduction in coordination costs also reduces the jobs of information and coordination intermediation like travel agents and even middle administrative jobs. Many skills are therefore become obsolete. ICT therefore substantially reduces the demand for the resources abundant in the low-developed countries in the global marketplace in this aspect. The effects have caused increasingly acute international as well as domestic disparities and poverty problems. (Among many others, International Labour Office, 2001; Warschauer, 2003; Katz and Rice, 2002; Norris, 2001)

At this stage of development, the technology divide is still formidable. The telecommunication infrastructures based on copper wire, cables and optical fiber are expensive to the poor countries. The emerging wireless technologies may allow the poor nations to surpass the technology divide. Moreover, advances in ICT have already reduced the cost of information transmission substantially. After the ICT infrastructure is established, internet communication is virtually costless between any two points on the globe. If the digital divides are due to the technological problems, then national and international inequalities will gradually fade over time as a result of the technological advances and infiltration. However, besides the mechanical process, information transmission also involves the linguistic process - the encoding of message by the sender and the decoding of message by the receiver. (Marschak, 1968) If the receiver cannot decode the sender's message, the ICT and the transmitted messages will be useless. The potential gains of the receiver and sender from the transmitted messages cannot be realized. It is the language divide that is likely to be long-lasting and formidable in the globalization process. Poor countries are not only marginalized in the world economy due to the technological reason, but also due to their illiteracy in English.

Our world has more than six thousand living speeches after evolution over millennia. (Motluk, 2002) According to estimations, in 1997, about 350 million people around the world speak English as a native language, representing some 6% of the world's population. Even taking into the consideration of the people of learning English as a second language and foreign language, there are still three-quarters of the world's population knows almost no English. However, 81% of international Web sites were in English. The English content in internet well out of proportion to the number of English speakers in the world. Moreover, predominate majority of software and hardware of ICT are constructed for English users. This language divide happens in other aspects of transnational communication. About 85% of international organizations employ English as one of their official languages, 85% of the world's film market is in English, and 90% of the published articles in leading journals of linguistics are in English. (Crystal, 1997, cited in Warschauer, 2003) Under the situation, literacy in English is essential to the developments of individuals, regions and nations. Even if everyone in the world is netted up could not empower those individuals who were English illiterate. Moreover, the problem of English exclusion is not likely to find a technological solution: the translation costs can be huge, especially given the need for continuing updating of the content. Finding the solution may also divert resources from more urgent needs. Without other solutions, it seems that nurturing the competence to exploit the potential benefits of the ICT is a vital job of schools and colleges. This imposes a whole range of values embodied in English on smaller cultures and hampers linguistic diversity. Moreover, to the poor countries that even ICT infrastructures are lacking and suffering from the vicious cycle of poverty and illiteracy, education seems to be a far-reaching, if not unreachable, solution.

2.1 The Linguistic Conflicts

The impact of ICT on the international conflicts and stabilities can be ambivalent, as was the impact of the earlier technological revolution. It depends on how we steer the evolution process.

Network externalities suggest that the value of a network is proportional to the number of people using it: the more people link to each others in the internet and global networks, the greater their utility, and the more they attracts. Under this mechanism, we can predict that in the long-run, only one market speech and writing system will survive for minimizing transaction costs in the globalization process and there will have no problems caused by linguistic divide. Even it is true, the political costs can be prohibitive. It seems that historically, language diverge rather than converge. As in the case of Roman language, one language becomes many languages. According to the cases documented in Castells (1997), many minorities are acting fierce campaign to upgrade the status of their ethnolect. Similar to any organizations, once an organization is formed, vested interests of the organization will tend to elongate and extend the power of the organization. Organization has life, so do the language communities. The vested interests associated with speech communities will be hostile to any possible displacement by foreign languages. The single market language long-run equilibrium will not be reached without fierce struggles. Language has long been a nationalism issue. This is exemplified by the struggles over bilingual education in the United States; the Quebecois, Basque, and Kosovar separatist movements; the battles over language and citizenship in post-Soviet countries; and language revitalization movements in Ireland (Gaelic), New Zealand (Maori), Morocco (Tamazight), and many other countries indicate the powerful role of language-based identity in today's world. (Warschauer, p. 93-94) French president Jacques Chirac even described the international prevalence of English as the ultimate act of intellectual colonialism, a 'major risk for humanity' which threatens to impose linguistic and cultural uniformity on the world. The perception results in the regulation that all web sites in France must provide their content in French. (Nunberg, 2000) The political forces among thousands of speech communities imply that multilingual patterns in the world are likely to last in the foreseeable future even technological innovations substantially reduce the costs of travel and telecommunications.

Even though we survive all the international struggles and conflicts until a single market speech and writing system realized in the long-run as theoretically predicted, is this mono-cultural environment favorable to our development and conducive to the survival possibility of human races? Similar to genetic diversity, is cultural diversity itself desirable for raising our survival possibility in the unpredictable future? If accidentally, a phonographic writing system is selected under the market mechanism, this will mean the disintegration of the natural habitats and the disappearance of thousands of natural speech communities. The tones, stories, songs, norms, beliefs, technology and knowledge, or the cultures in general will vanish with the speeches. Do we feel disgrace about the loss of Maya civilization due to the brutal behavior of our ancestors? Similarly, do we feel sorry about the losses of Sumerian and Egyptian civilizations that vanished under the struggles among different cultures? If we have chance to start over again, would we select to do something else for maintaining our cultural diversity? Now, it seems that we are in the cross-road to choose our future cultural environment.

It is quite likely that the inequalities and global tensions created by the exclusions from the knowledge economy will be increasing over time. The global economy has reached a stage that know-how replaces land and capital as the fundamental driving force of economic growth. Information, knowledge, interaction and communication are essential 'raw materials' for innovations and advances. Disparities in the access of information and communication technologies will result in an increasingly divided world. The divides will finally jeopardize transnational growth, peace and security.

Our urgent problem in this ICT era is to design an artificial writing system that is stable and self-sustaining to bridge the language-divides. The solution has to face the reality of national and cultural pride and dignity. Any feasible solution for the language divide has to be addressed in the context of mutual beneficial, transnational equity, poverty, human dignity, and quality of life among all speech communities.

Although Thompson (1977) has identified the problems of linguistic divide and proposed some possible technical and linguistic solutions, the problems are far from being solved. Up to now, there are no feasible technical solutions. The network externalities in ICT era and the drive for the gains from trade may result in a global market speech and writing system in the long-run. However, if we take into account of the political factors, the huge adjustment costs towards this long-run equilibrium may not be realistic. Based on the above understandings, and inspired by the suggestion in Thompson (1977), we introduce and create a system of natural logographs. We hope that the NL can make the scientific knowledge, news, advice, entertainment, communication and services available in a global context and allow the participation of the most less-developed segments of all societies and of the world. This will bring a quantum jump of our civilization by tremendously raising the productivity of information, promoting global division of labor and innovative activities, and mobilizing the resources of all speech communities in participating in the global development.

3 A Linguistic Solution

Speech is an integral part of interaction, creativity and communication processes that allow a speech community to function. Speeches embody the tones, rhythm, traditions, stories, habitats, values, jargons and in general, the philosophy, knowledge, feelings and memories of the respective speech community. Speech is an organizational capital that allows the speech community for efficient coordination and division of labor. The characteristics of a speech and its embodied coordination power to a speech community define the identity of the speech community. However, the vested interests and sentiments of the groups or individuals in any speech community generate the drives to seek the survival and prosperity of their speech and community. This protective tendency of each speech community has created strong linguistic barrier to the global division of labor. From a global perspective, speeches separates, raise costs, contributes to communication failure and conflicts among the speech communities. In this ICT era, the information asymmetries brought with the speech barriers result in income and opportunity inequities, poverty, cultural barriers, misunderstandings and international conflicts. In this section, we attempt to propose a linguistic solution to surpass the speech barriers and the potential international conflicts and instabilities, namely, the introduction of the natural logographs (NL).

Communications can be considered as an encoding, transmission and decoding process. Phono-communications require the potential receiver to understand the sounds of the encoder's messages. Logo-communications require the potential receiver to understand the logos of the encoder's messages. Under the phonographic writing systems, the encoding of the messages is based on speeches, different speeches result in different forms of encoded messages. As a result, the potential message-receivers must be familiar with the encoders' speeches as well as the phonetic values of the encoding letters. For logographic writing systems, the messages are encoded by logos, the potential message receivers do not need to know the speech of the encoder. As long as the logos of messages are known and have not changed, the messages can be transmitted over time and over different speech communities. Therefore, if we adopt a natural logographic system for transmitting messages across the world, most inefficiencies and problems caused by the language divides will be solved. The differences in information transmission between a phonographic and logographic environment can be understood by Table 1. Encoding messages in phonographs will result in writings as diverge as the speeches while the NL will provide the same logos for unlimited speeches. The communication barriers and hence coordination costs and conflicts will be substantially reduced. In the world of NL, when an individual has learned to write her speech in NL, she can understand all the scripts written by any speech community in the world. All the opportunities, information and benefits in the internet world will be open to **her.**

Table 1 Information Transmission, Phonographs versus Logographs

Phonographic environment:			
A speech sender →	A phonograph →	translation →	particular targeted receivers
B speech sender →	B phonograph →	translation →	particular targeted receivers
C speech sender →	C phonograph →	translation →	particular targeted receivers
Logographic environment:			
A speech sender →			
B speech sender →	Logograph → All receivers		
C speech sender →			

3.1 The Strengths and Weaknesses of Chinese Logograph[2]

Historically, all the primitive ancient writing systems like Sumerians, Egyptians and Chinese are logographic. Logos seems to be the most natural way in transmitting script messages. However, among the three well-known logographic writing systems, only the Chinese survives to the modern time. It will be very useful to review the evolution and characteristics of the Chinese for understanding the merits and demerits of the phonographic and logographic writing systems.

---

[2] Until recently, the author has limited knowledge on linguistic theories. I have to emphasize that the following discussions about the Chinese characters are abstracted from the work of Ping Chen (1996).

Ping Chen (1996) provides very useful discussions and review on the evolution and characteristics of the Chinese characters. We abstract his discussions on the Chinese characters that will inspire us about the desirable characteristics of a universal global writing system and its effects on the multi-speeches environment in the ICT era.

Define the basic unit in a script that corresponds to the smallest segment of speech represented in the writing as grapheme. English graphemes are letters, whereas Chinese graphemes are characters. Graphemes differ with regard to whether they encode pure phonetic values, or phonetic values together with meaning. Writing system are characterized as phonographic or logographic, depending upon whether they are mainly composed of phonographic or logographic graphemes. While the majority of modern languages have adopted phonographic writing systems, Chinese is the most important language to retain a logographic writing system. Chinese writing as a well-developed system dates back to the fourteenth century B.C. As is the case with other two ancient writing systems, Sumerian cuneiform and Egyptian hieroglyphs, most Chinese characters during the initial phase are logographic signs, indicating both the sound and meaning of the morphemes they represent. In the literature of traditional Chinese philosophy, these characters fall into three major groups according to the principles underlying their graphic structure, xiangxing 'pictographic', shishi 'ideograph', and huiyi 'compound indicative'. Xiangxing characters bear a physical resemblance to the objects they indicate. Examples are familiar characters like ri 'sun', yue 'moon', shan 'mountain', shui 'water'. Supplementary to the principle of pictographic resemblance is zhishi, which refers to the more diagrammatic method used to create characters that represent more abstract concepts. Examples are shang 'up', and xia 'down'. On the basis of xiangxing and zhishi characters evolved the third method, huiyi, which combines graphs of the first two categories on the basis of their semantics to create new characters that imply a combination of the meanings of the component parts. A good example is ming 'bright', which is made of two graphs, 'sun' and 'moon'.

All three groups share the feature that the characters were shaped in a way that attempt to capture the semantic content of the morphemes they represent in a more or less iconic fashion. Characters formed on the iconic principle constitute the bulk of the early stage of the Chinese writing system as represented by jiaguwen. We define the characters created based on the three principles as the natural logographs that iconize objects based on their nature and characteristics.

It is obvious that the iconic principle has some limitations. There are words for indicting complicated concepts or serving purely grammatical functions which are difficult to have natural logos. For recording increasingly complicated environments, similar to the Sumerians and Egyptians, Chinese turn to the method of phonetic borrowing, whereby the originally logographic characters are used as pure phonetic signs. Using the xingsheng semantic-phonetic method, some graphs are attached to cenemic syllabograms as semantic determinatives and some are attached to pleremic logograms as phonetic determinatives. Xingsheng provides an easy method to create a large number of characters on the basis of the existing stock of natural logographs, and consequently after the jiaguwen period it became the major principle by which new characters were made, bringing about a sharp increase in characters in the following two millennia. However, the cost for the convenience is the reduction of the natural coherence in the writing system and hence become increasingly difficult to learn among different speech communities.

Most experts in the field of Chinese linguistics would agree that the greatest shortcoming of the Chinese script, in comparison with phonographic Romanized writing systems, is that it is very difficult both to read and to write. With characters other than the xingsheng type, there is no cue whatsoever in the graphic structure as to the phonetic value. Moreover, as a result of attrition in the graphic structure, a large number of the graphemes of the xiangxing, zhishi, and huiyi categories discussed earlier have lost all traces of the iconicity of the original shape and ideas and become mere mnemonic symbols, which are known in the literature as jihao sign characters. The same happened to a large number of graphs that were incorporated into xingsheng characters as phonetic or semantic determinatives. According to the latest statistics, characters that compose such jihao constitute at least 20 percent of the characters in common use in modern Chinese. Students can do little with the characters beyond rote memorization.

The next serious shortcoming of the traditional Chinese writing is its complexity to learn and write. In modern Chinese there is an average of 11 strokes per character. In order to differentiate between characters, the configurations of these strokes are necessarily complex. As most of the graphic shape of the characters provides little or no indication of the shape, characteristics and speech of the matters, learning to read and write thousands of graphically complex characters becomes a massive mnemonic task. The success of this task demands a large amount of time and energy. It is estimated that 30 percent of the total class hours in Chinese primary and secondary schools are devoted to learning the Chinese language, and much of the time is spent on learning characters. A comparative study shows that the reading materials in language class up to year 4 in Chinese schools are only about one-sixth of the length of those at the comparable level in countries that use phonographic writing systems.

In addition, there are a large number of characters used as basic symbols in the Chinese writing system. It makes the Chinese writing system a very clumsy tool for many purposes. Due to the complicated nature of the graphic structures, the Chinese script is much less convenient than a phonographic system when it comes to indexing and retrieving, such as in cataloging, dictionary compilation, etc. , where the ordering of the writing symbols is involved. In many similar applications, the lack of uniformity in the ordering of characters stands in sharp contrast to the neatness of a phonographic system that uses far fewer basic symbols. The deficiencies of the Chinese script become even more apparent in the present-day information age with its widespread use of computers. The input and output facilities of the computer today is best suit for phonographic writing that makes use of a relatively small number of basic units combined in a systematic way to represent the language. Near the end of 1980s there were more than 700 input schemes for the Chinese script. This testifies to the tremendous amount of effort that has gone toward solving the problem. In spite of all the time and money invested in the endeavor, we have yet to see a scheme that is truly satisfactory and widely adopted.

In fact, in the last century, continuous attempts have been made to transform Chinese writing into phonograph. Comparing with the majority modern languages, Chinese writing is complex and hence slow in writing. The disadvantages in the Chinese writing system were considered as a cause for the underdevelopment in traditional China.

On the other hand, Chinese as a writing system has been serving numerous speeches for thousands of years. No one would deny that the character script does have its own strengths that have enabled it to survive as the sole major logographic writing system in the world. One of the most important merits of the Chinese script is its ability to span time and dialects. As characters can have different phonetic values in different times and at different places, they can be used to represent the Chinese language spoken in different periods and in different geographic areas. It is largely by virtue of this feature that it is much easier for present-day Chinese to read the writings of more than 2,000 years ago than for the users of a phonographic system, such as English, to read texts from very early times. To a certain extent, it is also by virtue of this feature that the Chinese people can communicate in writing even if they speak mutually unintelligible dialects. These strengths of the Chinese logographs have also drawn the attention of scholars from various fields including history and communication. (Gernet, 1972; Thompson, 1977; Bliss, 1965)

3.2 The Natural Logograph (NL)

We develop a system of natural logographs in order to solve the problems caused by the linguistic barriers. Appendix A presents the basic symbols (graphemes) of NL with some examples. Translations of some English and Chinese writings into NL are also attached to further illustrate the characteristics of NL in Appendix B. Appendix C shows the preliminary keyboard design for the writing system. A comparison of different writing systems is listed in Table 1.

For logical coherence and easy to be learned by every speech community, all NL are created under three principles only: the xiangxing 'pictographic', shishi 'ideograph', and huiyi 'compound indicative'. There are only 59 graphemes. The graphemes and their combinations created are used to indicate the characteristics and nature of all possible matters and events. This iconic writing system may enhance the logical reasoning and even creativity of the NL learners (Table 2).[3]

---

[3] According to Thompsons (1983) argument, it is said that the right hemisphere of the brain is involved in the processing to images and, presumably, also iconic symbols. This hemisphere, in addition to its graphic role, also is usually the one involved in creative and intuitive activities. Perhaps giving the right hemisphere of our brains a proper linguistic means might increase our level of creativity.

Table 2 Comparison between Different Writing Systems

Writing Systems	Graphemes	Simplicity	Morpheme Coherence	Tendency
Phonographs	26 letters (in English)	easy to learn in pronunciation	very weak internal logic	Diverge
Chinese Logographs	No structured graphemes	difficult to learn	weak internal logic	Converge
Natural Logographs	59 graphemes	easy to learn	strong internal logic	Converge

To reduce the complexity of the present writing systems, the NL characters have an average of about 4 strokes. Moreover, many multi-syllabic morphemes in Chinese logographs are represented by a single NL character, that is, compare to the Chinese logographs, most NL are 'multi-syllabic characters' or they are 'word-based logographs'. Similar to Chinese, literacy in NL is measured by how many characters, instead of words as in the phonographs, acquired by learners. Based on the experience in the usage of Chinese logographs, about 2400 characters or less of NL will cover 99 percent of the characters in publications in Modern Chinese. (Ping Chen, 1996) We expect that about the same number of characters will be able to encode every language in the world. These characters, based on the logic of huiyi 'compound indicative', are combined into bi- or multi-syllabic words to describe all other matters and events. This characteristic substantially enhances the variety of potential messages, the degree of precision and conceptual discrimination as well as the required flexibility to encode every speech in the world. This flexibility also allows NL to function under unforeseen circumstances with virtually unlimited potential in creating new words under the established logical framework, an essential characteristic of being a good global writing system.

To enhance the ordering of writing symbols, so that the logographs can be indexed and retrieved conveniently, there are only 59 basic symbols (graphemes). Moreover, the basic symbols can be divided into four classes: they are the classes of Nature, Tools, Human and Indicative Signs.

The NL is digitally friendly. On average, about three keys will be able to encode a NL character. Moreover, the input method can be easily accommodated in the conventional keyboard today as indicated in the Appendix III.

With only slight modifications for capturing the specific grammatical structure of different speeches, the NL is precise and flexible enough to encode all speeches. This characteristic enhances the survival possibility of all minority speeches and hence the cultural diversity embodied. Moreover, the slight modifications will have minimal effect on the effectiveness of message transmission across different speech communities.

The simplicity of the NL relative to other writing system is not trivial. The time and effort saved from writing and learning other complex writing systems can be used for innovations, maintenance of one's health or of the social functions that benefit his own generation and beyond. Complexity in writing results in inefficiencies and costly operations to an economy. In a competitive world, inefficient languages will not survive if its carrier, the writing community, disintegrates resulted from the inefficiencies. This applies to the civilization of human race as a whole.

3.3 The Possible Impacts of NL

Under the NL environment, once an individual has learned the NL to write her own speech, she will be able to read all written information of all speech communities in the world. At present, she has to learn all the speech-based and other writing systems before she is able to do so. This tremendous saving in communication cost will have tremendous impacts on all walks of our life and virtually eliminate all the problems generated by the language-divide in the internet.

As NL is independent to speeches, the world communities will have access instantaneously to a much larger pool of technologies and information when the pool is tremendously enriched by the NL writings of all speech communities in the world. Moreover, the NL has no displacement effect on any speech as all speeches can be expressed by the same logograph. Since everyone can tap almost all the benefits associated with internet under the NL environment, the speech minorities have less urgent needs to learn a market speech and the corresponding phonographic writing system. The results are therefore a Pareto improvement for all speech communities. The preserved cultural diversity, the flexibility and effectiveness of NL for communication over time and space may also enhance the survival of all human races and their civilizations. Moreover, the arrangement allows each speech community and her natural language to follow and complete its natural evolutionary processes. The linguistic conflicts caused by national and cultural dignity can be resolved in this aspect. The NL can therefore become the global glue in transnational bodies like the European Union, United Nations, OECD, APEC, and transnational corporations, rendering them organizationally effective and resolving majority and minority interests.

The NL allows direct communication between peoples of different speeches and colors. It enhances the transnational flow of ideas, cultures and belief without any costs of translation. This will promote higher endurance of cultural diversity among different speech communities and therefore a reduction in international conflicts and instabilities. At the same time, frequent interaction of different cultures will generate a more advance global civilization and possibilities. This crossbreeding opportunity will result in a boom in innovations and technological improvements.

Interestingly, the NL solution will be most beneficial to those speech communities that do not even have their own writing system. In such cases, the NL can be their natural writing system that will bring them all the benefits associated with it. In this sense, the solution is pro-poor, pro-weak and pro-diversity. The poorest members of the speech communities can be much better off, able to survive and prosper, and become better integrated into the global economy.

All of the above effects will result in a tremendous increase in aggregate supply as well as aggregate demand world-wide, in lowering unemployment rate and reducing income and productivity disparities. The demand for the software and hardware of the information industry will increase tremendously when the productivity of ICT tremendously increases due to the tremendous increase in the volume and reaches of the messages and information produced across the world.

These revolutionary transformations brought by the NL will result in the potential quantum jump envisioned in the ICT era.

If we compare with the other possible evolutionary path in the ICT era, the NL solution is much more superior. The network externalities associated with language adoption in the ICT era implies that there will be only one market writing system in the world in the long-run. In fact, this is supported by the observation that there is a gradual decline of many minority languages despite the surge of nationalism. In a phonographic environment, if the speech minorities hold on to their native speeches, it results in their marginalization. They have to face fundamental problems of basic survival and multiple difficulties with nutrition, literacy, and health. These problems will further reduce their chance of survival in the ICT era. They have either to adopt the market language that is costly and time-consuming in order to tap the benefits of the ICT or face the total destruction of their habitat along with their culture and knowledge embodied in their natural speeches. This process is jeopardizing the survival and evolution of all marginal speeches in the world.[4] The loss of cultural diversity will reduce the adaptability of human races in the uncertain future. The NL will generate no threats to any speeches but promoting their survival possibility by raising the productivity of all speech communities at the same time. The carrier of a speech is the speech community. As long as the habitat of the speech community survives, the speech survives. If culture is mainly embodied by speeches and cultural diversity is beneficial to our survival, then the NL will enhance the survival chance of human beings.

In general, NL can strengthen the fundamental of the information society and eliminate many destabilizing effects in the evolutionary process. It is a solution that has little infringements on the national and cultural dignity of all speech communities. The NL will drive the world towards one with a sufficient level of homogeneity to allow inter-cultural tolerance, interaction, friendship, trade, voluntary migration, labor mobility among all speech communities while allowing all speech communities to maintain their own speeches and cultures. The NL will build up the sentiment of 'Earthlings' to all speech communities. Therefore, it not only reduces international conflicts from the economic and political aspects, it also resolves the issue deep from the heart of the sentimental and identity fundamentals among all speech communities.

---

[4] Under a phonographic environment, apart from the market speech, all speeches will become marginal in the long-run if the market power among speech communities remain unchanged.

Under the NL world, the digital inequalities will be a temporary problem that will gradually fade over time as the ICT spreads due to technological improvements and the virtuous cycle brought by the global usage of the NL. Even machines can talk and real time machine translation are possible, there is still a vital role of the NL to play: it is the least costly and the most natural and inspiring way to enhance script communications between all speech communities.

4 Conclusion

It is unfortunate that the problems mentioned in Thompson(1977) have only become more serious and obvious while the proposed solutions have no signs to appear and realize in the foreseeable future. At the same time, the growing international disparities, increasingly intimate contacts among different speech communities and advances in destruction technology imply that cross-cultural understanding is essential for a secure global economy. A surprising fact is that the idea of having a universal symbolism for resolving the problems has been conceived more than 300 years ago. There is no better way to end this paper by citing the thinking of some pioneers to understand the importance of the issue and the contributions of the NL.

'A Universal Characteristic ... might be introduced if small figures were employed in the place of words, which would represent visible things by their lines and the invisible, by the visible, which accompany them.' 'This true method of a Universal Symbolism would ... guide the mind as do the lines drawn in geometry, and the formulas in arithmetic ...' 'This would be of service at first for easy communication with distant nations; but if introduced also among us, without however, renouncing ordinary writing ... would be useful in giving thoughts less absurd and verbal than we now have ...' 'I think these thoughts will some day be carried out, so agreeable and natural appears to me this writing ... for rendering our conceptions more real.' (1679, Gottfried Wilhelm Leibniz, cited in Bliss, 1965, p. 21)

'We are in the alarming position of having enormous control over the forces of nature, and very little reasoning power to guide our actions ...' 'Human thought requires an efficient method of symbolism such as no language yet supplies. If the keepers of our language maintain a die-hard attitude and succeed in preventing reasoned improvement the result will, I suggest, be that language will be less and less used for intellectual and rational purposes and relegated to an altogether inferior status as the symbols of sentiment and small talk.' 'This idea is also not new ...Leibniz realised the need of a reformed symbolism and method of thought. He imagined a universal symbolism of thought which would be understood by all nations, and by which thought itself would become accurate and quantitative.' (1930 Sir Richard Paget, cited in Bliss, 1965, p. 23)

'Today, it seems we have reached another economic saturation point. Our industrial economic system is hard pressed to generate all wealth needed to finance the social services we want, while still maintaining its own health. Before we fall into the same trap as those earlier administrators, and dissipate our resources in unnecessary disputes, we had best determine if there is a potential economic transformation involving higher levels of perceived wealth creation ... Masuda points to the capability of the combination of computers and communications to produce information. His studies lead him to claim that the economic potential of this next quantum jump step is greater than that produced by the industrial revolution.' (Thompson, 1977)

'When a new technology impinges on a socio-economic system, two classes of results can be expected. The first class consists of those cases where the significant impacts are the direct, first-order ones, and involves an intensification of current practices, the second class consists of those case where the higher-order impacts are the significant ones, and represents an extension into new practices. In general, the first class of interactions between a technology and a socio-economic system is related to cost-reduction activities and is characteristically labor-releasing, while the second class is wealth-creating, involves new enterprise, and is labor-absorbing ... the extensive or higher-order impact, the more magical and transformative, class is somehow inhibited, ' (Thompson, 1977),

After more than twenty years, it becomes obvious that we are still trapped in the first-order effects of ICT that has caused domestic as well as international tensions, conflicts and disparities. The fundamental constraint is still operating which inhibits the expected extensive class of interactions.

Thompson concluded that the world is again turned upside down and the need for an economic quantum leap is apparent. Echoing Thompson's point of view, leaving a harmony and pluralistic world by creating a NL is much more acceptable than leaving our future generations with polluted habitats and a planet bereft of its non-renewable resources. A pluralistic environment without the language barriers will increase the probability of finding solutions that will raise our innovative power and enhance our survival possibilities in the unforeseeable future.

At this point, because of coordination failures among thousands of speech communities, we are not sure whether the NL writing system will be automatically adopted in the global marketplace even though it is socially optimal to do so. However, we are quite sure that political will and consensus of international organizations on promoting the NL will make the rosy world promised by the ICT much faster to be realized than going through the market process although the long-run equilibrium may be the same. Until then, our world will never be the same. Will we live in a heavenly space where stagnation, hunger, cold, illiteracy, cultural conflicts and wars are just memories while our challenges come from the relentless Universe only? Will the tremendous costs of the linguistic divides soften the huge political barriers across thousands of speech communities? Will we have a global political leadership that can lead us to the 'promised land'of the ICT era? Now, the global stock of wealth and knowledge has made the problems of digital divide no longer technological nor linguistic, but a political issue that can only be solved by wisdom and leadership. Will God bless us?

References

American Council of Learned Societies (1942) The Chinese Language as a Factor in Chinese Cultural Continuity. Far Eastern Leaflets, Numbers 1-6, Washington, D.C., pp. 28-29; reprinted in: Essays on Chinese Civilization by Derk Bodde (Ed), Princeton University Press, 1981, Princeton, N.J..

Arcand Jean-Louis (1996) Development Economics and Language: the Earnest Search for a Mirage?. International Journal of the Sociology of Language 121: 119-157.

Bliss, Charles, K. (1965) Semantography (Blissymbolics). Semantography (Blissmbolics) publications, Sydney , Australia.

Castells, M. (1997) The Power of Identity. Blackwell, Malden, Mass..

Chen, Ping (1996) Toward a Phonographic Writing System of Chinese: a Case Study in Writing Reform. International Journal of the Sociology of Language 122: 1-46.

Gordon, Robert J. (2000) Does the New Economy Measure up to the Great Inventions of the Past. Journal of Economic Perspectives 14: 49-74.

International Labour Office (2001), World Employment Report 2001, Life at Work in the Information Industry. International Labor Organization.

Gernet, Jacques (1972) A History of Chinese Civilization, translated by J. R. Foster, Cambridge University Press, Cambridge.

Katz, James E. and Rice, Ronald E. (2002) Social Consequences of Internet Use, Access, Involvement, and Interaction. The MIT Press.

Lazear, Edward P. (1999), Culture and Language. Journal of Political Economy, 107(6): S95-S126; reprinted in 2002: The Economics of Language , Lamberton Donald M (ed), Edward Elgar.

Marschak, Jacob (1965) Economics of Language, Behavioral Science, 10 (2): 135-40; reprinted in 1996: The Economics of Communication and Information, Lamberton Donald M (ed), Edward Elgar.

Masuda, Yoneji (1975) The Conceptual Framework of Information Economics. IEEE Transactions on Communications, Vol. Com-23, No. 10: 1028-1040.

Motluk, Alison (2002) You are What You Speak. NewScientist, 30: 34-38.

Mo, Pak Hung (1995) Effective Competition and Economic Development of Imperial China. Kyklos 48(1): 87-103.

Norris, Pippa (2001) Digital Divide, Civic Engagement, Information Poverty, and the Internet Worldwide. Cambridge, University Press.

Nunberg, Geoffrey (2000) Will the Internet Always Speak English?*The American Prospect*, March 27-April 10 ; reprinted in 2002: *The Economics of Language*, Lamberton Donald M (ed), Edward Elgar.

Thompson, Gordon B. (1977), The World Turned Upside Down: Information Technology and the Linguistic Constraint, Telecommunications Policy 1 (2), 153-7; reprinted in 2002: The Economics of Language, Lamberton Donald M (ed), Edward Elgar.

Warschauer, Mark (2003) Technology and Social Inclusion, Rethinking the Digital Divide. The MIT Press.

Chapter 16
Agricultural Informationization in China

Wensheng Wang[1], Guangqian Peng[2] and Guangming Lu[3]

[1] Agricultural Information Institute, Chinese Academy of Agricultural Sciences, P. R. CHINA
[2] Business Administration Department, Wageninen University, THE NETHERLANDS
[3] Saidi Consulting Co. Ltd. (CCID), Beijing, P. R. CHINA

Abstract Types of rural-urban gaps exist and seem keep in extending in the mainland of China, although agriculture and rural lives have obtained significant enhancement since the "opening and reforming" policy started in 1980. Amongst these gaps, digital gap is critical itself, and may make other gaps wider. How to promote rural informationization construction effectively and efficiently is a great and new challenge to Chinese government and Chinese people nowadays. Meanwhile, the process of rural informationization also brings opportunities with new markets, new technology and new culture, etc. The first part of this chapter introduces the background about rural areas and rural informationization in China in brief. The second part studies the three phases of agricultural informationization first, then, gives focus on main types of service models and technology models of rural informationization. Furthermore, policy guidance and government (guided) projects or actions are introduced in the third part. Finally, this chapter ends with the significance and development direction of agricultural informationization in this transition country. We wish the information service models and technical models introduced here bring meaningful references for relevant people such as police-makers, basic-level officers, farmers, and agricultural information companies inside and outside the mainland of China.

1 Background

1.1 Background about Rural China

China is a big agricultural country with large number of rural population and broad rural areas. On one hand, 737 million people, namely, 56% of the total population, live in rural areas. On the other hand, the agricultural output value accounts for 15% of the total GDP, which means agricultural production still takes an important position for the national economy. In 2005, the output value of township enterprises accounts for 27.9% of the National GDP, 46.3% of the national industry value added, 27% of the financial income, and 40% of the foreign exchange earned through exports. The total output value from agriculture production and township enterprise, accounting for 43% of the national GDP, is an important factor to promote the economy and social development in the mainland of China. (China Statistics Yearbook 2005)

Although the rural economy has obtained rapid development since the opening and reforming policy was started in 1980, its growth rate still lagged heavily comparing with the growth rate of urban economy, and the development gap is getting wider. Currently, there are 21.48 million rural poors still facing the problem of food and clothing and 35.5 million people with low-income in China. In 2006, the per capita disposable income for urban residents is 11759 Yuan RMB, while the average net per capita income for farmers is 3587 Yuan RMB (Fig. 1). In other words, the urban-rural income ratio is 3.28:1. The following figure shows the per capita income gap between rural and urban residents during 2000-2006 (SCLGPO, 2007; Sina news report, 2007).

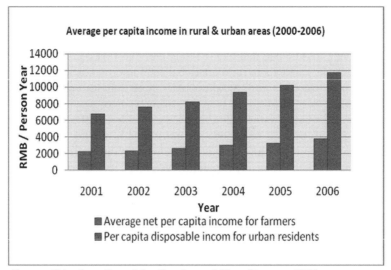

(Source: China State Council Leading Group Office of Poverty, 2007)

Figure 1 Average per capita income in the urban & rural area (2000-2006)

Except per capita income gap, other types of gaps between urban and rural areas exist including infrastructure gap, education gap, medicine and health gap, social security gap, and digital divide, etc. Digital divide is making the above other gaps wider and wider especially in less-developed parts of China, namely, the western and middle China. Therefore, to accelerate agricultural informationization and to narrow digital divide has obtained high attention from and is a big challenge for Chinese government and Chinese people.

1.2 Background about Agricultural Informationization in China

The following part introduces about rural Internet penetration, rural telephone penetration, rural radio and television penetration, rural personal computer penetration and agricultural website construction in China (CNNIC 2007b; Lu 2007b).

Rural Internet Penetration Rate Internet penetration rate was just 5.1% with 737 million rural residents, while it reached 21.6% with urban residents at the same time. Table 1 below shows this Internet gap. Comparing with the situation at the end of 2006, Internet gap was narrowed slightly in the first half of 2007. An important reason leading to this gratifying change is the massive growth of rural student Internet users[1]. Currently, the amount of rural student Internet users has increased from 6.7 million (at End 2006) to 15.75 million (at Middle 2007), accounting for 42.1% of the total rural Internet users. In other words, the increasing rate of rural student Internet users is as high as 135.1%.

Table 1 Internet penetration rate compared between urban and rural areas

	Rural Areas	Urban Areas	Total
Internet Users Amount (Million Persons)	37.41	124.59	162.00
Penetration Rate (%)	5.1	21.6	12.3

(Source: CNNIC 2007b)

Rural phone Penetration All administration villages having phones was realized in 22 provinces or municipalities at the end of 2006 such as Beijing, Shanghai, Jiangsu, Zhejiang, Tianjin, Shandong, Guangdong, Fujian, Liaoning, Hebei, Jiangxi, Helongjiang, Jilin, Ningxia, Inner Mongonia, Hainan, etc. Meanwhile, 98.7% of administration villages and over 116 million rural households had phones. The amount of rural households having phone has increased 2.5 times during the last six years. In more detail, 28.1% of rural residents had fixed phone, while 35.3% of them had mobile.

The amount of mobile users has increased faster than the amount of fixed phone users. Figure 2 shows the amount of fixed phones owned by per hundred rural households during 2000-2006. (Lu 2007b)

---

[1] Internet users are those citizens 6 years old or over 6 years old and using Internet at least once per half year. (CNNIC 2007a)

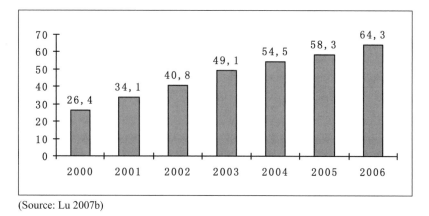

(Source: Lu 2007b)

Figure 2 The amount of fixed phones owned by per hundred rural households (2000-2006)

Rural Radio and Television Penetration The comprehensive rate of population covered by radio and television increased from 86.02% and 87.68% respectively in 1997 to 94.5% and 96% respectively in 2006. Figure 3 below shows the amount of colourful TV owned by per hundred rural households. (Lu 2007b)

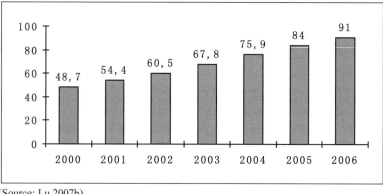

(Source: Lu 2007b)

Figure 3 The amount of colorful TV owned by per hundred rural households (2000-2006)

Rural PC Penetration The rate of households owning personal computer (PC) was 2.4% in rural areas in 2006. Although this rate is very low comparing with that rate in urban areas (41.5%) at the same time, it had grown rapidly from the historic perspective, especially when considered that the rate in rural areas was just 0.5% in 2000 and the base amount of rural households in China is huge. There was around 30 million PC owned by rural households at the end of 2006, and this is not a small number. Figure 4 shows the amount of PC owned by per hundred rural households. (Lu 2007b)

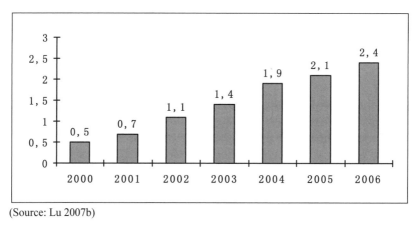

(Source: Lu 2007b)

Figure 4 Amount of PC owned by per hundred rural households (2000-2006)

Agricultural-related Website Construction   There were 6389 agricultural-related websites at the end of 2006, accounting for 0.81% of the total amount of websites (788400) in China at the end of 2006. They mainly distributed in the eastern and coastal provinces or municipalities. For example, 50.38% of agricultural-related websites located in Shandong, Beijing, Zhejiang, Jiangsu and Guangdong. Only rare amount of agricultural-related websites located in Western China. Meanwhile, when sorted by operators, 82.56% of agricultural websites were operated by enterprises, 11% by government offices, 2.6% by agricultural education or research organizations, and very rare percentage by farmers themselves. (Lu 2007b)

2 Current Status of Agricultural Informationization in China

2.1 Development Phases of Agricultural Informationization in China

Currently, agricultural informationization in China is still at the initial stage. It has undergone three development phases as shown below, when sorted by the breadth and depth of agricultural-related application of information and communication technology (ICT). (Wang 2007)

2.1.1 Starting Phase (End 1970s – End 1980s)

ICT have started to be applied in agriculture and in rural areas in China since the middle of 1970s. At the end of 1970s, the first big-sized computer Felix C-512 was imported and used in agriculture for agricultural science calculation, mathematical programming model and statistical analysis, etc. Since then, modern information technology (IT) started to be used in agriculture in China, which is a symbol showing the agricultural informationization was started. The research on the computer application in agriculture was the main features for this phase.

At the beginning of 1980s, State Leading Group Office of Electronic Revitalization was established. It made the strategic guidance, which is "reforming traditional industry and promoting national economic development through computer" and "Paying attention to application and promoting the development with computer industry". Meanwhile agricultural expert systems started to be researched at the beginning of 1980s, including expert advisory systems on wheat fertilization on Shajiang soil, on cultivation techniques, on breeding new varieties, on pest and disease control, and on identification and control of weeds. These expert advisory systems were used broadly with types of corns. Meanwhile, a significant amount of administrative and research staffs got tempered.

2.1.2 Basic Construction Phase (Beginning 1990s – End 1990s)

Internet appeared at the beginning of 1990s, which accelerated the construction of information infrastructure and the application of computers, and brought fundamental changes to information collecting tools and service models. Since then, the rural informationization in China entered a phase of laying foundation. The main feature of this phase is that the main lines of networks, as the main infrastructure of informationization, were constructed. Besides, the IT application agriculture became broader and deeper.

The construction of information infrastructure obtained continuing development through 1990s. The research on IT application in agriculture was broadened with contents involving all professional areas in agriculture. A patch of achievements owning independent intellectual property rights (IPR) were obtained, including "the demonstration project of intelligent IT application in agriculture", "the agricultural expert decision-making system and IT system", etc. Meanwhile, the exploration and application of those technologies such as "agricultural 3S technology", "precision agriculture" and "virtual agriculture" obtained high attention. Since the middle of 1990s, the website of Chinese Agricultural Science and Technology (www.cast.net.cn) and other agricultural-related websites at province or city level started to be operated. All of these have contributed into significant bases for the further development of rural informationization in the long run.

2.1.3 Rapid Development Phase (since 2000-)

The features of this phase include: emphasizing the rural information service and the broad application of Internet and database technology in agriculture. It is a symbol that the rural informationization in China entered a rapid development phase. During this phase, more rural information infrastructure was constructed, more information resources were explored, greater organization systems of information services were built up, IT was applied with broader areas, and the research of cutting-edge technology was strengthened.

"Spark plan – rural informationization action" was activated by Ministry of Science and Technology in 2001. The state information center was established in Ministry of Science and Technology in 2004 and "the spark project of making people rich through science and technology" was initiated later on. 188 110-service centers were set up in 20 provinces or municipalities in 2005, while types of service forms such as remote satellite receivers, television and video were provided, and showed strong vitality.

2.2 Information Service Models and Technical Models in Rural China

2.2.1 Typical Service Models of Rural Informationization

Since entering the new century, information services have played more and more important roles in the economic and social development of rural China. Some successful information service models that disseminate technology and market information and serve rural development have appeared. They are classified below for feature analysis.

First, information service models can be sorted according to the transmission vectors into the following three types: traditional service model, Internet service model and mixed service model (Zhong 2004; Huang 2006; Liang 2006; Wang et al. 2006; Wang 2007).

Traditional information service model

With traditional information service model, types of information about agricultural resources, practical technologies, agricultural markets, and policy and regulations are transmitted to farmers to guide the production and sale of agricultural products through traditional media such as radio, television, telephone, and newspapers and journals. The service process of the traditional model is shown in figure 5 below.

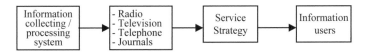

Figure 5 The process of the traditional information service model

The traditional service model has the features such as being easy to get started, wide dissemination and low cost, but is with the disadvantages such as single direction of information dissemination and receiving information passively by users.

Internet information service model

With Internet service model, different forms of information resources are transmitted to rural users through Internet to guide and organize the production and sale of agricultural products. The service process is shown in figure 6 below.

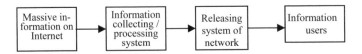

Figure 6 The process of Internet information service model

Different from the traditional service model, Internet service model has advantages such as diversified service providers, the wide range of information users, massive amount of information, and timeliness, etc. Meanwhile, it is with disadvantages such as high service cost and repeated construction of information resources, etc.

Fixed information service model

Fixed information service model is an innovated service model which transmits information through comprehensively using traditional and modern media and integrating agricultural information resources, according to local conditions and taking appropriate manners. The service process of this model is shown in figure 7 below.

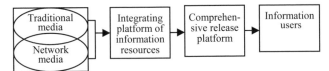

Figure 7 The process of fixed information service model

The fixed service model integrates traditional service model with Internet service model, makes full use of the advantages of diversified media. This service model can meet variety of demands from different information users in different industry and in different areas.

Second, information service models can be also sorted according to information service providers into the following seven types, including: the government-leading promotion model, rural professional association model or the self-service model of cooperative economic organizations, the wholesale markets radiation and diffusion model, dragon-head enterprises integration model, professional information companies or website market operation model, leading households and brokers demonstration model, and the international cooperation anti-poverty model. These seven models are introduced below and are called collectively as the management and organization model of rural information services. (Zhong 2004; Wang 2007)

The government-leading promotion model

In this model, the leading role is played by the government. The rural informationization is promoted by governments at variety of levels through constructing variety of public information service platforms such as information centers and information stations, etc.

Service station

With service stations, county information service centers are established relying on science and technology offices at county level, and extended downward to build township information service stations. In some villages with high demands for information, village information points are set up relying on village committee and leading farming households. By these ways, a comprehensive information service organization with three levels (namely, county, township and village levels) is established. The process of service stations is shown in figure 8.

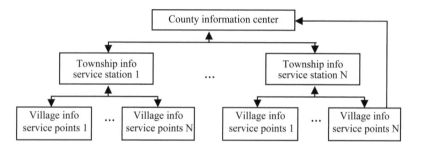

Figure 8 The process of service station model

- **Agricultural technology service hall**

An agricultural technology service hall, such as the one invested and built by the agricultural bureau in Gaocheng city in Hebei Province, integrates multifunctional information services and provides one-stop service to farmers. The service hall in Gaocheng city, with a construction area of 108 square meters and located in the downtown, can be divided into seven service areas: agricultural expert advice area, agricultural query service area with touching screens, demonstration area of agricultural productions, real-time information release area, screen area of agricultural popular science films, reading area of agricultural technology books, and Internet query and release area of agricultural information.

The structure of agricultural technology service hall is shown in figure 9.

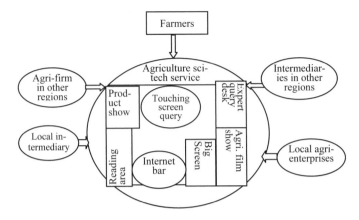

Figure 9 The structure of agricultural technology service hall

Expert workstations

Expert workstation model is a technology information service model combining multi-disseminators of information. With expert workstations, the daily works are managed by enterprises or professional association, while the government offices of information services cooperate to provide full service, to formulate development plans, to design management manners of experts and expert workstations, etc. Specific information service organizations are built by enterprises and professional associations.

They are responsible for the sale of agricultural products on one hand, and for transmitting agricultural technology information upward to the government and downward to the farmers on the other hand. The expert employees are responsible for researching, exploring and promoting new and high technology, and are responsible for providing technology training to farmers. Meanwhile, farmers are both disseminators and users of information.

On one hand, they conduct agricultural production in scientific and standard ways according to technical guidance from experts and according to market information from enterprises.

On the other hand, they disseminate information to each other and feedback information to expert workstations. Figure 10 shows the structure of expert workstations.

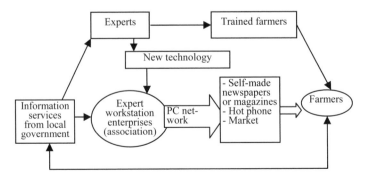

Figure 10 The structure of expert workstations

- **Science and technology 110**

Currently 188 110-service centers have been established in 20 provinces or municipalities. The service forms include telephone counseling, remote satellite receiver, television, and video, etc. Through calling "science and technology 110", farmers can obtain voice advice about cultivation, breeding and feeding, markets and resources.

- **Three electrics in one**

"Three electrics in one" is an information service model promoted by Ministry of Agriculture in rural China. The "three electrics" are: telephones, televisions and computers. The pilot works of "three electrics in one" was conducted in broad area in 2005. Six cities and fifty counties with certain foundations were selected for the pilot works. The pilot works were expected to lead to the achievement that all farmers owning telephones, televisions or computers can obtain timely agricultural information. And "the last one kilometer" problem with agricultural information services is expected to be resolved in this way.

Rural professional association model or self-service model of cooperative economic organizations

With professional association model, farmers producing the same or similar products are organized by leading farmers in a volunteering way in counties, townships or villages, where large amount of certain agricultural products are produced and certain types of information are demanded eagerly. Professional associations are self-managed and self-serviced by farmers themselves. Professional associations provide information about techniques, markets or policy to farmers. Some of them also purchase production materials or help sale products for farmers. In some villages, regional cooperative economic organizations are established to provide self-service in a volunteering way with a village or a village farmer group as a unit. This service model is similar to professional association model in the form and in mechanism of production information services, but its service contents are not limited to certain agricultural products or certain fields. Figure 11 shows the structure of professional association model or cooperative economic organization model.

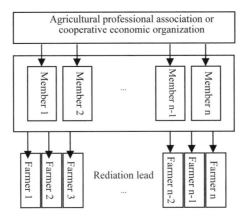

Figure 11 The structure of professional association model or cooperative economic organization model

The wholesale market radiation and diffusion model

With this service model, information services are provided relying on multi-functions of wholesale markets such as commodity distribution, pricing, information collection and releasing functions. Types of information about trade prices, trade amounts, and supply and demand changes in wholesale markets are distributed to neighboring regions, to the whole province or to the whole country through the collecting and releasing system of agricultural information such as market information centers or market information websites. Meanwhile, market management levels and trade efficiency get improved through the introduction of electronic clearing system. Figure 12 below shows the structure of this model.

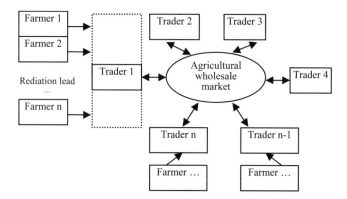

Figure 12 The structure of the wholesale market radiation and diffusion model

Dragon-head enterprises integration model

With dragon-head enterprise integration model, dragon-head agricultural-related enterprises, namely, leading agricultural enterprises, establish enterprise websites on Internet, collecting relative information online, release purchasing and selling information, guide farmers' production, purchase their products, and provide full services about producing, supplying and selling to farmers. With this service model, leading enterprises obtain profits while farmers obtain increased income and the solutions for the problems of "without both technology for production and markets for selling". Figure 13 shows the structure of dragon-head enterprises integration model.

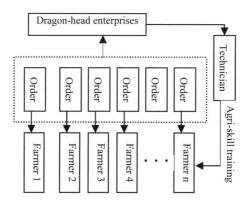

Figure 13 The structure of dragon-head enterprises integration model

Professional information company or website market operation model

Since 1990s, many information enterprises or commercial websites started to provide information services for farmers or for rural small- and middle-sized enterprises (SMEs), in order to obtain wider profit spaces and to expand business areas. The examples include Beijing Agricultural Information Communication Co. Ltd., Agricultural Doctor Web and Billion Farmer Web. Figure 14 shows the structure of this model.

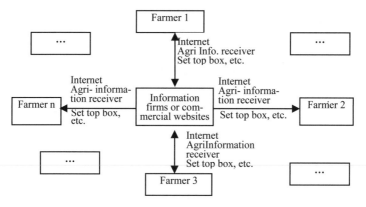

Figure 14 The structure of the professional information company or website market operation model

Leading farming household and broker demonstration model

With this service model, leading rural technology households and brokers, including farmer households which are specialized in cultivation, feeding, transporting or rural information services, collected broad information about technology, economy or markets through phones, televisions or Internet. They promote their neighboring farmers to product, process or sale certain types of agricultural products by face-to-face communication or by words and deeds, and realize specified and scaled production. Figure 15 shows the structure of leading farming households and brokers demonstration model.

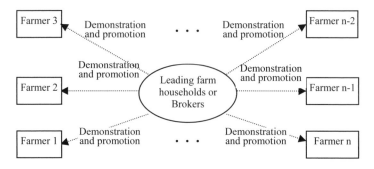

Figure 15 The structure of leading farming households and brokers demonstration model

International cooperation anti-poverty model

With this model, relative state ministries or committees cooperate with international organizations such as The United Nations Development Program to provide information services and to promote rural informationization. This model, mainly taking the form of pilot assistance projects, supports poverty regions to establish information agencies and organizations facing rural areas, purchases information equipments, and bring poverty-stroke areas out of poverty by serving farmers agricultural information. So far, five poverty alleviation information centers, ten poverty alleviation information stations at township level, and twenty two information points at village level have been established in five poverty counties located in Chongqing and Anhui.

2.2.2 Technology Models of Rural Informationization Services

In general, there are types of technical models to serve rural areas with agricultural information, including: traditional technical model, "three networks in one" model, "three electrics in one" model, "sky-earth technology" model, "three networks and one stock" model, and "3G mobile" new model, namely, "three electrics coupled plus one machine" model (Wang et al. 2006; Wang 2007). Each model has its own features, advantages and disadvantages. Suitable technical model should be selected during the service process of rural informationization according to the local conditions and the local user demands.

Traditional technical model

With this model, traditional media such as newspapers, magazines, books, blackboards, radio and televisions are used for information services. With the vast territory, types of development unbalances exist in China and "digital divide" is extremely serious. Although no modern technology used with traditional model, due to the limitation of being under-skilled and undereducated of farmers and the shortage of informationization equipments, tradition technical model is still the main and valid model for mountainous regions and for West-Middle China. The traditional model should not be ignored even in Eastern China where informationization level is higher and modern technical model is in usage.

"Three networks in one" model

With "three networks in one" model, telecommunication networks, Internet, and radio and television transmission networks are used in comprehensive and optimized way, to establish full-digital linking network systems and multi-media information networks which are with broadband information exchange and transmission, integrated professional works, and intelligent management and control. Through this multi-media network model, information services such as voice, data and video services are provided to users.

"Three electrics in one" model

As mentioned above, with this model, the "three electrics" such as telephones, televisions and computers are integrated together in a valid way for information services. In detail, databases of agricultural information are established by using computers and by collecting information from network environments; information and professional knowledge is available at any time for agricultural producers by using telephones, by phone voice automatic query systems and by expert advisory systems; hot topics involving agricultural production are communicated to farmers in the form of television programs through television broadcast systems. In this way, the "three electrics" such as telephones, televisions and computers are integrated together to provide farmers valuable information services timely and precisely.

Currently, "three electrics in one" model is advocated by Ministry of Agriculture as an important manner of rural informationization services. It is suitable for the regions with nice network infrastructure, with high demands for information and with advanced information technology.

"Sky-earth technology" model

Here, the sky means satellite communication technology, while the earth means ground transmission technology. This model takes the full advantages of satellite transmission such as broad covering areas, low operation cost and non-time limitation. Meanwhile, satellite transmission technology, ground transmission technology and the technology integrating the above two are combined to contribute into the practical rural information service platforms with a low cost.

"Three networks and one stock" model

This model was initiated as a technical solution for electronic government (e-government) in China. Here, the three networks, different from the three networks in "3 networks in one" model, mean inner networks, specific networks and outer networks and all of them are based on Internet. Inner networks are used inside certain government departments and are with systems such as government administration systems, internal management systems and business automatic workflow systems, etc. Specific networks, namely external specific network, cover several government departments and other cooperating organizations, and are used for communication between government departments. Meanwhile, outer networks are open to provide rich information to broad farmers. The stock means information resource stock, which is similar to the information resource databases in "three electrics in one" model.

The focus of "three networks and one stock" model is to provide security technology solution for the utilization of information resources in the process of developing informationization. This model is suitable for different levels of agricultural-related government offices, for different levels of security of information resources, authority management and information security services.

"3G mobile" model

3G mobile, namely third-generation mobile, is the new generation of movable communication system, which can combine voice communication with multimedia communication. It provides information services such as images, voice, web browsers, telephone conferences, information querying, etc. "3G mobile" model is possible to develop as an important technology model of rural informationization services, that is "three electrics coupled plus one machine" model (with telephones, TV, computers and mobiles), a model with significant development prospects.

2.3 Problems and Challenges for Agricultural Informationization in China

Certain problems exit and need to be solved urgently, although great achievements have been obtained with the construction of rural informationization and ICT have gotten broad application in agriculture and rural China. The main problems are (An 2005; Sun 2005; Wen 2006; Lu 2006; Wang et al. 2006; Lu 2007a; Wang 2007):

- Problems with the market mechanism of rural information. Currently, the leading role is played by the government in the construction process of rural informationization. The breadth and depth that enterprises involve in the informationization construction is far from being adequate, while farmers have limited smooth channels and limited motivation to participate into this great and historical process. If these problems with the informationization market mechanism fail to be resolved, rural informationization could not obtain healthy development. Meanwhile, it brings critical problems with the mechanism development of investment and financing for rural informationization. Currently, the investment channels and the manners of supervision and services are far from complex and perfect.
- Problems with the production mechanism of rural information contents. The rural informationization in China has mainly focused on infrastructure construc-

tion. The current situation of information content construction still stays far from the demands. Meanwhile, the localization of information content processing is a crucial issue needed to be resolved. How to collect local information and to transmit them in a way that is timely, precise and suitable for local farmers is a big challenge in the further process of rural informationization.

- Problems with the standardization of rural informationization. Eighty code standards about information classification have been issued in China so far. However, there is still without any code standard for agricultural information classification. This leads to problems that information and data are collected, coded and preserved in different forms instead of unit forms. Therefore, there is much less possibility to exchange and share information.

- Problems with the manners of motivating and organizing farmers. Generally, Chinese farmers are with low education and weak capability in receiving and using information. It is reported that the average education year amount is 6.79 years for rural labors. Meanwhile, 54.17% of farmers get less than middle education and 76.4% never get any technical training. That means most part of farmers have serious limited knowledge and weak consciousness about markets and informationization, and have weak capability to obtain and use information, How to motivate, organize and train farmers in a valid way to help them participate into the great process of rural informationization as both information providers and users is a challenge, which would decide the effectiveness and efficiency of rural informationization.

- Problems with finance and human resources. On one hand, information services rely on modern communication tools. However, finance shortage and equipment shortage exist broadly. This leads to backward information collection and procession, and low level of information service. On the other hand, human resources for informationization are in critical shortage, while many of them are with out-of-date knowledge structure, are difficult to fit the new and complex demands, therefore are far from being truly qualified. The obstacles with both finance and human resources are particularly critical at township and village levels. Many information services are difficult to be continued after the setting-up investment due to without further financial or intelligent support.

3. Government Police Guidance and Actions

3.1 Government Police Guidance for Agricultural Informationization

Currently, accelerating the process of informationization is looked as an important strategic task by the Chinese government. The following policy guidances were proposed on the sixteenth national representative congress of the Chinese communist party, including "using informationization to stimulate industrialization, and using industrialization to promote informationization", and "informationization is an inevitable choice to accelerate the industrialization and modernization in China". Nowadays, "promoting informationization vigorously" is taken as one of the main tasks in the process of economic reform and construction during the first twenty years in the new century.

Policy guidance of Chinese government also gives high attention to rural informationization. According to "2006-2020 National Informationization Development Strategy" issued by the State Council of China, the government policy involving rural informationization is to promote information service facing "san nong", namely, agriculture, rural areas and farmers. In details, rural network penetration rate should be enhanced with multiple accessing means and with acceptable prices for farmers; agriculture-related information resources should be integrated; non-profit information intermediary services should be regulated and perfected; urban and rural coordinating systems of information services should be established; farmers should be provided with information about suitable markets, science and technology, education, and sanitation and health, etc.; and surplus rural labors should be supported to flow reasonably and orderly.

Chinese government has realized that ICT takes a significant role in promoting agricultural development, in enhancing farmers' income, and in accelerating the rural economic and social development, and in advancing the construction of new countryside. Multiple government departments and offices are involved into the construction of agricultural and rural informationization, including Ministry of Agriculture, Ministry of Commerce, Ministry of Science and Technology, Ministry of Information Industry and National Meteorological Administration, etc.

There are several important projects and actions initiated and supported by Chinese government, including "golden agriculture" project, "every village covered" project, "three electrics in one" project, "12316" project, agri-food traceability systems project, and "modern remote education in rural schools" project, etc. "12316" is a national unit, specific and non-profit phone number for agricultural information services, which is started in service since 2006. The following part introduces several important projects and actions involving rural informaionization in details.

3.2 Government projects and actions

3.2.1 "Golden Agriculture" Project

"Golden Agriculture" project (GA Project) was one of the twelve state key electronic government projects. GA project was proposed on the third conference of the Joint Meeting of National Economic Information in December 1994. It aims to accelerate and to promote agricultural and rural informationization, to construct "Information Systems of Comprehensive Agricultural Management and Services", and to establish agricultural information systems meeting the demands for rural economic development. The construction core of GA project is the "state center of

GA project", and its main tasks are: (1) providing services involving with network control management and information exchange, including information exchange and sharing with other agriculture-related systems. (2) constructing and maintaining the state agricultural database group and its application systems. (3) coordinating the development of a unified standards and regulations for information collection and release, while conducting technologic guidance and management with regional centers and industry centers. (4) organizing agricultural modern information services and promoting exploration and application of types of computer application system such as expert system, geographic information systems (GIS), and satellite remote sensing information systems (SRSIS). The bases for the system construction of GA project are state key agricultural counties, middle- and big-sized agricultural markets, leading agricultural education or research organizations, and types of agricultural professional institutes or associations. (ChinaWeb 2007)

GA project is led by Ministry of Agriculture and cooperated by organizations such as National Development and Reform Commission,   National Food Authority, and Central Rural Work Leading Office, etc. Its main construction tasks for each stage are:

Stage I (1995-2000): transmitting data by using PSTN, China@Net, DDN, frame relay, BSTN, VSAT satellite mini-station, and the television inverse-way radio, etc; making sure that information from all levels and all departments can be transmitted, exchanged and kept in databases timely; organizing, coordinating and guiding the exploration of information resources, while building and perfecting state basic agricultural database groups; establishing application systems of macro-control and decision-making services of agricultural monitoring, forecasting, and early warning, including forecasting systems of crop yield and agricultural production situation; setting up disaster prevention system and agricultural service information systems; researching, developing and promoting software systems and application tools with great economic and social benefits; building remote sensing information processing systems, including state agricultural remote sensing center and regional sub-center, provincial agricultural remote sensing station, remote sensing information processing systems, etc.; constructing demonstration projects, and technology and education information networks.

Stage II (from 2000-2010): expanding the scale of information collection points to 3000; perfecting transmission and processing center of comprehensive agricultural information at province level; Extending the information center construction contents from state level to province level.

3.2.2 "Every Village Covered" Project

"Every Village Covered" project (EVC Project) was activated with the demand to coordinate urban and rural economic development; to solve problems involving with "three rural issues" (namely, issues related to agriculture, rural areas, and farmers), to construct a socialist harmonious society, and to implement the strategic objective of comprehensive construction of a well-off society. EVC project is comprised by the following sub-projects (Li 2007; *Informationization* editors 2007):

- "Every village on the phone works". This project was activated on January 2004. Under the organization of Ministry of Information Industry, this project is conducted by six operators in the way of "each operator responsible for certain patches". The six operators are: China Telecom, China Netcom, China Mobile, China Unicom, China Satcom, and China Railcom. The tasks for each stage are: (1) stage I (from 2004-2005): over 95% administrative villages should be on the phone at the end of 2005[2]; (2) stage II (2006-2010)[3]: continuing the "administrative villages on the phone works", improving rural telephone penetration rate, extending the phone project from administrative villages to natural villages, constructing types of rural information service platforms, and exploring and using rural applied information resources, while realizing "every village on the phone works and every townships to the Internet" at the end of 2010.
- "Every village covered by radio and television project". This project was activated in 1998 and organized by the coordinating office with leader members from The Central Propaganda Department, The State Administration of Radio Film and Television, National Development and Reform Committee, Ministry of Finance, Ministry of Education, Ministry of Agriculture and Ministry of Culture. The tasks for each stage are: (1) stage I (from 1998-2003): all administrative villages having accesses to electricity should be covered by radio and television. (2) stage II (from 2004-2006): almost all natural village with over 50 households and with electricity should be covered by radio and television. (3) stage III (from 2007-2010): almost all natural village with over 20 household and with electricity should be covered by radio and television; Meanwhile, over 8 television channels and over 4 radio channels should be available for these villages.

---

[2] This task was over-completed. On Nov. 24, 2005, 52304 administrative villages, instead of 14563 as designed, got to have phone owing to EVC project. Therefore, the phone penetration rate for administrative villages increased from 89% to 97.1%. (Statistics yearbook of China's information industry, 2007).

[3] The task for 2006 was over-completed too. The phone penetration rate for administrative villages increased to 98.9% at the end of 2006, to 99.13% at the beginning of Sept. 2007, and designed to reach 99.5% at the end of 2007. Almost all townships have accesses to be online, and parts of townships and administrative villages have broadband Internet in Eastern or Middle China. Meanwhile parts of townships have dial-up Internet in Western China. Jiangsu province was the first realizing that all administrative villages have broadband Internet and all natural villages with over 20 households have phones at the end of 2006. Meanwhile, all natural villages having phones are realized in Guangdong province (*Informationization* editors 2007).

So far, types of economic and social benefits are achieved through EVC Project, including expanded spaces for telecommunication industry development, improved farmers' living standards, maintained social stability in rural areas, and narrowed digital divide and promoted socio-economic development in rural areas in the long run.

3.2.3 Agri-food Traceability Projects

Food traceability is the ability to trace the history, application, or location of a food, feed, food producing animal or substance, or food direct package through all stages from production, distribution, to sale points, namely, from farm to fork (ISO definition; Wilson and Clarke 1998; Beulens et al. 2006). Food traceability was initiated in European Union (EU) as a response to the break-outs of Bovine Spongiform Encephalopathy (BSE) crisis in 1990s and is conducted in over 20 countries nowadays. Although obtaining high attention and quick development in China, food traceability researches and practices in this country is still in its initiative stage and mainly in the form of pilot projects. The food traceability researches and practices in China have the following characteristics (Wen 2006; Wang et al. 2007; Zhou and Zhang 2007):

- Some systems of agri-food traceability in China were started with meat industry. Some Chinese researchers suggest traceability system should be set up and completed first in pork industry because pork is with the highest consumption amount amongst meat products in China, while it in EU was started with beef. Later on, food traceability should be promoted with other types of food;
- Food traceability in China is currently confined to metropolis where are with aggregated consumers and high demand with food safety;
- The improvement of the systematization level of food producers and processors is an important determinant for the introduction of food traceability, based on the characteristics of China's small household production;
- It is highly urgent to strengthen other relative management measures and corresponding techniques.

Meanwhile, there are some problems with the Chinese agri-food traceability systems, including (ANCC 2006):

- Different product encoding systems but not only EAN.UCC systems are used in some industries or regions. EAN.UCC system or a generic code system which can converge with EAN.UCC system is in need to be promoted nationally;
- Tracking and tracing processes are often with fractures through the agri-food supply chains and networks (SCN);
- Traceability systems bring financial, technical and concept challenges with small- and middle-sized enterprises which are the major actors in food industries in the mainland of China.

Some main food traceability (pilot) projects are shown in Table 2 below

Table 2 Main agri-food traceability (pilot) projects in China. (Source: summarized by the chapter authors)

Project Name	Project Location	Organizations or Firms Involved	Relative Time	IT used or information system involved
State vegetable traceability system (www.safefood.gov.cn)	Shandong province	- Standardization Institute of Shandong Province; - Shandong local dragon-head firms involving in vegetable, fruits, meat and aquatic products.	Project started in 2003; The first trial operation started in Aug. 2004.	Enterprise-port management information system (MIS); Data platform of food quality and safety; Market-port traceability management (MNMT) system.
China beef traceability system (www.safebeef.cn)	Beijing city, Dalian city, Shaanxi province	- China Agricultural University; - China Huaxin Homologous Tech. Ltd. - Several firms involving with beef production, distribution and sales.	Project started in Nov. 2004	RFID; Electronic MNMT technology;
Beijing traceability system of quality and safety of agri-food (vegetable) (www.atrace.org)	Beijing city	- Beijing agricultural Bureau; - 40 firms involving vegetable production and distribution; - Over 120 markets, supermarkets, convenience stores or cafeteria.	- Project started in Beginning 2006; - The system set up recently	Information inquiry technology including Internet, cellphone short message, phone and multimedia;
Inquiry system of agri-food quality and safety information of Shanghai (www.ancc.org.cn/sub/viewsub.asp?id=175)	Shanghai city	- Shanghai agri-information Co., Ltd.; - Shanghai office of GS1-China; - Companies producing vegetable, poultry eggs, corns, fruits or mushroom; - 50 domestic or international supermarkets.	Project started in 2003; Trial operation started on 1st January, 2004	Information inquiry systems (including sub-systems such as supermarket multimedia inquiry, Internet inquiry or phone inquiry systems); Production MNMT systems; Statistics analysis systems;

System	Province	Organizations	Timeline	Technology
Pork traceability system (www.jxqinglian.com/castback.aspx)	Zhejiang province	- Qinglian food Ltd.;	Project started in 2005; Enterprise inside traceability realized in Beginning 2006; Whole SCN traceability realized in Feb. 2007	-
Traceability system of yuanshan Hetian chick supply chains (www.yshtj.com)	Fujian province	- Standardization Institute of Fujian Province; - Yuanshan Hetian Chick Development Ltd.	- Project started in 2005 and completed in April 2007.	-
Food traceability system of century three-agriculture (www.f-race.com)	Bejing	- Bejing Century 3-agricultural Tech. Develop. Center	-	IT including modern database MNMT tech.; network tech.; and barcode tech.; Systems including traceability inquiry system; terminal advertising MNMT system of traceability; information systems of markets and stores.

3.2.4 Modern Remote Education Project in Rural Schools

Modern remote education project conducted with rural primary and secondary schools, by taking advantage of modern information technology, aims to transmit qualified education resources, to improve education and teaching quality and to enhance management efficiency and effectiveness, to further qualify teacher groups, to promote the sharing of qualified education resources, to resolve types of bottlenecks involving rural education in China such as the shortage of education and teaching resources, the shortage of rural teachers, and the shortage of teaching quality, and finally to promote the compulsory education in rural China. (SDRC 2007)

Based on pilot works, the remote education project with rural schools was permitted by the State Council and activated by Ministry of Education, State Development and Reform Committee, and Ministry of Finance. It was designed rural secondary schools, by taking around five years since 2003, should be equipped with computer classrooms, satellite teaching and learning acceptation points, while rural primary schools equipped with CD players and sets of CD-ROM for teaching and study.

Until 2006, with 200 million Yuan RMB from State Development and Reform Committee and Ministry of Finance, with 505 million Yuan RMB from local governments, computer rooms have been established in 39.8 thousands of rural secondary schools, satellite teaching and studying acceptation systems have been built in 218.8 thousands of rural primary schools, and CD player and sets of CD-ROM have been provided to 93.5 thousands of rural primary schools. 80% of the total designed tasks involving the remote education project have been completed. Further, the designed construction tasks are completed earlier than planned in Xinjiang Construction and Production Corps and five provinces such as Guizhou, Qinhai, Tibet, Ningxia and Xinjian.

4 Conclusion

4.1 The Coming Five to Ten Years is Crucial for Agricultural Informationization

To construct socialism new countryside and to promote the national informationization are long-term development strategy taken by the Chinese government. These two strategies would not be changed in the coming 20-30 years. Rural informationization is a cross-cutting area involving both of the two strategies. Strongly supporting policy and actions have been made by the government to promote rural informationization and to make sure of its significant prospect. To certain extent, rural informationization is a key area in Chinese informationization in the long run.

In the short term, the coming five to ten years is crucial for the development of agricultural informationization in China, although the Internet penetration rate is as low as around 5% in rural China (Lu 2007a). The reasons are: on one hand, rural information markets have been activated and rural residents have started to accept types of informationization terminals; on the other hand, middle school students are the main rural Internet users, which will participate social activities and become a key forces to promote ICT application in rural China in the coming five to ten years; furthermore, constructing socialism new countrysides is proposed as a strategic objective by Chinese government, while developing agriculture and building new countrysides become a key part amongst the national construction tasks in the new period. Therefore, the macro-environment for ICT application in agriculture and in rural China will be further perfected with the strong and various policy supports from the state government.

4.2 The Development Direction of Agricultural Informationization

E-commerce, network communities and rural comprehensive information management will be the main direction for the development of rural informationization in China. First, e-commerce would have broad development spaces because of the remoteness and traffic un-convenience in most parts of rural China. With e-commerce platforms, farmers can trade production materials and agricultural products while integrate the small-scale of production with big markets (Huang 2006). Meanwhile, rich cultural resources exist in rural China. Through network communities, farmers having similar interests in traditional cultures such as customs and local opera can communicate with each other with less regional obstacles. Therefore, network communities would help to promote the mutual cultural communication amongst farmers and villages, to break the close and preservative tradition in rural society and to widen farmers' insights. Third, rural social comprehensive information management is meaningful for the comprehensive management of the production and social life in countryside, for the improvement of operation efficiency and management level in rural society, and for the strengthening of the rural cohesion. (Lu 2007a)

In conclusion, harmonious development in both rural and urban areas will be realized and the design of the new socialism countryside will become true at the end, if majority of Chinese farmers are able to benefit from the modern ICT, to take advantage of ICT to narrow the gap between the urban and the rural and to narrow the gap between traditional agriculture and modern industry civilization.

References

An X (2005) Probe on theoretical basis and development mechanism of rural informationization. *Modern information*. 25:24-25

ANCC (2006) China's food safety traceability coding should be on the international track. http://bbs.ancc.org.cn/dispbbs.asp?boardid=21&id=2032. Accessed 16 November 2007

Beulens AJM, Coppens LWCA., Trenekens JH (2006) Traceability requirements in food supply chain networks. In: Trenekens J.H (ed) Supply chain management. WUR, Wageningen

ChinaWet (2007) Golden agriculture project. http://www.china.com.cn/Chinese /zhuanti/283749.htm. Accessed on 16 November 2007

CMII (2007) Statistics yearbook of China's information industry (the integrated part). Chinese Ministry of Information Industry(CMII), Beijing

CNNIC (2007a) Statistics report on the Internet development in China. China Internet Network Information Center (CNNIC). http://www.cnnic.cn/index/0E/00/11/. Accessed on 02 December 2007

CNNIC (2007b) Statistics report on the Internet in rural China. China Internet Network Information Center (CNNIC). http://www.cnnic.cn/html/Dir/2007/09/07/4769.htm. Accessed on 02 December 2007

Huang H (2006) Probe of rural informationization and its realizing manners in China. *Economy and exploration of sci-technology information*. 16:91-93

Informationization Editors (2007) New progresses appear continuously with "Every Village Covered" project. *Informationization*. 6:80-82

Li C (2007) To promote the "every village covered by radio and television" project in the new period. Guangming Daily. 04 January 2007

Liang J (2006) The status and technical countermeasures for the construction of new countryside in China. *Journal of Nanjing Agricultural University*. 6:25-27,38

Lu G (2006) Research on main bodies of agricultural and rural informationization. *China's information world*. 12:46-48

Lu G (2007a) The rural information organizations and their structure administration based on capital accumulation in rural society in China. Post-doctor report

Lu G (2007b) Report on the agricultural and rural informationization in China (2006-2007). CCID Consulting Co. Ltd

SCLGPO (2007) Status of poverty alleviation and development in rural China. China State Council Leading Group Office of Poverty (CSCLPO), Beijing

Sina news report (2007) The income gap between urban and rural areas is being widened The income ratio is 3.28:1 in the last year. http://www.sina.com.cn. Accessed on 16 November 2007

SDRC (2007) A guidance on the government's investment and support to agriculture. Issued by the State Development and Reform Committee. http://www.sdpc.gov.cn/zjgx/t20070703_145973.htm. Accessed December 2 2007

Sun C (2005) General situation of agricultural information technology and countermeasures in China. *China Science and Technology Information*. 24:166-167

Wang D, Wang W, and Min Y (2006) Pattern and application of information service in rural China. *World agriculture*. 8:15-18

Wang Y, Zheng Y, Wang F et al (2007) Application of RFID-based traceability system of safety and quality information through the whole supply chains and networks of multi-regional pork. *Agricultural Network information*. 8^+:54-60

Wang W (2007) Service models and operation mechanism of rural informationization in China. Economy and Management Press, Beijing

Wen T (2006) Problems staying with the rural informationization when the government withdraws. www.ruralchinawatch.org. Accessed 02 December 2007

Wen X (2006) The current situation and the development of traceability application. http://bbs.ancc.org.cn/dispbbs.asp?boardID=21&ID=2922&page=1. Accessed 06 November 2007.

Wilson TP, Clarke WR (1998) Food safety and traceability in the agricultural supply chain: using the Internet to deliver traceability. *Supply chain management.* 3: 127-133

Zhong Y (2004) Case study on information service in rural China. FAO report. http://202.127.45.55:7001/pub/agri/ztzl/xxgzjyjl/faoxxfw/index.htm. Accessed on 16 November 2007

Zhou Y, Zhang l (2007) Traceability system in food safety management: the international developments and trends in China. International symposium on certification and traceability for food safety and quality. 18-19 October 2007, Beijing

Chapter 17
Mobile Communications Market in China

Sunanda Sangwan[1], Chong Guan[2] and Louis-Francois Pau[3]

[1] Associate Professor, Nanyang Business School, Nanyang Technological University, SINGAPORE
[2] Doctoral Candidate, Nanyang Business School, Nanyang Technological University, SINGAPORE
[3] Professor, Rotterdam School of Management, Erasmus University, THE NETHERLANDS

Abstract China's mobile communications market presents unique marketing challenges. With a high subscriber growth rate but polarized and stratified consumer adoption trends, an investigation into the current status of this market will improve our understanding on how the market is evolving. In this chapter we analyze market characteristics of mobile communications with an objective to better comprehend the dynamics of the largest mobile subscribers market. Using secondary data we identify industry related and end-user related trends to infer our conclusions.

1 Introduction

The China mobile communications market is dynamic and has experienced large growth over the last decade, particularly in terms of the total numbers of subscribers. Recent Statistics show that the number of mobile phone subscribers in China has reached nearly 540 million and mobile phone adoption rate and user numbers have surpassed the fixed-line subscribers (See Table 1). This data also shows that mobile users increased by 78.32 million in numbers in 2007 while the number of fixed-phone users number increased by a marginal 1.52 million during the same period (mii.gov.cn).). This makes China the world's largest mobile phone subscriber market with the mobile penetration rate nearly 40 percent exceeding the fixed line penetration rate. The number of mobile subscribers is expected to exceed 600 million by 2010 (Embedded Research Network 2007). Hence China continues to present a potential for business and marketing opportunities for both international and local manufacturers and operators.

P.O. de Pablos, M.D. Lytras (eds.), *The China Information Technology Handbook*,   299
DOI: 10.1007/978-0-387-77743-6_17, © Springer Science+Business Media, LLC 2009

Table 1 Fixed-Line and Mobile Subscribers in China, 2004 - 2007 (in millions and as a % of population)

	January 2004	January 2005	January 2006	January 2007	November 2007	Average year-over-year growth
Mobile users	277	340	398.80	467.41	539.38	19%
Penetration rate in %	21.31	26.00	30.34	34.62	39.95	-
Fixed-line Subscribers	269	316.00	352.99	368.85	369.3	11%
Penetration rate in %	20.69	24.17	26.85	27.32	28.3	-

Source: chinapop.gov.cn, emarketer.com, mii.gov.cn Ministry of Information Industry in China, 2007

These developments motivate us to investigate and understand the mobile communications market characteristics in depth. The objective of this chapter is to provide a brief survey and analysis of the major market characteristics of mobile communications in China. The chapter is organized as follows: the following section highlights the market developments at industry level contributing to the growth of this sector. The next section analyzes the end–user level market characteristics, followed by critical market trends in general. The final section investigates some of the challenges faced by mobile content providers and we conclude with insights for the future about the growth of the mobile communications market.

2 Industry Level Market Characteristics

2.1 Reorganization and Deregulation of the Telecom Industry

The telecommunications industry has been deregulated and reorganized in the past decade. The main objective of this restructure has been to develop the industry and to meet the high-growth demand in the domestic market (Sangwan and Pau 2005). Deregulation is also aimed to invite foreign direct investment to address the deficiency in central government investment funds and to introduce competition in the domestic market (fdi.gov.cn, Wang 2002). By channeling access to technological and other resources, the government wants to motivate local industry to be more competitive and efficient and eventually participate in the global market through joint ventures and other networks (Jiang and Tan 2005).

In 1995, the telecom business was reorganized, and China Unicom and China Telecom were formed. In subsequent developments, Ministry of Information Industry (MII) was established to introduce a fair, open and competitive business environment (ChinaUni-com.com, Jiang and Tan 2005). In 2001, further reorganization introduced new companies (mofcom.gov.cn), each with a focused objective: China Telecom (chinatelecom.com.cn) and China Network Telecom (China Netcom chinanetcom.com.cn) in the fixed-line business, China Mobile (chinamobile.com) and China Unicom (chinaunicom.com), in the mobile sector, and two smaller organizations China Satcom (China Satellite) and China TieTong (China Railway Telecom) in the supporting role (mofcom.gov.cn).

The government also focused on global participation and reached an agreement to join the World Trade Organization (WTO) in 1999. This committed China to allow foreign organizations to provide a wide range of telecommunication services through joint ventures with ownership of 49 percent (mofcom.gov.cn). Subsequently, China which has been the largest recipient of foreign investment among all developing nations for 15 years also experienced an increase in primary industries including the Telecom sector (fdi.gov.cn).

With its formal accession to WTO in 2001, its impact on several market developments can be observed. Custom tariffs for high tech products were lowered to allow cheaper imports of components to manufacture affordable mobile phones for Chinese and global consumers (customs.gov.cn). The government has gradually introduced regulations to reform the duopoly in the industry and a number of foreign telecom operators have entered the Chinese market. As a result prices of mobile products and services have also declined over time as indicated by the national price index (chinaprice.org.cn). For instance, mobile operators initially charged both the caller and the receiver for their services and the government facilitated operators to offer price competitive packages and free incoming calls. These efforts show a 13.6 percent decrease in 2007 in overall telecom charges [mii.gov.cn, 2008]. Similarly, cost and prices of the mobile phones, particularly manufactured in the domestic market continue to decrease but the product renewal has also sped up (Annual Report 2007, Kumar and Thomas 2006).

Most major foreign entrants in the mobile market have invested in R&D to incorporate new features and reduce cost and prices to gain local and global market share (Sangwan, and Pau, 2005). In 2004, Alcatel invested over €100 million for R&D in China, focusing on 3G technologies (SinoCast CBDN, 2005). Nokia, Ericsson and Siemens have also set up R&D units in 3G products in R&D areas like Chengdu (Kwong, 2000; SinoCast CBDN, 2005). Ericsson's spending for the first phase of its latest R&D investment in Guangzhou was US$15 million and its R&D expenditure is projected to increase over 30% each year within the next five years (SinoCast CBDN, 2005). China operates both GSM and CDMA networks. 3rd Generation mobile communication technology was launched by China Unicom, however, 3G is still in initial stages. There is insufficient demand and 3G application services available on the market are limited and costly. The mobile telecommunication services can largely be treated as homogeneous products with limited value added services.

The government continues to be a predominant stakeholder in the development of this industry. All providers of basic telecommunications services and mobile telephony are also state-owned enterprises and the government has effective control of this industry (Qing and Keun 2005, Kumar and Thomas 2006). The market is subject to regulations which give a preferential treatment of domestic companies, require technology transfer, and R&D activities form foreign organizations willing to enter the market. These features contribute to the non-tariff barriers against foreign entrants (Nie and Zeng, 2003).

2.2 Dual Oligopolistic Market

China mobile communication market presents typical dual oligopolistic character-istics. Despite the deregulation of the industry, the continuous dominance of the market by the two state owned mobile operators; the China Mobile Communica-tions (China Mobile) and the China United Telecommunications (China Unicom), has not shifted. China Mobile is currently the largest GSM (Global System for Mobile Communications) operator in the world with 369.34 million mobile phone subscribers by December 2007 (chinamobileltd.com), followed by China Unicom which operates both GSM and CDMA has nearly 150.28 million subscribers dur-ing the same period (chinaunicom.com.hk).

   Table 2 compares positioning of China Mobile and China Unicom on the basis of subscribers and revenue. Due to the liberalization and deregulation of the mo-bile operators market, the competition has increased and both foreign and domes-tic organizations are aiming at the growth opportunity; however the market is still dual oligopoilstic (Yaobin et al 2007). It is to be noted that fixed-line operators, China Telecom and China Netcom introduced a Personal Hand-phone System (PHS), a low-cost 2G wireless standard phone often referred to as "Xiaolingtong" ("little smart") in as a mobile substitute. Xiaolingtong is perceived by many con-sumers as a less appealing version of the mobile phone, with very basic voice and text messaging functions, a weaker signal and no roaming ability. Since 2005 the Xiaolingtong user growth has slowed down and was negative in 2006 (Annual Report of China Telecom, 2006). Up to August 2007, there were 89.58 million Xiaolingtong subscribers which can be connected to 3G services (mii.gov.cn). It

Table 2 Market Share of China Mobile and China Unicom

		2002	2003	2004	2005	2006	Dec. 2007
China Mobile	Revenue (RMB)	163730	171870	198300	235800	286300	na
	(US $)	20991	22035	25423	30231	36705	
	Share (%)	76.49	72.04	73.20	75.24	77.71	
	Subscribers*	1.38	178	221	264	317	369.34
	Share (%)	66.99	65.93	66.17	67.18	68.76	
China Unicom	Revenue (RMB)	50330	66705	72620	77700	82140	na
	(US $)	6453	8552	9310	9962	10531	
	Share (%)	23.51	27.96	26.80	24.78	22.29	
	Subscribers*	68	92	113	129	144	150.28
	Share (%)	33.01	34.07	33.83	32.82	31.24	
Total	Revenue (RMB)	214060	238575	270920	313500	368440	
	(US $)	27444	30587	34733	40193	47236	
	Subscribers*	206	270	334	393	461	519.26

Source: (mii.gov.cn) * figures in millions

remains to be seen how this segment would benefit form 3G (Yuan et al 2006). In addition, the emergence of Internet communication poses some threat to mobile operators' voice services, but Internet communication is not supported by the government until now. Thus, the PHS and Internet communications do not constitute a decisive impact on China's mobile market, which still can be seen as a typical dual-oligopolistic market.

China Mobile revenue share has been on average 75 percent of the total market with an average of 66 percent of the total number of subscribers. This suggests that China Mobile generates higher average revenue per user (ARPU) than its nearest competitor China Unicom. This can be explained by the variety of value-added services (VAS) offered by it. Its VAS revenue (RMB 69.31 billion or $9 billion) in 2006 accounted for 23.5 percent of its total revenue. China Unicom earned VAS revenue of RMB 11.543 billion ($988 million), or 12.2 percent of its total revenues in the same period (China Telecom Weekly, 2007). This illustrates the demand for VAS is on increase with growth in purchasing power and intensity of mobile usage.

3 User Level Market Characteristics

3.1 Income Based Market Segments

With a GDP growth rate of an average of 8 percent during the last decade (indexmundi.com), consumers have experienced a high increase in their purchasing power. The distribution of income structure shows that average annual disposable income per head in 2006 was 11,759 Yuan, (1469.9US$) a 10 percent increase from the year before (XFN 2007, uschina.org 2006). According to a Gallup study based on the sample of 15,000 adults across China, the average household income has increased by nearly 250% over the last decade (Gallup 2007). Cumulated with overall lower manufacturing costs, it is estimated that a consumer in China can, on average, buy nearly four to five times in goods and services per dollar as compared to his counterpart in USA (Fishman, 2004, Chu 2005). High and middle-income households constitute rapidly growing market segments of the population. These developments have directly contributed to the higher, frequent change, multi-brand and multiple unit adoption of mobile telephony (Annual Report2007). These trends also show the probability of increased ARPU and higher revenue generation in the industry.

Geographically, the eastern and southern provinces of China are economically more developed, and are major drivers for revenue growth in this sector with branded product purchase and high VAS usage (Ramstad, 2004). It is estimated that the average consumption of an urban household in Shanghai is almost three times the national average (PricewaterhouseCoopers, 2004). The current consumption of mobile value added services is largely concentrated in urban areas. With mobile phone functionalities continually being upgraded and average product and service prices on decrease, there is a higher likelihood for urban consumers to continue to show preference for branded and high-end units irrespective of the higher prices (Ramstad, 2004).

Per-capita income of the rural population is estimated to be only one third of the per-capita disposable income of urban China (Xinhua News Agency, 2007). But irrespective of income disparities the rural market segment is becoming the driver and sustaining factor for the mobile industry even if the ARPU is expected to be lower (Nolan, Zhang and Liu 2007). This is supported by the fact that more than half of China Mobile's new subscribers in the year 2006 and 2007 were from rural areas (Asia Pulse Provider, 2007). As urban markets become saturated, China Mobile and China Unicom are also expanding their network in the rural areas. Innovative marketing strategies and new marketing models have increased the mobile adoption in all demographic segments. Domestic manufacturers have largely focused on the market share based on lower labor costs, lower purchasing power market segment, and low profit-large market share strategy (Dean, 2003). Domestic handset manufacturers have realized the significance of low-end R&D to meet the global competition and to serve the bottom market segments (Qing and Lee, 2005). In the first half of 2007, around 72 million homemade mobile phone sets were sold in China (Annual Report, 2007) and this generated 84.58 billion RMB (1.57US$) revenue, an increase of 25.5 percent from 2006, and on average of 5.5 percent (Annual Report, 2007). Clearly the rural and the bottom market segment has benefited from local brands.

The growth of the mobile communications consumer market can be explained by the market characteristics of any typical developing country where first-time buyers form a large part of the consumer market segment. The penetration level is still short of saturation with near 40% (see Table 1), but this projects growing market potential in this stratified market.

3.2 Lifestyle based Market Segment: High ARPU

For the young working adult segment a mobile phone is a lifestyle statement along with an advance communication and entertainment center. China Mobile received more than 25% of its revenue from value added services in 2007, and its voice business revenue has declined. In 2007 nearly 25 million units of high-end smart phones were sold and this sale contributed to 16% of total market in China (Annual Report, 2007). For this segment, comprising of young entrepreneurs and professionals mobility constitutes a life style element and demand comes from desire to upgrade or replace their current hand sets. Technological innovations such as 3G for high data transfer will contribute older technologies to become obsolete and require consumers to constantly upgrade. This is one factor that contributes to sustaining the growth in this industry (Dittrich and Duysters 2007, Weaver 2005).

This segment spends most on value added services but price sensitivity of these services has also contributed to this polarization of the content services market. It is estimated that 55% of mobile users in China are young working adults between the ages of 25 and 35 years. In urban areas like Guangzhou, mobile penetration rate for the young population between 21 to 30 years is about 92% (Weichao 2007). The total revenues generated by mobile value-added service providers in China is expected to grow from about US$565 million in 2003 to around US$1.9 billion in 2008 (Boltz and Corney, 2005). Revenue from China Mobile's value-added business accounted for 23.5 per cent of its total operating revenue in 2006 (Chinadaily 2007).

Amongst value added services, ringtone downloading is the most widely accepted service. Other services include downloading pictures, accessing Internet, using MMS, surfing on WAP websites, and downloading mobile phone games (iUsersurvey 2006). Guessing games, news alerts and information inquiries are other value added services on growth (China Daily, 2007). Demands and 3G facilitation presents mobile music and mobile video a rapid development momentum (China Mobile Value-added Services Report, 2006).

Demand for non-voice business, including mobile newspaper, mobile payment, and mobile tracking reports is growing and mobile operators now face the challenge of managing the future growth of mobile content (SinoCast China IT, 2007). Services like message-on-demand and stock trading are increasingly being used (Xu, 2003). For example, subscribers can visit the website of SOHU and subscribe to customized news on sports and entertainment. This allows them to receive the latest news via their handsets on a regular basis. China Mobile charges of mobile news depend on service providers (SP), but on average RMB2.00 (US$0.2) per new piece or RMB 30.00 (US$3.75) per month (news.xinhuanet.com, 2007). Service providers are thus differentiating themselves by integrating mobile content and value-added services on SMS (short messaging services), MMS (Multi-media Messaging Services), WAP (Wireless Application Protocol), and IVR (Interactive Voice Response).

This market size and scale enables China's portals and other stakeholders like service providers to earn large profits on their mobile value-added service through alliances and networks with third party content and service providers (China Mobile 2008). They are innovative in introducing services conducive to this brand-swapping and price sensitive segments (Campbell, 2005). Current regulations also support mobile operators who can retain 15% of the message fee and have exclusive rights for operating SMS services. NTT DoCoMo's success in Japan has provided Chinese mobile operators with valuable experience in developing a business model. Learning from DoCoMo's model, the market has consolidated alliances between mobile operators and third-party content providers and portals have been formulated (Fjermestad et al. 2006, Mylonopoulosm and Sideris 2006) Subsequently, China Mobile introduced the Monternet program and service providers can now access the carrier's mobile network at any place to provide nation-wide service (Carey 2005, Xu, 2003). This is also known as the "one-stop shop, China-wide service" arrangement. China Mobile keeps between nine and twenty percent of the traffic revenue and the content service providers receive remainder of the revenue (Xu 2003, China Mobile Value-added Services Report, 2006).

3.3 Low ARPU Market: Short Messaging Services (SMS) Usage

Future growth of mobile value added data services in China depends on the existing SMS, based on the GSM standard. Chinese mobile phone users sent 429.7 billion short messages in 2006, a 41.0 percent increase from the year before (mii.gov.cn). This translates to about 78 SMS per month per user as compared to 61 SMS in US, 70 in the UK and 180 MSS per month in Japan. SMS generated a revenue of about RMB 42.9 billion (US$5.4billion) in 2006. SMS is limited to a maximum of 160 characters as compared to 140 in India, but it is an economical and cost effective way to communicate.

Sending one short message costs RMB0.10 (US$0.01) (news.xinhuanet.com 2007) against a regular one-minute telephone call which costs RMB0.40 or 0.25 (US$0.05 or 0.02) (soft.zol.com.cn 2008, Xu 2003). On average, each user spends RMB21 (US$2.57) on SMS per month. Some Internet portals like SINA.com and Sohu.com also allow users to send SMS via their PCs to the handsets of mobile phone users, but given the low PC penetration rate of around 15%, this is not a viable option and neither is it in direct competition with the mobile SMS. The success of SMS is largely a result of its low cost and convenience, but is also attributed to relatively reserve attitude of Chinese toward open communication and self-expression (Reid and Reid 2004). SMS based mobile commerce and mobile marketing is being increasingly adopted and accepted. Personalized services like SMS novels are viewed to be successful in the Chinese market (China Daily, 2005). The service enables mobile phone users to read a novel by receiving an 'episode' in a SMS message every day, costing about RMB 0.50 (US$0.06) for each episode.

Operators and service providers have also profited from SMS based information services provided by several businesses. A joint SMS centre, called MOBNIC (Mobile Network Information Centre), was jointly launched China Mobile, China Unicom, the China Mobile Communication Association and other service providers. Its services enable users to visit corporations' "SMS-based websites". Users can send a specific number or code via an SMS message to access the "SMS website" of a business to receive free interactive information services. A 160 character message with 40% space for sponsored advertisements is then sent to the user. This advertising offers small and medium-sized enterprises (SMEs) an opportunity for low cost marketing (China Daily, 2005). This growth in mobile messaging has had an impact on the development of m-commerce and mobile advertising. Mobile advertisements are predominantly SMS based but other services such as color ringtones, WAP browsers, voice services are generating value for the end-users (securities.com). By 2010 mobile advertising is projected to generate near RMB two billion (iResearch 2008).

3.3 Preference for Prepayment Price Mechanism: Low ARPU

Prepaid price mechanism is the prevalent mode of transaction necessitated by China's current telecom business environment. It has significantly contributed to the diffusion of mobile telephony all over the world (Smirlis et al 2004). Although there has been an increase in minutes of usage over the years, generally the new subscribers are from low income and low usage market segment and yield low average revenue per user (ARPU). It is reported that China Mobile's ARPU has declined from RMB431 (US$52) (chinamobilehk.com) in 1997 to RMB96 (US$12) in 2007. This may partially be explained by declining costs of the mobile services but largely by the growth in low-use subscribers who use pre-paid services mode. Around 67% of China Mobile's total subscriber base are on the prepaid plans (chinamobilehk.com).

Preference and adoption of prepaid mechanism can be explained by several factors. In low income segments it allows users better control over their spending. As prepaid users do not have to register their address with the operator it extends more privacy to the user than with subscription plans (Fan, 2000, Gow and Ihnat 2004). Pre-paid services are also favored by China's Telecom operators because of market and procedural irregularities associated with the back-end-billing or post-paid payments (Boltz and Comey, 2005). The market is not established in its regulations and their implementation, and post-paid strategy has caused operators revenue loses from unpaid bills (York, 2001). Back-end billing and collection systems are evolving, and all stakeholders are in the process of learning and adoption.

Most consumers do not use credit or debit cards and China continues to be largely a cash culture economy (Laforet and Li 2005). Because of this undeveloped billing system, mobile operators are also not able to sell third-party financial services. Even if the technological advancement has increased operational capacity, and lowered operational costs, banks in China have their own individual credit and debit card billing system. Their transactions cannot be routed through a centralized computer system until systems are standardized or replaced by a collective system marketing efforts to encourage customers to switch to subscription plans and use third-party services, have therefore achieved limited success.

4 Conclusions

It is evident that the mobile communications market in China is undergoing reforms but it also faces several challenges that are negatively affecting revenue and profits generation and has slowed down the growth of the mobile industry. These include market irregularities relating to illegal and unwanted content; forced subscription of services without users prior consent; underdeveloped billing methods; and declining ARPU and other revenues (Sangwan and Pau 2005, Qing and Keun 2005). In an attempt to rectify some of the issues, China mobile suspended MMS licenses of some of its operators for providing MMS services to users without prior permission. A national survey undertaken by third party researchers on a sample of 90,000 mobile users across China showed 76% of total respondents were satisfied with two large mobile operators (Interfax China 2007). User showed dissatisfaction with higher service charges and poor signal quality. Better policy measures and managerial implementation can diminish such market irregularities.

Market is consolidating where several small service providers are either being eliminated or being merged with larger organizations (China Daily, 2005). China's Mobile operators are forming their own value-added service (VAS) consortium to avoid dependence on the third party content and service providers. This strategy also displaces existing service providers and the two mobile operators, China Mobile and China Unicom, have gained dominant market positions. This allows them to exercise significant negotiating power over third-party service providers. Introduction of competition through policy and managerial interventions will accelerate growth in the industry. These measures can motivate introduction of new products and services generating higher user satisfaction.

The 2.5g based value added service acceptance is growing and recently China has allowed market test of indigenous TD-SCDMA 3G services. These offers higher quality graphics, richer content and interactivity and are premium priced than the established SMS-based services. Implementation of international 3G services has been on delayed until the Olympic games of summer 2008. But success of China's 3G policy will relate to user acceptance of value added content for higher ARPU. It is also expected that with 3Gs launch, every operator will receive its license. TD will not be the single standard, most popular WCDMA will also be used although China will protect its domestic standard TD by giving it priority for 2 years' protect time. Future success of the mobile industry may thus depend upon innovation of services, market consolidation, improved policy and management structure and effective marketing strategies.

References

Annual Report on China's Mobile Phone Market 2005-2006, 2006-2007; CCID Consulting http://www.ccidconsulting.com/. Accessed 25th Jan., 2008.

Asia Pulse, Several Issues 2007 http://site.securities.com.ezlibproxy1.ntu.edu.sg/docs.html?pc=CN&sv=EMIS&pub_id=ASIAPULSEHK Accessed 25th Jan., 2008.

Boltz, Paul W. , Corney, Charles C.(2005) Spread your content far and wide. *The China Business Review*. March-April.

China Daily. : Several Issues

China Telecom Weekly 08-2-8 Interfax http://site.securities.com.ezlibproxy1.ntu.edu.sg/docs.html?pc=CN&pub_id=IFCTW&sv=EMIS Accessed 8th Feb., 2008

China Mobile Value-added Services Report, 2006, Research In China. (2007). http://www.researchandmarkets.com/reportinfo.asp?report_id=452588 Accessed 8th Feb., 2008

China Mobile (2008) Excellent Financial Performance Favorable Profitability, China Mobile Limited Announces 2007 Interim Results, 16 August 2007 http://www.chinamobileltd.com/doc/pr/2007/20070816.htm Accessed 25th Jan., 2008

Dean, T. (2003) The fight for China's handset market, The China Business Review **30** (6), pp. 28–31.

Dittrich, Koen, Duysters, Geert. (2007) Networking as a Means to Strategy Change: The Case of Open Innovation in Mobile Telephony. Journal of Product Innovation Management, 24(6), p510-521.

Embedded Research Network (2007) Nokia's cell phone sales skyrocket in China

Fan, Z. (2000)"China Unicom fights against delinquent accounts". Qilu Night. April 5, 2000.

Fjermestad, Jerry; Passerini, Katia; Patten, Karen; Bartolacci, Michael R.; Ullman, David (2006) Moving toward mobile third generation telecommunications standard: the good and bad of the 'anytime/anywhere' solutions Communications of AIS, 2006(17), 2-33.

Fishman, Ted C. (2004) The Chinese Century. The New York Times Magazine. July 4, 2004.

Gallup (2007) A Weak Driver of a Strong Economy Challenges in China's Move Toward Consumption-Oriented Economic Growth Gallup Chinese Consumer Study: 1994 -2006 http://media.gallup.com/WorldPoll/PDF/WPChinaTFExecSummary.pdf, The Gallup Organization, Princeton, NJ.

Gow Gordon A. and Ihnat Mark (2004) Prepaid Mobile Phone Service and the Anonymous Caller Surveillance & Society 1(4), 555-572.

iResearch (2007) What were China's 450 million mobile users "Searching" for 2007/01/23 http://english.iresearch.com.cn/search_engine/detail_news.asp?id=8145

Jiang Yu and Kim Hua Tan (2005) The evolution of China's mobile telecommunications industry: past, present and future. *International Journal of **Mobile** Communications*, 3(2), 1-1.

Kotabe Masaaki & Jiang Crystal (2006) Three Dimensional, *Marketing Management.* 15(2), 39.

Kumar Keval J. and Thomas Amos O. (2006) Telecommunications and Development: The Cellular Mobile 'Revolution' in India and China, *Journal of Creative Communications*, 1(3), 297-309.

Kwong, 2000 Kwong, Regis (2000) Tomorrow's Telecoms: Who Will Win China's Phone Wars? Asiaweek, December 1, Hong Kong, 1-1.

Laforet, Sylvie; Li, Xiaoyan (2005) Consumers' attitudes towards online and mobile banking in China. *International Journal of Bank Marketing*, 23(5), 362-380.

Mylonopoulos, Nikolaos; Sideris, Ioannis. (2006) Growth of Value Added Mobile Services Under Different Scenarios of Industry Evolution, Electronic Markets, 16(1), 28-40.

Nie, Winter, Zeng, Hongjian. (2003) The Impact of China's WTO Accession on Its Mobile Communications Market. *Journal of Business and Management*, Spring 9(2).

Nolan, Peter; Jin Zhang; and Chunhang Liu. (2007) The Global Business Revolution and the Cascade Effect : Systems Integration in the Global Aerospace, Beverage and Retail Industries. Palgrave Macmillan.

PricewaterhouseCoopers (2004) 2004/2005 Global Retail & Consumer Study from Beijing to Budapest. 5-6.

Qing . M. and K. Lee (2005), Knowledge diffusion, market segmentation and technological catch-up: The case of the telecommunications industry in China, *Research Policy* 34 (6), . 759.

Ramstad. E. (2003), New game, many winners, *Far Eastern Economic Review* 166 (34), 28–29.

Reid Fraser J.M., Reid Donna J. (2004) Text appeal: the psychology of SMS texting and its implications for the design of mobile phone interfaces, *Campus-Wide Information Systems*, 21(5),196 – 200.

Sangwan, Sunanda, Louis-Francois Pau. (2005). Diffusion of Mobile Phones in China, *European Management Journal*, 26(5).

Smirlis Yannis G., Despotis Dimitris K. , Fiala J. Jablonsky, (2004) Identifying "Best-Buys" In The Market Of Prepaid Mobile Telephony: An Application Of Imprecise Dea. International *Journal of Information Technology and Decision Making* 3(1), 167-177.

SinoCast CBDN 2005, Sinocast LLC, The Financial Times Limited sinocast.com Accessed 8th
    Feb., 2008
Wang, Wei (2002) China's Access to WTO: Impact on Telecommunications and Internet Infor-
    mation Services. China's Integration with the World Economy: Repercussions of China's
    Access to the WTO. Chapter 11.
Weaver, G. (2005) The Mobile Phone Industry: A Strategic Overview, *Reed Electronics Re-
    search*, June 2005.
Weichao Nancy (2007) Everyday necessity of Teens: The use of mobile phones for young people
    in Macau and Guangzhou China East Asia Media New Media Conference 2007
    http://cea.cci.edu.au/?q=node/154 Accessed 8th Feb., 2008
Wu J.,(2006) Operations: OEMs and EMS, iSuppli Market Watch, 6(10), p.5.
Xinhua Online (2005). TD-SCDMA insiders say trial went badly. June 24, 2005.
Xu, Yan.(2003) Mobile Data Communications in China. *Communications of the ACM*. Decem-
    ber 2003. 46(12).
Yaobin Lu, Yuanyuan Dong, Bin Wang (2007) The mobile business value chain in China: a case
    study. *International Journal of Electronic Business*, 5(5), 460.
York, Tom (2001). China's Exploding Wireless Industry. Impulse Magazine. October 2001
Yuan, Yufei; Zheng, Wuping; Wang, Youwei; Xu, Zhengchuan; Yang, Qing; Gao, Yufei (2006)
    Xiaolingtong versus 3G in China: Which will be the winner? *Telecommunications Policy*, 30
    (5/6), 297-313. Accessed 8th Feb., 2008

Chapter 18
Logistics and IT Services in China Outsourcing in the Manufacturing Industries

Yen-Chun Jim Wu

Professor, Dept. of Business Management, National Sun Yat-Sen University, Taiwan. CHINA

Abstract Outsourcing has been one of the most popular activities among enterprises worldwide for nearly a decade. By outsourcing non-core technologies to professional manufacturers abroad, firms can minimize their operating costs. After its admission to the WTO, China has attracted an increasing number of investing foreign enterprises. The local enterprises in China are facing a more complicated environment. To serve different customers both at home and from abroad, they will restructure their organizations and adjust their operation strategies. They also consider if the external resources and facilities can meet their needs. Complete development of logistics infrastructures in China will be the key to successful operations for the local enterprises. Our research discusses logistics services provided by outsourced suppliers in China for domestic and foreign customers and how the need to serve different customers affects their organization. This study is from the viewpoint of outsourced suppliers in China, by attempting to understand customer logistic service criteria, IT services, customer selection criteria, and the difficulties and future challenges facing Chinese enterprises.

1 Introduction

During the past decade of rising global markets, prosperous development of international trades and worldwide technological advancement, the distances between countries have been shortened. In the past, due to lack of advanced communication technology, enterprises could not outsource parts of their operations to low-cost countries. With the latest technological development, it is now possible for them to reduce their operation costs through outsourcing. This has caused restructuring and adjustment in the global supply chain. Amidst the current trend of globalization, China, with its competitive edge in resources and environment as well as gradual market deregulation, has seen increasing domestic economic demands. To connect to the global supply chain, well-planned logistics infrastructure development is a vital measure for each country in enhancing its own competitiveness. Good logistics infrastructures can help effectively boost national productivity and promote national economic developments.

Enterprise operations also require the assistance of logistics infrastructures to enable fast product delivery to customers, increase operation efficiencies and

P.O. de Pablos, M.D. Lytras (eds.), *The China Information Technology Handbook*,   311
DOI: 10.1007/978-0-387-77743-6_18, © Springer Science+Business Media, LLC 2009

achieve business goals. As the global market changes structurally, many foreign investors are drawn to the rising countries, among which China constitutes an irresistible, large market in particular with its advantageous geographic location, abundant resources and cheap labor. Facing such a globalization trend and powerful external forces, the PRC government is required to further deregulate and open up the market. Meanwhile, the local enterprises are facing a more diversified variety of customers both at home and from abroad. Mutual trust is the primary requirement of foreign enterprises toward suppliers in developing countries—the former expect the latter to meet their operating needs. Suppliers in developing countries also try to satisfy the needs of local and international customers to maximize profits. Different customers require different logistics services (Liker and Wu 2000) Long-term partnerships between supplier customers will eventually affect operation and management. Therefore, to facilitate operation and management, the supplier must evaluate its abilities and partner with suitable customers with which to build long-term partnerships in order to achieve win-win situations. To meet the needs of different customers, they have to adjust their operation strategies to adapt themselves to the drastic changes in the external environment. These enterprises need to evaluate if their operations can survive the changes in the external market and make responding strategies.

Ever since its reform and opening up in 1979, China has experienced rapid economic growth that infuses vigor into the consuming market. In addition to the growing productivity brought by continuous influx of foreign investments, local product distributions and rapid development of foreign trade activities have rendered the current logistics infrastructures in China unable to meet the actual needs. After its entry into the WTO, China made many promises on issues regarding market investment deregulations. These promises are expected to promote economic development in China and, meanwhile, bring more opportunities along with challenges for both local and foreign enterprises. This study is mainly intended to discuss about the difficulties and challenges confronting local enterprises in China after the PRC's entry to the WTO and analyze the current logistics development in China.

Based on the viewpoint of the logical enterprises, this research attempts to find out the differences among Chinese suppliers in their logistics services for different customers and responses to different customer demands. In addition, the study also discusses the criteria of customers in evaluating the logistics services and analyzes the influence and difficulties in management level for the Chinese enterprises to enter the international market. The study also attempts to provide further understanding of the criteria of the Chinese suppliers in forming partnerships with local customers and foreign ones. Finally, the study explores the challenges for the local enterprises from the external environment. From the above-mentioned analysis, the study is intended to provide a clear picture about the current logistics development in China after its WTO admission.

2 Review of the Literature

Before the reforms, all the planning of production and distribution in China was the sole responsibility of the PRC government. What products to be manufactured and the production volume were only decided by the government. In addition, the distribution channels back then were also strictly restricted (Jiang and Prater 2002). According to many existing studies, the logistics development in China was rather slow, indicating the problems of underdevelopment of logistics and transportation back then (Speece and Kawahara 1995). Logistics services were provided exclusively by the central government or local authorities who rarely offered value-added logistics services (Powers 2001). The private sector was only allowed to do internal transportation and warehousing but not logistics business. Meanwhile, the lack of third-party logistics providers also resulted in management inefficiency (Hong et al. 2004). In 1978, the PRC government launched a series of economic reforms which allowed the establishment of new logistics systems and the participation of different types of enterprises in logistics activities. In addition, the manufactures were given the autonomy to choose their logistics providers (Luk 1998).

- Ever since its WTO admission and the popularity of e-course, China, a vast land with abundant resources, have started to see booming economic development (Jiang and Prater 2002). With increasing logistics development, many of the local manufactured began to outsource their logistics operations. After its WTO entry, China would gradually loosen its restrictions on investments by foreign logistics providers, elevating the local logistics system development into the model of free market. Meanwhile, as the local logistics providers in China lack the ability to provide high-level logistics services, the deregulation of logistics policy can encourage the entry of foreign logistics providers to provide more advanced logistics services (Hong et al. 2004). Jiang and Prater (2002) further indicated that while these local enterprises and foreign ones share the same logistics and distribution problems in China, they would have to improve their enterprise models and further integrate their value chains in this fiercely competitive environment. Gould (2002) also pointed out that China's entry to the WTO would cast a significant influence in its logistics development particularly in the following aspects:
- Liberalization of China's customs, taxation and tariff structure.
- Changes in China's legal system to meet the regulations of international trade organizations.
- Reengineering of large-size national enterprises.
- Benefits of mid- and small-size private enterprises from China's WTO admission.
- Increase of foreign investments in China.

In addition, he also suggested that, after the WTO entry, the key of successful operation for both local and foreign enterprises in China would lie in close connections with their local partners and frequent reevaluation of the partnerships to establish and maintain effective performance matrixes. Facing the changes in the external environment, the local Chinese manufacturers should evaluate and adjust their operation strategies. As indicated by Easton (2003), the PRC government has invested heavily on the construction of logistics and transportation infrastructures while the manufactures have also strived to develop new logistics competences to provide better services and reduce operation costs. Handfield and Mccormack (2005) discussed the strengths and weaknesses of Chinese suppliers from the viewpoint of foreign enterprises by using the SCOR model to analyze the operation competences of Chinese manufacturers. The SCOR model is a process reference model that can provide explanations of the relationships among partners in the supply chain. According to their findings, the Chinese suppliers are advantageous in manufacturing planning and production scheduling but relatively weak in cross-function and cross-company planning. In addition, the Chinese suppliers are unable to adjust the fluctuating product demands in the external market and lack of logistics competences and real-time transportation ability. Despite their high-level delivery procedures, they have relatively low control over products shipped out of the factory. Pyke et al. (2002) used questionnaires to discuss the differences among three types of enterprises in China in their implementations of advanced production technologies. Pyke et al. (2000) also studied the local enterprises and foreign enterprises in China, trying to find out differences between them in their manufacturing strategies and supply chain management. He discovered that, even though the Chinese enterprises had developed a certain level of manufacturing policies, their concepts of supply chain management were still behind those of their western counterparts. From the above-mentioned studies, it can be seen that the Chinese manufacturers are generally insufficient in logistics competences and concepts. To solve this problem, Handfield and Mccormack (2005) suggested the Chinese suppliers should have administrative supports and suitable organizational structures. Meanwhile, a coordination mechanism should be established, such as a cross-function team, regular review meeting, global outsourcing contract and evaluation process of the performance of translators and suppliers.

3 Methodology and sample

This study focused on suppliers in the manufacturing industry in Shanghai, China. In the latest Annual Urban Competitiveness Report (Li 2005), Shanghai ranks first, and Shanghai is also ranked by Forbes (2005) as one of the top three Chinese commercial centers. As the most advanced industrial and business city, Shanghai has better infrastructures for both foreigners and local citizens as well as more advanced communication infrastructures. The logistics in Shanghai are far more developed than in other Chinese cities because the government has worked hard on infrastructure development in Shanghai to attract more foreign investment. Moreover, its port is one of the most important trade ports in the world, so the port allows foreign enterprises to ship their products abroad promptly. Almost all Top 500 companies around the world have been stationed in Shanghai. We focus on manufacturers from the automotive, telecommunication and computer, and household appliance and electronic product industries. Our sample selection was based on the Annual Urban Competitiveness Report (Li 2005) and the Shanghai Suppliers and Manufacturers Directory (SMERT 2002).

The unit of analysis for the survey is the supplier-customer dyad focused on their one largest-dollar volume product for the dyad. In sample screening, only suppliers with both domestic and foreign customers were selected when foreign customers accounted for more than 10 percent of their annual sales. In addition, we required to have basic communication infrastructures, such as e-mail and fax, for communication with foreign customers. Since there were many firms do not meet these criteria, suppliers who met the requirements were contacted by telephone, email, or fax before the questionnaires were sent out to ensure data consistency. The actual data collection process started in early June and ended in late July of 2005. After sample screening, a total of fifty-six suppliers met the requirements in this study, and 41 returned questionnaires were returned with response rate of 73 percent. Among the responses, 26.8 percent were from the automotive industry, 29.3 percent from the communication and computer industry, 24.4 percent from the household appliance industry, and 19.5 percent from the electronics industry. To boost the response rate, each supplier who had participated in this study was given reasonable honorarium fees and promised a summary report of the research findings and promised confidentiality.

Supplier characteristics are listed in Table 1. Among the forty-one suppliers, more than 50% of these suppliers are joint ventures. The investment ratio shows that most suppliers have more investments from Chinese investors than foreign ones, perhaps because the Chinese government restricted foreign investments in the past, limiting foreign investors to hold not more than 50% of company shares.

Most suppliers in this study are middle-sized firms with 100 to 500 employees. According to the regulations governing enterprise scale standards in China, a company with a business volume of less than 300 million RMB is considered a middle- and small-sized enterprise.

Among the returned samples, when judged according to their business volumes, most are middle- and small-sized enterprises. About three quarters of them have been established for over five years. The questionnaires were answered mostly by middle managers, followed by top managers. These suppliers mainly serve foreign customers from the US and Asia while most of their Asian customers are from Taiwan, Japan, and Korea. Foreign customers account for a major portion of the business volumes of these suppliers. Therefore, it can be expected that, to better serve their foreign customers, the suppliers will provide more services. Our study later shows that the suppliers have higher satisfaction rates with foreign customers. The questionnaire in this study was designed based on the Likert scale to measure the importance of each service provided by the suppliers. Each question was answered on a five-point scale with five points indicating very important, four points for important, three points for fair, two points for unimportant and one point for very unimportant. The questions covered the following issues: logistics services the supplier provides for domestic and foreign customers, actions taken to meet different customer needs, evaluation of customers' logistics criteria from the viewpoint of the supplier, satisfaction rate with customers, management of the suppliers, criteria of customer selection, and challenges encountered by the supplier. The questions were designed to discover the difference in importance of supplier services when serving different customers. The variable setting in the questionnaire was based mainly on expert opinions and literatures related to logistics and China. A t-test was conducted on local and foreign customers of these suppliers to find out if there is a significant difference in the importance of their needs for logistics services.

Table 1 Sample Characteristics

	Sample	
	n	%
Industry		
Automotive	11	26.8
Tele. Com. & Computer	12	29.3
Household Appliances	10	24.4
Electronics	8	19.5
Respondent Position		
First-line manager	7	17.1
Middle manager	22	53.7
Top manager	12	29.2
Ownership		
Chinese	18	43.9
Foreign	2	4.9
Joint Venture	21	51.2
Joint Venture Ratio		
Chinese over 50%	13	61.9
Foreign over 50%	8	38.1
Years Since Establishment		
< 5 years	10	24.4
5 ~ 10 years	21	51.2
> 10 years	10	24.4
Annual Sales in 2004		
< 30 millions	18	43.9
30 ~ 300 millions	22	53.7
> 300 millions	1	2.4
Employees		
< 100 workers	2	4.9
100 ~ 500 workers	22	53.7
501 ~ 1000 workers	11	26.8
> 1000 workers	6	14.6
Largest Foreign Customer in Sales		
US	16	39.0
Korea and Japan	9	22.0
Taiwan	6	14.6
Europe	5	12.2
Others	5	12.2
Annual Sales in 2004 for Domestic Customer (Ratio)		
< 50%	17	41.5
> 50%	24	58.5
Annual Sales in 2004 for Foreign Customer (Ratio)		
< 50%	29	70.7
> 50%	12	29.3

4 Analysis

4.1. Logistic Services Provided by Suppliers

As far as the provided logistics services are concerned, overall speaking, a stark statistical difference exists in all activities between the local customers and the foreign customers while there is no significant difference in the warehouse operations required by the suppliers from the four industries (See Table 2-5). The major logistics services they provide are processing, assembly and packaging, overpacking, as well as warehouse-related operations such as receiving, order picking, shipping, and goods return. Since the operations of the automobile industry require a lot of components, warehousing plays a role of significant importance in the logistics operations. The inventory management and return goods management are issues that both local and foreign customers highly value. Unlike the automotive industry, the other three industries place more emphasis on return goods management.

The electronic industry, in particular, values product storage and monitoring. In distribution services, the requirements of foreign customers of each industry are almost the same—transshipment and tracking, which suggests the two services are greatly valued by foreign customers while domestic customers desire direct overseas delivery. In distribution, the foreign automotive enterprises attach great importance particularly to emergency transportation and tracking in the hope of fully monitoring transportation status and achieving on-time delivery while their Chinese counterparts emphasize more on prompt product delivery by suppliers to other countries. In leasing services, both domestic and foreign customers pay considerable attention to maintenance services, warehouses, and facilities.

The information and communication services provided by the forty-one suppliers in this study for their domestic and foreign customers include the Internet, e-mail, bar-coding and scanning, electronic data interchange, warehousing management system, and transportation management system. In the three industries, all the foreign enterprises regard highly of the establishment of information systems which they expect to be helpful in providing real-time information about production and sales for the references in planning future demands of products and raw material procurements.

Therefore, e-mails and electronic information communications are important methods for them to exchange information with suppliers and customers. Meanwhile, both local and foreign enterprises value technologies of bar coding and scanning which can enable quick inventory check and effective production planning. The survey results indicate growth in the use of Internet and e-mail by domestic customers. Meanwhile, domestic customers are using e-commerce more frequently while the automotive and electronics industries are applying the vendor-managed inventory (VMI) to monitor inventory and production. In transportation, most foreign customers are using road transport, followed by air transport and water transport while the major transportation models of the domestic customers are road transport, rail transport, and inland water transport.

In customer services, the suppliers in this study provide their foreign and domestic customers with assistance services, customization services, operation performance analysis, and consulting services. Foreign customers have higher requirements for customer services and expect the suppliers to provide more information about their operations, more supports and customized services. Their foreign customers have a higher need for customer services while the use of customer services by domestic customers, though less frequent, is showing signs of growth.

4.2. Actions Taken by Suppliers to Meet Customer Needs

In response to different customer needs, suppliers would try to fulfill these needs based on available resources (See Table 2-5). In warehousing services, all suppliers in this study provide their foreign customers with the following value-added services: use of a scanning system, accurate forecasting of inventory demand, and handling instruction reinforcement and package reinforcement.

All the suppliers of the three industries seek precise prediction of inventory in order to meet customer demands of different stages. They will improve their related operations so as to meet the demands of both local and foreign customers.

The three industries all highlight the importance of packaging. The foreign customers would request the suppliers to improve the packaging and to provide product identification systems to facilitate product processing. The foreign customers of the electronic industry, in particular, would prefer the suppliers to have products assembled at locations closer to export and direct delivery to overseas while their local counterparts would like the suppliers to provide warehouses. In contrast, for domestic customers, suppliers from the communication, computer and electronics industries would build or purchase warehouses to fulfill their needs in time. In storage services, suppliers provide their domestic and foreign customers with services such as handling monitoring, delivery confidence, and security system investment. In distribution, suppliers provide both domestic and foreign clients with services such as emergency delivery and tracking, but they also provide more diversified modes of distribution for foreign customers.

Table 2 Automotive Industry: Logistic Services Provided and Actions Taken by Suppliers to Meet Foreign Customer and Local Customer Needs

	Logistics Service for Foreign Customer	Actions Taken for Foreign Customer	Logistics Service for Local Customer	Actions Taken for Local Customer
Warehouse Services	Processing, assembly, packaging	Accurate forecasting of inventory	Processing, assembly, packaging	Package reinforcement
	Overpacking, Inventory management	Use of scanning system	Overpacking, Return goods management	Reinforcing handling instructions
	Receiving, order picking, shipping & cross-docking	Improving handling instruction	Receiving, order picking, shipping & crossdocking	Accurate forecasting of inventory
Distribution Services	Trans-shipment	Providing different modes of distribution	Tracking	Making emergency delivery
	Tracking	Making emergency delivery	Direct delivery to overseas	Providing different modes of distribution
Leasing Services	Providing repairing services	Purchasing own warehouse	Providing repairing services	Purchasing own warehouse
	Providing warehouse equipment	Providing warehouse	Providing warehouse equipment	Providing warehouse
Technology	Internet & E-mail	Building logistics system for customer	Internet & e-mail	Investment in IT
	Bar-coding & scanning	Integrated communication system	Electronic data interchange	Joint investment in IT
	Electronic data interchange	IT outsourcing	Bar-coding & scanning	IT outsourcing
	Vendor-managed inventory		Vendor-managed inventory	
Transportation	Road transport	Training in transportation skills	Road transport	Complete document for transport
	Air transport	Complete document for transport	Intermodal transport	Transportation mode change
	Water transport	More careful selection of carriers	Rail transport	Use of third party logistics
	Rail transport		Inland Water transport	Rescheduling routing
Customer Services	Operational performance analysis	Providing customized services	Operational performance analysis	Exclusive service dept for customer
	Providing assistance services	Exclusive services dept for customer	Distribution & warehouse	Providing customized services
	Providing customization services	Providing assistance services	Process planning	Providing assistance services
			Providing assistance services	

All variables are statistically significant at 0.05.

Through information provided by the suppliers, foreign customers can be aware of delivery status. For domestic customers, in addition to the above-mentioned distribution services, the suppliers can also choose to offer coordinated transportation.

In leasing services, suppliers would purchase warehouses for foreign customers and provide existing warehouses of their own to serve domestic customer needs.

Table 3 Tele. Com. & Computer Industry: Logistic Services Provided and Actions Taken by Suppliers to Meet Foreign Customer and Local Customer Needs

	Logistics Service for Foreign Customer	Actions Taken for Foreign Customer	Logistics Service for Local Customer	Actions Taken for Local Customer
Warehouse Services	Return goods management	Package reinforcement	Receiving, order picking, shipping & crossdocking	Use of scanning system
	Processing, assembly, packaging	Use of scanning system	Inventory management	Building warehouses
	Inventory management	Use of nearby assembly sites for export	Overpacking	Accurate forecasting of inventory
	Storage & monitor	Accurate forecasting of inventory	Return goods management	Reinforcing handling instructions
Distribution Services	Direct delivery to overseas	Making emergency delivery	Trans-shipment	Coordinated transportation
	Trans-shipment	Tracking & feedback	Direct delivery to overseas	Making emergency delivery
Leasing	Providing warehouse equipment	Providing warehouse	Providing warehouse equipment	Providing warehouse
	Providing repairing services	Purchasing warehouse	Providing repairing services	Purchasing own warehouse
Technology	Internet & E-mail	Building logistics system for customer	Internet & E-mail	Investment in IT
	Bar-coding & scanning	Investment in IT	Electronic data interchange	IT outsourcing
	Electronic data interchange	Joint investment in IT	E-commerce	Joint investment in IT
	Enterprise resource planning	IT outsourcing	Bar-coding & scanning	Building logistics system for customer
Transportation	Road transport	Taking better security measures	Rail transport	More careful selection of carriers
	Air transport	Getting customers to provide their own transport	Road transport	Taking better security measures
	Intermodal transport	Complete document for transport	Inland Water transport	Getting customers to provide their own transport
	Rail transport	Training in transportation skills	Air transport	Rescheduling routing
Customer Services	Providing assistance services	Exclusive service dept for customer	Operational performance analysis	Setting up feedback mechanism
	Operational performance analysis	Providing customized services	Logistics consulting services	Providing customized services
	Logistics consulting services	Providing assistance services	Providing customized services	Exclusive service dept for customer

All variables are statistically significant at 0.05.

Table 4 Household Appliances Industry: Logistic Services Provided and Actions Taken by Suppliers to Meet Foreign Customer and Local Customer Needs

	Logistics Service for Foreign Customer	Actions Taken for Foreign Customer	Logistics Service for Local Customer	Actions Taken for Local Customer
Warehouse Services	Return goods management Overpacking Processing, assembly, packaging Inventory management	Use of scanning system Package reinforcement Reinforce handling instruction Accurate forecasting of inventory	Receiving, order picking, shipping & crossdocking Overpacking Processing, assembly, packaging	Package reinforcement Use of scanning system Accurate forecasting of inventory Use of nearby assembly sites for export
Distribution Services	Trans-shipment Tracking	Tracking & feedback Making emergency delivery	Direct delivery to overseas Trans-shipment	Making emergency delivery Tracking & feedback
Leasing Services	Providing repairing services Providing warehouse equipment	Lease outsourcing Purchasing own warehouse	Providing warehouse equipment Providing repairing services	Purchasing own warehouse Providing warehouse
Technology	Bar-coding & scanning Internet & E-mail Warehousing management system & transportation management system Electronic data interchange	Integrated communication system IT outsourcing Joint investment in IT Building logistics system for customer	Internet & E-mail Bar-coding & scanning Electronic data interchange Enterprise resource planning	Integrated communication system Building logistics system for customer Investment in IT Joint investment in IT
Transportation	Road transport Air transport Rail transport Inland Water transport	Training in transportation skills Rescheduling routing More careful selection of carriers Getting customers to provide their own transport	Road transport Rail transport Inland Water transport Intermodal transport	Rescheduling routing Changing transportation mode More careful selection of carriers Training in transportation skills
Customer Services	Operational performance analysis Distribution & warehouse process planning Providing assistance services	Providing assistance services Providing customized services Exclusive service dept for customer	Providing assistance service Distribution & warehouse process planning Logistics services consulting	Exclusive service dept for customer Providing assistance services Providing customized services

All variables are statistically significant at 0.05.

Table 5 Electronics Industry: Logistic Services Provided and Actions Taken by Suppliers to Meet Foreign Customer and Local Customer Needs

	Logistics Service for Foreign Customer	Actions Taken for Foreign Customer	Logistics Service for Local Customer	Actions Taken for Local Customer
Warehouse Services	Liability insurance; Return goods management; Overpacking; Processing, assembly, packaging	Use of scanning system; Reinforcing handling instruction; Accurate forecasting of inventory; Package reinforcement	Return goods management; Storage & monitor; Overpacking; Processing, assembly, packaging	Building warehouses; Package reinforcement; Accurate forecasting of inventory; Use of scanning system
Distribution Services	Tracking; Trans-shipment	Making emergency delivery; Tracking & feedback	Direct delivery to overseas; Trans-shipment	Coordinated transportation; Provide different modes of distribution
Leasing Services	Providing warehouse equipment; Providing repairing services	Providing warehouse; Lease outsourcing	Providing repairing services; Providing warehouse equipment	Lease outsourcing; Providing warehouse
Technology	Bar-coding & scanning; Enterprise resource planning; Internet & E-mail; Electronic data interchange	IT outsourcing; Investment in IT; Integrated communication system; Joint investment in IT	Internet & E-mail; Bar-coding & scanning; Vendor-managed inventory; Electronic data interchange	Joint investment in IT; Investment in IT; Building logistics system for customer; IT outsourcing
Transportation	Air transport; Road transport; Water transport; Inland Water transport	More careful selection of carriers; Rescheduling routing; Forming firm's own transportation fleet; Taking better security measures	Rail transport; Road transport; Water transport; Inland Water transport	Rescheduling routing; Changing transportation mode; Training in transportation skills; Getting customers to provide their own transport
Customer Services	Distribution & warehouse process planning; Providing assistance services; Operational performance analysis	Exclusive service dept for customer; Providing consulting services; Providing customized services	Providing customized services; Distribution & warehouse process planning; Providing assistance services	Providing assistance services; Exclusive service dept for customer; Providing customized services

All variables are statistically significant at 0.05.

In information services, suppliers would establish logistics systems for foreign customers or integrate with customer information systems. Considering their resources, suppliers would probably outsource information services since it is possible that their information technologies cannot integrate with those of foreign customers and there may be many difficulties in integration. And suppliers cannot build information technology system themselves. Therefore, the suppliers would choose outsourcing to prevent unnecessary waste of resources.

For domestic customers, the suppliers would have joint investment with them on IT communication infrastructures to prevent integration problems. In transportation, since the transportation system in China cannot satisfy the needs of most foreign customers, improvement should be made by providing training in transportation management skills, carefully selecting among carriers and instituting better security measurement criteria.

Improvement in transportation services for domestic customers can be made by changing transportation modes, rescheduling routing, getting customers to provide their own transport and choose the third party logistics services. The major difference between domestic and foreign customers in transportation is that the former can select transportation modes more beneficial for them while the latter can only choose from the limited number of local carriers since the government in China restricts the entry of foreign carriers. In addition, the foreign customers prefer those suppliers who are careful in selecting transportation suppliers. The electronic industry especially highly emphasizes the safety standards of transportation. Due to the sophistication of electronic products, transportation of such products requires extreme caution. Each of the industries has come to the gradual realization that self-operated logistics will only hinder their operations and, therefore, start to outsource to external logistics service providers. Nevertheless, they would only outsource parts of their logistics operations to one or several providers or even to foreign ones. They would not outsource only to one provider in order to reduce risks. When providing customer services, suppliers would set up exclusive customer services departments. For different types of customers, suppliers would also provide customization and assistance services. Meanwhile, each of the suppliers also establishes a feedback mechanism to respond to customer needs quickly. In the example of the communication industry, the suppliers would improve their products based on customer opinions, allowing customers to participate in product design.

4.3 Customer Logistics Performance Criteria

Suppliers come to an awareness of customer requirements for different logistics services and performance valued by customers when serving them. This study attempts to discuss the criteria of logistics performance valued by customers from the viewpoint of suppliers (See Table 6-7).

Table 6 Customer's Logistics Performance Criteria (I)

	Industry			
	Automotive		**Tele. Com. & Computer**	
	Foreign Customer	Local Customer	Foreign Customer	Local Customer
Warehouse Services	• Product damage rate • Warehouse capacity • Inventory accuracy • Accuracy in order picking & shipping	• Inventory accuracy • Warehouse capacity • Product damage rate • Accuracy in order picking & shipping	• Inventory accuracy Product damage rate • Package reliability • Accuracy in order picking & shipping	• Inventory accuracy • Accuracy in order picking & shipping • Storage reliability • Product damage rate
Distribution Services	• Delivery reliability • On-time delivery	• Delivery reliability • On-time delivery	• Delivery reliability • On-time delivery	• Delivery reliability • On-time delivery
Technology	• Real-time information • Flexibility • System reliability • Responsiveness	• Real-time information • Accuracy • Information availability & stability • Flexibility	• Responsiveness • Real-time information • System reliability • Flexibility	• Real-time information • Information availability & stability • Accuracy • Responsiveness
Transportation	• Speed • Carrier reliability • On-time delivery • In-transit damage rate	• Speed • In-transit damage rate • On-time delivery • Shipping costs	• In-transit, loading & unloading time • On-time delivery • Shipping costs • Speed	• On-time delivery • In-transit damage rate • Speed • Shipping costs
Customer Services	• Order fulfillment rate • Reliability • Service level • Quality consistency	• Cost reduction • Service level • Quality consistency • Reliability	• Order fulfillment rate • Delivery speed • Order fulfilling rate • Quality consistency	• On-time delivery • Cost reduction • Responsiveness • Order fulfillment rate

All variables are statistically significant at 0.05.

In warehousing services, domestic customers tend to value product damage rate, inventory accuracy, accuracy in receiving, order picking and shipping, and package reliability because, after warehousing operations, the use of different transportation modes will result in risks in the transportation process. Meanwhile, for foreign customers, order picking accuracy is very important in that any error in order picking will cause unnecessary damage. Inventory accuracy provides references for foreign customers to purchase based on their needs. With better inventory accuracy, foreign customers can prevent unnecessary purchases while suppliers can control their inventories more effectively not only to lower their own operation costs, but also to better serve customer needs. There is no significant difference between domestic and foreign customers in their focus on warehousing performance.

Table 7 Customer's Logistics Performance Criteria (II)

| | Industry | | | |
| | Household Appliances | | Electronics | |
	Foreign Customer	Local Customer	Foreign Customer	Local Customer
Warehouse Services	● Package reliability ● Inventory accuracy ● Product damage rate ● Accuracy in order picking & shipping	● Accuracy in order picking & shipping ● Inventory accuracy ● Package reliability ● Storage reliability	● Inventory accuracy ● Package reliability ● Product damage rate ● Accuracy in order picking & shipping	● Accuracy in order picking & shipping ● Inventory accuracy ● Product damage rate ● Storage reliability
Distribution Services	● On-time delivery ● Delivery reliability	● Delivery reliability ● On-time delivery	● On-time delivery ● Delivery reliability	● On-time delivery ● Delivery reliability
Technology	● Real-time information ● Accuracy ● Responsiveness ● System reliability	● Information availability & stability ● System reliability ● Responsiveness ● Accuracy	● Real-time information ● Accuracy ● Information availability & stability ● Flexibility	● Flexibility ● Information availability & stability ● Real-time information ● Responsiveness
Transportation	● Speed ● Shipping costs ● On-time delivery ● In-transit damage rate	● In-transit damage rate ● Shipping costs ● Carrier reliability ● Speed	● In-transit damage rate ● On-time delivery ● Speed ● In-transit, loading & unloading time	● Carrier reliability ● Speed ● Shipping costs ● On-time delivery
Customer Services	● Delivery speed ● Quality consistency ● Order fulfillment rate ● Service level	● Cost reduction ● Stockout & replenishment rate ● On-time delivery ● Order fulfillment rate	● Quality consistency ● Order fulfillment rate ● Delivery speed ● On-time delivery	● Cost reduction ● Responsiveness ● On-time delivery ● Order fulfillment rate

All variables are statistically significant at 0.05.

However, domestic customers pay more attention to goods storage reliability since warehouses are provided by the suppliers. In delivery performance, the requirements of both domestic and foreign customers are delivery reliability and on-time delivery.

In information, they both value real-time information, response rate, information availability, accuracy, flexibility, and system reliability. Based on information provided by their suppliers, customers can forecast the size of future orders. To monitor product status at any time, the foreign customers would expect the suppliers to provide real-time and precise information based on which they can predict the size of next orders.

All the foreign customers emphasize the reliability of the information systems, expecting the suppliers to exchange related information more effectively. There is no great difference between the local customers and foreign ones in their requirements of information. They are mainly different in the fact that the former attach more importance to the availability and stability of information. In transportation performance, foreign customers pay more attention to delivery speed, in-transit, loading and unloading time, on-time delivery, shipping costs, and in-transit damage rate. The foreign customers hope to have faster and on-time delivery of products while domestic customers value in-transit damage rate, on-time delivery, delivery speed, especially for shipping costs. In addition to the above-mentioned performance criteria, customers of suppliers in the electronics and household appliance industries also highly value transportation reliability. In customer service performance, foreign customers weigh order fulfillment rate, delivery speed, product quality consistency, and service level while domestic customers are significantly different from foreign ones in their emphasis on cost reduction. For all domestic customers in each industry, cost reduction is one of the most important operation goals. In addition, domestic customers also stress the importance of on-time delivery while most of their performance criteria are the same as those of foreign customers.

4.4 Impacts on Supplier Management

The need to serve different customers will likely influence the organization management of suppliers. According to the survey results in this study listed in Table 8, all suppliers agree that the most direct impact on supplier is the human resource-related issues with an average point of 4.517 (4.033 for information technology, 4.147 for internal operation and 3.259 for customer service). The most prominent in human resources are personnel training and personnel exchange with customers, hiring of overseas managers, personnel skills re-training, and organization restructure. The suppliers think their employees generally lack in the trainings and knowledge about logistics. Through their cooperation with the customers, the suppliers can have a clearer picture of the whole supply chain process and learn more know-how. By employing foreign personnel, they expect themselves to meet the ever-changing market demands and to know better about the operations of their foreign customers and the different product demands of different customers. More importantly, the suppliers think organization reengineering is definitely necessary for the complexity in their organization structures poses a great difficulty for operation and integration.

Table 8 Impacts on Management of Suppliers

		Mean
Human Resource Management		
Personnel training & personnel exchange with customers		4.639
Hiring of overseas managers		4.487
Personnel skills re-training		4.482
Organization restructure		4.440
	Grand mean	4.517
Technology		
Information technology Adoption		4.070
Developing information technology system & purchasing management software		4.068
Building communication platform to share information with customers		4.050
Integration of internal information with customer information		3.982
	Grand mean	4.033
Internal Operation		
Obtainment of international professional certifications/licenses		4.407
Establishment of customer service level & operation performance indicators		4.335
Investment in IT systems		4.215
Business process re-engineering		4.178
Seeking support from other firms & government		3.917
Adjusting internal resource to meet the customer expectations		3.832
	Grand mean	4.147
Customer		
Understanding customer's business model		4.087
Forming a partnership (alliance)		4.009
Risk management, customer data confidentiality		3.752
Contract agreement		3.710
Monitoring the process & quality services for supplier		3.680
Exchanging knowledge & information with customer		3.590
Participation in product design		2.561
	Grand mean	3.259

5-point Likert scale. 1 (least important); 5 (very important).

As for impacts on information, suppliers are likely to take the following actions to serve different customers: adopt information technology, develop information technology system and purchase management software, establish an information platform to share information with customers, or integrate internal information with customer information to effectively integrate all resources. To allow communications and information exchanges with foreign clients, the suppliers must establish information systems. Seeing the growing complexity in operations, the suppliers should also choose the systems that can integrate all the information regarding raw materials, production and sale. Based on the integrated information, the suppliers can predict future demands more effectively. Internal operations influence is the most conspicuous in the obtainment of international professional certifications/licenses and establishment of customer service level and operation performance indicators, investment in IT systems and business process re-engineering. Most foreign companies are only interested in working with Chinese suppliers that have an internationally recognized quality system such as ISO 9000 or QS 9000 (Ting 2004). Also, suppliers consider investments of the suppliers on IT systems through which the operation procedure and organization can be further integrated. The acquisition of international professional certificates by the suppliers can assure customers of their capability of effective operations and in-time satisfaction of different customer demands even in case of emergency. By setting customer service standards and performance indexes, the suppliers can monitor and smooth their operation processes. The establishment of information systems and organization restructuring will in turn affect the internal operations of the suppliers. Other influences include seeking support from other firms and government and adjusting internal resource to meet the customer expectations. In customer management influence, research results in this study show that suppliers of each industry desire to understand their customer's business model and form a partnership while exchanging information and knowledge with their customers. Meanwhile, risk management is very important in regard to supplier-customer cooperation. Even with contractual agreement, customers are still likely to change contract contents or even fail to honor the contract. Finally, customer data confidentiality is also something suppliers should be careful about.

4.5 Customer Selection Criteria of Suppliers

As presented in Table 9, among domestic and foreign customers, the suppliers in this study have a higher satisfaction rate with the latter.

When cooperating with their customers, the suppliers always try to satisfy the needs of customers in many aspects. With limited resources, suppliers have to concentrate and distribute their resources to the most suitable customers. However, it is interesting to see that the suppliers at the same time are far more pleased with working with their foreign customers than with local ones. Therefore, suppliers will select the most beneficial customers based on their resources and partnership with the customers. The analysis in this study is intended to find out some

Table 9 Satisfaction Rates of Four Industries for Foreign and Local Customer

Industry	Foreign Customer		Local Customer		
	Mean	Std. Error	Mean	Std. Error	Sig.
Automotive	4.400	0.516	2.700	0.483	**
Tele. Com. & Computer	4.364	0.505	2.182	0.751	**
Household Appliances	4.200	0.632	2.400	0.699	**
Electronics	4.375	0.744	1.875	0.354	**

**p< 0.05 (Paired T-test). 5-point Likert scale. 1 (least important); 5 (very important).

criteria for suppliers in customer selection. When selecting foreign customers, the major criteria of the suppliers in this study are customer coordination with the supplier, customer reputation, order fulfillment rate, reasonable customer demands, customer trustworthiness, and business dependency.

As shown in Table 10, supplier's criteria for selecting domestic customers are significantly different from those for selecting foreign customers. The major consideration for suppliers in domestic customer selection is "Guanxi" (people connections), which is unique in the China area. The suppliers in China tend to choose domestic customers they are familiar with to prevent unnecessary risks. Through "Guanxi," suppliers and customers can enhance their partnership and build up mutual trust in cooperation. Roberts and ArndtI (2005) suggest to cultivate Chinese partners is necessary for U.S. corporate investor. Meanwhile, it is easier for suppliers to obtain more resources by working with such customers. Other criteria for suppliers in selecting domestic customers are transaction frequency, years of cooperation, customer reputation, and business dependency in sales. In selecting local customers, the suppliers would make their decisions mainly based on the transaction frequency and the number of years of cooperation, indicating that the Chinese enterprises emphasize long-term and stable partnerships.

Table 10 Customer Selection Criteria of Suppliers

Industry	Foreign Customer	Local Customer
Automotive	● Coordination with supplier ● Order fulfillment rate ● Business dependency in sales ● Customer reputation ● Reasonable customer demands ● Customer trustworthiness	● Guanxi* ● Reasonable customer demands ● Business dependency in sales ● Transaction frequency ● Coordination with supplier ● Loyalty
Tele. Com. & Computer	● Customer's reputation ● Considering supplier's operation ● Customer trustworthiness ● Coordination with supplier ● Customer's operation performance ● Commitment	● Guanxi* ● Years of cooperation ● Customer reputation ● Business dependency in sales ● Coordination with supplier ● Transaction frequency
Household Appliances	● Business dependency in sales ● Coordination with supplier ● Customer's reputation ● Order fulfillment rate ● Reasonable customer demands ● Customer trustworthiness	● Order fulfillment rate ● Years of cooperation ● Guanxi* ● Customer reputation ● Coordination with supplier ● Business dependency in sales
Electronics	● Customer trustworthiness ● Coordination with supplier ● Transaction frequency ● Years of cooperation ● Customer reputation ● Loyalty	● Guanxi* ● Transaction frequency ● Customer reputation ● Reasonable customer demands ● Order fulfillment rate ● Customer trustworthiness

All variables are statistically significant at 0.05 except for "Guanxi".

4.6. Difficulties and Challenges for Suppliers

From the above discussion, in order to serve different customer needs, suppliers will provide more services to satisfy customers. Such an action will not only influence the operations of the suppliers but also bring both internal and external difficulties and challenges. As shown in Table 11, all suppliers in this study gave an average point of more than four when evaluating the importance of issues related to difficulties and challenges in their human resources, indicating that there is still room for improvement in human resource management of these suppliers. What they need most is professional logistics managers. With the complexity of logistics procedures and the difficulty of integrating them, only experienced professional logistics managers can be competent enough to control all the operations. This problem is consistent with the findings of Balfour's report (Balfour 2005). Balfour (2005) addresses the shortage problem of senior managers in China. In the process of decision making, they are lacking in related management knowledge and leadership so they do not how to solve the problems when they communicate with the foreign partners and respond to the changing internal and external environments.

Table 11 Other Difficulties and Challenges for Suppliers

	Mean	Std. Error
Customer		
Conflict in culture	4.462	0.505
Contract Change	4.392	0.628
Inability to respond to customer demand	4.244	0.634
Concerns about IT confidentiality by customers	4.244	0.699
Customers do not consider the supplier condition	4.244	0.734
Customer outsourcing with multiple suppliers	4.202	0.813
Difficulty information integration with customers	4.171	0.738
Week coordination with customers	4.058	0.846
Contract complexity	3.985	0.908
Government		
Lack of transportation and communication infrastructure	4.595	0.547
Low logistics integration by government	4.462	0.636
Union power	4.343	0.728
Legal policy restriction	4.121	0.812
Complicated customs procedures	3.955	0.714
Excessive non-procedural practices at customs	3.937	0.755
Shipping costs & taxes	3.762	0.830
External Environment		
Competition with other firms	4.545	0.636
Failing to adapt to external changes	4.490	0.637
Regional protectionism	4.452	0.677
Unidentified competition superiority	4.224	0.690

5-point Likert scale. 1 (least important); 5 (very important).

In China, there are currently many trained logistics personnel but few have actual business experience. Furthermore, the general lack of logistics concepts and international business knowledge among supplier employees also causes many problems with foreign customers. In addition to the lack of professional skills among employees, suppliers are also facing challenges of poor management performance because their organizations are too complicated to manage. Suppliers are also confronted with problems of finance and introducing information technology. There is a significant difference among suppliers in regard to the problem of lack of professional skills and international business knowledge among employees. Other challenges are shown in Table 11. In problems related to customer services, all forty-one suppliers agree that culture conflict is the most difficult challenge. In addition, the frequent contract changes by the customers, inability to respond to customer demand, confidentiality concerns by the customers are also challenges suppliers face when dealing with customers.

In issues related to government, all supplier respondents agree that inferior infrastructures, logistics integration, and unions are the key reasons for low logistics performance. According to previous studies on logistics development in China, infrastructure insufficiency has long been considered a major problem for logistics in China. Moreover, the government is apparently not working hard enough to integrate logistics. This study also finds that supplier operations are influenced by union power. Roberts (2005) find that the rights of the workers are waking up. Furthermore, Suppliers in China suffer their greatest challenge in regional protectionism, failing to adapt to external changes, or unidentified competition superiority when dealing with the external environment.

5 Conclusion

From the above analysis, it can be told that the Chinese suppliers facing problems that come from both internal and external environments. In addition, the foreign customers and local ones are paying significantly different levels of attention to related operations while there are noticeable differences in the satisfaction rate of the suppliers to their foreign and local customers. Such findings indicate that, for the Chinese enterprises, there is still room for improvement in their operations. In the past, the logistics management of the manufacturing industry were mainly self-operated or commissioned to state-run transpiration organizations. Compared with foreign counterparts, the production concept, production method, management method, logistics management concept and operations of the Chinese enterprises were relatively underdeveloped. Furthermore, due to the weak industrial foundation in China, the logistics development of the local manufacturers was far behind the modern standards. As the Chinese market is emerging and attracting more and more foreign investments in recent years, the Chinese manufacturers are aware the failure of their management to meet the current market demands. Particularly after China's entry to the WTO, the trend of international logistics will inevitably push development of the local manufactures. If leaving their traditional production methods and organization structures unchanged, these Chinese enterprises are surely expected to see problems of low efficiencies, high consumption and limitations in their logistics management. In addition, the lack of logistics knowledge among them will cause misunderstanding of and resistance against the modernization of their logistics, making it more difficult for the reengineering of the traditional logistic industry. Despite its rapid growth in recent years, the logistics development in China does not bring more substantial benefits for local enterprises. Even though the PRC government has gradually loosened its regulations on logistics development policy, there is still a significant gap between the policy and actual needs. In addition, the disagreement between the PRC government and local governments in policy implementations also results in more obstacles for enterprise operations, consuming more time and resources without further enhancing enterprise operation efficiency. Facing more fierce market competition, the Chinese enterprise can expect a more complicated environment which can bring more opportunities for improvement and more challenges for both the enterprises and the government.

References

Balfour F (2005) The state's long apron strings. Business Week, August.

Easton RJ (2003) On the edge: The changing face of supply chain management in China. Accenture.

Forbes (2005) The top 10 cities in China. Forbes China.

Gould SA (2002) After WTO membership, China's next steps. Supply Chain Management Review 6(3):13-14.

Handfield RB, Mccormack K (2005) What you need to know about sourcing from China. Supply Chain Management Review 9(6):28-36.

Hong J, Chin ATH, Liu B (2004) Logistics outsourcing by manufacturing in China: A survey of the industry. Transportation Journal 43(1):17-25.

Jiang B, Prater E (2002) Distribution and logistics development in China: The revolution has begun. International Journal of Physical Distribution & Logistics Management 32(9):783-798.

Li PF (2005) Annual report on urban competitiveness. Social Sciences Academic Press, Beijing, China.

Liker JK, Wu YC (2000) Japanese automakers, U.S. Suppliers and supply-chain superiority. Sloan Management Review 42(1):81-93.

Luk STK (1998) Structural changes in China's distribution system. International Journal of Physical Distribution & Logistics Management 28(1):44-67.

Powers P (2001) Distribution in China: The end of the beginning. The China Business Review 28(4):9-12.

Pyke D, Farley J, Robb D (2002) Manufacturing technology and operations in China: A survey of stated-owned enterprise, private firms, joint ventures and wholly-owned foreign subsidiaries. European Management Journal 20(4):356-375.

Pyke D, Robb D, Farley J (2000) Manufacturing and supply chain management in China: A survey of stated-, collective-, and privately-owned enterprises. European Management Journal 18(6):577-589.

Roberts D (2005) Waking up to their rights. Business Week, August.

Roberts D, ArndtI M (2005) It's getting hotter in the east. Business Week, August.

SMERT (2002) Shanghai suppliers and manufacturers directory, 1st ed. Shanghai Far East Publishers, Shanghai, China.

Speece MW, Kawahara Y (1995) Transportation in China in the 1990s. International Journal of Physical Distribution & Logistics Management 25(8):53-71.

Ting A (2004) Outsourcing in China. Industrial Engineer 36(12):46-50.

Chapter 19
China's Perspectives on the Development of IT

Ying HOU[1] and Yufan HAO[1]

[1] Faculty of Social Sciences and Humanities, University of Macau, Macau, P.R. CHINA

Abstract With the rapid development of private computer (PC), digital communication apparatus and Internet, information technology (IT) has infiltrated into almost all the aspects of social life. Information technology is broadly and loosely defined as "technology involved in acquiring, storing, processing and distributing information by electronic means (including radio, television, telephone, and computers)."(Collin 2002, 194) UNESCO extends this concept to encompass "computers and their interaction with people and machines, and associated social, economic and cultural matters."(Gupta 2007) Thus IT development involves technology concerning information on the one hand, and its humane and social influences on the other. In China, the past decade has witnessed a rapid informatization with a top down, state-led pattern and a campaign style, which enabled China to emerge as a leading player with the most seductive market in the worldwide waves of IT. However, as a double edged sword, IT development in China has also contributed to the growth of "an increasingly wired society" (Cheng 2005, 45) which, together with the dynamic IT market, inversely influences the government's policies and behaviors within and beyond the latitude of IT. (Cheng 2005, Lagerkvist 2005, Zheng 2005). Therefore, the Chinese government faces a dilemma between economic prosperity with the benefit of IT and threats brought by IT development to the regime survival and stability. The future development of IT in China to a certain extent may depend on the multilateral interactions and cooperations among government, market and society rather than the unidirectional motivation from top state leaders to the market or to the society.The purpose of this paper is to examine the feature of IT development in China over the past decade as well as the challenges faced by the Chinese government. Through analyzing the current issues and problems in IT development, this paper tries to present a Chinese perspective on the issue and the possible response from the government in the future.

1 An Overview: IT Development in China over the Past Decade and Current Situations

IT development in China is a top down, state-led process. As early as in the aftermath of Cultural Revolution, Deng Xiaoping's famous assertion of "Science and

P.O. de Pablos, M.D. Lytras (eds.), *The China Information Technology Handbook*,   335
DOI: 10.1007/978-0-387-77743-6_19, © Springer Science+Business Media, LLC 2009

technology are the first productivity" and Chinese Communist Party's (CCP's) re-kindling the "four modernizations" (industry, agriculture, national defense as well as science and technology) have laid a foundation for Chinese IT development.

It was included in a series of China's national science and technology projects such as the 863 Plan, Torch Plan (huo ju ji hua), Star Lit (xin ghuo ji hua), the Climb Plan (pan deng ji hua) and the 973 Plan. But it was not until 1993 that China officially kicked off the overall informatization through a series of "Golden Projects" launched by the central government. Since then, IT has progressed rapidly in the development of five areas: legal and regulatory framework, e-government, telecommunication, IT industry, and Internet, all demonstrating a gradually weakening of governmental control. (Figure 1)

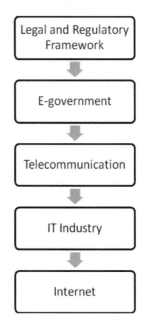

Figure 1 Five Aspects of Informatization in China

1.1 Legal and regulatory framework

Providing a supportive legal and regulatory framework is the foremost step of Chinese government's efforts for IT development. In 1993, the State Council ratified the establishment of National Economic Information Joint Committee in order to plan, organize and coordinate all informatization projects in the whole country. In 1996, the State Council set up the State Council Informatization Leading Office (SCILO) composed by the ministers from more than twenty ministries to organize and coordinate the informatization in the country. Since then, both central and local governments established informatization as an important role in the national economic and social development, and informatization became a powerful trend in the country. In 1997, SCILO held the first National Informatization Meeting in Shenzhen and passed the *Outline of the National Informatization Development Plan* which provided a regulatory framework for informatization, especially the information infrastructure and the development of network. In 1998, SCILO was merged into the newly founded Ministry of Information Industry which was in charge of the whole nation's electronic manufacture, telecommunication and software industry. In 2000, the 10th *Five-year Plan for National Economy and Social Development* formulated some more concrete strategies to enhance the development of informatization and to improve its infrastructure. In 2006, *The State Informatization Development Strategy (2006-2020)* was published by General Office of the CPC Central Committee and General Office of the State Council set forth China's goals in informatization development for the next 15 years.

Under this context, many laws and regulations – such as *China Internet Domain Name Regulations, Regulations on Telecommunications of the People's Republic of China, Electronic Signature Law*, etc. – were made and went into effect to promote informatization. Moreover, a telecommunication law based on the existing regulations has been put on the legislation plan of the standing committee of the National People's Congress (NPC) in 2006. (Chinese Business View 2007) In addition, many local regulations regarding to IT industry and service have come into force since 2000 as a response to the booming e-business.[1]

The continuously improved legal and regulatory framework makes it possible for the overall development of informatization in China, which first and foremost reflects the development of e-government.

1.2 E-government

E-government in China has undergone three overlapping stages:

1. The stage of Office Automation (OA). As early as in the mid-1980s, Chinese central and local governments began to use the modern office equipment such as computer, fax and photocopier to process official information. All kinds of vertical and lateral internal office nets known as Local Area Networks (LANs) were gradually set up to improve the efficiency and quality at the all levels of the government.
2. The stage of improving the capacity and quality of administration by providing the online information. In 1993, the "Three Golden Projects" – Golden Custom, Golden Bridge, and Golden Card – launched by the Chinese government opened the era of e-government in China, which were later expanded to a series of golden projects in the professional sectors varying from economic to many other social service fields. (Table 1) Based on these golden projects, more than

---

[1] For China's laws and regulations on IT, see China-law.org. http://www.china-law.org/

Table 1 Golden Projects

Projects	Authorities & Proprietor	Functions & Goals
Golden Custom	Ministry of Foreign Trade, Customs	Push the electronization of customs declaration services, including the internal network of customs clearance and the electronic law-enforcement system of external port.
Golden Bridge	Ministry of Electronics, Jitong Co.	Construct the infrastructure for informatization, including the ground backbone network, satellite communication network, wireless mobile data users access network, etc.
Golden Card	People's Bank of China, Ministry of Electronics, Ministry of Internal Trade, Great Wall Computer Co.	Establish a modern, practical and integrated electronic money system, form a financial card management system geared to both China's basic conditions and international standards, and popularize the financial card in the nationwide.
Golden Macro	National Development & Reform Commission, Ministry of Finance, Ministry of Commerce, People's Bank of China, State-owned Assets Supervision and Administration Commission, State Administration of Foreign Exchange, Customs, State Statistics Bureau	Promote the interaction and cooperation among the departments of macroeconomic management on the basis of e-government network platform.
Golden Tax	Ministry of Finance, National Tax Bureau, Ministry of Electronics	Informatize the tax collection system, strengthen the state's management to the value-added tax and prevent the tax fraud.
Golden Wealth	Ministry of Finance	Build a computerized financial network system to manage the budget, payment and accounting covering the governments at all levels.
Golden Agriculture	Ministry of Agriculture, National Development & Reform Commission, State Grain Administration	Construct an agricultural integrative management and an information system.
Golden Quality	General Administration of Quality Supervision, Inspection and Quarantine	Enhance quality supervision transparency and services of all levels of government, form an integrative quality supervision network, and informatize law-enforcement in the quality supervision system.

Golden Audit	National Audit Office	Transform the reactive audit system to a more proactive one by having a secure platform for information sharing and for tracking and checking accounts.
Golden Social Security	Ministry of Labor and Social Security	Better manage the increasing labor force covered by the national insurance system and offer retirement and medical information to the insured.
Golden Shield	Ministry of Public Security	Strengthen central police control, responsiveness, and crime-fighting capacity.
Golden Water	Ministry of Water Resources	Use IT to collect, transfer, store, and manage water resources and enhance the efficiency of the water conservancy.
Golden Intellect (CERNET)	Ministry of Education	Promote the librarian resources sharing, academic exchange and research cooperation; improve teaching methods, environment and quality.
Golden Tour	National Tourism Administration	Enhance the government's capacity in managing tourism and providing services for e-commerce.
Golden Land	National Development & Reform Commission, Ministry of Land &Resources	Provide the informational and technological support for national resources protection and the prewarning of geologic hazards.
Golden Credit	State Administration for Industry and Commerce	Establish an internal network in the whole system of Administration for Industry and Commerce; Construct a system of trademark registration and automatic management; provide to the society online services such as enterprise registration, enterprise annual inspection, complaint, etc.

(Source: China Online 2003, Wang 2007, Qiang 2007)

40 ministries and governmental departments launched the "Government Online Project" to popularize the construction of portal websites of government departments at all levels. Till the end of 2006, the rate of website owned by governments at all levels has amounted to 85.6%, 35% much greater than it was in 2003. (Wang 2007, 7-8)In addition, as of June 2007, there were 31,093 domain names and 15,334 websites under gov.cn (CNNIC 2007), whereas there were only 4,615 domain names and 3,294 websites under gov.cn at the end of 2000 (CNNIC 2001). During this stage, the governmental websites focused on providing all kinds of information to the public and promoting the openness of administrative information. At the beginning of 2007, the *Regulations on Governmental Information Openness* were passed by the standing committee of the State Council in order to standardize the administrative information openness and transparency of governmental units. Today most of Chinese governmental

departments provide on their websites the information including relevant laws and policies, the introduction and structure of the organization, etc.

3. The stage of providing governmental service online. While different governmental departments vary at the levels of constructing their portal websites, many of them have gradually transformed from providing online information to offering more and more online service to the public since 2003. For example, Beijing government opened the online service for fee payment on its portal website to facilitate its citizens to pay various fees, polling message and lodging complaints.

1.3 Telecommunication

China's state-led informatization is also reflected in Chinese government's efforts to liberate the telecommunication market. Before 1994, Chinese telecommunication services were provided by the only one state-owned telecommunication operator – China Telecom, which was under the control of the former Ministry of Posts and Telecommunications. In 1994, as the result of breaking monopoly, China Unicom was created by three ministries – Ministry of Electronics, Ministry of Electricity and Ministry of Railways – to compete with China Telecom in the long-distance and mobile markets. In 1998, the Ministry of Posts and Telecommunications was replaced by the Ministry of Information Industry under the context of institutional reform. As a result, China Telecom experienced two reconstructions. In 1999, China Telecom was first separated and restructured into three new operators – China Telecom, China Mobile and China Satcom – to run the fixline, mobile and satellite communication services respectively. In 2002, China Telecom was geographically split into North and South parts: the former kept 30% of the network resources and merged with China Netcom founded in 1999 to be the new China Netcom which later also incorporated Jitong Corporation and served the 10 Northern provinces; the latter remained to be China Telecom and kept 70% of the network resources and served the 21 Southern provinces. In addition, the division of the Ministry of Railways resulted in a new telecommunication operator – China Railcom in 2000. Thus five state-owned companies – China Telecom, China Netcom, China Mobile, China Unicom, and China Railcom – were finally formed and competed in Chinese telecommunication market. Till 2005, China Telecom has possessed 60% of the Chinese fixed-line market, and China Mobile has been the largest mobile operator in China with holding 65% of the Chinese mobile market (Qiang 2007, 43).

After China's entry into World Trade Organization (WTO), some foreign companies such as Spain's Telefónica and Britain's Vodafone began to participate in China's telecommunication market (Qiang 2007). As a response to the competition of foreign telecommunication players as well as the applications of the third generation telecommunications networks (3G), a new wave of restructuring China's telecommunication operators has been underway for a long time.

At the beginning of 2008, a government reshuffle plan was adopted by the National People's Congress, which would create the Ministry of Industry and Information integrating the original Ministry of Information Industry (MII) and the relevant functions of the National Development and Reform Commission (NDRC), the Commission of Science, Technology and Industry for National Defense and the State Council Informatization Office (Xinhua News Agency 2008). The institutional reshuffle will make it possible for the implementation of the long-awaited restructuring of China's telecommunication. According to a widely spreading plan, China Mobile is expected to be combined with China Railcom to be the new China Mobile. China Unicom will be split into two parts: the Global System for Mobile Communications (GSM) business will be integrated into China Netcom; and the Code Division Multiple Access (CDMA) business will be incorporated into China Telecom[2].

On the other hand, China now possesses the largest fixed and mobile telephone market in the world. According to the statistics of Ministry of Information Industry (MII), China's total number of telephone subscribers in 2006 exceeded 800 million, including 367.812 million fixed telephone subscribers and 461.082 million mobile telephone subscribers (MII 2007). Although the number of new fixed telephone subscribers in 2006 decreased, the number of new mobile telephone subscribers maintained a steady growth. (Figure 2) In addition, another kind of personal handy phone system services called Xiaolingtong or Little Smart provided by China Telecom and China Netcom has widely spread in the cities and witnessed an explosive growth because of its lower tariffs and one-way charging comparing with mobile phones. Until June 2005, there were nearly 80 million subscribers of Xiaolingtong throughout 600 cities in China (Yuan 2006, 297).

Despite its rapid popularization, Xiaolingtong nowadays has to face the future challenge of 3G, which has been under heated discussion in China. (Yuan 2006) Although so far no 3G license has been granted by Chinese government, a survey shows that more than 70% of Chinese cell phone users will use 3G.[3] In addition, even though many uncertainties exist in the allocation of 3G licenses due to the restructuring of Chinese telecommunication operators, there are signs that China Mobile has the chance of obtaining such a license based on time division-synchronous code division multiple access (TD-SCDMA) which was developed by Chinese company Datang Mobile and became one of the three standards for 3G in the world.[4]

---

[2] See the special coverage about restructuring of China's telecommunication in sohu.com. http://it.sohu.com/s2005/dianxinchongzu.shtml. Accessed 17 March 2008.

[3] See New China News Online, "More Than 70% of Cell Phone Users Will Buy 3G Mobile Phone" Resource document. New China News Online. http://news.xinhuanet.com/tech/2007-01/01/content_5556380.htm. Accessed 27 October 2007.

[4] See New China News Online, "The Uncertain Factors in Chinese Telecommunications Tend to be Clear" Resource document. New China News Online. http://news.xinhuanet.com/tech/2007-01/06/content_5572171.htm. Accessed 27 October 27 2007.

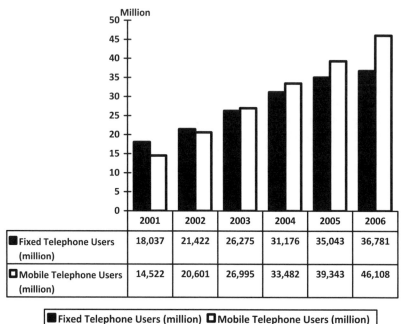

	2001	2002	2003	2004	2005	2006
■ Fixed Telephone Users (million)	18,037	21,422	26,275	31,176	35,043	36,781
☐ Mobile Telephone Users (million)	14,522	20,601	26,995	33,482	39,343	46,108

■ Fixed Telephone Users (million) ☐ Mobile Telephone Users (million)

Figure 2 The Number of Telephone Subscribers 2001 – 2006

Data Source: Statistics in the website of MII http://www.mii.gov.cn/col/col169/index.html

1.4 IT industry

Here the IT industry mainly refers to the electronic, hardware and software industry. The structure of Chinese IT industry has experienced three stages of transformation:

1. Transformation from the unitary defense-focused industry to the development of both military and civil industry;
2. Transformation from producing consumer products to the production focusing on investment, consumer and component;
3. Transformation from the unitary hardware production to the development of both hardware and software industry.

Since the mid-1980s, Chinese IT industry has grown rapidly under the support of the government. On the one hand, Chinese government encouraged the IT enterprises to participate in the foreign market by adopting the "go abroad" strategy. On the other hand, the government offered a series of preferential policies to attract foreign investment. Many national electronic information industrial zones

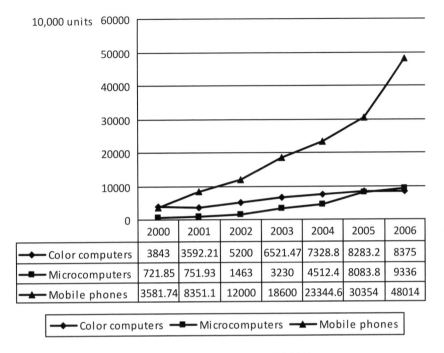

10,000 units	2000	2001	2002	2003	2004	2005	2006
Color computers	3843	3592.21	5200	6521.47	7328.8	8283.2	8375
Microcomputers	721.85	751.93	1463	3230	4512.4	8083.8	9336
Mobile phones	3581.74	8351.1	12000	18600	23344.6	30354	48014

Figure 3 China's Major Electronic Information Products 2000-2006

Data Source: State Council Informatization Office 2006, China Unicom 2007.

and parks were thus established all around the country. In this sense, Chinese IT industry has grown rapidly. In 2006, Chinese IT industry had the sales revenue of 4.75 trillion Yuan, an increase of 23.6% over the same period in the last year (China Unicom 2007). (Figure 3) By purchasing IBM's personal computing business in 2004, Lenovo Group Limited becomes the third largest PC maker in the world.

Moreover, with vast labor resources and low production cost, Chinese IT industry has been able to keep its comparative advantage in the markets of light electronic goods in a rather long period of time. Pearl River Delta and Yangtze River Delta are thus emerging as the two agglomerations of Chinese IT industry. According to the report of World Bank, the whole Chinese IT market still faces some "ironies": "Although China is a leading exporter of semiconductors, it still needs to import chips to meet local needs; although Chinese firms export third-generation (3G) mobile technologies, these same technologies have yet to be commercialized in the mainland; Although Lenovo, China's leading personal computer (PC) firm is the third largest in the world, there are only an estimated 65 million computers in a country with a population of over 1 billion people." (Qiang 2007, 55)

1.5 Internet

China's network construction was initiated with the support from foreign research group in 1987. On April 20, 1994, the *National Computing and Networking Facility of China (NCFC)* project opened a 64K international dedicated line to the Internet through Sprint Co. Ltd of the United States and achieved a full-functional connection to the Internet, which enabled China to be officially recognized as a country with full functional Internet accessibility. Since then, Internet has gained a booming growth in China. According to the statistics of China Internet Network Information Center (CNNIC), up to June 30, 2007, there were 67.1 million computers connected to Internet and 1.311 million websites in China (CNNIC 2007). Furthermore, the Chinese mainland has 9.18 million domain names of which 67% were CN domain name. Under this context, e-business encompassing the models such as business to business (B2B) and business to consumer (B2C) expand quickly in the nationwide. In 2003, only 39.15% of the enterprises advertised on Internet and 8.02% did online procurement, whereas the two scales increased to 55.94% and 36.48% in 2004 (Ministry of Commerce 2006). Moreover, Chinese e-commerce revenue was 2.2 billion US dollars in 2000, yet it attained to 84.2 US dollars in 2005 (Qiang 2007, 110).

A more impressive fact is the boom of Internet users and its effects on the emergence of the civil society in China. According to the statistics of CNNIC, 25 million Internet users were added in China in 2007 and the total number of Internet users reached 162 million including 122 million broadband users, which made China rank as the second largest size of internet users in the world (CNNIC 2007, 9), only after the United States. For Chinese Internet users, Internet has become an important channel of information. According to the statistics of CNNIC, by the end of June 2007, about 75% of Chinese Internet users read the news and utilized the search engines online (CNNIC 2007). As a public space and an important tool for communication, Internet offers an access to Chinese people to express their opinions and dissents in the online forums or blogs, and even to organize collective actions, (Zheng 2005, Cheng 2005, Zhao 2007), which unavoidably exerts more and more impacts on Chinese government's domestic and foreign policies (Hao 2006), and even threatens the regime stability.

2 Current Issues and Problems

Despite the swift growth, some important issues and problems block the further development of IT in China, which can be demonstrated in the following five facets: (1) the deficiency in legal and regulatory framework; (2) the uneven development of IT development; (3) the inefficiency of IT applications; (4) the problem of information security; (5) the lack of human resources in IT area.

2.1 The Deficiency of Legal and Regulatory Framework

First, up to now, China is still in need of an overarching legal and regulatory framework for IT development that clearly defines the rights and responsibilities of the agencies and players concerned. As a result, the governmental departments at different levels often form various institutions and formulate some overlapping even conflicting regulations, leading to the confusion and inefficiency of the administrative management as regards to IT Different governmental departments often do not have communications when they are in charge of the same IT sector. Moreover, some administrative provisions are too complex to be operated. Secondly, there are no specific laws protecting the privacy and the intellectual property rights in China, which hampers the development of China's e-business and discourages the independent innovation of Chinese enterprises as well as the confidence of foreign investors.

2.2 The Uneven Development of IT development

The uneven development of IT in China reveals in two aspects: firstly, China encounters a digital divide in the course of informatization, which refers to a great gap not only between China and developed countries as regards to the technological innovations, but also between urban and rural areas, east coastal regions and central as well as western regions inside China. On the one hand, although China's IT industry has developed rapidly since the 1980s, China lags behind in the core technologies, which makes the domestic IT industries cost a lot to get the licenses of these technologies. On the other hand, the IT development is mainly in the coastal area in the east of China, which is characterized by the two agglomerations in Pearl River Delta and Yangtze River Delta. According to a statistics, none of the top ten provinces of high informatization is in the west of China, whereas the four least informatized provinces exist in the west.[5] As to the gap between urban and rural areas, according to the statistics of CNNIC, 76.9% of the 162 million Internet users live in urban areas by the end of June 2007, and the urban penetration rate reached 21.6%, whereas the rural penetration rate was of only 5.1% (CNNIC, 2007).

Secondly, the swift development of IT has driven the sharp urbanization and industrialization in China. However, China's urban-centered development strategy widened the gap between urban and rural areas. For example, in 2004, 10 coastal provinces in China received 110.2 billion Yuan of investment in telecommunications, whereas the 21 provinces in central and western China only received 57.94 billion Yuan (Zhao 2007, 99-100). As a result, Chinese society becomes greatly

---

[5] See New China News Online, "Digital divide Drags China's Rank in World Informatization". Resource document. New China News Online. http://news.xinhuanet.com/newmedia/2006-04/17/content_4436495.htm. Accessed 27 October 2007.

divided by region, income, and profession. Moreover, China's Gini coefficient index attained to .447 in 2005, which was higher than the United States and reflected the great inequity in China nowadays (Zhao 2007, 102).

2.3 The Inefficiency of IT Applications

Even though IT has developed exponentially in China, the level of IT application
is still at a primary stage. Firstly, the utility ratio of infrastructure and IT resources
is low. On the one hand, many informatization investments bear low returns; and
the imbalance between supply and demand exists commonly, due to the overin-
vestment and under-consumption, which is quite often seen in telecommunications
sector. In some regions, local government blindly launches many informatization
projects for political vanity. On the other hand, the existing IT facilities have not
been properly used and developed, which drops behind 10-20 years compared
with the developed countries (China Labor Market 2006). Secondly, the inadequate research and development (R&D) and technological innovation also contribute to the inefficient use of IT resources.

2.4 The Problem of Information Security

For Chinese government, the information security encompasses two facets: (1) the
protection of data and privacy; and (2) the monitoring of the information. On the
one hand, the explosive growth of Internet severely challenges the Chinese government's capacity in protecting data and privacy against the shock of emergency
as well as against all kinds of viruses and spy software. For example, the communication traffic caused by the earthquake off the southern tip of Taiwan in December 2006, and the rapid spread of the virus named "Panda Burning Joss Sticks"
which swept across China by infecting millions of computers, challenged Chinese
government's capability in offering the public security in an information age.
Moreover, tens of thousands of Trojan and BotNet delivered by the intelligence
agencies seriously endanger China's national security.[6]

On the other hand, the rapid development of IT facilitates the information flow,
challenging the government's monopoly of information in China. Especially, the
diverse means of communications such as Internet and satellite-based TV make it
easy for the circulation of the news and ideas unfavorable to the government. In
addition, IT also helps to boost the growth of the civil society face à face the state

---

[6] See New China News Online, "Rampant Network Spies Pry into State Secrets". Resource
document. New China News Online. http://news.xinhuanet.com/mil/2007-10/30/content_
6972946.htm. Accessed 10 November 2007.

and offers an access for individuals to organize collective actions threatening the regime's stability.

2.5 The Lack of Human Resources in IT Area

The rapid development of IT also sheds the light on the increasing demands for IT professionals. The supply of IT professionals particularly the senior talent cannot meet the demand. According to the report of Ministry of Education, in 2005, there were 600 thousand software practitioners among which only 40 thousand were senior professionals, whereas the number demanded by the software industry was about 1 million, including 60,000 senior professionals (China Labor Market 2006). Similarly, China's online games industry meets a shortage of experienced game designers and project managers, which hamper the growth and the competitiveness of China's online games industry.

3 Government's Dilemma and Response

Since 1993, China has given IT a prior role in the economic development. The 16th Communist Party of China (CPC) Congress identified the two-way strategy of "driving the industrialization through informatization and spurring the informatization through industrialization" (CPC Center Committee General Office, State Council General Office 2006), which provides a new way for industrializations. China's IT experienced an explosive development, but it has also resulted in a series of problems such as digital divide. Furthermore, the Chinese government has to face the dilemma between economic prosperity in virtue of IT and the threats of information explosion to the national security and regime survival. As a response, Chinese government tried to combine the growth-oriented strategy and the social justice on the basis of the "scientific outlook on development", which has been repeatedly emphasized in the 11th Five-Year Plan. Later, in "the State Informatization Development Strategy (2006-2020)", the strategy of China's informatization during these 15 years is summarized as "overall planning, resources sharing, deepening applications, seeking practical results, facing market, basing on innovation, combining military and civil use, as well as being safe and reliable."(CPC Center Committee General Office, State Council General Office 2006)

Therefore, in the near future, China's IT development will follow two tracks: the efficiency highlighting innovation on the one hand, and the justice intending to reduce the digital divide on the other. As a major supporter, the Chinese government will try to play a service-oriented role by providing a favorable environment for IT development and improving e-government. Thus a benign interaction among government, market, and society is expected to gradually form so as to replace the unilateral top-down governing. (Figure 4)

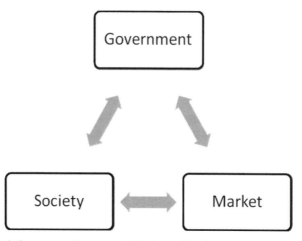

Figure 4 The Relations among Government, Market and Society

3.1 Government: E-Government and Others

Promoting the informatization in economic and social life may continue to be a strategic emphasis of the Chinese government. Meanwhile, the government tends to change its role from a controller to a moderator in IT development with an effort to ameliorate the public service. Firstly, the functions of e-government may be strengthened. Despite the abundant information provided by the governmental departments at all levels, the "information island" of these governmental portal websites may be integrated to promote the synergy among different departments and establish the integrity system for the enterprises and individuals. Based on this, more and more e-services targeting the citizens and businesses may be provided and popularized to the streets, communities and villages. In the near future, the Chinese government may increase the content of e-services, expand its scope and enhance its quality.

Secondly, the government has promised to offer a sound environment for the IT development in the future. First of all, a consistent and supportive legal and regulatory framework may be gradually established. According to "the State Informatization Development Strategy (2006-2020)", nine measures will be adopted to ensure the coordination and continuity of informatization: (1) improving the strategic research and policy system of informatization process; (2) deepening the institutional reform in the informatization; (3) perfecting related financing policy; (4) accelerating the formulation of the application norms and technological standards; (5) promoting the legal construction of informatization; (6) enforcing the governance on Internet; (7) increasing the supply of IT professionals; (8) strengthening the international exchanges and cooperations; (9) improving the managing institutions for the informatization(CPC Center Committee General Office, State Council General Office 2006).

Second, the state's information security system may be strengthened after the completion of "Golden Shield Project". In the past a decade, many legal and technical measures have been taken by the government to protect the national information security. In the legal aspect, a series of laws, orders, regulations, and provisions have been detailedly prescribed in almost every respect of the administration of networks and domain names as well as the network security (China Internet Information Center 2002). In the technical aspect, the "Golden Shield Project" starting in 1998 has erected a Great Firewall for China with the censorship and supervision system. A "two-tiered network structure", in which "the lower deck screens users, while the upper deck edits the content of foreign data sets" (Cheng 2005), has been established by the government to keep the public from the information unfavorable to the government or to the regime survival. In addition, about 30,000 cyber police monitor the networks everyday to combat cyber crimes and hackers. Meanwhile, it seems that the government, instead of totally blockading the network, only filters and sanitizes the unfavorable information and leaves a relative freedom to the public (Hao 2006).

3.3 The Role of Market: Innovation and others

For the Chinese authorities, innovation means "more scientific discovery and technological invention", "the organic synthesis of related technologies to develop competitive products and industries", and "absorption, digestion and re-innovation of introduced technologies, with a focus on building up innovation capability and creating more IPR on the basis of extensive utilization of resources worldwide" (Wu 2007).

Indeed, the shortage of core technologies has been the Achilles Heel of Chinese enterprises when competing with their foreign counterparts in the world IT market. Therefore, Chinese government gives the market-oriented innovation to a prominent role in the coming informatization. In "the Outline of National Plan for Medium to Long-term Scientific and Technological Development (2006-2020)", innovation was identified as a strategic entity associated with "two wings": the applications of IT infrastructure and the technological breakthroughs in the basic fields of IT industry such as integrated circuit, key electronic components, and software (CNII 2006). Some further steps may be taken by the government in the following aspects:

1. The enterprises especially the large ones are encouraged with preferential tax privilege to become the major players in the technological innovation and application, as well as the upgrade of the industrial structure (CCITC 2006).
2. The government may take measures to stimulate R&D, with an increasing of R&D investment of more than 2.5% of the GDP to booster innovation (Wu 2006), and to encourage coordination between industry and research institutions.

3. The government may ameliorate the environment of IT human resources, by popularizing the basic IT knowledge and application capabilities in the nation-wide.

3.4 To Improve Social Justice

The social justice and equality remain a major concern of the Chinese government in the near future. The 17th CPC Congress in October 2007 reiterated the "scientific outlook on development" and the notion of "constructing a harmonious society" (Hu 2007). In the field of IT, bridging the digital divide remains a main task of the government in coordinating urban and rural economic and social development. On the one hand, the government promises to balance urban and rural IT development under the scheme of building a "new socialist countryside". In order to promote the agricultural informatization, the government may increase the investment in IT infrastructure and provide more public access to Internet with free or low cost in rural areas. Moreover, the information service ranging from education, health care to endowment treatment will be delivered to the peasants. On the other hand, the imbalance between different regions, particularly between east and west regions economically developed and backward areas will be taken into account. The government will still focus on expanding the network as well as popularizing the information service in the central and western regions.

4 Conclusion

In short, the past three decades has witnessed a considerable development of IT in China, which is characterized with a top down, state-led informatization. Five aspects – legal and regulatory framework, e-government, telecommunication, IT industry, and Internet – show this one-way reaction and weakening control of the Chinese government. Meanwhile, although IT boom contributes a lot to China's impressive growth and the emergence of a civil society, it leads to many economic, social and even political problems: the distemperedness of legal and regulatory framework, the inequality of IT development, the inefficiency of IT applications, the insecurity of information handling, and the deficiency of human resources in IT area. As a response, the Chinese government changes its passive reaction to an active engagement in the future development of IT. While it will continue to advance the development of informatization with an emphasis on innovation, it may take into account the promotion of balanced social development. Furthermore, even though the government remains to be a crucial player in China's informatization in recent future, it will try to act as a moderator rather than a controller or a manager in this course through providing a favorable environment based on a consistent legal and regulatory framework and service-oriented e-government. In this sense, a multiple interaction between government, market and society will continue.

References

Cheng, Tun-jen (Ed.). (2005). *China under Hu Jintao: Opportunities, Dangers, and Dilemmas*. River Edge: World Scientific Publishing Company, Inc.

CCITC (China Chain International Tax Consultancy). (2006). The State Announced the Preferential Tax Policies to Encourage the Enterprises' Technological Innovation. Resource document. China Chain International Tax Consultancy http://www.ccitc.net.cn/news/newsdetail.asp?T_ID=5&D_ID=2681. Accessed 1st November 2007.

China Internet Information Center. (2002). The Overview of Laws and Regulations for the Internet Management. Resource document. China Internet Information Center. http://www.china.org.cn/chinese/zhuanti/192893.htm. Accessed 25 October 2007.

Golden Bridge Project (2003), Resource document. China.org.cn. http://www.china.com.cn/ chinese/zhuanti/283721.htm. Accessed 25 October 2007.

China Labor Market. (2006). Five Ministries Issued the Report for the Demand of Four Kinds of Professionals. Resource document. China Labor Market. http://www.lm.gov.cn/gb/news/2006-03/20/content_110323.htm. Accessed 27 October 2007.

Chinese Business View. (2007). Our Anticipations for Telecommunication in 2007. Resource document. Chinese Business View. http://hsb.huash.com/2007-01/11/content_6034190.htm. Accessed 27 October 2007.

China Unicom. (2007). The Yearly Report of Chinese Information Industry. Resource document. China Unicom. http://www.chinaunicom.com.cn/profile/xwdt/ndbg/file37.html #电子信息产业发展情况. Accessed 27 October 2007.

CNII (China Information Industry Net). (2006). The Outline of National Plan for Medium to Long-term Scientific and Technological Development (2006-2020). Resource document. China Information Industry Net. http://www.cnii.com.cn/20060808/ca369603.htm. Accessed 29 October 2007.

CNNIC (China Internet Network Information Center). (2001). The 7th Statistical Survey Report on the Internet Development in China (Jan. 2001). Resource document . China Internet Network Information Center. http://cnnic.cn/download/2003/10/13/91443.pdf. Accessed 25 October 2007.

The 20th Statistical Survey Report on the Internet Development in China (July 2007). Resource document. China Internet Network Information Center. http://www.cnnic.net.cn/uploadfiles/pdf/2007/7/18/113918.pdf. Accessed 25 October 2007.

Collin, S.M.H. (2002). Dictionary of Information Tech*nology (3rd edition)*. London: Peter Collin Publishing.

CPC Center Committee General Office, State Council General Office. (2006). The State Informatization Development Strategy (2006-2020). Resource document. New China News Online. http://news.xinhuanet.com/newscenter/2006-05/08/content_4522878.htm. Accessed 27 October 2007.

Gupta, Vibha and Mehtab Alam Ansari. (2007). Impact of Information Technology on Societal Development and E-Governance. *Electronic Journal of Academic and Special Librarianship*, 8(1), http://southernlibrarianship.icaap.org/content/v08n01/gupta_v01.htm. Accessed 25 October 2007.

Hao, Yufan. (2006). Dilemma of Openness. EAI (East Asia Institute). http://www.eai.or.kr/english/common/junior_past_view.asp?filename=/english/upfile/project/pjcontent/EAI%20Working%20Paper%20Series1_Hao.pdf. Accessed 27 October 2007.

Harwit, Eric and Duncan Clark. (2001). Shaping the Internet in China: Evolution of Political Control over Network Infrastructure and Content. *Asian Survey* 41(3), 377-408.

Hu, Jintao. (2007). Hold High the Great Banner of Socialism with Chinese Characteristics and Strive for New Victories in Building a Moderately Prosperous Society in all. Resource document. China Daily Online. http://www.chinadaily.com.cn/china/2007-10/25/content_6204663.htm Accessed 3 November 2007.

Lagerkvist, Johan. 2005. "The Rise of Online Public Opinion in the People's Republic of China." *China: An International Journal* 3(1) (March): 119-130.

MII (Ministry of Information Industry). (2007). Statistics of National Communication Development in 2006. Resource document. Ministry of Information Industry. http://www.mii.gov.cn/art/2007/02/09/art_169_28756.html. Accessed 27 October 2007.

Ministry of Commerce. (2006). *Report for Chinese E-Business 2004-2005*. Resource document. Ministry of Commerce. http://xxhs.mofcom.gov.cn/subject/dzshwbg/index.shtml. Accessed 25 October 2007.

New China News Online. (2007). *Internet Guide 2007 (Simple version)*. Resource document. New China News Online. http://news.xinhuanet.com/hlw/2007-01/10/content_5587999.htm. Accessed 27 October 2007.

Qiang, Christine Zhen-Wei. (2007). *China's Information Revolution: Managing the Economic and Social Transformation*. Washington, D.C.: World Bank.

State Council Informatization Office. (2006). China Informatization Development Report 2006. Resource document. State Council informatization Office. http://download.xinhuanet.com/it/document/info_report2006.doc Accessed 25 October 2007.

Wang, Changsheng (Ed.). (2007). *Blue Book of Electronic Government: China E-Government Development Report (No.4)*. Beijing: Social Sciences Academic Press.

Wilson III, Ernest J. and Adam Segal. (2005). Trends in China's Transition toward a Knowledge Economy. *Asian Survey*, 45(6), 886-906.

Wu, Zhongze. (2006). Innovation: China's New National Strategy Address at the Opening Ceremony of China-EU Science and Technology Year. Resource document. European Commission. http://ec.europa.eu/research/iscp/eu-china/pdf/vm_wu_speech_en.pdf. Accessed 29 October 2007.

Xinhua News Agency. (2008). Highlights: China Launches Sweeping Institutional Restructuring of Gov't. Resource document. Xinhuanet. http://news.xinhuanet.com/english/2008-03/11/content_7765398.htm. Accessed 17 March 2008.

Yuan, Yufei, Wuping Zheng, et al. (2006). Xiaolingtong versus 3G in China: Which will be the winner? *Telecommunications Policy*, 30, 297-313.

Yusuf, Shahid and Kaoru Nabeshima. (2007). *Strengthening China's Technological Capability*. Washington, DC: World Bank.

Zhao, Yuezhi. (2007). After Mobile Phones, What? Re-embedding the Social in China's 'Digital Revolution'. *International Journal of Communication*, 1, 92-120.

Zheng, Yongnian and Guoguang Wu. (2005). Information Technology, Public Space, and Collective Action in China. *Comparative Political Studies*, 38(5), 507-536.

Chapter 20
Electronic Government in China

History, Current Status, and Challenges

Yue "Jeff" Zhang[1]**, Li Richard Ye**[1]**, Zhiyang Lin**[2]** and Quan Lin**[2]

[1] California State University, Northridge, USA
[2] Xiamen University, P.R. CHINA

Abstract This chapter focuses on China's e-government practices. Compared to other world economic powers, the Chinese government has been slow in adopting the Internet technology in carrying out its administrative and public service functions. As China's Information technology infrastructure improves and its Internet user population continues to grow, however, the government has become increasingly convinced by the significance and benefits of conducting its business online. The chapter reviews the evolution of e-government in China, examines its current status, identifies the unique problems and challenges China faces, and highlights recent Chinese government initiatives that promise to dramatically change China's e-government landscape.

1 Introduction

On June 30, 2007, the number of Chinese Internet users reached a new record of 162 million, a number that is the second largest in the world, behind only that of the United States (CNNIC, 2007). With such a large Internet population, e-businesses are booming in China. Since the early 1980s, China has embarked on a journey of economic modernization through market-oriented reform and opening to the outside world. Such policy changes have led to stunning progresses for the country, both in terms of economic output (measured in GDP) and structure (i.e., the increasingly larger proportion of private sector in the nation's economy). Contrasting with its remarkable economic achievements, however, China's political structure has yet to undergo a fundamental change.

P.O. de Pablos, M.D. Lytras (eds.), *The China Information Technology Handbook,*   353
DOI: 10.1007/978-0-387-77743-6_20, © Springer Science+Business Media, LLC 2009

The high concentration of political power in the hands of the ruling party – Chinese Communist Party (CCP), the lack of transparency in government operations and decision-making, and the fledgling rule of law conspire to create an environment within which a multitude of social ills emerge, including rampant corruption, enormous waste of pubic funds and resources, and an alarming disparity both among social classes and among different regions in the country (Kurtenbach, 2005; XinhuaNet, 2006). Democratizing the government, strengthening rule of law, and increasing the participation of Chinese citizens in the political processes and general affairs of the society have become critical to China's healthy development in the future decades into an open, stable, and responsible member of the world community. The Internet, with its openness for information flow and information sharing, is seen as a strong vehicle for people to exchange ideas and to interact. Leveraging the Internet for government operations and for the interaction between governments and citizens – "electronic government" or "e-government," is believed to have the benefits of "cost effectiveness in government and public operations, with better and continuous contacts with citizens," and "greater transparency and accountability in public decisions, powerful ways to fight corruption, the ability to stimulate the emergence of local e-cultures, and the strengthening of democracy (The Center for Democracy & Technology, 2002) ."

Influenced by the outside world, and pushed by its own people, especially the social elite, the Chinese government is now also implementing e-government initiatives (Li et al, 2004), a desirable trend that should be encouraged and facilitated by the international community.

2 The Dawn of China's e-Government

On June 8, 1994, the General Office of the State Council of the People's Republic of China released the Announcement on Issues Regarding the "Three-Golden Projects", thus launching the information system (IS) projects of Golden Bridge (information infrastructure), Golden Customs (information systems connecting China's customs) and Golden Cards (information systems for credit cards). In later years, more initiatives would be added to the list, which eventually grew to become the "Twelve Golden Projects", covering such governmental IS application areas as macroeconomic policy support, taxes and budgeting, real-time statistical information flows, product quality monitoring and control, water resources management and flood control, and agricultural technology information services. These are the early efforts to digitize the Chinese government's administration of major economic activities of the nation (CNNIC, 2007).

In 1997, a national conference on informatization was held, at which the "National Informatization Vision 2000" was outlined, and the Chinese Internet was introduced into the list of national infrastructure development. A national internetworking center was proposed. Later in the same year, under the delegation of the State Council Informatization Steering Committee, the Academia Sinica (Chinese

Academy of Sciences) established the China National Network Information Center (CNNIC). In 1998, the Ninth National People's Congress passed a law to establish the Ministry of Information Industry (MII), which essentially joined two former government bodies, the Ministry of Post and Telecommunications, and the software and telecommunications portion of the Ministry of Electronic Industry, to become a new government entity in charge of the industry of digital products and services, telecommunications, and software industry, in an effort to further the modernization of the country's information technology (IT) infrastructure. In 1998, Qingdao (Tsingtao), a tourism and industrial city on the northeast coast of China, established the first public-oriented government website, Qingdao Government Public Information Net, symbolizing the birth of a local e-government in China (Li, Wang, and Gao, 2004). Then came the defining moment of China's e-government initiative: on January 22, 1999, more than forty central government ministries and bureaus held the "Launching Meeting of the Government Online Project." China's national e-government officially began its operation. On New Year's Day, 2006, the main website of the Central People's Government of the People's Republic of China - www.gov.cn - was officially launched (CNNIC, 2007).

In May 1999, the Government Online Project launched the first 50 provincial and prefecture level government online pilot projects. On May 17, 1999, the 31st World Telecommunication Day, government domain names registered under gov.cn sharply increased to 1,470, among which 720 government ministries/entities provided WWW services for the public. The standardization of Chinese government domain name system was proposed (XinhuaNet, 2003). As of late 1999, the ministries participating in the Government Online Project had increased to 66 from the initial 48. As of 2000, there were over 2,300 government websites in the "gov.cn" domain (Anonymous, 2000).

3 Strategies for Advancing China's e-Government

China's e-government efforts have been seen as the means toward "improving the national competitiveness of China". The e-government initiatives are believed to provide the following significance and benefits (National Officials Training Text Compilation and Evaluation Steering Committee, 2004):

1. It will meet the urgent demand for improving the capability of governance, improving effectiveness of government operations, and improving the level of public service of the Chinese government.
2. It will be a means to meet the challenges of globalization after China's entry to the WTO.
3. It will provide opportunities to stimulate and propel both the information industry and the national economy as a whole.
4. It will set an example for informatization in other aspects of the country.

In 2002, the State Council Informatization Steering Committee issued the Guiding Opinions on the Construction of Electronic Government, outlining the operational principles of e-government (The State Council Informatization Steering Committee, 2002):

- Centralized planning, with strong guidance and top-down control
- Demand-driven, with emphases on building unified network platforms and incremental growth
- Integrating resources and mobilizing related information industries
- Unifying standards and ensuring system security.

The Guiding Opinions also mandated the continuation of the existing "Golden Projects," and the expansion of the list from three to twelve (see Table 1).

The Guiding Opinions also set the goals for China's e-government for 2000-2005 as follows (The State Council Informatization Steering Committee, 2002):

1. Developing an integrated e-government network
2. Developing and optimizing major operational systems (including such systems as the aforementioned "Three Golden Projects")
3. Planning and developing important government information resources
4. Advancing public services
5. Establishing basic security assurance systems for e-government networks and information systems
6. Perfecting e-government standards
7. Training and testing government officials for e-government implementation
8. Accelerating the development of legal systems to facilitate e-government

Table 1 The "Twelve Golden Projects (eGov China 2004)"

Project Name	Starting Time	Purpose
Golden Bridge (Jin Qiao)	1994	Information infrastructure
Golden Cards (Jin Ka)	1994	Credit card system
Golden Customs (Jin Guan)	1994	Foreign trade and customs
Golden Tax (Jin Shui)	1994	Tax management
Golden Agriculture (Jin Nong)	1994	Agricultural service, forecast, and management
Golden Security (Jin Bao)	1999	Social security
Golden Water (Jin Shui)	2001	Flood and drought monitoring and forecasting
Golden Shield (Jin Dun)	2002	Public safety (police) information
Golden Quality (Jin Zhi)	2002	Product quality monitoring and control
Golden Auditing (Jin Shen)	2002	Auditing information management
Golden Macro (Jin Hong)	2002	Macroeconomic management information system
Golden Budget (Jin Cai)	2006	Government finance and budget management

4 The Status of China's e-Government

From 2002 to 2004, CCW Research, a spin-off of China Computer World Magazine specializing in information and communications technologies (ICT) consulting and research, conducted annual surveys and assessments of e-government websites. The samples of the survey and assessment included 32 major cities in China, as well as all the national-level ministries and bureaus. The 2004 survey and assessment found that the overall service quality level of the e-government websites reached 6.3 on a 10-point scale, the first time they achieved a passing grade (as compared to 4.8 in 2002). The functionalities and contents of the websites had experienced rapid progresses. Yet the functionalities of the government websites still did not reach passing level of 6 points out of 10, while the contents of the websites passed 7 points (CCW Research, 2004). The report presented the following findings and conclusions:

- quality varied widely among ministerial websites;
- the openness of government information is yet to be improved, in that the information published was often obsolete and very limited in amount, and the governmental business procedures published were unclear or incomplete;
- functionalities were largely under-developed, in that most of the websites could not support online inquiry or tracking of a transaction/application, or support searches on governmental business procedures or rules;
- the websites of ministries of the Central Government had satisfactory performance in providing contents, yet failing performance in providing service functionalities (such as searching, tracking, interaction, and transaction), with a low average score of 4 on a 10-point scale;
- at the provincial/city government level, the overall website quality had strong correlation with the economic development level of the province/city of interest, and such correlation was more prominent among lower-level governments (prefectures and counties) than among provincial governments;
- There was a clear pattern of digital divide among different geographical regions that were at various stages of economic development: from 2002 to 2004, in the three surveys, the top-10 cities were mostly on the more developed east coast, whereas the lowest-scoring cities were all in the relatively underdeveloped western region.

Electronic Government Magazine, the leading trade magazine in the field of e-government in China, sponsored a nationwide survey in 2003-2004, and published the 2003-2004 China City Governments Web Portals Assessment Report (Electronic Government Magazine, 2004). The survey examined and rated 336 cities of prefecture-level and higher (which covered almost all the cities at those levels), and ranked the cities according to the assessment and rating. The survey found that 303 cities of the 336 surveyed (90.2%) had established a city government web portal. Among the cities, 33 had portals at relatively higher level of quality, accounting for 9.8% of the cities. There were, however, 33 cities that did not have a web portal, also accounting for 9.8% of the cities surveyed. The survey used five categories of criteria in assessing the web portals: contents, interaction, timeliness and currency, personalization, and transparency. The average scores of the cities surveyed on these five categories were 58%, 23%, 37%, 31%, and 25%, respectively. While the contents of the city web portals received the highest score (58%), the interaction functionality received the lowest score (23%), with transparency not much better (25%).

In 2005, CCW Research conducted a new round of survey and assessment of e-government websites of 69 ministries/bureaus, 31 provinces, 32 provincial capitals and major cities, 201 prefecture-level cities, and 201 counties. The study found that the overall quality of the e-government websites were comparable with that of the previous year, with the ministerial websites scoring just below, and the provincial websites just above, the passing level. Among the provincial-level governments, Shanghai and Beijing achieved outstanding levels at 8.3 and 8.0, respectively. The prefecture-level and county-level governments received scores comparable with those of the previous year, at 5.4 and 5.1, respectively (CCW Research, 2005).

The low scores could be attributed again to a lack of functionalities. Most government websites did not really provide services to the public. Overall, the "information" function of government websites was nearly mature, but the "interaction" and "transaction" functions were far behind. The survey also found that the enthusiasm of citizens to participate in the public and social affairs was a driving force for the improvement of e-government. As more and more citizens went on line, the public not only had stronger needs for accessing government information, but also were more eager in participating in public affairs, thus forcing government websites to go beyond information publishing to provide government-citizen interaction capabilities.

There was, however, again a strong pattern of digital divide between the more developed eastern (coastal) region and the less developed central and western (inland) regions: of the top-10 major city websites, only one was from the western region. In contrast, of the bottom-10 major city websites, only one was near the east coast (CCW Research, 2005).

More recently, the eBusiness Center at Peking (Beijing) University and CCW Research conducted a joint, nationwide study of web portals of 289 prefecture-level cities, 32 major cities, and 31 provincial governments (eBusiness Center at PKU and CCW Research, 2007). The main findings of the study are:

- the overall quality of China's government web portals was improving;
- online interaction and transaction capabilities were still very underdeveloped;
- content publishing was the best, while online service remained far behind;
- most city government web portals seemed to be content with staying at low levels, with only very few being able to break through to higher levels of interaction and transactions;
- Willingness to serve, awareness to serve, and the general attitude towards serving the citizens determined the quality and functions of city government web portals.

5 Obstacles Facing China's e-Government Development

While China has become the fourth largest economy in the world (AFP, 2006), due to its large percentage of rural population, its per capita GDP is still ranked below 100 among all countries (CIA, 2006). At 162 million, China's Internet population still accounts for only about 12.3% of the country's total population of 1.3 billion, lower than the global average of 17.6% (CNNIC, 2007). Despite notable reforms and the increasing openness that have occurred during the last two decades, the Chinese government remains secretive and controlling, more often steered by calculated wills of political factions than by rationally designed policies, operating in changeable, sometimes unpredictable ways rather than following laws, procedures, and the wills of its citizenry. Consequently, much needed citizen- and service-orientation remain elusive to China's e-government endeavors, and further progress will most likely depend on its success in confronting and overcoming the following issues and challenges.

1. Values, philosophy, attitudes, and habits:
   - There is a lack of "serving the citizens" mentality (Electronic Government Magazine, 2004; eBusiness Center @ PKU and CCW Research, 2007) and a lack of law-abiding attitude (eGov China 2004, 2004).
   - Between the two components of e-government" – "e" (the technological means) and "government" (the government services to citizens and the procedures of providing such services), there are far more emphases on the former. The tendency is to use a government website as an image booster rather than as a vehicle to better serve citizens (eGov China 2004, 2004; Zhang, 2006), which in turn often leads to a waste of resources (Xue and Huang, 2001; Electronic Government Magazine, 2004).
   - There is a lack of willingness to open and share government information, resulting in information islands that are isolated from one another (eGov China 2004, 2004).
   - There is no recognition of the need to reform government functions or processes, leading to simple and "mechanical" migration of existing (inefficient/ineffective) government procedures on line, without much-needed government process reengineering (eGov China 2004, 2004; Electronic Government Magazine, 2004; Zhang, 2006).

2. Architectural planning and design of the systems
   - E-government philosophy and models are not adopted or applied (Electronic Government Magazine, 2004; eBusiness Center @ PKU and CCW Research, 2007).
   - No integration of government services and sharing of resources; public service functions are insignificant/unnoticeable (Electronic Government Magazine, 2004; eBusiness Center @ PKU and CCW Research, 2007).
   - Repetitive construction of infrastructure (Xue and Huang, 2001; Electronic Government Magazine, 2004).

- Most government websites are only at the beginning stage of static information publishing; most have minimal or no interaction or transaction capabilities (Electronic Government Magazine, 2004; eBusiness Center @ PKU and CCW Research, 2007).
- Published information or available services lack depth or largely insufficient (Electronic Government Magazine, 2004; Zhang and Shen, 2006; eBusiness Center @ PKU and CCW Research, 2007).

3. Security of systems; balance between security and openness
- Network security zoning and control are inappropriate, causing either poor public service due to insufficient information availability, or poor security due to inappropriate information releasing (Xue and Huang, 2001; eGov China 2004, 2004).
- Internal monitoring and control are largely absent(eGov China 2004, 2004).
- There is insufficient certification services for e-government system(eGov China 2004, 2004).
- Disaster recovery and emergency response are often not in place (eGov China 2004, 2004).

4. Resources limitations
- There is insufficient budget allocation for the projects (eGov China 2004, 2004).
- There is a shortage of IT professionals for development and maintenance of government websites (eGov China 2004, 2004).

5. Environment for e-government
- Legislatures conducive to e-government initiatives are few and far in-between (eGov China 2004, 2004; Zhang, 2006).
- Changes in public awareness and cultures are needed to facilitate and support e-government (Zhang and Shen, 2006).

6. Disparities
- Large gaps remain among regions (Xue and Huang, 2001; eGov China 2004, 2004; Zhang *et al*, 2006);
- Even within the same region, there are significant disparities among different governmental departments/bureaus (Zhang and Shen, 2006; Zhang *et al*, 2006).

Accordingly, the following actions/countermeasures have been recommended: (1) better strategic planning; (2) measuring and assessing e-government performance/effectiveness; (3) providing financial subsidies for poorer regions to bridge the digital divide; (4) establishing and enforcing technical standards; (5) fostering stronger demand among citizens and businesses for e-government services; (6) creating internal motivational and incentive mechanisms for local governments to adopt and implement e-government; (7) providing sound guidance for local governments on e-government projects; (8) providing operational training in the use of e-government systems; and (9) promoting the utilization, not just building, of the government websites to reap the benefits of e-government (Zhang and Shen, 2006; Wang, 2007).

6 International Research on e-Government in China

The advent and growth of China's e-government movement have naturally attracted attention from the outside world, leading to several research studies on China's e-government conducted by international as well as Chinese scholars. Ma, Chung, and Thorson (2005) studied the evolution of China's e-government initiatives, mostly from the central government's documents (executive orders, regulations, resolutions, etc.), involving the cases of Beijing, Nanjing, Shenzhen, and Nanhai, all major cities or industrial cities in the more prosperous eastern region. The study focused mainly on the relationship between economic development (requiring information decentralization) and administrative control (information centralization). Holliday and Yep conducted a survey of the websites created by Chinese central government agencies, and by some of the leading provincial and city governments (Holliday and Yep, 2005). They employed a coding frame developed for two studies of British e-government sites commissioned by the National Audit Office (NAO) in 1999 and 2002, which enumerated the existence of certain types of e-government service features without measuring the level of performance or sophistication. Along with their Chinese counterparts (e-government researchers), Holliday and Yep came to the conclusion that "progress is currently limited to surface change rather than fundamental reworking of the governance system" (Holliday and Yep, 2005). As an exploratory measure, the survey conducted in this research only noted the existence ("Yes or No") of a certain website feature. Future studies will need better designed metrics in order to measure an e-government system's performance.

Zhang, Lin and Lin (Zhang, et al 2006) conducted a more thorough assessment of 53 cities/counties in all Chinese provinces except Tibet. For each city/county, not only was the city/county government's web portal visited and assessed, three other bureaus that are closely related to citizens' life were also visited and assessed: Education, Price Administration, and Labor and Social Security. Their study found that overall, e-government in China was still relatively underdeveloped (see Figure 1). They also found that, compared to city government web portals, the quality and performance of individual governmental units' websites fared far worse, and that regional differences remained an important factor in China's development and social transition, as evidenced in the adoption and implementation of e-government practices. While the west and central regions were lagging behind the east region in general, the regional gaps were much more magnified among peer governmental units' websites than among peer city government portals (see Figure 2). Moreover, it was noted that many governmental websites at the department/bureau level were difficult to find or navigate; an ordinary citizen may have neither the knowledge about governmental structure nor the searching capability to locate such sites. As a result, the study proposed that an "index measuring ease of access" be introduced in the future when assessing the quality of government websites.

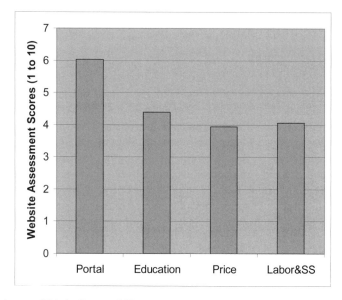

Figure 1 Average Website Scores of City Government Portal and Three Bureaus
Source: Zhang, et al (2006)

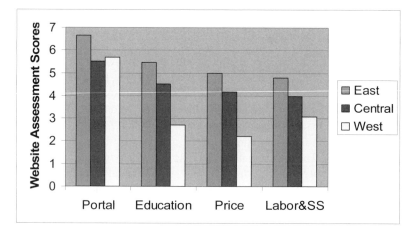

Figure 2 Website Scores by Governmental Unit, by Region
Source: Zhang, et al (2006)

A follow-up study by Zhang, Lin, and Lin (Zhang, et al 2007) also explored Chinese citizens' opinions on e-government benefits, important issues, and perceived critical success factors of e-government in China. Participants of the study reported that they found the amount of resources at their local e-government inadequate, and that it was difficult to express their opinions and concerns about local affairs through e-government portals. Overall, these findings confirmed the view that China's e-government practices continue to exhibit a lack of citizen service orientation.

7 Outlook for e-Government in China

Yukai Wang, a professor at Beijing University School of Government Administration, a member of the National Informatization Consultation Committee, and an e-government expert, laid out his view of the "Ten mega-trends" for China's e-government development (Wang, 2007):

1. The central government's goal of establishing a "harmonious society" mandates the development of a service-oriented e-government.
2. "People-centered," "social harmony," and "sustainable development" will become new values in e-government development.
3. Government reform will receive a higher priority, and continuing e-government development will lead to a higher level of transparency, accountability, effectiveness, and efficiency of government operations.
4. Informatization in rural China will accelerate.
5. A citizen-centered, service-oriented e-government will lead to more innovations.
6. Back-end application integration of the government portals will lead to more powerful front-end service functions and capabilities.
7. Increased funding in e-government development in the central and western regions will further shrink the digital divide between regions.
8. Cross-department online coordination and collaboration will increase, leading to breakthroughs in novel applications that better serve businesses and citizens.
9. Instead of image improvements, future e-government projects will focus on providing real, more practical user benefits.
10. Greater efforts will be concentrated in exploring a low-cost approach to building effective, highly integrated e-government systems.

Following these trends, the Chinese government is currently embarking on a significant campaign of government reform: making government information public. Issued by the State Council, China's new "Government Information Disclosure Act (State Council, 2007)" mandates that governments of county-level and higher must make eleven categories of government information public, and that township governments must make eight categories of government information public. The outlets for such information disclosure include "government gazettes,

government websites, press conferences, and newspapers, radio, and television."
With government websites being a prominent channel, the Act will certainly pro-
vide impetus for an intensified effort in China's e-government development.To
answer the calls for a clear, nationwide, high-level road map for e-government in
China, the State Council Informatization Office recently also issued the National
Electronic Government Framework (State Council Informatization Office, 2006).
Outlined in the Framework are general requirements for China's e-government:

- Leverage the roles of e-government in regulating the economy and monitoring
  markets
- Focus on improving community management and providing public service
- Focus on the development and utilization of government information resources
- Establish information sharing and process collaboration mechanism.

The goals set by the Framework to be achieved by the year 2010 are:

- Complete a nationwide, unified e-government network
- Establish basic directory and exchange systems and information assurance in-
  frastructure
- Achieve interoperability among key application systems
- Establish a preliminary system of laws and regulations
- Make government portals the primary channel for government information dis-
  closure
- Achieve online processing capability for at least 50% of administrative licens-
  ing applications

As China's economy continues to grow, as China plays an increasing important
role in the global economy and other aspects of globalization, and with the 2008
Summer Olympic Games in Beijing serving as an immediate catalyst, the Chinese
government is being presented with unprecedented opportunities as well as challenges. E-government, with its unique power to collect and disseminate information, to connect the citizens and the government, and to facilitate mass participation in political and social affairs and processes, will no doubt be an instrumental
component in China's modernization quest. With a 162-million-strong and growing Internet population that is demanding an increasing level of control over their
personal and social lives, China e-government movement has truly come of age.

References

Anonymous (2000). Government Online Project Has Shown Positive Effects. China Information
    Review, 2000, No.2, 13-15, http://www.wanfangdata.com.cn/qikan/periodical.Articles/
    zgxxdb/zgxx2000/0002/000205.htm, accessed November 1, 2007.
AFP (2006). China's economy fourth biggest in world after sharp growth in 2005, Yahoo! News,
    http://news.yahoo.com/s/afp/20060125/bs_afp/chinaeconomy, accessed January 31, 2006.

CCW Research (2004). China's Government Websites Evaluation Research Report. http://grp.topoint.com.cn/zyzx/view.asp?id=448&cc=2&Number=1, accessed October 20, 2007.

CCW Research (2005). 05Chinese Government Website Assessment Report came Out: Most Sites Failed. http://xxj.liuzhou.gov.cn/xxhyw/qgdt/P020051216347883591933.doc, accessed October 20, 2007

CIA (2006). Rank Order - GDP - per capita (PPP), in The World Factbook, http://www.cia.gov/cia/publications/factbook/rankorder/2004rank.html, accessed March 20, 2006.

CNNIC (2007). Major events in the Internet Development in China, 1993-2006. http://www.cnnic.net.cn/html/Dir/2003/10/22/1001.htm, accessed November 1, 2007.

CNNIC (2007). The 20th Report on the Development Status of Internet in China, http://www.cnnic.net.cn/uploadfiles/doc/2007/7/18/113843.doc, accessed August 20, 2007.

The Center for Democracy & Technology (2002). The E-Government Handbook for Developing Countries. http://www.cdt.org/egov/handbook/, accessed September 20, 2005

eGov China 2004 (2004). 2004 China e-Government White Paper. http://www.eceb.com.cn/articleview/2006-4-13/article_view_1195.htm, accessed October 15, 2007.

Electronic Government Magazine (2004). China City Governments' Web Portal Assessment Report Published. http://it.sohu.com/20041012/n222456569.shtml, accessed November 1, 2007.

Holliday, I. and Yep, R. (2005) E-Government in China, Public Administration Development, 25, 239–249.

Kurtenbach, E. (2005). Gap Between China's Rich, Poor Alarming, AP (Yahoo! News) http://news.yahoo.com/s/ap/20050921/ap_on_bi_ge/china_wealth_gap, accessed September 21, 2005.

Li, Q., Wang, J., and Gao, H. (2004). The New e-Government Training Course Textbook, in "Party and Government Cadres and Civil Servant High/New Technology Training Series" (in Chinese), Science Press, Beijing, China.

Ma, L., Chung, J., and Thorson, S. (2005). E-government in China: Bringing economic development through administrative reform, Government Information Quarterly, Vol.22, 20–37.

National Officials Training Text Compiling and Steering Committee (2004). Informatizatin and Electronic Government, People's Publishing House, Beijing, China.

eBusiness Center at PKU and CCW Research (2007). 2006-2007 Nation-Wide Government Web Portal Assessment Research Report. http://www.ccwresearch.com.cn/pinggu/2006pinggu.pdf, accessed October 20, 2007.

The State Council, People's Republic of China (2007). The People's Republic of China Government Information Opening Regulation. http://www.gov.cn/zwgk/2007-04/24/content_592937.htm, accessed October 30, 2007.

The State Council Informatization Steering Committee (2002). Guiding Opinions on the Construction of Electronic Government, http://www.dzsw.org/dzswlw/ShowArticle.asp?ArticleID=3956, accessed October 20, 2007.

The State Council Informatization Office (2006). National Electronic Government Framework. http://www.nbit.gov.cn/homepage/show_view.aspx?id=1870&catid=355, accessed October 20, 2007.

Wang, Y. (2007). Forecast: Ten Magatrends in 2007 for e-Government Development in China. Informatization (magazine), accessed at the Central People's Government Website of China, http://www.gov.cn/zfjs/2007-03/09/content_546606.htm, accessed October 15, 2007.

Xinhuanet (2003). News Background: Looking Back to Major events of the Government Online Project, http://news.xinhuanet.com/newscenter/2003-02/24/content_741590.htm, accessed November 3, 2007

XinhuaNet (2006). Promoting the "Tertiary Distribution," Alleviating Disparity in Wealth, http://news.xinhuanet.com/misc/2006-03/09/content_4282106.htm, accessed March 10, 2006.

Zhang, W. and Shen, Y. (2006). Solutions to the Development of e-Government for Prefecture-Level Cities in China. http://www.eceb.com.cn/articleview/2006-4-26/article_view_1695.htm, accessed November 2, 2007.

Zhang, Y. (2006). The Current Problems in and Development Strategies for China's e-Government. http://www.eceb.com.cn/articleview/2006-4-29/article_view_1856.htm, accessed November 1, 2007.

Zhang, Y., Lin, Z., and Lin, Q. (2006). The Readiness for and Current Status of E-Government in China. Proceedings of the National DSI Conference (November 2006, San Antonio , Texas, USA), 29251-29256.

Zhang, Y., Lin, Z., and Lin, Q. (2007). Chinese Citizens' Opinions on e-Government Benefits, Issus, and Critical Success Factors. Presented on the National DSI Conference (November 2007, Phoenix, Arizona, USA).

Chapter 21
Software Evolution for Evolving China

Hongji Yang[1], Feng Chen[1], Yong Zhou[2], Mingyan Zhao[2], Yuxin Wang[2] and He Guo[2]

[1] De Montfort University, Leicester, UK
[2] Dalian University of Technology, Dalian, China

1 Introduction

Software systems need to evolve continually to cope with ever-changing software requirements. Constant innovation of information technology and ever-changing market requirements relegate more and more existing software to legacy status. From the moment a software product is released, the race against time and aging begins. Organisations are in fear of their legacy systems, as maintaining these systems is a significant drain on the organisation's resources. They are also afraid of replacing them, as these legacy systems are enormously valuable assets. Having stood the test of time and evolved, they provide the most accurate statement of current business practices. Legacy systems, then, are not an issue that can be simply thrown away.

Software evolution is a process of conducting continuous software reengineering. In other words, software evolution is repeated software reengineering [76]. The purpose of software reengineering is both to position existing systems to take advantage of new technologies and to enable new development efforts to take advantage of reusing existing systems. Software reengineering has the potential to improve software productivity and quality across the entire life cycle. The Conference on Grand Challenges in Computing Research organised by the UK Computing Research Committee was held in March 2004. The report shows that the software evolution (GC6) is a key co-theme within a more general grand challenge addressing dependable software engineering.

In this Chapter, we provide an overview of current software evolution research in evolving China. In Section 2, we introduce the background and some basic concepts of software evolution research. Section 3 elaborates software evolution themes by reviewing the state of the art. We have tried to explore current trends of software evolution in the UK and USA and then discuss the demanding issues in software evolution research. Section 4 is devoted to the reviews of software evolution research in China. There are many Chinese researchers who have paid much attention to transformation and reengineering of software changes and artifacts. We have classified several views to support the contribution, e.g., software architecture evolution,

P.O. de Pablos, M.D. Lytras (eds.), *The China Information Technology Handbook*,   367
DOI: 10.1007/978-0-387-77743-6_21, © Springer Science+Business Media, LLC 2009

software dynamic evolution, software evolution with modern paradigm, etc. Based on previous reviews, Section 5 shows our speculations to the hot issues of software evolution in China in the foreseeable future and Section 6 is a summary.

2 Background and Basic Concepts

In this section, we will introduce the background of software crisis and legacy crisis, present an overview of software evolution, and define basic concepts related to software evolution and software reengineering.

2.1 From Software Crisis to Legacy Crisis

No one will doubt today that information systems are business-critical for almost all institutions. However, too much software currently being produced is late, over budget, and does not perform as expected; yet software costs are rising all the time. The fact that the software development industry is in a crisis has been recognised since 1969. Problems associated with the software crisis have been caused by the character of software itself. F. P. Brooks [5] claims the following properties of large software systems:

- Complexity: This is an essential property of all large pieces of software, essential in that it cannot be abstracted away from. This leads to several problems:

    - Communication difficulties among team members, leading to product flaws, cost overruns, and schedule delays.
    - It is difficult or impossible to enumerate all the states of the system, which makes it impossible to understand the system completely.
    - It is difficult to get an overview of the system, so maintaining conceptual integrity becomes increasingly difficult;
    - It is hard to ensure that all loose ends are accounted for.
    - There is a steep learning curve for new personnel.

- Conformity: Many systems are constrained by the need to conform to complex human institutions and systems (e.g., the tax regulations of a state).
- Change: As it is used any successful system will be subject to change to enhance its capabilities, or even apply it beyond the original domain, as well as to enable it to survive beyond the normal life of the machine it runs on and to be ported to other machines and environments.
- Invisibility: For complex software systems there is no geometric representation, as is available to the designers and builders of complex mechanical or electronic machines or large buildings. There are several distinct but interacting graphs of links between parts of the system to be considered (e.g., control flow,

data flow, dependency, and time sequence). One way to simplify these, in an attempt to control the complexity, is to cut links until the graphs become hierarchical structures [47].

As one of the most important areas of computer science, software engineering had its origin as a solution to the "software crisis". Many methods and techniques have been hailed as the solution to the software crisis and however in practice only small gains in productivity have been achieved and few of these methods pay any attention to the problems of maintaining and enhancing the developed software. Estimates show that 65-75% of total software costs are subsumed in maintenance activities [56]. This number has undoubtedly increased and is increasing at an accelerating rate. The result is that even if the promised large improvements in development speed by the use of new methods do eventually appear they will have little impact on total software costs since any gain from increased development will be swallowed up by the increased maintenance cost. Concern is growing that the development of new software is outpacing the ability to maintain it. In the current decade, four out of seven programmers are working on enhancement and repair projects. With large portions of software budgets being devoted to maintenance, few resources remain for new development. If these trends continue, eventually no resources will be left to develop new systems, and people will enter the Middle Ages of the information age, referred as "legacy crisis" [54].

2.2 Software Evolution

Evolution describes a phenomenon that is widespread across many domains. Natural species, societies, cities, concepts, theories and ideas all evolve over time, each in its own context. In most situations, evolution results from concurrent changes in several, even many, of the properties of the evolving entity or collection of entities. Individual changes are generally small relative to the entity as a whole, but even then their impact may be significant. In areas such as software, many allegedly independent changes may be implemented in parallel. As changes occur as a part of the overall evolution, properties no longer appropriate may be removed or may disappear and new properties may emerge [32]. Software evolution is the sub-domain of the software engineering discipline that investigates ways to adapt software to the ever-changing user requirements and operating environment.

2.2.1 Laws of Software Evolutions

The observation of software systems continuing changes was first put forward by Belady and Lehman. They termed this dynamic behaviour of software systems *evolution* and carried out empirical research on about 20 releases of the OS/360 operating system. The investigation led to five "laws" of software evolution [27]. After then, Lehman and his colleagues worked on the FEAST/1 project and FEAST/2 project, three new laws were identified and over 50 rules were provided [30].

Lehman clarified classification scheme distinguishing three types of programs, i.e., S-type, P-type and E-type, and defined that an E-type program is a computer program that solves a problem or implements a computer application in the real world domain indicated that E-type software supports E-type applications and the latter must also evolve. The results of their studies are based on observation, which have become known as Lehman's laws [28] (Table 1):

A practical issue is how to break these laws to prolong the life of the software systems. The first and second laws are especially interesting and will be discussed in detail.

2.2.2 Software Changes and Software Evolution Approaches

Large-scale industrial and commercial software systems usually have a long life-span, e.g., sometimes twenty years or more. The consequence of software aging, as described in [48], is a growing inability to keep up with the market by introducing new features, reduced performance and decreased reliability. Many such applications do not remain static after their original development phase, as they tend to evolve continuously during their lifetime. There are four main reasons for changing software [76]:

Table 1 Lehman's Laws of Software Evolution

Law No.	Law name	Law description
1	Continuing Change	An E-type program that is used must be continually adapted else it becomes progressively less satisfactory.
2	Increasing Complexity	As a program is evolved its complexity increases unless work is done to maintain or reduce it
3	Self Regulation	The program evolution process is self regulating with close to normal distribution of measures of product and process attributes
4	Conservation of Organisational Stability (invariant work rate	The average effective global activity rate on an evolving system is invariant over the product life time.
5	Conservation of Familiarity	During the active life of an evolving program, the content of successive releases is statistically invariant.
6	Continuing Growth	Functional content of a program must be continually increased to maintain user satisfaction over its lifetime
7	Declining Quality	E-type programs will be perceived as of declining quality unless rigorously maintained and adapted to a changing operational environment.
8	Feedback System	E-type Programming Processes constitute Multi-loop, Multi-level Feedback systems and must be treated as such to be successfully modified or improved

- To be perfective. These changes are made to improve the product, such as adding new user requirements, or to enhance performance, usability, or other system attributes. These types of changes are also called enhancements.
- To be corrective. These changes are made to repair defects in the system.
- To be adaptive. These changes are made to keep pace with changing environments, such as new operating systems, language compilers and tools, database management systems and other commercial components.
- To be preventive. These changes are made to improve the future maintainability and reliability of a system. Unlike the preceding three reactive reasons for change, preventive changes proactively seek to simplify future evolution.

Software systems could not be inescapable to change. Changes to software artifacts and related entities tend to be progressive and incremental, which are driven by feedback from users and other stakeholders. Every software system that is being used needs to be changed. Software is only finished when it is no longer in use. The activities of software change can be divided into three categories: maintenance, reengineering, and replacement [54].

- Software maintenance is the modification of a software product after delivery to correct faults, to improve performance or other attributes, or to adapt the product to a changed environment. Maintenance is an incremental and iterative process in which small changes are made to a system without major structural changes.
- Software reengineering involves more extensive changes than maintenance but conserves a significant portion of the existing system. These changes often include restructuring the system, enhancing functionality, or modifying software attributes. Software reengineering falls between the two extremes of system replacement and continued maintenance.
- Software replacement requires rebuilding the system from scratch and is resource intensive. Replacement is carried out when reengineering is not possible or cost-effective. Systems can be replaced incrementally where reengineering works as a preparatory step before beginning an incremental replacement effort.

2.2.3 Software Complexity and Modern Software Paradigms

In the past decades, software developers created massive, monolithic software programs that often performed a wide variety of tasks. Difficulties in designing, implementing and launching computer-based systems increase exponentially with the size of the system. However, there has been a shift from the development of massive programs containing millions of lines of code, to smaller, modular, pieces of code, where each module performs a well defined, focused task or a small set of tasks, rather than thousands of different tasks, as used to be the case with old legacy systems. The computer industry is always looking for ways to handle complexity and improve software development productivity as well as the quality and longevity of the software that it creates. Object-orientation, component-based development, patterns, and distributed computing infrastructures are examples of new approaches that have aided in this quest [13]. Of course, these modern software paradigms are also capable of dealing with changes.

Since the birth of modern computers, it has been witnessed the progressive move from low-level abstractions to high-level. In terms of mainstream programming, there has been a progressive move from structured programming to object-oriented programming, and more recently to agent-oriented programming. It can be predicted that more advanced software development paradigms will be available in the future and therefore that evolution techniques for emerging development paradigms will be needed. In the following sections, we will introduce object-oriented, component-based, service-oriented, and agent-based techniques, which are the mainstreams at current stage [23]. When software evolution is carried out, techniques needed may relate to these paradigms directly or indirectly.

2.2.3.1 Object Oriented Paradigm

An object-oriented approach to the development of software was first proposed in the late 1960s. However, it took almost 20 years for object technologies to become widely used. As time passes, object-oriented technologies are replacing classical software development approaches [50]. Object-oriented software is easier to maintain because its structure is inherently decoupled. This leads to fewer side effects when changes have to be made and less frustration for the software engineer and the customer.

2.2.3.2 Component-based Paradigm

Component-based paradigm is probably one of the most significant techniques that have occurred during the last decade. Components target the large-scale composition of software, while maintaining simplicity in that composition. Software components aim to succeed in the area of software reuse. Components are neither an alternative nor competing with object-oriented programming. These are two orthogonal and complementary concepts. Software components are all about binary reuse, strict interface/implementation separation and application development by assembly, while object-oriented programming is an approach for fine-grained code development: the coding of core routines, algorithms and data structures. Object-oriented programming can be used for component development and even as glue between components. From a view of software evolution, an important property of components is that the interfaces also hide the age of the components, permitting cooperation of legacy components and newly created system parts. This also implies that there should be a strong relationship between techniques for reengineering and techniques for construction.

2.2.3.3 Service Oriented Paradigm

As defined by the World Wide Web Consortium, A Web service is a software system identified by a URI, whose public interfaces and bindings are defined and described using XML [62]. Its definition can be discovered by other software systems. These systems may then interact with the Web service in a manner prescribed by its definition, using XML based messages conveyed by Internet protocols.

Web services are software building blocks that can be assembled to construct the next generation of distributed business applications. Web services rely on the functionalities of publish, find, bind and the components of a Web Service model include Service Providers, Service Broker and Service Requester. Web Services are defined by their interfaces in particular about how they describe their functionality, how they register their presence, and how they communicate with other Web Services. People who want to use Web Services could connect to the Universal Description Discovery and Integration (UDDI) centre to search for the required services. The information about the Web Services described by Web Service Description Language (WSDL) can be acquired. And the users could use the Simple Object Access Protocol (SOAP) to transfer the requirement information and receive the real service [61].

Today, Web services are emerging as the new "standard" architectural style. This new architectural style and the software lifecycle it implies are extremely attractive because they can effectively address the demands for short development cycles, distributed development and global user base, at the same time [58]. The Service Oriented Architecture (SOA) is the most flexible approaches based on the following reasons [19]:

- reduction of interface complexity,
- decentralised software development,
- explicit separation of business logic and service mediation logic, and
- technical independency of service participants.

Using Web services technologies to implement a distributed system does not magically turn distributed object architecture into SOA, nor are Web services technologies necessarily the best choice for implementing SOAs. Nevertheless, Web services are increasingly becoming an adequate technology for the partial implementation of features of an SOA.

2.2.3.4 Agent-based Paradigm

An agent is an encapsulated computer system that is situated in a certain environment and that is capable of flexible, autonomous action in that environment in order to meet its design objectives. A multi-agent system (MAS) can be defined as a loosely coupled network of entities that work together to make decisions or solve problems that are beyond the individual capabilities or knowledge of each entity [25]. Individual agents are easier to construct and understand than large monolithic systems and agent-oriented approaches can significantly enhance the ability to model, design and build complex, distributed software systems. Because of the autonomy and intelligent nature of agents, agent-oriented techniques are a design metaphor for Web services, where agents are needed both to provide services, and to make best use of the resources available. A number of efforts have recently begun to integrate the agent and Web service communities, which enable agents to use Web services' infrastructure and to extend the Web services model with the benefits of agent technology [7].

2.3 Software Reengineering and Terminology

Reengineering is necessary when we are confronted with *legacy systems*. These are systems that are still valuable, but are notoriously difficult to maintain. The goal of reengineering is thus to come to a new software system that is more evolvable, and possibly has more functionality, than the original software system. The reengineering process is typically composed of three activities, as captured by the so-called *horseshoe model*. First, reverse engineering may be necessary when the technological platform of the software system (language, tools, machines, operating system) is outdated, or when the original developers are no longer available. This activity is typically followed by a phase of *software restructuring* in which we try to improve crucial aspects of the system. Finally, in a *forward engineering* phase we build a new running system based on the new, restructured, model.

There are a number of techniques related to software reengineering. All of them aim at supporting the understanding and the reuse of assets from the previous development. Without covering all of them, the following key terms provide a clear scope and taxonomy of the domain of software reengineering [3, 9, 54, 55, 76]:

- *Reengineering* is the examination and alteration of a subject system to reconstitute it in a new form and the subsequent implementation of the new form. The process of reengineering computing systems involves three main steps: reverse engineering, restructuring, and forward engineering.
- *Forward engineering* is the traditional process of moving from high-level abstractions and logical, implementation-independent designs to the physical implementation of a system.

- *Reverse engineering* is the process of analysing a subject system to (1) identify the system's components and their interrelationships and (2) create representations of the system in another form or higher level of abstraction.
- *Restructuring* or *refactoring* is the transformation from one representation form to another at the same relative abstraction level, while preserving the subject system's external behaviour (i.e., functionality and semantics) yet improves its internal structure. Refactoring makes reuse of both the domain knowledge and the source code.
- *Program understanding* or *program comprehension* is a term related to reverse engineering. Program understanding implies that understanding begins with the source code while reverse engineering can start at a binary and executable form of the system or at high-level descriptions of the design. Program understanding is comparable with design recovery because both of them start at source code level.
- *Design recovery* or *reverse design* is a subset of reverse engineering. Design recovery recreates design abstractions from a combination of code, existing design documentation (if available), personal experience, and general knowledge about problem and application domains.
- *Program transformation* is an act of changing one program into another. The term program transformation is also used for a formal description of an algorithm that implements program transformation. The languages in which the program being transformed and the resulting program are written are called the source and target languages, respectively.
- *Model transformation* is a mapping of a set of models onto another set of models or onto themselves, which can be broken into two broad categories: model translation and model rephrasing. In the former, a model is transformed into a model of a different language, and in the latter, a model is changed in same modelling language.
- *Redocumentation* is the creation or revision of a semantically equivalent representation within the same relative abstraction level. The resulting forms of representation are usually considered alternate views (for example, data flow, data structures, and control flow) intended for a human audience. Redocumentation is the simplest and oldest form of reverse engineering and can be considered to be an unintrusive, weak form of restructuring.
- *Reverse specification* is a kind of reverse engineering where a specification is abstracted from the source code or design description. Specification in this context means an abstract description of what the software does. In forward engineering, the specification tells us what the software has to do. However, this information is not included in the source code. Only in rare cases, it can be recovered from comments in the source code and from the people involved in the original forward engineering process.
- *Recode* involves changing the implementation characteristic of the source code. Language translation and control flow restructuring are source-code-level

changes. Other possible changes include conforming to coding standards, improving source code readability, and renaming program items.

- *Redesign* involves changing the design characteristics. Possible changes include restructuring a design architecture, altering a system's data model as incorporated in data structures or in a database, and improving an algorithm.
- *Respecify* involves changing the requirement characteristics. This type of change can refer to changing only the form of existing requirements (i.e., taking informal requirements expressed in English and generating a formal specification expressed in a formal language, such as Z). This type of change can also refer to changing system requirements, such as the addition of new requirements, or the deletion or alteration of existing requirements.

3 The State of the Art

In this section, we will elaborate software evolution themes by reviewing the state of the art. We have tried to explore current trends of software evolution in the UK and USA and then discuss demanding issues in software evolution research.

3.1 Research Methods

This section discusses the research methods applied in the studies of software evolution, which link the new knowledge coming from research to the process leading to outcomes. Software evolution belongs to software engineering, aiming to be a rigorous discipline and enable the successful production of software (high quality products at the lowest possible cost). Being a kind of computer science and like all kinds of engineering, the majority of software engineering research is constructive. Constructive research refers to the new contributions being developed. A new contribution can be a new theory, algorithm, model, framework or a method. Since software engineering always involves complex action and interaction of human beings, empirical research is also required to investigate such situation. Hence, the research methods in software evolution research area include both empirical and constructive research.

There are two prevalent views on software evolution, often referred to as the 'what' and 'why' versus the 'how' perspectives [11, 32, 33]. The 'what' and 'why' view focuses on software evolution as a scientific discipline. It studies the nature of the software evolution phenomenon, and seeks to understand its driving factor, its impact, and so on. It requires interdisciplinary research involving non-technical aspects such as human psychology, social interaction, complexity theory, organisational aspects, legislation and many more. The 'how' view focuses on software evolution as an engineering discipline. It studies the more pragmatic aspects that aid the software developer or project manager by providing and improving means, processes, activities, languages, methods, tools to direct, implement and control software evolution.

3.2 Two Approaches

3.2.1 Formal Methods

Formal methods can be defined as mathematically based languages, techniques, and tools for specifying and verifying systems. Baumann [4] states that reverse engineering methods must be based on a sound foundation, which entails formal denotation semantics, because if these methods should extract the wrong information during reverse engineering process, this wrong information could lead to new errors in the reengineered programs. Formal methods can also increase the understanding of a system by revealing inconsistencies, ambiguities, and incompleteness that might go undetected [10]. In the area of reverse engineering, formal methods have been put forward as a means to

- formally specify and verify existing systems in particular those already operating in safety-critical applications,
- introduce new functionalities, and/or
- take advantage of the improvement in systems design techniques [97].

Formal methods can be classified into the following five classes or types, i.e., Model-based, Logic-based, Algebraic, Process Algebra and Net-based (Graphical) methods, which should consist of some essential components: a semantic model, a specification language (notation), a verification system/refinement calculus, development guidelines and supporting tools [76]:

- The semantic model is a sound mathematical/logical structure within which all terms, formulas and rules used have a precise meaning. The semantic model should reflect the underlying computational model of the intended application.
- The specification language is a set of notations which are used to describe the intended behaviour of the system. This language must have a proper semantics within the semantic model.
- Verification system/refinement calculi are sound rules that allow the verification of properties and/or the refinement of specifications.
- Development guidelines are steps showing the use of the method.
- Supporting tools involve proof assistant, syntax and type checker, animator, and prototype.

There are at least two advantages of using formal methods as the foundation of software reengineering. First, formal methods can help software engineers to acquire a rigorous and precise description of the system being reengineered, therefore greatly increasing the quality of the new system. Second, automation is one of the key goals of reengineering. By applying formal methods, it is possible to automate more of the process of reengineering [76].

3.2.2 Cognitive Method

Compared to formal methods, cognitive methods rely mainly on domain knowledge. In order to jump from one level up to another abstract level in the process of reverse engineering. One has to throw away some information. No method can guarantee that such a throwing away of information is appropriate [41]. This implies that the abstraction is creative work. In order to achieve correct and practical abstraction, a knowledge base is necessary.

A cognitive model describes the mental process or faculty of knowing a software system [51]. A hierarchy of cognitive design elements to support the construction of a mental model was defined in [57], which explains how to improve program understanding by supporting the actions of identifying software artifacts and the relations between them, by browsing code in delocalised plans, and by building abstractions. These actions comprise canonical reverse-engineering activities.

Two common approaches to program understanding are a functional approach emphasising cognition by what a system does and a behavioural approach emphasising how a system performs [51].

- The functional approach is bottom up and deductive, relying more on the knowledge of the implementation domain to produce higher level of abstractions that may map to the application domain and the system's functional requirements.
- The behavioural approach is top down and inductive, using hypothesis postulation and refinement to match artifacts derived from knowledge of the application domain onto the related software system.

3.3 Research Domains

In order to provide an overview of important research themes in software evolution, we summarise some of the most important research domains listed below [1, 2, 12, 29, 31, 45]:

- *Requirements evolution.* The main objectives of *requirements engineering* are defining the purpose of a software system that needs to be implemented. Requirements evolve because requirements engineers and users cannot predict all possible uses of a system, because not all needs and (often mutually conflicting) goals of the various stakeholders can be taken into account, and because the environment in which the software is deployed frequently changes as well.

- *Architecture evolution.* Based on a description of the software requirements, the overall software architecture (or high-level design) and the corresponding (low-level) technical design of the system can be specified. These are inevitably subject to evolution as well.
- *Runtime evolution.* Many commercial software systems that are deployed by large companies need to be constantly available. Halting the software system to make changes cannot be afforded. Therefore, techniques are needed to change the software while it keeps on running. This very challenging problem is known under a variety of terms, including *runtime evolution, runtime reconfiguration, dynamic adaptation* and *dynamic upgrading.*
- *Language evolution.* When looking at languages, a number of research directions come to mind. The first one is the issue of co-evolution between software and the language that is used to represent it. The second challenge is to provide more and better support for evolution in the context of multi-language software systems. A third challenge is to improve the design of languages to make them more robust to evolution. This was the case for object-oriented programming, aspect-oriented programming, component-oriented programming, and so on.
- *Data evolution.* In information systems and other data-intensive software systems it is essential to have a clear and precise description of the database schema. So it explores in detail how to evolve such schemas.
- *Software evolution process.* This research is to find the software process model that is most appropriate to facilitate software evolution [2], which aims to reduce cost, effort and time-to-market, to increase productivity and reliability, or to affect any other relevant properties.
- *Software evolution management.* If proper support for measuring quality is available, this can provide crucial information to determine whether the software quality is degrading, and to take corrective actions if this turns out to be the case. Numerous software metrics have been proposed, studied and validated as measures of software quality characteristics such as complexity, cohesion, coupling, size and many others [12, 52]
- *Modernisation with new paradigms.* SOA provides a new paradigm in which a user-oriented approach to software is taken. The software is developed in terms of which services are needed by particular users, and these users should be able to easily add, remove or adapt services to their needs. A service-oriented approach thus promises to be inherently more flexible than what is available today. Other development paradigms such as agile software development, aspect-oriented software development, model-driven software development, agent-oriented development, and many more can provide productivity, higher quality, and more adaptable and maintainable software.

3.4 Representative Reengineering Environments

3.4.1 Maintainer's Assistant and FermaT

One of the most important successes of Maintainer's Assistant (MA) [6, 75, 76] is that it is based on a wide spectrum language, which defines syntax and semantics formally. Maintainer's Assistant (MA) employs transformation techniques to derive a specification from a section of code and to transform a section of code into a logically equivalent form. MA has features as follows:

- It acts, initially, on existing program code as a tool to aid comprehension (possibly by producing specifications) and only the program code is required for the processing;
- The system can work with any language by first translating, i.e., with a stand-alone translator into WSL and changes are made to the WSL program by means of transformation;
- The system incorporates a large, flexible catalogue of transformations. The applicability of each transformation is tested before it can be applied;
- The system is interactive and incorporates an X-Windows front end and pretty printer called the Browser;
- The system includes a database structure to store information about the program being transformed, such as the variables assigned to within a given piece of code;
- The system includes a facility to calculate metrics for the code being transformed.

Maintainer's Assistant has evolved into an industrial-strength reengineering tool, FermaT [71, 72, 76], which allows transformations and code simplification to be carried out automatically. The FermaT tool was also designed to use WSL and has applications in the following areas:

- Improving the maintainability of existing mission-critical software.
- Translating programs into modern programming languages. FermaT often translates program written in obsolete assembler language to more modern languages such as C.
- Extracting reusable components from the current system, deriving their specifications, and storing the specifications, implementation, and development strategy.
- Reverse engineering existing systems to high-level specifications, followed by subsequent reengineering and evolutionary development.

3.4.2 CStar and Elbereth

Both CStar and Elbereth [16] are the results of the research conducted at the Software Engineering Laboratory of University of California at San Diego. Elbereth is a Java Reengineering Tool based on Star Diagrams. It provides powerful ways to view all the uses of a variable, method or class in the context in which it is used. It also supports the recording and recall of plans for system-wide changes, meaning that the tool not only provides visualisations of a program, but of a programmer's work as well. CStar is a C Reengineering Tool based on Star Diagrams. It provides much the same functionality as Elbereth, but for C. It is more mature in some ways, supporting capabilities such as building a star diagram for all variables of a particular type.

They based their approach to reverse engineering on abstraction, and identified three kinds of abstractions: problem domain, structural, and logical. Problem domain abstractions correspond to concepts from a program's application area. Structural abstractions are used to eliminate implementation details and redundant information. Logical abstractions are properties that can be logically derived from code.

The goal in logical abstraction is not to generate abstract program description, but to be able to determine the validity of specified properties of a program's context/action pairs.

3.4.3 Chopshop Project

The Chopshop project [24] is carried out in the School of Computer Science, Carnegie Mellon University. It aims at providing practical analysis and visualisation tools to assist with real software engineering task. Chopshop is guided by a number of aspirations:

- To focus on commonly-used programming languages.
- To provide analysis that is efficient even when applied to very large systems.
- To provide analyses with firm theoretical foundations-the results of the analyses should be translated into claims about the behaviour of analysed programs.
- To present results at different levels of abstraction appropriate for the task at hand.

A program slicing tool Chopshop has been built, which computes the dataflow dependencies of C code and displays them using a variety of abstraction mechanisms. Chopshop is a reverse engineering tool to help programmers understand unfamiliar C code. A new dataflow analysis technique is developed, which is a modular generalisation of static program slicing. It gives more understandable results than standard formulations of slicing. The user can select several sources and sinks of information, and Chopshop shows how data flows from the sources to the sinks.

3.4.4 Rigi Project

The Rigi-Environment (also known as Rigi-System) [46] is a reverse engineering tool developed over more than ten years within the framework of the Rigi-Project at the University of Victoria. The Rigi-Environment uses reverse engineering to reconstruct the architectural features of a legacy system. The structure of software is defined as an accumulation of architectural features to build a mental image or model of the software system. In other words the Rigi-Environment is a reverse engineering system to extract, navigate through, analyse and document the structure of a software system.

The Rigi-Environment is very flexible and was created to be used in several domains. This can be for example database systems, graphic systems or operating systems. It is also very scalable, which means it is able to handle large legacy systems with up to 5 million lines of code. The Rigi-Environment is able to split a system into different viewpoints. This can help the user to understand the relationship between the structural elements. A viewpoint of a system can be provided in different ways (views) like resource-flow relationships or flow charts. The Rigi-Environment also provides the possibility to show several abstraction levels of the same view.

3.4.5 PURe Project

The aim of the PURe research project is to develop calculi for program understanding and reengineering. Formal techniques that have traditionally been developed for and applied to forward engineering of software are applied in reverse direction, i.e. for the understanding and reengineering of existing (legacy) program code.

The UMinho Haskell Software is a repository of software, written in the functional programming language Haskell, which is being developed in the context of various research and educational projects. The objective is to enable use and reuse of software across project boundaries. In particular, software developed in the context of the Research. PURe Project is collected into the UMS repository and the UMS repository is roughly partitioned into two parts:

- Libraries: a hierarchical library of reusable modules.
- Tools: a collection of tools.

The libraries offer reusable functionality. Each tool bundles part of the library functionality behind an interactive or command-line interface.

3.4.6 Renaissance Project

The Renaissance project at Lancaster University is an ESPRIT funded research project into software reengineering and software evolution. The principle business objectives of the Renaissance partners are to improve their capability to offer commercial services in the area of system evolution and to increase their return on investment in their software assets. To meet these objectives, the Renaissance project has established the following technical objective:

- Support application evolution from centralised to distributed client-server architectures.
- Support the recovery of system family designs and subsequent evolution using existing CASE tools.
- Support evolution through the reuse of sub-systems recycled from existing systems.
- Provide a method for project managers to assess the costs, risks and benefits of evolution options.
- Integrate all of this support into a systematic method to support system evolution.

3.4.7 ISVis (Interaction Scenario Visualiser)

The purpose of ISVis is to support the browsing and analysis of execution scenarios, derived from actual program executions. It is useful during software engineering tasks requiring a behavioural understanding of programs, such as design recovery, architecture localisation, design/implementation validation, and reengineering. The key features of ISVis are its use of visualisation techniques to depict the large amounts of information available to a user, and the notion of recurring scenarios, or "interaction patterns", as abstractions which help bridge the gap between low-level event traces and high-level design models. Users of the system might be software designers, programmers, testers, or maintainers. The process of using ISVis requires several phases:

- static analysis of the subject program
- instrumentation of the source code to track interesting events
- usage of the instrumented system in particular scenarios to generate program event traces
- analysis of the event traces using the ISVis graphical views
- recording of models created by the user

While this system is intended to handle object-oriented (OO) programs, its architecture allows for "global" functions, meaning that a completely procedural program can be analysed as well. The interaction events being analysed include messages (function invocation/return), and can be extended to object creation/destruction and data read/write.

3.4.8 SNiFF+ (Wind River Workbench)

SNiFF+ is an open, extensible and scalable cross-platform source code engineering tool for C, C++, FORTRAN, Java, CORBAIDL and other languages. The main goal in developing SNiFF+ was to create an efficient and portable environment with a comfortable user interface. SNiFF+ is tailored for large multi-developers projects.

Wind River Workbench, Desktop Edition is Wind River's development suite for native application development. It is the next-generation product based on the Eclipse platform, and replaces the SNiFF+ product line. Workbench, Desktop Edition retains most of the features of SNiFF+ while providing enhanced functionality.

3.4.9 Imagix 4D

Imagix 4D helps software developers understand complex or legacy C, C++ and Java software. By using Imagix 4D to reverse engineer and document your code, you're able to speed your development, enhancement, reuse, and testing. Eliminate bugs due to faulty comprehension. Get new hires on board faster. Spend time engineering, not reading through code.

A comprehensive program understanding tool, Imagix 4D enables you to rapidly check or systematically study your software on any level - from its high level architecture to the details of its build, class, and function dependencies. You can visually explore a wide range of aspects about your software - control structures, data usage, and inheritance. You can review the software metrics and quality checks to identify and eliminate problem areas in your software. You're also able to create design documentation automatically; further leveraging the information Imagix 4D collects about your software.

3.5 Demanding Issues

One of the main difficulties of software evolution is that all artifacts produced and used during the entire software life-cycle are subject to changes, ranging from early requirements over analysis and design documents, to source code and executable code. Much attention should be paid to the following demanding issues when a software system is evolved:

- the evolved system should be reliable,
- the evolved system should be functional,
- the evolved system should be efficient, and
- the cost of evolution should be acceptable.

The above issues must be satisfied; otherwise, it leads to high cost of a software system and sometimes, it implies the redesign of the whole system, which requires huge investment, with significant risk that the new systems may fail to deliver the required services [43].

4 Research of Software Evolution in China

Since the beginning of the 90's, the scale of software system becomes larger, the structure becomes more complex, and the lifetime becomes longer in China. The number of systems constructing from scratch reduces while developing on existing systems increases gradually. Chinese software developers have realised the importance of the software evolution and many scientists and scholars are engaging in software reengineering research. Among them are researchers in Beijing University, Central South University, Institute of Computing Technology (ICT) in Chinese Academy of Sciences, Dalian University of Technology, Fudan University, Jilin University, Nanjing University, Nanjing University of Aeronautics and Astronautics, Northeastern University, University of Science and Technology of China, Shanghai Jiaotong University, South East University, Xi'an Jiaotong University, Xi'an University of Technology, Yunnan University and Zhejiang University. We will discuss them in detail in the following sections.

4.1 Software Requirement Change and Domain Analysis

It's a persistent aim and basis of software evolution for software developer to control software change. Jiong Jia introduces a new object-oriented requirement analysis method, the ORDIT modelling method [26]. Changing objects based on use case are identified by Yinhui Wang, who describes the changes of functional requirement [65, 66]. A strategy of scope decision of changing components is addressed and a tracing approach of change information is presented. Several important properties of software change propagation in software lifecycle are clarified as well. Figure 1 shows the evolution process by software requirement change.

The systematic approach for achieving the goals of using the domain knowledge is called Domain Engineering. Domain engineering does not serve only the building of new systems; it also enables systematic use and reuse of the domain knowledge in order to support the establishment, maintenance and evolution of software systems. There exist many different domain models such as domain feature model, domain functional model, domain dynamic model, domain object model, domain information model, domain data dictionary, etc. However, feature modelling is considered as the greatest contribution of domain engineering to software engineering. In order to identify the relation among software requirements, a approach based on feature traces in software evolution is proposed by Wangen Huang [22].

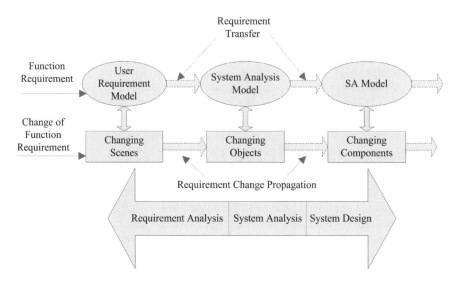

Figure 1 Evolution process by software requirement change

4.2 Software Architecture Evolution

Software evolution consists of a series of complex change activities. Software complexity decides that the research of managing software evolution should start from software architecture level, which is the early production of software life cycle. It is much necessary to study software architecture evolution management deeply [42].

Software architecture based method for software evolution is becoming main trend method for evolving large complex systems. Well defined components are the prerequisites to applying the method. In the component based software development, we may add components, delete components and modify different relations of components to achieve software evolution [86]. The relations among the components can be represented with basic component operations so that software architecture can be abstracted as the component algebra structure [83, 84]. According to the messages which a component can receive and send, the component interface definition framework is extended by Wangen Huang and Songqiao Chen to depict four kinds of composition operations and six kinds of component evolution operations formally. Meanwhile a component composition model based on messages is employed, and component running paths are defined [21].

The study of software architecture evolution management by Xiaohua Zhang shows that software architecture evolution management mainly contains five parts [82]: multiple versions, optional component, variant component, optional and variant component and the relation of/between optional component and variant component. An integration model SAEM (Software Architecture Evolution Management) is proposed, which integrates architectural and configuration management concepts in a single representation. All architectural changes can be precisely captured and clearly related to each other at both the fine-grained level of individual architectural elements and at the coarse-grained level of architectural configurations. Yan Zhang has analysed the demand of component evolution for the software configuration management and managed the relations of the components with the direct chart for tracing the relations of the components and the evolution [85]. Xin Peng has paid attention that component library plays an important role in the Component Based Software Development (CBSD) [49]. However, there are still some difficulties in practice when reusing, maintaining and adapting components. A main difficulty is that most component libraries are lack of Configuration Management (CM) support. Hence a configuration management framework, which can put component libraries under systematic version and configuration management, is presented in [87].

Gang Li proposed a transformation approach used to generate formal component specification automatically [36]. The completeness of specification and correctness of transformation is given in [64]. The proposed approach can control the granularity and span of transformation better, and confirm the completeness of specification and correctness of transformation to some extent. Meanwhile vertical reuse is implemented during the course of the transformation, and the models and specifications built by it have some adaptability to requirement variation. Yinghui Wang et al studied the ripple-effect analysis of the software architecture evolution which is based on the reachable matrix [68, 69]. An analysis framework for ripple effect of software architecture evolution on two levels is proposed, which is the foundation to manage, control, utilise, measure software architecture evolution in quantity [14, 37, 60].

4.3 Runtime Evolution

Most researches on runtime evolution are also based on software architecture (SA). As Internet and wireless network make the runtime environment much more dynamic and open, software becomes more and more complex and difficult to maintain. Gang Huang, Hong Mei, Fuqing Yang etc. proposed a software maintenance and evolution method based on Software architecture at run-time (RSA), which is implemented by reflective software middleware [20]. RSA can help maintainers understand and reason the run-time system. Moreover, RSA helps to keep SA consistent in the whole software lifecycle. RSA regards component and connection as "white box" entities to describe running system accurately and completely, and meantime, expand traditional SA description language to describe RSA from the view of formal.

Xinlin Ye, Wenyun Zhao, Tao Jiang [78] have carried on the technical analysis in view of architecture's evolution and the reconfiguration, which supports to add, delete, replace component and change component type dynamically.

Inspired by typing system and process construction methods of Pi-calculus, Hongquan Gong and Yueqiu Qian proposed an interaction based component model [34, 35]. To ensure the correctness of interaction behaviours of component ports and channels, service port type and channel type are introduced. Meanwhile the static and dynamic evolution rules are proposed and method for recovering from inconsistent state is presented. Under the frame of the D-ADL [15], the refinement relations among different levels guarantee the application integrity and the evolution uniformity.

Online evolution supported by a dynamic software architecture is proposed in [79]. Ping Yu indicates that architecture information is reified as explicit and manipulability entities to organise a runtime architecture meta-model, which is causally connected to software implementation and specification. By using reflection mechanism, the evolved architecture meta-model modifies running system, and updates specification simultaneously to ensure system consistency, integrity, and evolution traceability. Based on this model, a visualised integrated development platform entitled Artemis-ARC is also successfully implemented [59]. It supports component and service design, development and assembly for dynamic evolution.

4.4 Software Evolution Process

4.4.1 Software Evolution Process Model

At present, the research and improvement of the software process have already become a hotspot in software engineering field. Tong Li form Yunnan University proposes an approach to modelling and describing software evolution processes [38]. A formal software process model was constructed to effectively support software evolution. Six progresses have been made in this research:

- Firstly, five important properties of software evolution processes are analysed.
- Secondly, a Petri Net is extended with object-oriented technology and Hoare Logic and a formal evolution process meta-model (EPMM) is proposed.
- Thirdly, based on EPMM, an object-oriented evolution process modelling language (EPML) is designed.
- Fourthly, based on EPMM and EPML, a semi-formal approach to modelling software evolution processes is proposed.
- Fifthly, an approach is proposed to capture and extend concurrency in an inefficient model segment.
- Finally, an approach is proposed to decompose a function into a code segment which consists of finer functions which are easy to be realised.

Yao Guo etc from Beijing University have given the definition of software reengineering and the process model [18]. They propose a software reengineering framework and give the activity what should be considered in the entire process of carrying on a software reengineering practice.

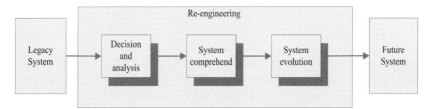

Figure 2 Basic framework of software reengineering

Figure 2 gives a basic framework of software reengineering process. A software reengineering process mainly consists of three parts that are decision-making analysis, system understanding and system evolution.

Ping Yang etc. from Shanghai Jiaotong University carried on research on the analysis and design of software evolution process [77]. The proposed process model supports software parallel engineering on four aspects: standardising, the role model, resources model, stratification, which supports the progress of standardisation, configurable software evolution.

A new method is proposed by Yousheng Zhang and Xiong Li, using algebra theory to research the evolution process of software system and provide methods that express the results of evolution by graphs [39, 40].

4.4.2 Software Evolution Operational Language

The description of software evolution operation has become the hot spot of Software Evolution research. It supports the automation of software evolution for enhancing the visibility of the software evolution activity, through the records of software evolution operation activity. Shengbin Ren etc. [53] from Central South University have conducted the research based on logical and software architecture operational semantics. A Software Evolution Operational Language (SEOL) is proposed to describe the software evolution operations. The syntax and structural operational semantics of SEOL are studied; what's more, a method to analyse the semantic equivalence is also illustrated. The application of SEOL is described through two instances: program evolution and model evolution. SEOL has rigorous grammar and explicit semantics and its semantics equivalence analysis methods are simple and feasible. SEOL has already developed its editor and analysis tool as a plug-in unit in Eclipse platform.

4.4.3 Software Evolution Metrics or Measurement

Software measurement can evaluate software evolution process to gain the understanding and make the software in control [88]. Measurement of software can also predict software evolution process and evaluate other elements from known characteristics. Improving analysis by measuring data is helpful to ensure efficiency in software involution process [22]. Software involution is to add new characteristics in software system to meet the new demands or remove some unused characteristics. It is not only a process which generates from nothing to something, but also a process which transforms the software. Lingxiao Zheng and Tong Li have also conducted research of measurement in supporting software evolution process and strategy by data gathering that improves original software system to adapt to the changed circumstance [89]. From software process viewpoint, there are two data collecting strategies: Top-Down way and Bottom-Up way [8].

4.5 Software Evolution with Modern Techniques

4.5.1 Agent based Software Evolution

An agent based model (including software evolution based on agent model, modelling and analysing multi-agents system and dynamism of multi-agents system) for software evolution caused by change of computing environment is proposed by Jianfeng Zhan [80, 81].

Firstly, an architecture description language, MA ADL, which is based on CSP formalism and suitable for multi-agents system, has been proposed. In MA ADL, the organisation and behaviours of multi-agents system are specified and analysed on four different abstraction levels: component, agent, organisation and system.

Secondly, from a perspective of software architecture, the dynamism of multi-agents system is defined on four different dimensions. Through decomposing the system into four different dimensions, the span of multi-agents system can be divided into static segment and dynamic change segment.

Thirdly, a new dynamic reconfiguration method is proposed. With the efforts in the phase of agent-oriented modelling and analysing, mutual dependency and cyclic dependency relationship can be reduced to linear dependency ones. Several cases show that the legacy system can adapt to new environment through the new requirement and adapting its low-level technology.

4.5.2 AOP based Software Evolution

Software system is often required to add some new public functions which are distributed in many components of the system. A general method is to insert code into each corresponding class, which would be a trivial task but may increase the risk of introducing errors and destroy the structure of the system. To solve this problem, an Aspect-Oriented Programming (AOP) based software evolution approach based on .NET is introduced by He Guo [17]. By using joinpoints, the proposed approach can insert new code into the evolving system without any modifications to the existing class structures. This method can avoid directly modifying the original code, reduce errors, and protect the structure of system [63].

4.5.3 SOA based Software Evolution

Service-oriented computing in Internet open environment has brought new business model. Xiaoxing Ma, Ping Yu, Xianping Tao, Jian Lv proposed a concerted dynamic coordination service-oriented architecture [44] to refine the original abstract software architecture specification into a built-in runtime architecture. On the one hand it preserved the information of the system architecture for evolution decision. On the other hand it made full use of inheritance and polymorphism, and facilitated the system dynamic adjustment. By using this technology in Web services and enterprise computing environment, they design and implement a corresponding support platform with characteristics of the dynamic service based software evolution.

4.5.4 Internetware

Under the influence of application, platform and technological development, the configuration of software evolves unceasingly. As a result of the popularisation of the Internet as a new computation environment, the traditional software configuration is gradually unable to adapt the development and application under the environment of Internet, therefore the new configuration and technology of software need to be studied. The Internetware based on the environment of Internet is the trend of development of the software in the future. For this new software configuration, Professor Fuqing Yang of Beijing University, Professor Jian Lv of Nanjing University, Zhi Jin of Chinese Academy of Science Mathematics Research institute, Leqiu Qian of Fudan University all have made the indication that named it Internetware. Based on the traditional Internet application mode, the Internetware will further deepen the resources sharing under the opening environment, regard content of the information, application, computation resources and service connection as the network resources, implement the spanning from information Web to Software Web through the connection of resources [74].

Internetware is built upon the coordination of the heterogeneous, autonomous software entities in the open coordination environment. But it is very difficult to select the honest coordination software entities with dependable quality of services to build the trusted Internetware because of the openness and dynamic of the Internet. Trust relationships among software entities will provide important information about the selections of trusted coordination entities. The trust relationships are always changing along with the co-operations of software entities. However, the existing trust models cannot support the automatic formation and update of the trust relationships among entities, and cannot reflect the dynamic attribute of the trust relationships. Yuan Wang, Jian Lv etc. present a trust measurement and evolution model for the Internetware [67]. The model abstracts the process of the trust measurement, transfer and combination rationally and provides a reasonable approach to form and update trust relationships automatically. This model is helpful to solve the problem of the trustworthiness of the Internetware.

4.6 Data Evolution

Data is an important issue of the software evolution. Zhongqun Wang studied the data-driven mechanism for software reuse and data evolution, which makes Information system more flexible and meet user requirements [70]. This technology is based on object-oriented data dictionary used to control the dataflow to achieve the greatest degree of software reuse, including software design, coding, testing and documentation, etc. The framework has been developed [73], focusing on data evolution with information exchange standards XML and XML schema. The method has been introduced to large institutions or enterprises software evolution projects, providing a comprehensive and scientific guidance.

4.7 Tools Developed in China

Academic and Industry both have developed a number of tools for software reengineering. Some of them have been introduced in previous section, e.g. Rigi, IS-Vis, Sniff +, Imagix4D. A couple of reengineering tools have been developed by Chinese researchers and engineers. The majority of these tools support static reverse engineering. Three of Chinese developed tools will be introduced as follows:

4.7.1 JBPAS (Jade Bird Program Analysis System)

Jade Bird project [20, 89], by the leading commitment of Peking University, is the key technological research projects in China. The core of Jade Bird project is developing integration assembly environment of application system based on reusable components, Jade Bird Software Production Line System, including software industrialized production technology, engineering development, and the corresponding methods support system tools, standards and norms, as well as areas of development platforms, providing the infrastructure for the development of China's software industry.

With the independent intellectual property rights, Jade Bird project is an R & D project that was completed by China, which represents the current highest standard of China's software engineering. JBPAS is one of the main products of Jade Bird project.

JBPAS is reverse engineering tools, which is a component in Jade Bird III system. It is composed of a C++ parser and a group of front-end analysis tools, which can statically analyse C++ programs taking advantage of incremental analysis techniques. It organises information, assists user in understanding and generates object-oriented system design documentation and Rose documents varying from different user requirements [20, 89].

4.7.2 Artemis-ARC

Artemis-ARC is developed by Xiaoxing Ma, Ping Yu, Xianping Tao, Jian Lv in Nanjing University [44]. A dynamic coordination architecture is proposed to facilitate service-oriented applications' dynamic adaptation to the evolving Internet environment and user requirements. The software architecture of a service-oriented application is reified as a first-class runtime object that defines the architectural context for each service or component deployment instance with an intrinsic mechanism. Artemis-ARC provides a visualised integrated environment for the development, execution and monitoring of service-oriented applications and their dynamic adaptations.

4.7.3 SASMSP

In order to adapt to the opening environment of Internet and the variable requirements of users, software systems should be able to adjust themselves dynamically. SASMSP (Software Architecture Space-Based Model Supporting Platform), developed by Changyun Li, Ying Li, Jian Wu and Zhaohui Wu's Research Group in Zhe Jiang University, is designed for this purpose [35]. The core of SASM supporting platform is an architecture based, dynamic evolution oriented software application model, which is constructed by reflection technology. Its meta-level is a layer with tree-like structure, between which there exit refinement relations, and its base-level is composed of physical components. The meta-level and base-level are associated in the form of cause and effect. Different layers of architecture provide views and management means at different abstraction levels to the users, which meet the variable requirement of various roles from management layer to operation layer. The online adjustment can modify base-level so as to evolve application system.

4.8 Observations

During the recent 20 years, researches on software evolution in China achieved very rapid growth. Due to the space limit, many papers and reports reviewed when preparing this section are omitted. Following summary is organised on the research groups in the leading Chinese universities and institutes.

- Fuqing Yang, Hong Mei and Jiaxiao Sun's group in Beijing University are focus on research of software reuse, software reverse engineering, software reengineering and internetware.
- Songqiao Chen, Yousheng Zhang, Wangen Huang's research group works on software component operation and its evolution whose members include both of Central south university and Hunan University.

- In Institute of Software of the Chinese Academy of Sciences, Hu Cheng, Jian-feng Zhan and Mingshu Li pay attention to software dynamic evolution and software process evolution.
- Zhi Jin and Xufeng Zhu's group from Institute of Computing Technology in The Chinese Academy of Sciences researches on software requirement engineering and domain engineering.
- Lifu Wang and Yinghui Wang's group by Beijing University and Xi'an University of Technology is engaged in research of software architecture evolution and software requirement change tracking.
- In Fudan University, the research interests of Leqiu Qian, Wenyun Zhao and Xin Peng's group are software evolution and reuse.
- Jian Lv and Xiaoxing Ma's group in State Key Laboratory for Novel Software Technology of Nanjing University conducts the software dynamic and online evolution researched.
- Baohua Zhao from the Department of Computer Science and Technology of University of Science and Technology of China studies on software reuse and testing.
- Tong Li from Yunnan University gives much more contributions for software evolution process model and metric data collection.

5 Discussion and Recommendations

Software evolution research is playing a very important role in software engineering. To keep the pace with the world, the Chinese academy and industry are facing the great chances and grand challenges. In this section, we hope that the following discussions can provide a red thread for future work by 'when', 'who' and 'what' dimensions.

- With development of Internet, software becomes more open, dynamic and changeable. The software theory, method and techniques will be adjusted accordingly to meet this challenge and software evolution techniques are becoming more and more important. It is time to treat software evolution as a core technology and strengthen software evolution research and practice as a driving force for innovation in China.
- During the literature review of software evolution in China, we found two interesting phenomena: that most researchers working on software evolution in China have cooperated with each other, and that most researchers in China have tight relationships with the overseas Chinese academicians. They are the main forces in software evolution research in China.
- Compared to the UK and USA, there is still a large discrepancy in the area of software evolution research and application. The main problems are:

- The intent of reusing and retrofitting the legacy systems was inadequate: we recommend to strength it by education.
- The knowledge of software engineers was not adequate in general: we recommend to strength it by education.
- Fundamental theoretical researches are rare, e.g. more than 20 years program transformation research for Maintainer's Assistant Environment: we recommend that the funding bodies invest more on fundamental and theoretical research.
- Commercialisation of scientific research results was limited, e.g. FermaT software: we recommend that more technology centres should be established to transfer the research results.

6 Summary

In this chapter, we first give a general overview of software evolution research background and define basic concepts related to software reengineering. Then, we review the state of the art of software evolution research and summarise the software evolution research in China. Finally, based on previous reviews, we show speculations to the hot issues of software evolution in future China. Followings are key points of this chapter:

- Many methods and techniques have been hailed as the solution to the software crisis, however in practice only small gains in productivity have been achieved. The development of new software is outpacing the ability to maintain it, referred as "legacy crisis".
- Software evolution is the sub-domain of the software engineering discipline that investigates ways to adapt software to the ever-changing user requirements and operating environment.
- Change and Complexity are inherent properties of software systems. Software systems continue to grow in complexity at a rapid pace, resulting in systems that are increasingly complex to build and evolve to meet changing requirements.
- The research methods in software evolution research area include both empirical and constructive research.
- Techniques of software evolution can be classified into two groups. They are based on formal or cognitive methods.
- The main difficulty of software evolution is that all artifacts produced and used during the entire software life-cycle are subject to changes, ranging from early requirements over analysis and design documents, to source code and executable code. Hence the most important research domains in software evolution are requirements evolution, architecture evolution, runtime evolution, language evolution, data evolution, software evolution process, software evolution management and modernisation with new paradigms.

- Chinese software developers have realised the importance of the software evolution and many scientists and scholars are engaging in software reengineering research.
- The Chinese government, the industry and the academy should pay more attention on software evolution research and build a more co-operative model to face the grand challenge of software evolution.

References

[1] Abran A, Moore JW, Bourque P et al (2004) Guide to the Software Engineering Body of Knowledge (SWEBOK): IEEE
[2] Ajila SA, Kaba BA (2007) Evolution Support Mechanisms for Software Product Line Process. Journal of Systems and Software
[3] Arnold RS (1992) A Road Map Guide to Software Re-engineering: IEEE Computer Society Press
[4] Baumann P, Fassler J, Kiser M et al (1994) Semantics-based Reverse Engineering. Technical Report 94.08, Department of Computer Science, University of Zurich, Switzerland
[5] Brooks FP (1987) No Silver Bullet: Essence and Accidents of Software Engineering. IEEE Computer 20(4): 10-19
[6] Bull T (1995) An Introduction to the WSL Program Transformer. Technical Report, University of Durham, England
[7] Chen F, Yang H, Guo H et al (2004) "Agentification for Web Service", 28th IEEE International Computer Software and Application Conference (COMPSAC'04), Hong Kong, pp. 514-519
[8] Chen Z (2007) Approach to Measuring Developers during Modeling Formal Software Evolution Process. Computer Engineering and Design 28(21): 5305-5307
[9] Chikofsky EJ, Cross JH (1990) Reverse Engineering and Design Recovery: a Taxonomy. IEEE Software 7(1): 13-17
[10] Clarke EM, Wing JM (1996) Formal Methods: State of the Art and Future Directions. ACM Computing Surveys 28(4): 626-643
[11] Cook S, He J, Rachel H (2001) "Dynamic and Static Views of Software Evolution", IEEE International Conference on Software Maintenance (ICSM'01)
[12] Cook S, Ji H, Harrison R (2000) Software Evolution and Software Evolvability. University of Reading. Technical Report
[13] Frankel DS (2003) Model Driven Architecture - Applying MDA to Enterprise Computing: Wiley Publishing, Inc.
[14] Fu J, Wang Y, Qian L (2001) DCF-Based Component Evolution. Computer Sciences 28(1): 21-24
[15] Gong H, Zhao W, Xu R et al (2004) A Research on Pi Calculus Based Component Evolution. Acta Electronica Sinica 32(12A)
[16] Griswold WG, Chen MI, Bowdidge RW et al (1997) Tool Support for Planning the Restructuring of Data Abstractions in Large Systems. Technical Report CS97-559, Software Engineering Laboratory, University of California at San Diego
[17] Guo H, Liu T, Chen F et al (Mar. 2007) Design and Implementation of a Software Evolution Strategy Based on AOP. Journal of Dalian University of Technology 47(2): 270-275
[18] Guo Y, Yuan W, Chen X et al (1999) Reengineering: Concepts and Framework. Computer Sciences 26(5): 78-83

[19] Herr M, Bath U, Koschel A (2004) "Implementation of a Service Oriented Architecture at Deutsche Post Mail", Lecture Notes in Computer Science 3250, Springer, ECOWS 2004, Erfurt, Germany, pp. 227-238

[20] Huang G, Mei H, Yang F (2004) Runtime Software Architecture Based On Reflective Middleware. Science in China (Series E): Technology Science 34(2): 121-138

[21] Huang W, Chen S (2007) Component Composition Operations and Component Evolution Based on Messages. Journal of Chinese Computer Systems 128(7): 1217-1220

[22] Huang W, Chen S (2007) Measuring Software Architecture Evolution Based on Component Combination Operations. Computer Sciences 34(9): 245-248

[23] Huhns MN (2004) "Software Development with Objects, Agents, and Services", 3rd International Workshop on Agent-Oriented Methodologies (Keynotes), Vancouver, Canada

[24] Jackson D, Rollins EJ (1994) "Abstraction Mechanisms for Pictorial Slicing." IEEE Workshop on Program Comprehension, pp. 82-88

[25] Jennings NR (2000) On Agent-Based Software Engineering. Artificial Intelligence 117: 277-296

[26] Jia J, He X (2003) A Method for Modeling Evolving Requirements. Computer Engineering and Applications 5: 70-72

[27] Lehman MM (1980) "Programs, Life Cycles, and Laws of Software Evolution", IEEE Special Issue on Software Engineering, pp. 1060-1076

[28] Lehman MM (1997) "Laws of Software Evolution Revisited", LNCS 1149, pp. 108-124

[29] Lehman MM, Ramil JF (2001) "An Approach to a Theory of Software Evolution", 4th International Workshop on Principles of Software Evolution

[30] Lehman MM, Ramil JF (2002) "An Overview of Some Lessons Learnt in FEAST", Workshop on Empirical Studies of Software Maintenance (WESS'02)

[31] Lehman MM, Ramil JF (2002) Software Evolution and Software Evolution Processes. Annals of Software Engineering 14(1-4): 275-309

[32] Lehman MM, Ramil JF (2006) Software Evolution and Feedback: Theory and Practice. Chichester, U.K.: John Wiley & Sons

[33] Lehman MM, Ramil JF, Kahen G (2000) "Evolution as a Noun and Evolution as a Verb", Workshop on Software and Organisation Co-evolution (SOCE'00)

[34] Li C (2005) Research on Architecture-Based Software Dynamic Evolution. PhD Thesis, College of Computer Science and Technology, Zhejiang University

[35] Li C, Wu J, Wu Z (2006) A Service-Oriented Software Model Supporting Dynamic Evolution. Chinese Journal of Computer 29(7): 1020-1027

[36] Li G, Liu X (2002) Evolution Transformation in Automatic Generation of Formal Component Specification. Computer Engineering and Applications 8: 69-72

[37] Li H, Li B, Guo R (2007) Application Research of Orthogonal Software Architecture Design and Evolution Method. Application Research of Computers: 78-82

[38] Li T (2007) An Approach to Modelling and Describing Software Evolution Processes. PhD Thesis, De Montfort University, England

[39] Li X (2002) Study on Software Evolution Based on Component Operations. Master Thesis, Hunan University

[40] Li X, Zhang Y (2005) Study on Software Evolution Based on Component Operations. Computer Engineering and Applications 9: 46-48

[41] Li Y (2002) Automating Domain Knowledge Recovery from Legacy Software Code. PhD Thesis, De Montfort University, England

[42] Lin Y, Zhang Y (2006) Research on Software Configuration Management Supporting Evolution of Components. Computer Engineering and Design 27(19): 3595-3597

[43] Liu X, Yang H, Zedan H et al (2000) "Speed and Scale Up Software Reengineering with Abstraction Patterns and Rules", International Symposium on Software Evolution, Japan

[44] Ma X, Yu P, Tao X et al (2005) A Service2Oriented Dynamic Coordination Architecture and Its Supporting System. Chinese Journal of Computer 28(4): 467-471

[45] Mens T, Demeyer S (2008) Software Evolution: Springer

[46] Muller H, Orgun M, Tiley S (1993) A Reverse Engineering Approach to Subsystem Structure Identification. Software Maintenance: Research and Practise 5: 181-204

[47] Parnas DL (1979) Designing Software for Ease of Extension and Contraction. IEEE Transaction on Software Engineering 5(2): 128-138

[48] Parnas DL (1994) "Software Aging", 16th International Conference on Software Engineering, Sorrento, Italy, pp. 279-287

[49] Peng X, Zhao W, Zhu C (2004) A Configuration Management Framework Supporting Evolution of Components. Computer Engineering and Applications 32: 1-4

[50] Pressman RS (2001) Software Engineering: A Practitioner's Approach (5th Ed): McGraw-Hill

[51] Qiao B (2005) Evolution of WEB-based Systems in Model Driven Architecture. PhD Thesis, De Montfort University, England

[52] Ratzinger J, Sigmund T, Vorburger P et al (2007) "Mining Software Evolution to Predict Refactoring", International Symposium on Empirical Software Engineering and Measurement (ESEM'07)

[53] Ren S, Yu S, Chen S et al (2007) Logic-based Software Evolution Operational Language and Structural Operational Semantics. Journal of Chinese Computer Systems 128(6): 1031-1036

[54] Seacord RC, Plakosh D, Lewis GA (2003) Modernizing Legacy Systems: Software Technologies, Engineering Processes, and Business Practices: Addison Wesley

[55] Sendall S, Hauser R, Koehler J et al (2004) "Understanding Model Transformation by Classification and Formalization", Workshop on Software Transformation Systems (part of 3rd International Conference on Generative Programming and Component Engineering), Vancouver, Canada

[56] Sommerville I (1995) Software Engineering, 5th Edition: Addison Wesley

[57] Storey MD, Fracchia FD, Muller HA (1997) "Cognitive Design Elements to Support the Construction of a Mental Model During Software Visualization", 5th Workshop on Program Comprehension (WPC'97), Dearborn, USA, pp. 17-28

[58] Stroulia E, El-Ramly M, Sorenson P (2002) "From Legacy to Web through Interaction Modeling", International Conference on Software Maintenance (ICSM'02), Montrzal, Canada, pp. 320-329

[59] Tan G, Li Y Research on Software Dynamic Evolution and Its Application. Master Thesis, Dalian University of Technology

[60] Tan G, Zhang S (2001) Study on Dynamic Simulation and Evolution of Hierarchical Message Bus Based Software Architecture. Computer Sciences 28(3): 75-77

[61] W3C (2004) Web Services Architecture. http://www.w3.org/TR/2004/NOTE-ws-arch-20040211, W3C Working Group

[62] W3C (2004) Web Services Architecture Requirements. http://www.w3.org/TR/2004/NOTE-wsa-reqs-20040211, W3C Working Group

[63] Wang B, Sheng J, Gui W (2007) Aspect-oriented Software Architecture and Software Process for Management Domain. Computer Engineering and Applications 33(15): 82-85

[64] Wang X, Wang Q, Mei H (2005) An Approach to Online Evolution of Component Based Software. Chinese Journal of Computer 28(11): 1890-1893

[65] Wang Y (2007) Change Propagation Mechanism Analysis of Software Function Requirement. Chinese Journal of Computer 30(11): 2035-2032

[66] Wang Y, Liu Y, Wang L (2004) A Dynamic Evolution Model Based on Static Point Transition. Chinese Journal of Computer 27(11): 12-17

[67] Wang Y, Lv J, Xu F et al (2006) A Trust Measurement and Evolution Model for Internetware. Journal of Software 17(4): 683-690

[68] Wang Y, Wang L (2005) Research about Model and Ripple Effect Analysis of Software Architecture Evolution. Acta Electronica Sinica 33(8): 1381-1386

[69] Wang Y, Zhang S, Liu Y et al (2004) Ripple-Effect Analysis of Software Architecture Evolution Based on Reachability Matrix. Journal of Software 15(8): 1107-1115

[70] Wang Z, Xie X (2003) Software Reuse and Evolution Techniques in MIS. Journal of Anhui University of Technology and Science 18(2): 26-31

[71] Ward M (2001) "The FermaT Assembler Re-engineering Workbench", IEEE International Conference on Software Maintenance (ICSM'01), pp. 659-662

[72] Ward M, Zedan H (2007) Slicing as a Program Transformation. ACM Transactions on Programming Languages and Systems 29(2)

[73] Wu J, Ding Q (2004) Study of System Evolution Environment. Journal of Nanjing University of Aeronautics & Astronautics 36(1): 117-120

[74] Xue Y, Xu R, Qian L (2004) A Summary of Internetware - a New Software Modality under the Internet Computing Environment. Computer Engineering and Applications 14: 38-41

[75] Yang H (1991) "The Supporting Environment for A Reverse Engineering System - The Maintainers Assistant", IEEE Conference on Software Maintenance, Sorrento, Italy, pp. 13-22

[76] Yang H, Ward M (2003) Successful Evolution of Software Systems: Artech House, Inc.

[77] Yang P, Xu L, Chen Y (2002) Analysis and Design of the Evolutions in Software Process. Computer Applications and software 3

[78] Ye X, Zhao W, Jiang T (2004) Research on Dynamic Architecture Technology Supporting Evolution & Re-configuration. Computer Engineering and Applications 7: 95-98

[79] Yu P, Ma X, Lu J et al (2006) A Dynamic Software Architecture Oriented Approach to Online Evolution. Journal of Software 17(6): 1360-1371

[80] Zhan J (2002) Researches on Software Evolution and Dynamism Under the Circumstances of Internet. PhD Thesis, Institue of Software Chinese Academy of Sciences

[81] Zhan J, Cheng H (2006) Specification and Evolution of Agent From a Perspective of Software Architecture. Journal of Computer Research and Development 39(12): 1543-1549

[82] Zhang X (2005) Study on Software Architecture Evolution Management. Master Thesis, Chongqing University

[83] Zhang Y (2004) Architecture-based Software Development Model. Computer Engineering and Applications 34: 29-33

[84] Zhang Y (2004) Study on Component Operations and Software Evolution. Computer Applications 24(4): 20-22

[85] Zhang Y (2007) Research on the Software Configuration Management Of Evolution of Components. Computer and Digital Engineering 35(4): 32-34

[86] Zhang Y (2007) Study on Methods for Description of Software Architecture and Software Evolution Based on Algebra Theory. PhD Thesis, Fudan University

[87] Zhao N, Zhao J, Li T (2007) Process Model Supporting Software Evolution - SDDM. Computer Engineering and Applications 43(13): 61-63

[88] Zhao N, Zhao J, Li T (2007) Software Process Model Supporting Software Evolution - SDDM II. Computer Engineering 33(14): 73-75

Chapter 22
E-Commerce in China: Culture and Challenges

Jeffrey Hsu

Information Systems, Silberman College of Business, Fairleigh Dickinson University, USA

Abstract The development of e-commerce in China has been of interest to many throughout both the scholarly and business communities. Certainly, a nation which claims one of the largest populations of Internet users, together with a dominant role in the global economy, would be expected to be a major player in e-commerce. However, because of the impacts of various variables, constraints, as well as the makeup of the population and its Internet users, e-commerce in China has evolved differently, and has unique characteristics compared with e-commerce from other nations and markets. An analysis of the current state of e-commerce in China, followed by an analysis of the factors which impact upon China's e-commerce, provide insight into its development of electronic business. The role of culture, which is another key factor, is also discussed. From here, a look to future trends and directions is provided.

1 Overview and Introduction

The growth of e-commerce has been a global phenomenon, and the influence of business and commerce being conducted over the Internet has been dramatic and wide-reaching. The ability to conduct business, from consumer purchases to large scale B2B transactions, globally using the Internet has been far-reaching and significant (Turban et al. 2006).

Certainly, China, being a major player in terms the global economy, having a large population and many Internet users, may be assumed to have a well-developed state of e-commerce. However, in reality, the development of e-commerce in China has been different from, and in many ways, has lagged behind, that of the United States, Europe, and Asian countries such as Japan (Wong, Yen, and Fang 2004).

What is the state of e-commerce in China? Based on previous research and studies conducted, China's e-commerce is in many respects a varied and complex situation which in some ways parallels development in the West and other parts of Asia, but in other aspects is different and unique in terms of its dynamics and

P.O. de Pablos, M.D. Lytras (eds.), *The China Information Technology Handbook,*   401
DOI: 10.1007/978-0-387-77743-6_22, © Springer Science+Business Media, LLC 2009

usage. Since e-commerce, even if focused solely on China, is such a large subject, the focus in this chapter will be mainly on B2C (business to consumer) e-commerce. There are studies which have addressed the development of B2B e-commerce in China, but that is an entire topic in itself (Hu, Wu, and Wang 2004; Andersen et al. 2004).

There are a number of issues which have impacted upon the acceptance, and usage, of e-commerce in China. They relate to the state of government, business practices and customs, language, culture, and a number of other variables. Business issues such as trust, logistics, payment systems, guanxi, and unique aspects of Chinese culture and society all make e-commerce in China a unique set of challenges and opportunities.

Particular attention is given to issues relating to the cultural aspects of Chinese culture and society which can impact not only the usage of e-commerce in general, but also, more specifically, the design and content of web sites which are directed towards Chinese audiences. Some of these issues include the basic differences between Chinese and American/Western cultures, family and collective orientations, religion and faith, color, symbolism, ordering and risk/uncertainty. This chapter will focus on these issues and discuss the present, and projected future state of e-commerce in China.

2 Internet Use and E-Commerce

The growth of e-business and e-commerce, globally, has been significant. Recent trends have placed the level of internet usage worldwide at 1.3 billion, which translates into a penetration rate of roughly 20%, based on the estimated total population, showing a 265% growth from 2000. Clearly, the trend has been increasing, and indicates strong growth and increases in the use of e-commerce on a worldwide basis (www.internetworldstats.com 2007)

If considered from the perspective of Internet connectivity and usage, China's potential e-commerce market can be considered as one of the largest in the world. From less than a million in 1997, by 2000 the number of computers connected to the Internet in China was at least 9 million (CNNIC 2000), and the number of users exceeded 22 million (CNNIC 2001). Based on a more recent report, there were at least 80 million Internet users in China reported in 2003, up from 68 million in 2002 (UNCTAD 2002) with the number increasing since then. This is a very large increase given that the number in Japan in 2003 at around the same time was significantly less at roughly 65 million (CNNIC 2004). The latest report puts the estimate at 210 million (Jesdanun 2008). Despite this large figure, it represents less than 10% of the population of China, however the actual number may actually be higher based on the fact that many persons share computers and that the reporting may not account for these additional users in many cases (Lu and Buhalis 2006; eBusiness Forum 2001). Without a doubt, China is now considered one of the top five nations in terms of Internet use, and as some experts predict, China is making strides towards having the second largest population of web surfers in the world, after the United States.

Certainly, this fact, and together with knowledge of the benefits that e-business and e-commerce can bring, have been noted. One of China's major newspapers, the People's Daily, reported that there are a projected 2 million new positions in e-commerce related fields which are expected by 2013, even though at the time the article was published, there were no more than 100,000 currently in that field (People's Daily 2003). There has been a push to offer e-commerce in Chinese colleges, and there are tens of thousands of graduates who have majored in e-commerce (Zhang, Li, and Lin 2005; Li and Zhang 2003). There are also e-commerce research institutes which have been started, the first of which was the E-Commerce Research Institute at X'ian Jiaotong University.

Certain firms, notably Haier, known for its refrigerators and household appliances, are examples of Chinese enterprises which have more fully embraced the e-commerce revolution, and there are several studies which examine their work in this area (Li and Chang 2004; Chang and Li 2003)

To put in better perspective the current level of e-commerce in China as compared to the United States, while China has a population in excess of 1 billion, and an economy which is robust, its levels of e-commerce are paltry compared to that of the U.S. In the year 2000, for example, e-commerce sales were over $5 billion dollars in the U.S., while China reported only around $100 million.

Clearly, there is a vast potential market in China which has yet to be expanded and tapped to its fullest potential.

3 Internet and Web Users in China

Despite the large total population in China, only a small percentage of people actually have access to a computer and the Internet. A rough estimate is that only about 10% of the population in China have this kind of access and communications capability. In fact, there are reported to be only 40.3 computers for every thousand persons living in China (World Bank 2002).

There are several characteristics specific to Internet users in China. It should be noted that while there is a very large potential market in China, the type of user who would be using the Internet actually forms a kind of subculture within the general population, with specific characteristics being younger age, having higher income and educational levels, and a tendency for users to be located in urban and metropolitan, rather than rural areas (Li and Buhalis 2006).

In effect, both for Internet use and for e-commerce market potential, China could be viewed essentially as two countries in one. The large cities, coastal provinces, and other areas with greater population, business, industry, and larger numbers of educated persons (Beijing, Shanghai, Guangzhou, etc.) comprise the areas where Internet usage is generally higher. Many of the people in these areas earn incomes in excess of $1,000, which is a general figure for the point from which Chinese start to purchase goods which are not basic necessities (Jiang and Prater 2002; Powell 2002).

In contrast to this, many of the Chinese living in the more rural, "Third World" interior regions of the country have limited incomes, infrastructure, and do not readily have access to the Internet, e-commerce, or the like. To put the differences in perspective, only 20% of Chinese websites comes from these areas, and only 30% of the Internet users (Wong, Yen, and Fang 2004). There have been some developments in the more remote, Western regions of the country, so over time, there may be a reduction in the differences between the coastal, urban cities and the Western provinces. In particular, there are cases where the unique products (carpets, camel-hair blankets, local clothing items) produced in the western provinces, including those comprising the Silk Road, were marketed and advertised via the Internet. In addition, advances in terms of improving wireless mobile, telecommunications, and Internet infrastructures are taking place (Davidson, Vogel, and Harris 2005).

One area which could have greater impact and penetration would be through the use of mobile phones with Internet capability. While the lack of Internet-enabled computers is frequently cited as a reason why more Chinese are not online, a survey by CNNIC (2003) revealed that technical knowledge of computer usage may be one main reason hindering many Chinese from being a part of the e-commerce and Internet revolution, However, mobile phones are more universally available, lower priced, are considered to be easier to use, and therefore may be a boon to the growth of the B2C m-commerce market in China (Wong, Yen, and Fang 2004) .

4 The Chinese Web Surfer

What are some of the characteristics of the Chinese web surfer? How do Chinese Internet users make use of the Internet? There are a number of factors which can impact upon the use of the Internet in China. Of course, depending on one's geographic area, the availability of the Internet can range from non-existent to readily available. There are also limitations in terms of cost, given the salary and income levels of the Chinese, for which there can be a wide disparity. Restrictions placed by the government and slow access speeds are also variables in Chinese internet access. In spite of these potential problems, the Chinese are very enthusiastic about getting onto the Information Superhighway. In fact, according to CNNIC (2001), the number of users is increasing by 33% per year, while the total number of web sites has increased dramatically.

Most of the users of the Internet in China are from the major cities, including Beijing, Shanghai, and Guangzhou. While the majority of China population is found in rural areas, there is a strong tendency for Internet users to be concentrated in cities and urban areas. A strong focus on urban issues, concerns, and interests should therefore be taken into account when designing for a Chinese audience e-commerce site, rather than a focus on rural areas.

Generally, more males than females (roughly twice as many) are online, and most of they are young. The majority of Internet users are less than 25 years of age. Many of these have a college education, are students, and/or have a professional employment in government or industry.

As for usage patterns and trends, the main uses for the Internet in China are to communicate via e-mail messaging, and the like; obtain information about various subjects and do research online; and for entertainment (such as playing on-line games, etc.) Most of the usage in China is centered on these communication, information gathering/research and entertainment purposes. While some inroads in terms of online sales have been made, in general the main use of the Internet in China is not to purchase goods. In many cases, the use of the Internet can be used to facilitate a sale, by allowing a consumer to determine who is selling what, where a sale is being held, obtaining detailed information on products, or perhaps submitting an "order" which will ultimately be finalized at a store. In general, only a few categories of low priced goods are purchased online and delivered to one's home, without the need to physically visit the store (Wong, Yen, and Fang 2004).

As such, the use of the internet and more specifically e-commerce oriented web sites are used more for information and product research, gaining information on stores and prices, and providing technical and post-sales support.

The types of sites that Chinese web surfers visit include those which are produced in China and directed towards the Chinese Internet population, extensions of well-known Internet brands, such as China-focused versions of Yahoo! Or Google China, and those which target Chinese language audiences but may not be produced in, or specifically focused toward, a specific country (Dou, You, and Ma 2003).

5 Government

Even though China is making strides towards the development of a knowledge economy, and also is making inroads in improving technology and infrastructure (Wilson and Siegel 2005),   there are aspects of government which impact upon Internet use, and e-commerce.

There are the elements of censorship, control, and restrictions associated with the use of the Internet. There have been attempts to restrict access to pornographic sites, sites which are sponsored or contain information which are considered unfriendly to the government, restrictions in terms of online video postings, and also anything which can be considered "harmful" to the government and people (ECT News Network 2008).

6 Business Issues and E-Commerce in China

6.1 Trust, Reputation and Guanxi

No discussion of the Internet and e-commerce would be complete without a discussion of several key issues relating to Chinese e-commerce, and in many ways, business in general. Since e-commerce is nothing more than a new form of doing business, the cultural aspects of Chinese society as they relate to business and trust are important to examine.

While the potential market in China for the Internet is indeed huge and many Chinese are eagerly getting online every day, only a small percentage of online users (roughly 20%) have done any shopping online. A lack of familiarity with this medium makes consumers cautious about embracing this new means of shopping. Some of the factors which may discourage online purchases include the need to provide one's personal and financial information online, which some would feel uncomfortable with; the inability to see and physically examine what one is buying as in a store, and also a lack of trust in terms of any enterprise which is not "brick and mortar" and exists only in the form of web pages and sites (Quaddus, Xu, and Hoque 2005; Efendioglu and Yip 2004).

Another factor can be the lack of what can be called "reputation systems" in China. Before making an online purchase (or an online auction), users in the U.S. frequently check out the reputation of the firm one is planning to do business with; conversely, businesses may want to know something about the credit and trust worthiness of the customer. In the U.S., there are services such as bizrate.com to rate online retailers, the "feedback" system in place on eBay, and various other means to find out about online merchants, and for auctions, about buyers. The availability of useful and accurate reputation services is generally lacking in China; it may not readily exist for particular retailer or industry; where it exists, the information may be misleading and not that meaningful (Li and Wang 2005). The establishment of some better means from which consumers can find out about the reputation of, and previous customer experiences with, online businesses would be helpful to promote public trust in e-commerce (Li and Wang 2005).

For good relations, especially those relating to business, it is important to maintain good guanxi ("relationship" in Chinese). The definition of guanxi could be expressed as the existence of connections in order to secure favor in personal relations (Brunner, Chan and Zhou 1989). While important in interpersonal relationships, guanxi is especially critical in business, where having guanxi can considerably improve how well a firm can do. Clearly, this is one aspect of a business relationship which is not the most easily accomplished using the Internet.

In Chinese business there is often a need and expectation for face to face contact to exist in order to build up a sense of trust. This relates back to Hofstede's notion of individualism-collectivism, where Chinese culture, based on the under-pinnings of Confucianism, is generally collective (Hofstede 1997). Confucianism also is in favor of the evaluating a partner's past and present behavior, which is a prerequisite for trust. Therefore, when dealing with uncertainty, which is the case of business, the need still exists for some kind of face to face contact. This is further supported by the connection between collectivism and high power-distance, which is contrary to general expectations that e-commerce is a low power-distance activity (Hofstede 1997). Clearly, one of the problems that e-commerce is facing in China may be due to a lack of trust both in online retailers and in the concept of buying something without face-to-face contact and without guanxi (personal relationship between parties).

In general, the implementation of guanxi in business is conducted using face to face meetings, and emphasizes the importance of relationships as a bridge to conducting business. Clearly, the existence of personal relationships, having meetings and meals together, and other personalized aspects of Chinese business are contrary to a generally more impersonal approach using electronic transactions in place of personal relationships; the ability to move from traditional approaches to doing business to new forms is one of the challenges which affects the growth and further development of e-commerce in China.

6.2 Payment Issues

One key stumbling block to a greater acceptance, and consequently, development of, B2C e-commerce in China has been the lack of effective and reliable electronic payment systems. In particular, the credit card, one of the enabling payment methods for most B2C e-commerce, while widely available and used by many in the U.S., Europe, and many other countries, is not widely used in China. Instead, the preferred payment method is usually cash, and the use of cash could be considered to be part of the "consumer culture" there (Stylianou et al. 2003).

In China, the most commonly accepted form of payment is cash. In a nation long accustomed to cash transactions, many stores and merchants accept only cash. In general, credit cards have remained largely the domain of foreign tourists, hotels, and some restaurants, for example. The widespread availability of credit cards is not yet a phenomenon which exists, so not only is electronic payment not yet widespread, it will not become so until there is a well-developed technological infrastructure for processing large volumes of credit card transactions. According to Ortolani (2005), the credit card penetration rate in China is around 1%, a very low figure by any standard. One reason for this may be the perception that credit cards are insecure, and the fact that running up a debt using a credit card is a negative financial state (Fannin 2003; Tan and Wu 2002).

As such, ordering online is made more difficult in that most of the transactions need, consequently, to be completed using some form of payment on delivery method, such as cash on delivery (COD). While many consumers in China actually have bank debit cards (90% of all Chinese bank cards in use), they may not be the best medium for e-commerce due to concerns about security, since the consequences of having one's checking account raided for example, can be serious. Another option which is growing in use is the payment for goods at the post office, where the pickup of goods can also be done. This is an especially good option for those persons who do not have home mail delivery, and is growing in popularity (Wong, Yen, and Fang 2004).

There is a need for the development of a comprehensive and widely available technology-based payment infrastructure, together with greater availability and acceptance of credit cards, before e-commerce in china can grow in terms of larger volume and greater acceptance.

Another possibility which has been examined as having potential is expanding e-commerce (actually m-commerce) through the use of Internet-enabled mobile phones. It has been reported that in China, there are significantly more mobile phones being used which have Internet capability rather than have personal computers. Because online purchases can be billed to a user's mobile phone bill, the further development of m-commerce would help to improve the volume of commerce since it removes the problems of not having credit cards, and also the need to pay on delivery (Wong, Yen, and Fang 2004; Ortolani 2005).

In summary, problems with payment methods are holding back the development and expansion of China's e-commerce, however there are a number of viable alternatives which can be used to alleviate the problem over time. The development of more sophisticated infrastructure and more easily available credit in the form of credit cards would go a long way towards making e-commerce for consumers a much more viable option.

6.3 Shipping and Distribution

One key to the development of e-commerce is the need for an efficient and effective distribution and shipping infrastructure. In the U.S. and other countries which have well-developed infrastructures, information flows can move efficiently through different parts of the supply chain, and there are various choices and options for shipping and delivering goods. For instance, the use of RFID (radio frequency identification) can be of benefit in terms of the management of supply chains.

The infrastructure in China, on the other hand, while improving, still has a great many aspects which are inadequate based on both current and projected future demands. Having evolved from a rigidly controlled three tier system of distributors and wholesalers, with central government control (Jiang and Prater, 2002) it was not set up for the needs of a global economy. In addition, foreign companies were not allowed to conduct distribution operations either for their own businesses, or for others. Instead, the goods needed to be passed along to the appropriate distribution company within the centrally-planned, 3 tier network described previously. Moreover, even shipping goods within China (across provinces) would incur additional costs, because of policies instituted for the purposes of regional and provincial protectionism, with the estimate being additional charges in the range of 30-40% (Jiang and Prater 2002; Goh and Ling 2002).

From a practical B2C e-commerce perspective, the problem of infrastructure limits the development of greater levels of e-commerce. Because of the lack of sufficient railways, highways, air freight, and other means of prompt and efficient shipping, the delivery of goods is problematic. While the existence of nationwide shipping systems such as Fedex, DHL, and UPS in the U.S. and other nations allow for efficient delivery, in China the choices are far fewer and less efficient. For most deliveries, postal mail and express mail are the main options. As a result, what would take a few days in the U.S. to ship across the country could likely take a week or several weeks in China (Su and Adams 2005; Jiang and Prater 2002; Goh and Ling 2002).

Information flows through the supply chain and other forms of business information are also not well-developed in China, and the data available may be limited to a certain region or area, rather than nationally or enterprise-wide. For example, while persons in the U.S. take for granted the existence of phone books, in China a phone book is not always readily available, may only be in Chinese, and frequently are limited in their coverage. In connection with this, if China is to improve in terms of the supply chain and the movement of products and raw materials, modernization of the existing structures and channels is needed. However, some Chinese firm in Shanghai and Hong Kong have started using RFID networks and technologies, which is the beginning of a trend towards the use of e-logistics in China's business (Davison, Vogel, and Harris 2005).

The needs of China's expanding economy, which already provide a large proportion of goods to the world, together with the effects of admission to the World Trade Organization (WTO) and a desire to fully embrace and develop e-commerce, have encouraged the development of a better infrastructure system in China. This, together with the planned improvements in the telecommunications and Internet infrastructure should have impacts to help improve the level of e-commerce in China over the long run.

In short, improvements are needed in terms of the Internet and telecommunications infrastructure in China, which can help to meet the volumes of use which exist even now, and for the growth which is expected in the future. In addition, before China can have improved levels of e-commerce as it exists in the U.S., there will need to be improvements in terms of better shipping, freight, and transport infrastructures.

7 E-Commerce Buying Patterns

Another reason for the lagged development of consumer B2C e-commerce in China is due to the buying patterns and habits of the Chinese. As mentioned earlier, the idea of cash purchases and on-the-spot buying has been considered the modal means of purchasing goods, with the added expectation of having physical contact and inspection of the merchandise in question. In order words, a Chinese consumer is accustomed to going to a store, actually taking in hand and examining the merchandise to make a purchase decision, and then paying for the item in cash. The idea of viewing a description or photo of an item, paying for it using a credit card, and then expecting prompt shipment to one's door is not familiar, nor preferred (Wong, Yen, and Fang 2004) .

Because of this tradition and past buying experiences, many Chinese consumers are hesitant to purchase items online. This is especially the case because there is a lack of trust towards online merchants, a reluctance to pay before receiving the merchandise, and minimal post-sales service (problems with goods are deferred back to the manufacturer, in most cases). Moreover, the competition in the Chinese retail market is such that often there are many retail stores located in a city and urban region, and price competition often results in an abundance of bargains and sale items. Various incentives including free local delivery or in-store pickup, contribute to making online buying not such a convenient or attractive option, especially when ordering online may involve the need for shipping charges (Wong, Yen, and Fang 2004).

As a result, the main types of merchandise purchased online are books, audio and music, and video/DVD products. These are products which are generally uniform in quality, do not vary from store to store, and are generally low priced. So the need for physical examination, to verify quality/brand, and post-purchase service are less of a consideration. In addition, the problem of shipping is less of an issue, since the postal service can be used to send these kinds of smaller items, and the ability to pay on receipt is available (Wong, Yen, and Fang 2004).

Another class of products which sells well online in China are computers and computer equipment. Generally, computers are not ordered online and shipped to the customer. Instead, the transactions are facilitated and confirmed online, while the actual pickup and payment is done in a physical location within the same city where the computer store and/or manufacturer is located. Clearly, the need for physical contact is still a factor in the Chinese retail business, even with the availability of the Internet (Wong, Yen, and Fang 2004).

In summary, it can be found that the major emphasis of e-commerce is in selling low-priced items such as books, music, and movies/video, which can easily be shipped through the mail service and paid for upon arrival. Larger and "big ticket" items would not typically be purchased online. However, the Internet is frequently used to find out about desired products and do other buying research, on higher-priced, "big-ticket" items.

8 Chinese Culture and E-Commerce

8.1 Culture

Previous work in consumer research has indicated that cultural familiarity is important in affecting consumer behavior. If given the choice between several Internet portals which are similar in content, with one more culturally familiar, the one with the cultural emphasis would tend to be preferred (Dou, Yoo, and Ma 2003; Briley et al. 2000). The use of cultural symbols, connotations, coverage of pertinent stories, use of specific designs and colors, and the like all can have an impact on the acceptance and adoption of a specific site or portal. The applicability of culture in promoting adoption of e-commerce sites in China, for example, may be related to the ability for familiar cultural elements to make the process of accepting new information and approaches easier. These are based on the Theory of Diffusion of Innovation (Dou, Yoo, and Ma 2003; Rogers 1983). Closely related to this is the concept of target consumer ethnocentrism, which states that persons who are more focused on and desiring of receiving information related to his/her ethnicity would be more favorably inclined towards sites which contain these cultural elements. (Iyer and Taube 2002; Shimp and Sharma 1987).

Culture is an important part of a successful web site or e-commerce business, since instead of working within the cultural confines of a single nation, such as that of the United States, cultural boundaries are crossed. China, a country with literally centuries of history and culture, certainly would have cultural issues which come into play.

Culture can be considered a man-made part of any human environment. This definition includes not only the material features of the human environment, but the conceptual features - the beliefs, science, myths, religions, laws, and other tenants, held by a group of people. A widely used definition of culture is derived from Hofstede's book (1997), in which culture is likened to mental programs, or "software of the mind," using the analogy of computer programming.

The effect of culture on e-commerce is important, since in many cases the goal of a web site is to market something – a product, service, or idea. According to Mooij (1998), culture is a fundamentally important aspect of marketing. It is important for marketers of one cultural system to understand and adopt the cultural strategy of the system/nation it is attempting to market to (Penazola 1998). There are a number of cultural aspects which need to be addressed, whether they be attitudes, behavior, or values. Marketing strategies and tactics, which may work well in one culture, could result in dismal failure in another (Su and Adams 2005).

Some of the important considerations include properly targeting the local culture, the use of effective symbols and meanings, managing social relations, and understanding cultural identities and ethnicity (Penazola 1989; Bouchet 1995). In addition, when focusing on the Chinese market, such aspects as family orientation, importance of Confucianism, and group orientation make up a unique approach to life and viewing the world, which results in important differences from Western cultures (Scarborough 1998; Lai 2001).

As a starting point, it would be useful to examine what are some of the distinctive aspects of Chinese culture, especially those which could relate in some way to the marketing and effectiveness of e-commerce web sites. Chinese culture is unique, and two commonly used terms express this: Zhong Guo, the Chinese word for the country itself, means "the center of the world," expressing belief that China is unique and an important force in the world. In addition, Guo Qing reflects the fact that China is a special, important country which has its own distinctiveness and uniqueness.

In general, culture was characterized by Nathan (1998), as the traits which define the uniqueness of a culture, which differentiate it from others. In the case of Chinese versus Western culture, these differences are described by Xing (1995). In general, Chinese culture is characterized as being intuitive, aesthetic, introverted, self-restrained, dependent, procrastinating, implicit, patient, group-oriented, and emphasizing continuity. This is in contrast to Western cultures, which are thought of as being more rational, scientific, extroverted, aggressive, independent, active, explicit, impatient, individualistic and change-oriented.

8.2 Hoefstede's Dimensions of Culture

One of the major frameworks of culture, which is related to the design of e-commerce web pages, web sites, and information systems in general, is Hofstede's Dimensions of Culture. These concepts were highlighted in his work (Hofstede 1997; Hofstede 2001).

There are a number of cultural dimensions which are important, including power-distance, uncertainty avoidance, collective/individual, and long versus short term orientation. China is a country which exhibits higher levels of power distance, which implies an acceptance of greater levels of unequal power distribution. Therefore, authority and control is more tolerated and accepted in China (Hofstede 1997; Hofstede 2001).

The Chinese also tend towards lower uncertainty avoidance, a strong long-term orientation, and an emphasis towards the collective over the individual. These could explain some characteristic traits of the Chinese including regarding anything new and different in a more negative manner, an emphasis on the opinions of groups and peers, a focus towards less expression, and conformity to societal trends and more traditional, established practices. A low tolerance for ambiguity and uncertainty is also present. These are characteristics which can be related not only to the previous and current development of e-commerce, but also to what challenges exist in further development with an eye towards the future (Hofstede 1997; Hofstede 2001).

8.3 Other Cultural Models and Frameworks

Aside from Hofstede (1997), there is also Appadurai's (1991) Five Dimensions of Cultural Flow, and King's Towns and Landscapes (1991), all relevant theories of globalization. Appadurai attempted to capture the ways in which cultures relate to and influence each other. These include the following five dimensions:

Table 1 Appadurai's Five Dimensions of Global Cultural Flow (1991)

Ethno-scapes	Flows of people—users and the Internet
Finanscapes	Currency and stock exchanges – Internet and e-commerce
Ideo-scapes	The distribution and proliferation of state and counter-state messages over the Internet
Mediascapes	Images of media and information
Techo-scapes	Technological products and equipment for the Internet

King (1991) claims that the Internet allows "the global diffusion of information, images, professional cultures and sub-cultures, supported by international capital flows." Both of these models support the concept that culture exists on, and is an important component of, the Internet, and should be taken into account whenever a web site is intended to be globalized.

In addition, combined with this are some specific characteristics of the Chinese, which are important to consider when targeting websites and pages for e-commerce and related purposes.

First, there are elements of traditional Chinese culture, which even in our modern-day society still carry weight. These include the influences of Chinese philosophy, including Confucianism (mentioned below), Taoism, and Buddhism. The influences of these helped to create a sense of practicality, together with philosophical views of life, in Chinese culture.

Some of the traditional values which are important to be aware of when interacting with Chinese culture include respect for the elderly and social status, "face", the use of color, and various traditions which are associated with various aspects of life. These traditional values and profiles below in the table.

Table 2 Chinese Cultural Traditions, adapted from Lee (1986)

CULTURAL TRADITION	DESCRIPTION
Respect for Social Status	Gender, age, job status, government authority, law.
"Face"	Importance of "saving face"; avoiding embarrassment
Education	Education is highly valued in Chinese traditional culture.
Dragon	An important symbol in Chinese culture.
Color	Red symbolized "happiness"
	White and black symbolize "mourning"

Unlike the United States and other Western cultures, Chinese culture is influenced by Confucianism, in which the notions of societal harmony, and of respect for family and elders. As discussed by Xing (1995), many Chinese attach a sense of importance to being a part of a group, rather than emphasizing their own individuality. In addition, Confucianism emphasis the moderate, "middle" path to things, instead of being to one or the other extreme.

In addition, there are a number of other characteristics of Chinese culture which are of importance when examining e-commerce in China. These include the conservative nature of Chinese society, the respect for conformity and authority, brand loyalty, and resistance to new products and ideas. In general, compared to Western societies, the Chinese are generally more conservative, and tend to avoid uncertainty, while preferring continuity and a more conservative view of the world. As a result, using an entirely new form of shopping and buying is likely to bring about resistance (Scarborough 1998; Jing 1993).

Attitudes towards marketing and advertising differ from the West in that authority is respected, and when a respected figure is seen promoting a product, it tends to improve sales. In addition, attention to social aspects such as conformity to norms and worries about the opinions of others are more a factor in China than in the West (Jing 1993; Yau 1988). Also, brands and brand loyalty seem to be rather strong in Chinese cultures and may be given emphasis when doing e-commerce (Yang 1989).

In connection with this, there is an emphasis on tradition over innovation, and as such some new products and services may be met with some resistance and skepticism, especially if it is viewed as being "socially unacceptable" at its early stages (Yang 1989). It could be possible to generalize these tendencies based on the fact that the Chinese are more concrete and traditional in their thinking, as opposed to the West, where there may be a stronger influence of abstract thinking and imagination (Li 1998).

Other interesting insights include the important of emphasizing the geographical areas in which Chinese users are residing and accessing the Internet, understanding the role of language, and engaging the transitional aspects of Chinese culture.

According to a study conducted by Lai (2001), many Chinese Internet users are more interested in and concerned with the news and information which relates to their immediate geographical area (city, municipality, or province). For instance, if someone resides in Beijing, he or she would have greater interest in Internet delivered content if it is focused on Northern China and the Beijing area rather than Guangzhou or Jiangxi, for example. Local services, or those which focus on a certain region, and deliver information such as local news, weather, or chat would have the most appeal. For instance, in the Sina.com site, the highest hit rates were reported on the Beijing and Shanghai local news and information, and also "city union" chat services (Sina Survey in Major Cities of China 2001). As a result, regionally-oriented e-commerce may be more effective than that directed towards China as a whole. After all, China is considered to be comprised of at least two or more distinct nations or countries.

Language also appears to be a key factor. While many of the sites which currently existing on the Internet are presented in English and may be Western-culture oriented, many experts predict that the Internet will continue to become more global-oriented in the coming years, and that the influence of China will contribute to a major shift in this current trend (Gupta 2001). Language is an important part of China's cultural tradition, and therefore the effective use of Mandarin Chinese in Chinese web sites appears to be of critical importance (Woodfield 1995)

This is particular true in China, where Mandarin is considered the official and main language, unlike Hong Kong or Singapore, where there is a much stronger bilingual emphasis, and many people are well versed in Chinese, English, and other languages. While it is true that many Chinese, especially those who are younger and college educated, have studied and can communicate effectively in English, it appears that overall, the preference and emphasis of communications is in Chinese. This could be attributed not only to the ease of communicating in the native language, but also due to a sense of tradition and pride in using Chinese. In addition, there are expressions, phrases, nuances and shades of meaning in Chinese which cannot always be expressed in the same way in English. The attention to and creation of e-commerce sites which are in Chinese is therefore a crucial element to the acceptance and usage of e-commerce sites in China, especially by those which are created by multinational firms not based in China (Dou, Yoo, and Ma 2003).

9 Conclusion and Future Trends of E-Commerce in China

Based on all indications, there appears to be a bright future for e-commerce in China, however at the present time there still exist a number of issues and considerations which are hindering further growth, deployment, and expansion.

While China claims the second highest number of Internet users in the world behind the United States, those who use the Internet make up only a small portion (10% or less) of the total Chinese population. Generally, the younger, higher income, and better educated persons, and those who reside in the major cities and coastal areas, make up the bulk of Internet users. However, there has been some progress made in terms of improving the telecommunications and communications capabilities in general, and a realization of the need to give more attention to enhancing technology in the more remote regions of China.

Many of the trends which are present in the U.S. and Europe are being seen in China, including interests in further development of B2B (business to business) e-commerce, the increased interest and availability of online auction sites (Lin and Li 2005), e-tailing, and the use of newer technologies such as RFID (Davison, Vogel, and Harris 2005) and web technologies (Xu, Jiang, and Ma 2005). However, the major use for the Internet by most Chinese is not so much to make purchases, but rather communications through e-mail, finding out about news and happenings, for educational purposes, and for doing research into products and services.

Despite the ability for many Chinese to read and speak English, the preference is for sites which are produced in Mandarin Chinese. These sites may include China-focused portals of global brands (Yahoo!, Google), sites which are focused on China, and also locally developed and hosted sites.

Improvements in infrastructure can help bring about greater availability of the Internet to a greater portion of the population in China. There have been additions and improvements made to the Internet infrastructure, to the creation of fiber-optic lines, and also a $151 billion commitment towards the creation of a national infrastructure for telecommunications. This development is a result of the Ninth National People's Congress, which wanted to make China a viable player in telecommunications by the year 2010. One of the broad goals, overall, is to make China the IT center of the world (Quan, Hu, and Wang 2005). The advancements proposed would help to expand coverage, allow for more readily available Internet access, wireless capabilities, and bring service to previously more remote, inaccessible areas.

The availability of cell phones, even by those who do not have or use a computer, can also contribute to the demand for e-commerce. A large portion of the over 300 million cell phones being used in China have the ability to access the Web, so there is a greater market in terms of potential users, when m-commerce is considered (Martinsons 2004). In fact, while some claim that China does not at this time have true e-commerce as it exists in the United States, there seems to be a strong possibility for growth in m-commerce given that cell phones have achieved greater coverage than computers in many parts of China, and the total population, overall.

Payment issues are another crucial consideration, since the low incidence and use of credit cards in China severely limit the facilitation of payments for purchases made online. Instead, less convenient means such as payment on delivery, payment at the post office, and billing through cell phones (for m-commerce transactions) are currently in use. Underlying this is the lack of an infrastructure to support a high volume of electronic credit card and other financial transactions.

Shipping, logistics, and related issues also hinder online transactions, and prompt shipment of goods is not currently that easily accomplished in China. More frequently, the customer must pick up, and pay for, purchases, at local stores, for products ordered online. Only goods such as music and video CDs/DVDs and book, for example, are typically shipped to the customer, and this usually through the post office.

A number of issues and considerations with relation to Chinese cultural and web site/e-commerce design were discussed, and clearly, there are a number of important considerations and issues which should be noted when creating a website or e-commerce site for Chinese audiences.

To start, the Chinese value the use of their own language. In China, using Mandarin Chinese implies respect and understanding of Chinese culture. Cultural traditions, while not quite as strong as in the past, still exist, and web designers need to be sensitive to the many complexities of a civilization which has developed over thousands of years. These include varied considerations such as cultural traits, Confucianism, traditions, and characteristics of Chinese consumers.

Business aspects are also to be considered. China's business environment is different, and understanding the dynamics would be a useful prerequisite. The social aspects of guanxi (relationship) and its role in business is also important to understand, as is its impact upon e-commerce. In online transactions, the role of these relationships is minimized, and therefore may be considered by some to be contrary to established means of conducting business.

Having discussed at length about the past and current states of B2C e-commerce in China, it would be useful to look at the future of electronic commerce in this nation of over 1 billion people. While there are limitations which current exist, based on the payment, infrastructure, consumer attitudes, and the availability of the Internet to larger numbers of users; further growth and development, especially with government support, is indicating further growth and prospects in this area. As mentioned, there are forecasts for vast increases in employment needs for electronic commerce positions over the next decade.

In conclusion, marketing and selling over the Internet in China is a complex endeavor, which is gaining in popular and growing, but has been up to this moment limited by a number of factors and limitations. Over time, it is expected that these limitations can be overcome, and that the B2C e-commerce (and m-commerce) will likely be an important part of the Chinese consumer's means for shopping and buying in the future.

References

Andersen, K. et al, (2004). B2B e-Commerce—Agricultural Export from China, *Proceedings of ICE'04 Conference*, 534-540.

Appadurai, A., in King, A.D. (ed.) (1991). *Culture Globalisation and the World-System*, Macmillan Press Ltd, SUNY-Binghampton, 1991

Bouchet, D. (1995). Marketing and the Redefinition of Ethnicity. In Costa, J., & Balmossy, G. (ed.) *Marketing in a Multicultural World*, London: Sage Publications.

Briley, D., Morris, M, and Simonson, I. (2000). "Reasons as carriers of culture: dynamic versus dispositional models of cultural influence on decision making," *Journal of Consumer Research*, 27, 2, 157-178.

Brunner, J.A., Chan, C. S. and Zhou, N. (1989). "The role of guanxi in negotiation in the Pacific Basin," *Journal of Global Marketing*, 3(2), 58-72, 1989

CNNIC (2004, 2003, 2001, 2000). "Survey of Chinese Internet Users, *Semi-Annual China Internet Report.*

Chang, T., and Li, P. (2003). How to Succceed in e-Business by Taking the Haier Road, *Competitiveness Review*, 13, 2, 34-45.

Davidson, R., Vogel, D., and Harris, R. (2005). The e-transformation of Western China, *Communications of the ACM* , 48, 4, 62-67.

Dou, W., Yoo, B., and Ma, L. (2003) Computer Patronage of ethnic Portals*, International Marketing Review*, 20, 6, 661-677.

eBusiness Forum (2001). Doing e-Business in China, www.ebusinessforum.com

ECT News Network (2008). China Dismantles 44,000 Sites in Anti Porn Offensive, 1/13/08

ECT News Network (2008). China Moves to Limit Online Video Posting, 1/3/08.

Efendioglu, A., and Yip, V. (2004). Chinese culture and e-Commerce, 16, 45-62.

Fannin, R. (2003). The eBay of China, *Chief Executive*, Aug/Sep. 2003, 31-32.

Goh, M. and Ling, C. (2002). Logistics Development in China, *International Journal of Physical Distribution and Logistics Management*, 33, 10, 886-917.

Gupta, A.F. (2001). Internet and the English Language. Retrieved on July 14, 2002, from the World Wide Web: http://www.fas.nus.edu.sg/staff/conf/ poco.paper6.html.

Hofstede, G. (2001). *Culture's Consequences: Comparing Values, Behaviors, Institutions, and Organizations Across Nations*, 2/E, Beverly Hills CA: Sage.

Hofstede, G. (1997). *Cultures and Organizations: Software of the Mind.* New York: , Mc Graw-Hill. .

Hu, Q., Wu, X., and Wang, C. (2004). Lessons for Alibaba.com: government's role in contracting," *Info Journal*, 6, 5, 298-307.

Iyer, L., and Taube, L. (2002). Global e-commerce: rationale, digital divide, and strategies to bridge the divide," *Journal of Global Information Technology Management*, 5, 1, 43-69.

Jesdanun, A. (2008). China Catching Up to US in Number of Web Surfers, *Associated Press/ECT News Network*, 1/21/08.

Jiang, B. and Prater, E. (2002). Distribution and logistics development in China, *International Journal of Physical Distribution and Logistics Management*, 32, 9, 783-798.

King, A.D. (1991)(ed.) *Culture Globalisation and the World-System*, Macmillan Press Ltd, SUNY-Binghampton, 1991

Lai, J. (2001) *Marketing Web Sites in China*, Minor Thesis, RMIT, 2001.

Lee, S.M. (1986) *Spectrum of Chinese Culture*, Pelanduk Publications (M), Selangor Darul Ehsau.

Li, C.H., (1998) China: *The Consumer Revolution*, New York: Wiley.

Li, Z. and Wang, S. (2005). The Foundation of e-Commerce—Social reputation Systems- A Comparison between America and China, *Proceedings of ICEC'05*, X'ian China, August15-17, 230-232.

Li , P. and Chang, (2004), A Holistic Framework of E-Business Strategy, *Journal of Global Information Management*, 12, 2, Apr-Jun, 44-62.

Lin, Z. and Li, J. (2005). The Online Auction Market in China, *Proceedings of ICEC'05*, X'ian China, August15-17, 123-129.

Li , L. and Buhalis, D. (2006). E-commerce in China: the case of travel, *International Journal of Information Management*, 26, 153-166.

Ortolani, A. (2005). Chinese begin Paying by Cellphone, *Wall Street Journal*, Feb 2, p. 1

Papadopoulou, P, Andreeou, A., Kanellis, P., and Martakos, D. (2001). Trust and relationship building in electronic commerce, *Internet Research*, 11, 4, 322-332.

People's Daily (2003). The Passport for Golden Bowls. Retrieved July 16, 2003   from http://www.people.com.cn/GB/paper447/10148/929507.html. (in Chinese)

Penazola, L.N. (1998). Immigrant Consumer Acculturation, in Srull, (ed.) *Advances in Consumer Research*, Provo, UT: Assn. For Consumer Research.

Powell, B. (2002). China e-commerce. *Fortune Magazine*, March 4.

Quaddus, M., Xu, J., and Hoque, Z. Factors of Adoption of Online Auction, *Proceedings of ICEC'05*, X'ian China, August15-17, 93-100.

Quan, J., Hu, Q., and Wang, X. (2005). IT is Not for Everyone in China, *Communications of the ACM, 48, 4, 69-72.*

Scarborough, J. (1998). Comparing Chinese and Western Culture Roots, " *Business Horizons*, Nov. 1998.

Shimp. T. and Sharma, S. (1987). Consumer ethnocentrism: construction and validation of the CETSCALE, *Journal of Marketing Research*, 24, August, 280-289.

SINA Survey (2001). SINA Survey in Major Cities of China.

Stylianou, A. Robbins, S., and Jackson, P. (2003). Perceptions and Attitudes About eCommerce Development in China, *Journal of Global Information Management*, April- June, 11(2), 31-47.

Su, Q. and Adams, C. (2005). Will B2C E-commerce developed in one culture be suitable for another culture, *Proceedings of ICEC'05*, X'ian China, August15-17, 236-243.

Tan, Z. and Wu, O. (2002). Globalization and e-commerce: factors affecting e-commerce diffusion in China, *Communications of the AIS*, 10, 4-32.

Trappey, C, and Trappel, A. (2001). Electronic commerce in greater China. *Industrial Management and Data Systems*, 101, 5/6, 201-209.

Turban, et al., (2006). *Electronic Commerce: A Managerial Perspective 2006* (4th Edition), Upper Saddle River: Prentice-Hall.

UNCTAD (2002). E-commerce and development report, http://www.unctad.org/en/docs/ecdr2002summary_en.pdf,

Wilson, E. and Segal, A. (2005). Trends in China's Transition Toward a Knowledge Economy, *Asian Survey*, 45, 6, 886-906.

Wong, X., Yen, D., and Fang, X. (2004). E-Commerce Development in China and its Implication for Business. *Asian Pacific Journal of Marketing and Logistics*, 16, 3, 68-83.

Woodfield, A. (1995). The Conservation of Endangered Languages, CTLL Seminar of University of Bristol.

World Bank (2002). *World Development Indicators*, Washington DC: World Bank, 2002.

Xing, F. (1995). The Chinese Cultural System, *SAM Advanced Management Journal*, 60, 1, 1995, p. 14-20.

Xu, B., Jiang, L., and Ma, F. (2005). On the new B2B E-Business Enabling Platform, *Proceedings of ICEC'05*, X'ian China, August15-17,681-684.

Yang, C.F. (1989). A conception of Chinese consumer behavior. In *Hong Kong Marketing Management at the Crossroads.* Hong Kong: Commercial Press, 317-342.

Yau, O.H. (1988). Chinese culture values: their dimensions and marketing implications, *Journal of Marketing*, 22, 1988, pp. 44-57.

Zhang, X., Li, Q. and Lin, Z. (2005). E-Commerce education in China, *Journal of Electronic Commerce in Organizations*, 3, 3, 1-17.

Short Bios

Editors

Miltiadis D. Lytras is an Assistant Professor in the Computer Engineering and Informatics Department-CEID (University of Patras). His research focuses on semantic web, knowledge management and e-learning, with more than 100 publications in these areas. He has co-edited / co-edits, 25 special issues in International Journals (e.g. IEEE Transaction on Knowledge and Data Engineering, IEEE Internet Computing, IEEE Transactions on Education, Computers in Human Behaviour etc) and has authored/[co-]edited 12 books [e.g. Open Source for Knowledge and Learning management, Ubiquitous and Pervasive Knowledge Management, Intelligent Learning Infrastructures for Knowledge Intensive Organizations, Semantic Based Information systems] . He is the founder and officer of the Semantic Web and Information Systems Special Interest Group in the Association for Information Systems (http://www.sigsemis.org). He serves as the (Co) Editor in Chief of 12 international journals [e.g. International Journal of Knowledge and Learning, International Journal of Technology Enhanced Learning, International Journal on Social and Humanistic Computing, International Journal on Semantic Web and Information Systems, International Journal on Digital Culture and Electronic Tourism, International Journal of Electronic Democracy, International Journal of Electronic Banking, International Journal of Electronic Trade] while he is associate editor or editorial board member in seven more.

Patricia Ordóñez de Pablos is professor in the Department of Business Administration and Accountability, at the Faculty of Economics of The University of Oviedo (Spain). Her teaching and research interests focus on the areas of strategic management, knowledge management, intellectual capital measuring and reporting, organizational learning and human resources management. She is Executive Editor of International Journal of Chinese Culture and Managemen, Executive Editor of the International Journal of Learning and Intellectual, Editor in Chief of the International Journal of Strategic Change Management and Co-Editor of China Insights Today. She serves in the Editorial Board of more than 15 scientific journals and has co-edited books, like Web 2.0: The Business Model (Springer).

Authors

Al Davis is a strategy and entrepreneurship professor at the U of Colorado at Colorado Springs. Previously, he was CEO of Omni-Vista, VP of Engineering Services at BTG, a Director of R&D at GTE Comm Sys, and Director of the Software Technology Cntr at GTE Labs. He has held academic positions at George Mason U and U Tennessee, and temporary academic positions at Atma Jaya U in Yogyakarta (Indonesia); U Jos (Nigeria); U Politecnica de Madrid (Spain); U Technology, Sydney (Australia); and U Western Cape, Cape Town (South Africa). He was Editor-in-Chief of IEEE Software (1994-1998). He is an editor for J Systems and Software (1987-present) and was an editor for Comm ACM (1981-1991). He is author of Software Requirements: Objects, Functions and States (Prentice Hall), 201 Principles of Software Development (McGraw Hill), Great Software Debates (Wiley & IEEE CS Press), and Just Enough Requirements Management (Dorset House). He has published 100+ articles in journals, conferences and trade press, and lectured 500+ times in 20+ countries. He is a founder of IEEE International Conferences of Requirements Engineering, and served as general chair of its 1st conference in 1994. He has been a fellow of IEEE since 1994, and earned his Ph.D. in Computer Science from U Illinois in 1975. Find out more about him at http://web.uccs.edu/adavis.

Alexander Brem received his Diploma in Business Administration from the University of Erlangen-Nuremberg in 2004, and earned his PhD there in 2007. From 2004 to 2007, he was Senior Research and Teaching Assistant at the Chair of Industrial Management, University of Erlangen-Nuremberg, where he now works as Senior Lecturer. Moreover, he is Founder and Partner of VEND consulting GmbH, Nuremberg. His current research interests include idea and innovation management and strategic management in SMEs.

Ann Hickey is an associate professor of information systems and associate dean of the College of Business at the U of Colorado at Colorado Springs. Before beginning her academic career, she worked for 17 years as a program manager and senior systems analyst for the U.S. government. Her research focuses on requirements engineering and elicitation and has been published in journals including the Journal of Management Information Systems and the Requirements Engineering Journal, conference proceedings and other outlets. She is currently the Associate Editor-in-Chief for requirements for IEEE Software and has served on the program and organizing committees for requirements conferences and workshops. She earned her B.A. in mathematics from Dartmouth College and her M.S. and Ph.D. in Management Information Systems from the U of Arizona. Find out more about her at http://web.uccs.edu/ahickey.

Ants Kraus is a lecturer of operation management at the Estonian Business School. He received his M.B.A from the University of Tartu, Estonia, and his M.S. in electronics engineering from the Electrotechnical University of Saint Petersburg, Russia. His main research interest is operation management practice in different cultures. Ants Kraus is a member of the European Thematic Network for the Excellence in Operations and Supply Chain Management Education, Research and Practice.

Chong Guan is currently a doctoral candidate at the Nanyang Business School, Singapore. She hold her first degree from the Beijing University and her research is in the area of online user behavior.

David L. Olson is the James and H.K. Stuart Professor in MIS Chancellor's Professor at the University of Nebraska. He has published research in over 100 refereed journal articles, primarily on the topic of multiple objective decision making. He teaches in the Management Information Systems, Management Science and Operations Management areas. He has authored or co-authored 21 books, including Decision Aids for Selection Problems, Managerial Issues of Enterprise Resource Planning Systems and Introduction to Business Data Mining. He is a Fellow of the Decision Sciences Institute.

Desheng Dash Wu is the affiliated Professor in RiskLab at the University of Toronto and the Director of RiskChina Research Center at the University of Toronto. His research interests focus on enterprise risk management, performance evaluation in financial industry and credit risk. His work has appeared in several journals as International Journal of Production Research, European Journal of Operational Research, Expert Systems with Applications, Socio-Economic Planning Sciences, Computers and Operations Research, International Journal of System Science. He has served as Editor/Guest Editors/Chairs for several journals/conferences. He is a Member of the Professional Risk Managers' International Association (PRMIA) Academic Advisory Committee.

Dexiang Wu is a PhD candidate majoring in Management Science at the University of Science and Technology of China. His research interests are supply chain and risk management.

Doug Vogel is Professor (Chair) of Information Systems at the City University of Hong Kong and an AIS Fellow. His research interests bridge the business and academic communities in addressing questions of the impact of information systems on aspects of interpersonal communication, group problem solving, cooperative learning, and multi-cultural team productivity. Professor Vogel is especially active in introducing group support technology into enterprises.

Edward J. Lusk is currently a Professor of Accounting, the State University of New York [SUNY], College of Economics and Business, Plattsburgh, NY, USA and Emeritus: The Department of Statistics, The Wharton School, The University of Pennsylvania, Philadelphia, PA. USA. From 2001 to 2006 he held the Chair in Business Administration at the Otto-von-Guericke University, Magdeburg Germany. He has also taught in China at the Shanxi University of Finance and Commerce and the Chulalongkorn University Bangkok, Thailand. He as published more than 160 articles in peer reviewed journals including: The Journal of Political Economy, Statistics and Probability, The Accounting Review, Management Science, The Journal of the Operational Research Society, Gender, Work and Organizations, and Decision Support Systems.

Feng Chen is a research fellow in School of Computing at De Montfort University, England. He got his BSc degree in Computer Science from NanKai University, China, in 1991 and MPhil degree in Computer Science from Dalian University of Technology, China, in 1994. He received the PhD degree in software engineering from De Montfort University, England, in 2007. His current research interests include software engineering, software evolution, software reengineering for security enforcement and software architecture.

Guangming Lu, Senior lecturer in the College of Humanities and Social Science, Beijing Forestry University; Postdoctor of the Renmin University of China, majoring in ICT application in China, especially in rural area; Ph.D. of the Zhejiang University, majoring in agriculture economics, management and rural development; Master of the Shanxi University, majoring in philosophy of science and technology, particularly in the relation between technology development and society changes. Current research focuses on the impact of ICT on the society and social development.

Guangqian Peng, M.Sc in Supply Chain Management Information Systems in Business Administration Department, Wageningen University and Research Centre. Her research recently focuses on management information systems in food supply chains and networks, and E-commerce by SMEs, etc. She became an assistant professor in Guizhou University in 1999. She has participated or managed projects at regional or (inter-)national level. She has (co-)published books and academic articles in such presses and journals as Springer Science+Business Media, Yunnan Science & Technology Press, China Insights Today, Economy in length and breadth, Journal of Southwest Agricultural Univ., and Journal of Ecological Economics. E-mail: Guang-qian.Peng@wur.nl

Guisheng Wu is a professor at School of Economics and Management, Tsinghua University. Wu is considered the leading academic and researcher in the field of management of technological innovation in China. He has co-authored more than 5 articles in international journals such as Research Policy and Technovation. He also published 8 books and more than 130 journal articles in Chinese. The text 'Management of Technological Innovation' is widely used by students in Chinese university and institutes of technology.

He Guo is a professor in the School of Software at Dalian University of Technology, China. He got his BSc degree from Jinlin University, China, in 1982 and MPhil degree from Dalian University of Technology, China, in 1988. His research interests include software architecture and distributed computing.

Hongji Yang is a professor, the Head of Computer Science Division, in School of Computing at De Montfort University, England. He received his BSc and MPhil degree in Computer Science from Jilin University, China, and his PhD degree in Computer Science from Durham University, England. His research interests include software engineering and distributed computing. He was programme Chairing IEEE ICSM'1999, IEEE FTDCS'2001 and IEEE COMPSAC'2002.

Jeffrey Hsu is an Associate Professor of Information Systems at the Silberman College of Business, Fairleigh Dickinson University. He is the author of numerous papers, chapters, and books, and has previous business and IT experience in the software, telecommunications, and financial industries. His research interests include e-commerce, global IT management, human-computer interaction, IS education, and business intelligence. Dr. Hsu also serves on the editorial boards of several journals, and has worked on global education, distance learning, and curriculum development initiatives. Professor Hsu received his Ph.D. in Information Systems from Rutgers University.

L. Richard Ye is Professor of Information Systems in the College of Business and Economics, California State University, Northridge. He received his Ph.D. in Management Information Systems from the University of Minnesota. His research interests include expert systems, business value of information technology, and electronic commerce. His work has appeared in such journals as MIS Quarterly, Expert Systems with Applications, Information & Management, and International Journal of Man-Machine Studies.

Liang-Hung Lin is currently an Assistant Professor in Department of International Business, National Kaohsiung University of Applied Sciences. Dr. Lin is interested in the fields of technology management, strategic management and organizational management. He ever published academic papers in the Journal of Organizational Change Management, International Journal of Technology Management and Total Quality Management and Business Excellence.

Louis-Francois Pau is born in Copenhagen (Denmark). Since 2001, he has been part-time Professor of Mobile Business and Media, Rotterdam School of Management, part of Erasmus University. He is also Adjunct Professor at Copenhagen Business School since 2004.From 1990-1995, Prof. Dr. Pau was the Technical Director of Europe for Digital Equipment (now part of Hewlett Packard). After which, he moved on in to be the General Manager (CTO) of L.M. Ericsson's Networks Division untill 2003 ; he is since in charge of Technology management across L.M.Ericsson .

Maria Fernanda Pargana Ilhéu holds a PhD degree in Marketing at Sevilla University, and is a Professor of Marketing at ISEG. She is also the Director of the Portuguese-Chinese Chamber of Commerce, the Vice-President of EU-China Business Association, and a member of the Editorial Board of the International Journal of Chinese Culture and Management. She is a founding member of Asiânia, the Centre for Asian Studies at ISCTE Business School in Lisbon. Her research interests concern international marketing, international business and China.

Mikael Collan (D.Sc. econ & BA) is a Research Fellow at the Institute for Advanced Management Systems Research at Abo Akademi University, in Turku, Finland. Mikael is working for a consortium of Finnish industrial companies in a joint R&D project and has previously worked as a senior business consultant. His primary research is in real investment profitability analysis methods.

Mingyan Zhao is a senior lecturer in the School of Software at Dalian University of Technology, China. He got his BSc degree from Shenyang University of Technology, China, in 1995 and MPhil degree from Dalian University of Technology, China, in 2001. His research interests include software engineering and data warehouse.

Mo Pak Hung is an Associate Professor in Department of Economics, Hong Kong Baptist University. He receives his Ph. D from the University of Washington in 1991. Currently, he is studying and writing the mechanisms driving economic development, contemplating the possible evolution of the global economy and the institutions required for accommodating the evolution process. As a hobby, he develops a system of pictograph that may facilitate the harmony and prosperity of the global economy. As a professional economist, he studied and published on varieties of economic issues including Chinese economy and history, political system, economic development and consumer theory. It appears that he has solved some important mysteries about the evolution and stagnation of imperial China.

Ruth Alas is the Vice-Rector for Scientific Affairs and Head of the Management Department at the Estonian Business School. She has written twenty one management textbooks and more than 100 articles on the following subjects: Change management, Crises management, Fundamentals of Management, Human Resource Management, public and private sector management and Strategic Management.

Ru-Yang Hong is Ph.D. candidate in management science and engineering in the school of management at Zhejiang University, China. She received her M.A. in management science and engineering management from Zhejiang University and B.A. in machinery manufacture design and automation from Zhejiang University of Science and Technology. Now she is a senior lecturer in economics at Hangzhou Normal University. Her current research interest focuses on the interface between intellectual capital management and strategic management in the areas of corporate entrepreneurship, technological innovation, strategic network, and organizational learning.

Shouhua Wei is an associate professor at School of Business, Nanjing University. Before joining the university in 2007, Dr Wei received his PHD in Human Geography from Peking University in China in 2003 and then worked as a research assistant in Tsinghua University in China. His current research interests are in the areas of technological innovation management and industrial organization. He has co-authored 4 papers for International Conference Proceedings including Globalics (2004), International Association of Management of Technology (IAMOT, 2006), and International Symposium Management of Technology (ISMOT, 2007). He has also published one book, authored 10 book chapters and more than 30 journal articles in Chinese.

Sunanda Sangwan (PhD Rotterdam School of Management) is currently Associate Professor at Nanyang Business School in Singapore. She has earlier worked at Copenhagen Business School and the Erasmus University in the Netherlands. She has held visiting positions at the Trier University in Germany, the Imperial College in the UK and several other business schools in Central and Northern Europe. She has conducted training at MBA, EMBA level and executive development programs in Europe and Asia. She has published and made conference presentations in her research areas of Marketing and Information Systems at the local and international levels. She is on the editorial review board of International Journal of Electronic Commerce, Journal of Electronic Commerce, Journal of Management Information Systems, etc.

Sylvie Laforet is a Lecturer in Marketing at The University of Sheffield. She has researched and published in the areas of branding for more than a decade. She has worked on ESRC funded projects in innovation management in small and medium-sized enterprises and has published in this area. Recently, she has also researched in technology-based services. She has authored over 30 publications and has published in international journals. She has refereed journal articles, books, grants applications, has examined PhDs and has given talks on a number of issues in branding, packaging and consumer behavior at practitioners' conferences. She is a member of Academy of Marketing Science, British Academy of Management and Institute for Small Business & Entrepreneurship. She has taught marketing at undergraduate, postgraduate levels and has supervised at PhD level.

Tomas Eklund (D.Sc. econ & BA) is a researcher at the Institute for Advanced Management Systems Research (IAMSR) at Abo Akademi University, in Turku, Finland. He received his doctoral degree from the Department of Information Systems at Abo Akademi University in 2004, on the topic of using the self-organizing map for financial benchmarking. His primary research interests are in data mining, self-organizing maps, benchmarking and performance analysis, and text mining.

Varadharajan Sridhar is Professor in Information Management at the Management Development Institute, India. He received his Ph.D. from the University of Iowa, U.S.A. Dr. Sridhar's primary research interests are in the area of telecommunication management and policy and global software development. He has published his research work in European Journal of Operational Research, Telecommunication Systems, International Journal of Business Data Communications and Networking, Applied Econometrics and International Development, Journal of Regional Analysis and Policy, and Journal of Information System Security. He was the recipient of the Nokia Visiting Fellowship awarded by the Nokia Research Foundation. He is Associate Editor of International Journal of Business Data Communications and Networking and is on the editorial board of the Journal of Global Information Management.

Wensheng Wang, Chinese, In 1998 he was awarded DAAD scholarship for his PhD study in Bonn University, Germany, and obtained his PhD in agricultural economics in 2001. He is currently the deputy Director General of the Agricultural Information Institute of CAAS, Professor and PhD Supervisor, as well as Visiting Professor of Shandong University of Science and Technology. Since joining the Agricultural Information Institute of CAAS, he has led or jointly led more than 20 projects, including the national scientific and technological key project, namely the Research on China Rural Information Service Mode and Mechanism; and the National 863 Project, namely the Research on Networked Agricultural Remote Diagnosis Platform, and so on. He has published over 30 papers in journals and magazines home and aboard.

Xi Zhang is currently a PhD student in the USTC-CityU Joint Advanced Research Center (Suzhou), a collaborative scheme for PhD student supervision sponsored by University of Science and Technology of China and City University of Hong Kong. His research interests include software development management, distributed work, and knowledge management in Chinese enterprises, with more than 10 publications in these areas.

Xianjun Li is an associate professor at Department of Automitive Engineering, Tsinghua University. Dr Li joined the department in 2004 after he worked as a research assistant at the University. His current research interests are in the areas of technological innovation management in automobile industry. He has presided several key projects in technological innovation management in this sector for governments and enterprises. Li has authored 5 papers for International Conference Proceedings such as International Symposium Management of Technology (ISMOT, 2002), Globalics (2004), and he also published 3 books and more than 30 journal articles in Chinese.

Xiao-Bo WU is Professor of Management, at School of Management, Zhejiang University, Hangzhou, China. His first degree is B. EE. After five years' work as an engineer in Beijing and Hangzhou, he went back to Zhejiang University, got the M.S. in Energy Economics, PhD in Technology Management. He was the Post-Doctorate at AIT, Bankok, Thailand, visiting scholar at Cambridge University, Fulbright Scolar at Sloan School, MIT. His research interests include Innovation Management, Global Manufacturing and Strategic Management, Information Technology and Management Change. Now he is the vice dean of School of Management, and director of National Institute for Innovation Management.

Yen-Chun Jim Wu is Professor of Department of Business Management at National Sun Yat-Sen University, Taiwan. His papers have appeared in Sloan Management Review, IEEE Transactions on Engineering Management, International Journal of Operations & Production Management, International Journal of Supply Chain Management, Journal of the American Society for Information Science and Technology, International Journal of Physical Distribution & Logistics Management, International Journal of Logistics Management, European Journal of Operational Research, Transportation Research Part A, International Journal of Technology Management, and Journal of Enterprise Information Management. He is listed in Marquis "Who's Who in the World" and "Who's Who of Supply Chain in Asia". His research interests include supply chain management, technology management, and lean manufacturing. He holds a Ph.D. in Industrial & Operations Engineering from the University of Michigan, Ann Arbor, U.S.A.

Ying HOU is PhD. student in international relations at University of Macau, China. She obtained her undergraduate degree in French language and literature from Nanjing University, M.A. in international relations from Fudan University in 2001 and 2004. She has published the articles on international relations theory and Chinese President regime: "The Continental School in Theories of International Relations" (in Chinese), in World Economics and International Politics, No.276, August 2003, pp.26-31; and "Changing Diplomatic Functions of Chinese President", in Xiao Jialing, Tang Xianxing ed., Diplomacy of The Great Powers: Theory, Decision-making and Challenge (Shishi Press, Beijing, 2003), pp.417-440.

Yong Zhou is an Assistant Professor in the School of Software at Dalian University of Technology, China. He got his BSc degree from Chongqing University, China, in 1993 and MPhil degree from Gansu University of Technology, China, in

1996. Having worked in industry for eight years, he returned to Dalian University of Technology in 2004. His research interests include software process, quality-based software engineering and software architecture.

Yue "Jeff" Zhang is Associate Professor of Information Systems in the College of Business and Economics, California State University, Northridge. He received his Ph.D. in Business Administration from Oklahoma State University. His current research interests are electronic commerce, electronic government, information privacy, and virtual collaborations. He has published articles in refereed journals such as Communications of the ACM, Journal of E-Commerce Research, Journal of Internet Commerce, MIS Review, Journal of International Technology and Information Management, Journal of Database Marketing, and International Journal of Services and Standards, among others.

Yufan Hao is Professor of Political Sciences and Dean of Faculty of Social Sciences and Humanities at University of Macau. He obtained his MA and PhD from the Johns Hopkins University School of Advanced International Studies in 1984 and 1989. He has published widely on Chinese politics, Chinese foreign relations, U.S.-China relations, and American politics in such journals as Asian Survey, Asian Perspective, Journal of Democracy, Journal of Contemporary China, American Studies Quarterly, the China Quarterly, etc. His latest books include Chinese Foreign Policy Making (Social Science Academic Press, Beijing, 2007) and Chinese Foreign Policy Making: Societal Forces in Chinese American Policy Making, (Ashgate, London, co-edited, 2005)

Yuxin Wang is a senior lecturer in the Department of Computer Science and Engineering at Dalian University of Technology, China. He got his BSc degree and MPhil degree from Dalian University of Technology, China, in 1997 and 2001 respectively. His research interests include software engineering and software architecture.

ZHAO Jing-Yuan, Ph.D. in Management Science and Engineering, Chinese Academy of Sciences (CAS) and University Science and Technology of China, Post-doctor in Harbin Institute of Technology. Dr. ZHAO's expertise is in Regional Economy and Urban Management. She is the author of more than 40 articles and papers, and 2 monographs that focus on regional innovation management and policies, High-tech industry cluster, knowledge management, technology diffusion. She is the assistant dean of School of Management of Beijing Union University, the invited reviewer for the state newspaper West Times to provide economic strategies and policy analyses.

Zhenjiao Chen is currently a PhD student in the USTC-CityU Joint Advanced Research Center (Suzhou), a collaborative scheme for PhD student supervision sponsored by University of Science and Technology of China and City University of Hong Kong. Her research focuses on justice and conflict, harmony, cross-cultural psychology.

Zhiyang Lin is a professor in School of Management, Xiamen University, China. He received his Ph.D. in Business Administration from Xiamen University. His current research interests are organizational theory and marketing. He has published articles in top journals in China, such as Economy and Management,

China Industrial Economy, Journal of Xiamen University. Quan Lin is a Ph.D. student in School of Management, Xiamen University, China, and visiting scholar in School of Business, University of Washington. His current research interests are organizational theory, enterprise informatization strategy, electronic commerce, and electronic government. He has published articles in top journals in China, such as Economy and Management and China Industrial Economy.

Zhongyun Zhou is currently a PhD student in the USTC-CityU Joint Advanced Research Center (Suzhou), a collaborative scheme for PhD student supervision sponsored by University of Science and Technology of China and City University of Hong Kong. He serves now in the Knowledge and Innovation Management research group of the scheme. His current research interests include the adoption and utilization of new information technology (IT) applications, the roles and strategic value of IT for managing knowledge in distributed work groups.

Index